SCHOLARSHIP IN WOMEN'S HISTORY: REDISCOVERED AND NEW

Editor

GERDA LERNER

A CARLSON PUBLISHING SERIES

For a complete listing of the titles in this series,
please see the back of this book.

Women Against Women

AMERICAN ANTI-SUFFRAGISM, 1880-1920

Jane Jerome Camhi

CARLSON
Publishing Inc

BROOKLYN, NEW YORK, 1994

Please see the end of this volume for a listing of all the titles in the Carlson Publishing Series *Scholarship in Women's History: Rediscovered and New*, edited by Gerda Lerner, of which this is Volume 4.

Library of Congress Cataloging-in-Publication Data

Camhi, Jane Jerome, 1936-
    Women against women : American anti-suffragism, 1880-1920 / by Jane Jerome Camhi.
        p.   cm. — (Scholarship in women's history ; 4)
    Includes bibliographical references and index.
    ISBN 0-926019-65-1
    1. Women—Suffrage—United States—History. 2. Tarbell, Ida M. (Ida Minerva), 1857-1944. I. Title. II. Series.
JK1896.C26   1994
324.6'23'0973—dc20   94-20242

Typographic design: Julian Waters

Typeface: Bitstream ITC Galliard

Jacket and Case design: Alison Lew

Index prepared by Scholars Editorial Services, Inc., Madison, Wisconsin.

Printed on acid-free, 250-year-life paper.

Manufactured in the United States of America.

Contents

To my mother Tess, who was born before women could vote, and to my granddaughter Carmiel, who will grow up in a young country that has already seen one woman prime minister, I joyfully dedicate this book.

Editor's Introduction
to the Series

An important aspect of the development of modern scholarship in Women's History has been the recovery of lost, forgotten or neglected sources. In the 1960s, when the practitioners of Women's History were so few as to be virtually invisible to the general profession, one of the commonly heard answers to the question, why is there nothing about women in your text? was that, unfortunately, women until the most recent past, had to be counted among the illiterate and had therefore not left many sources. It was common then to refer to women as among the "anonymous"—a group that included members of minority racial and ethnic groups of both sexes, most working-class people, colonials, Native Americans and women. In short, most of the populations of the past. These ignorant and erroneous answers satisfied only those who wished to stifle discussion, but they did make the issue of "sources" an urgent concern to practitioners of Women's History.

To historians who had done work in primary sources regarding women, it was obvious that the alleged dearth of sources did not exist, but it was true that the sources were not readily available. In archives and finding guides, women disappeared under the names of male family members. The voluminous records of their organizational work were disorganized, uncatalogued, and not infrequently rotting in file boxes in basement storage rooms. Since few if any researchers were interested in them, there seemed to be little purpose in making them accessible or even maintaining them. There were no archival projects to preserve the primary sources of American women comparable to the well-supported archival projects concerning Presidents and male political leaders. There were only a few and quite partial bibliographies of American women, while the encyclopedic reference works, such as the *DAB* (*Dictionary of American Biography*) or similar sources traditionally neglected to include all but a small number of women notables.

When the three-volume *Notable American Women: 1607—1950: A Biographical Dictionary* appeared in 1971, (to be followed by a fourth volume in 1980), it marked an important contribution to sources on women.[1] This comprehensive scholarly work consisted of 1,801 entries, with a biographical essay and a bibliography of works by and about each woman under discussion. It readily became obvious to even the casual user of these volumes how few modern biographies of these notable women existed, despite the availability of sources.

The real breakthrough regarding "sources" was made by a "grand manuscript search," begun in 1971, which aimed to survey historical archives in every state and identify their holdings pertaining to women. This project was started by a small committee—Clarke Chambers, Carl Degler, Janet James, Anne Firor Scott and myself. After a mail questionnaire survey of 11,000 repositories in every state, to which more than 7,000 repositories responded, it was clear that the sources on women were far wider and deeper than anyone had suspected. Ultimately, the survey resulted in a two-volume reference tool, Andrea Hinding, ed., *Women's History Sources: A Guide to Archives and Manuscript Collections in the United States.*[2]

The project proved that there were unused and neglected sources of Women's History to be found literally in every archive in the country. Participation in the survey convinced many archivists to reorganize and reclassify their holdings, so that materials about women could be more readily identified.

The arguments about "illiterate women" and absence of sources are no longer heard, but the problem of having accessible sources for Women's History continued. Even after archives and libraries reorganized and reclassified their source holding on the subject, most of the pertinent materials were not available in print. Many of the early developers of Women's History worked on source collections, reprint edition projects and, of course, bibliographies. The rapid and quite spectacular expansion of the field brought with it such great demand for sources that publishers at last responded. The past twenty years have seen a virtual flood of publications in Women's History, so that the previous dearth of material seems almost inconceivable to today's students.

For myself, having put a good many years of my professional life into the development of "source books" and bibliographies, it did not seem particularly urgent to continue the effort under the present conditions. But I was awakened to the fact that there might still be a problem of neglected and forgotten sources in Women's History as a result of a conference, which Kathryn Sklar and I organized in 1988. The Wingspread Conference "Graduate Training in U.S. Women's History" brought together 63 representatives of 57 institutions of higher education who each represented a graduate program in Women's History. As part of our preparation for the conference, we asked each person invited to list all the dissertations in Women's History she had directed or was then directing. The result was staggering: it appeared that there were 99 completed dissertations and 236 then underway. This was by no means the entire national output, since we surveyed only the 63 participants at the conference and did not survey the many faculty persons not represented, who had directed such dissertations. The questions arose—What happened to all these dissertations? Why did so many of them not get published?

When Ralph Carlson approached me at about that time with the idea of publishing "lost sources" in Women's History, I was more ready than I would have been without benefit of the Wingspread survey to believe that, indeed, there still were some such neglected sources out there, and to undertake such a project.

We used the dissertation list from the Wingspread Conference as a starting point. A researcher then went through all the reference works listing dissertations in history and other fields in the English language from 1870 to the present. Among these she identified 1,235 titles in what we now call Women's History. We then cross-checked these titles against the electronic catalog of the Library of Congress, which represents every book owned by the LC (or to define it differently, every book copyrighted and published in the U.S.). This cross-check revealed that of the 1,235 dissertations, 314 had been published, which is more than 25 percent. That represents an unusually high publication ratio, which may be a reflection of the growth and quality of the field.

A further selection based on abstracts of the 921 unpublished dissertations narrowed the field to 101. Of these we could not locate 33 authors or the authors were not interested in publication. Out of the 68 remaining dissertations we selected the eleven we considered best in both scholarship and writing. These are first-rate books that should have been published earlier and that for one reason or another fell between the cracks.

Why did they not get published earlier? In the case of the Boatwright manuscript, an unusually brilliant Master's thesis done in 1939, undoubtedly the neglect of Women's History at that time made the topic seem unsuitable for publication. Similar considerations may have worked against publication of several other earlier dissertations. In other cases, lack of mentorship and inexperience discouraged the writers from pursuing publication in the face of one or two rejections of their manuscripts. Several of the most valuable books in the series required considerable rewriting under editorial supervision, which, apparently, had not earlier been available to the authors. There are also several authors who became members of what we call "the lost generation," historians getting their degrees in the 1980s when there were few jobs available. This group of historians, which disproportionately consisted of women, retooled and went into different fields. Three of the books in this series are the work of these historians, who needed considerable persuasion to do the necessary revisions and editing. We are pleased to have found their works and to have persisted in the effort of making them available to a wider readership, since they have a distinct contribution to make.

The books in this series cover a wide range of topics. Two of them are detailed studies in the status of women, one in Georgia, 1783-1860, the other in Russia in the early 1900s. Two are valuable additions to the literature on the anti-woman's suffrage campaigns in the U.S. Of the four books dealing with the history of women's organizations, three are detailed regional studies and one is a comparative history of the British and American Women's Trade Union League. Finally, the three biographical studies of eighteenth- and nineteenth-century women offer either new information or new interpretations of their subjects.

Eleanor Miot Boatwright, *Status of Women in Georgia, 1783—1860*, was discovered by Professor Anne Firor Scott in the Duke University archives and represents, in her words "a buried treasure." An M.A. thesis written by a high school teacher in Augusta, Georgia, its level of scholarship and the depth of its research are of the quality expected of a dissertation. The author has drawn on a vast range of primary sources, including legal sources that were then commonly used for social history, to document and analyze the social customs, class differences, work and religion of white women in Georgia. While her treatment of race relations reflects the limitations of scholarship on that subject in the 1930s, she gives careful attention to the impact of race relations on white women. Her analysis of the linkage made by Southern male apologists for slavery between the subordination ("protection") of women and the subordination of slaves (also rationalized as their "protection") is particularly insightful. The work has much information to offer the contemporary scholar and can be compared in its scholarship and its general approach to the work of Julia Spruill and Elizabeth Massey. When it is evaluated in comparison with other social histories of its period, its research methodology and interpretative focus on women are truly remarkable.

Anne Bobroff-Hajal's, *Working Women in Russia Under the Hunger Tsar: Political Activism and Daily Life*, is a fascinating, excellently researched study of a topic on which there is virtually no material available in the English language. Focusing on women industrial workers in Russia's Central Industrial Region, most of them employed in textile production, Bobroff studied their daily lives and family patterns, their gender socialization, their working and living conditions and their political activism during the Revolution: in political organizations, in food riots and in street fighting. The fact that these women and their families lived mostly in factory barracks will be of added interest to labor historians, who may wish to compare their lives and activities with other similarly situated groups in the U.S. and England. Drawing on a rich mixture of folkloric sources, local newspapers, oral histories, workers' memoirs and ethnographic material, Bobroff presents a convincing and intimate picture of working-class life before the Russian Revolution. Bobroff finds that the particularly strong mother-child bonding of Russian women workers, to which they were indoctrinated from childhood on, undermined their ability to form coherent political groups capable of maintaining their identity over a long period of time. Her thesis, excellently supported and well argued, may undermine some commonly held beliefs on this subject. It should prove of interest to all scholars working on gender socialization and to others working on labor culture, working-class activism, and class consciousness.

Rosemary Keller, *Patriotism and the Female Sex: Abigail Adams and the American Revolution*, is a sophisticated, well-documented interpretation of Abigail Adams's intellectual and political development, set firmly within the historical context. Compared with other Abigail Adams biographies, this work is outstanding in treating her seriously as an agent in history and as an independent intellectual. Abigail Adams emerges from this study as a woman going as far as it was possible to go within the limits of the gender conventions of her time and struggling valiantly, through influencing her husband, to extend these gender conventions. This is an accomplishment quite sufficient for one woman's life time. Professor Keller's sensitive biography makes a real contribution to colonial and women's history.

Elizabeth Ann Bartlett, *Liberty, Equality, Sorority: The Origins and Integrity of Feminist Thought: Frances Wright, Sarah Grimké and Margaret Fuller*, is another work of intellectual history. It attempts to define a common "feminism" emerging from the thought of these important nineteenth-century thinkers and concludes that feminism, in order to sustain itself, must balance the tensions between the concepts of liberty, equality, and sorority. The lucid, well-researched discussions of each woman's life and work should appeal to the general reader and make this book a valuable addition to courses in intellectual history and women's history and literature.

Mary Grant, *Private Woman, Public Person: An Account of the Life of Julia Ward Howe from 1819 to 1868*, is a sensitive, feminist study of Howe's life and thought up to the turning point in 1868, when she decided to dedicate her life to public activism in behalf of women. By carefully analyzing Howe's private letters and journals, the author uncovers a freer, more powerful and creative writer beneath the formal *persona* of the author of "The Battle Hymn of the Republic" than we have hitherto known. She also discusses in detail Howe's fascinating, never published, unfinished novel, "Eva and Raphael," which features a number of then taboo subjects, such as rape, madness and an androgynous character. This well-written biography reveals new aspects and dimensions of Julia Ward Howe's life and work.

Jane Jerome Camhi, *Women Against Women: American Anti-Suffragism, 1880-1920*, and Thomas J. Jablonsky, *The Home, Heaven, and Mother Party: Female Anti-Suffragists in America, 1868-1920*, are complementary studies that should be indispensable for any serious student or scholar of woman suffrage. They are, in fact, the only extant book-length studies of anti-suffragism. This important movement has until now been accessible to modern readers only through the somewhat biased lens of contemporary suffragists' observations. They consistently underestimated its scope and significance and did not engage with its basic paradox, that it was a movement by women against women.

Jane Camhi's comprehensive study of nationwide anti-woman's suffrage movements makes this paradox a central theme. Camhi analyses the "antis' " ideas and ideology and offers some thought-provoking theories about the competing and contradictory positions women took in regard to formal political power. Her insightful profile of a noted anti-suffragist, Ida Tarbell, is an additional contribution this fine book makes to the historical literature.

Thomas Jablonsky's study is focused more narrowly on the organizational history of the rise and fall of the movement. The book is based on extensive research in the organizational records of the anti-suffragists on a state and national level, the records of Congressional hearings, biographical works and the manuscripts of leaders. Jablonsky takes the "antis" seriously and disproves the suffragists' argument that they were merely pawns of male interest groups. He offers a sympathetic, but critical evaluation of their ideas. His detailed attention to organizational efforts in states other than the major battle-grounds—Massachusetts, New York and Illinois—make this book a valuable resource for scholars in history, political science and Women's History.

The four remaining books in the series all focus on aspects of women's organizational activities. Taken together, they reveal the amazing energy, creativity, and persistence of women's institution building on the community and local level. They sustain and highlight the thesis that women built the infrastructures of community life, while men held the positions of visible power. Based on research in four distinctly different regions, these studies should prove useful not only for the intrinsic worth of each, but for comparative purposes.

Darlene Roth, *Matronage: Patterns in Women's Organizations, Atlanta, Georgia, 1890-1940*, is a thoroughly researched, gracefully written study of the networks of women's organizations in that city. The author's focus on conservative women's organizations, such as the Daughters of the American Revolution, the Colonial Dames, and the African-American Chatauqua Circle, adds to the significance of the book. The author defines "matronage" as the functions and institutionalization of the networks of social association among women. By focusing on a Southern city in the Progressive era, Roth provides rich comparative material for the study of women's voluntarism. She challenges notions of the lack of organizational involvement by Southern women. She traces the development of women's activities from communal service orientation—the building of war memorials—to advocacy of the claims of women and children and, finally, to advocacy of women's rights. Her comparative approach, based on the study of the records of white and African-American women's organizations and leadership—she studied 508 white and 150 black women—is illuminating and offers new insights. The book should be of interest to readers in Urban and Community History, Southern History, and Women's History.

Robin Miller Jacoby, *The British and American Women's Trade Union Leagues, 1890-1925: A Case Study of Feminism and Class*, is a comparative study of working-class women in Britain and America in the Progressive period. Although parts of this work have appeared as articles in scholarly journals, the work has never before been accessible in its entirety. Jacoby traces the development of Women's Trade Union Leagues in Britain and America, exploring their different trajectories and settings. By focusing on the interaction of women's and labor movements, the author provides rich empirical material. Her analysis of the tensions and overlapping interests of feminism and class consciousness is important to feminist theory. Her discussion of protective labor legislation, as it was debated and acted upon in two different contexts, makes an important contribution to the existing literature. It also addressees issues still topical and hotly debated in the present day. The book will be of interest to labor historians, Women's History specialists, and the general public.

Janice Steinschneider, *An Improved Woman: The Wisconsin Federation of Women's Clubs, 1895-1920*, is a richly documented study based on a multitude of primary sources, which reveals the amazing range of women's activities as community builders and agents of change. Wisconsin clubwomen founded libraries, fostered changes in school curricula and worked to start kindergartens and playgrounds. They helped preserve historic and natural landmarks and organized to improve public health services. They built a sound political base—long before they had the right of suffrage—from which they trained women leaders for whom they then helped to secure public appointments. They worked to gain access for women to university education and employment and, in addition to many other good causes, they worked for world peace. Steinschneider's description and analysis of "women's public sphere" is highly sophisticated. Hers is one of the best studies on the subject and should prove indispensable to all concerned with understanding women's political activities, their construction of a public sphere for women, and their efforts and successes as builders of large coalitions.

Margit Misangyi Watts, *High Tea at Halekulani: Feminist Theory and American Clubwomen*, is a more narrowly focused study of clubwomen's work than are the other three, yet its significance ranges far above that of its subject matter. Watts tells the story of the Outdoor Circle, an upper-class white women's club in Hawaii, from its founding in 1911 on. Its main activities were to make Hawaii beautiful: to plant trees, clean up eyesores, preserve nature and rid the islands of billboards. To achieve these modest goals, the women had to become consummate politicians and lobbyists and learn how to run grassroots boycotts and publicity and educational campaigns, and how to form long-lasting coalitions. Above all, as Watts's fine theoretical analysis shows, they insisted that their female vision, their woman-centered view, become an accepted part of the public discourse. This case study is rich in theoretical implications. Together with the other three studies of women's club activities it offers not only a wealth of practical examples of women's work for social change, but it also shows that such work both resists patriarchal views and practices and redefines them in the interests of women.

Gerda Lerner
Madison, Wisconsin

Acknowledgments

Completion of this work was a historic event in my life. It marked a definite stage at which my development as a historian and my growth as an individual intersected to produce something new and different. My relationship to this work throughout its formative stages profoundly affected not only the ways I view myself as a scholar, but also how I feel about myself as a person. Like all historic events, however, it represented the culmination of numerous impulses and diverse influences. Whether these forces prevailed because of me or in spite of me is not easy to determine. Nevertheless I believe that somewhere along the way I assumed responsibility for channeling these impulses into the creation of this work.

It is a difficult task to identify all the strands that, woven together, helped make this work possible. Some of them have antecedents that go way back. These include the constant urging of my father, from earliest childhood, to hew out an area of concern that would become my special interest, as well as his insistence that I look to women for my models. I wish that he were here to share in the realization of what he meant to me. My mother's influence was somewhat more diffuse, but nevertheless as important. Resisting since childhood the model she offered me of a self-effacing wife and mother, I finally began to know her as an individual. This not only proved to be a rich and rewarding personal experience, but enabled me to appreciate those special qualities of love and devotion that a woman, raised in the tradition that her first duty was to those near and dear to her, can bring to family life. All of this broadened my understanding of the myriad possibilities of being a woman and brought me closer to the women of this book.

I shall always be indebted to the second great awakening of feminism in the late 1960s for enabling me to recover from the crippling effects of growing up a woman in the '50's. The women's movement helped to put me in touch with myself as a woman, take myself seriously as a person, and become sensitive to the experiences that, by virtue of my sex, I share with all women. Gradually pervading every aspect of my life, the movement had its most tangible effect on my intellectual life. I felt deeply the need to extend my sense of connectedness to women by reaching out through time to recover the past. I became committed to the idea of devoting myself to women's history.

On a practical level, this could have presented serious problems had it not been for the forbearance and tolerance of the Tufts University History Department. In particular I am indebted to Professor Nancy L. Roelker, my adviser throughout the years when I thought my scholarly bent lay in a different direction. Her kindness and consideration, as well as her faith in me, facilitated my highly unorthodox transition from Renaissance history to American women's history.

As for scholars in the field, I owe the deepest debt of gratitude to Professor Jill Conway of the University of Toronto for her continuous encouragement. She not only expressed her belief in the significance of the subject, but also gave careful thought to the many questions raised by this study. Unfortunately, it was not always possible to develop as many of the ideas suggested by her comments as I would have liked.

I am indebted on two levels to the support given me by the American Association of University Women. By awarding me a fellowship they not only made it possible for me to devote a year of uninterrupted work to my research, but also helped to legitimize what I regard as pioneering efforts in a new field.

To Howard Feinstein I owe a special debt of gratitude for helping me to realize that it is possible to gain a better understanding of the past by becoming more in touch with the present.

I also deeply appreciate the warmth and support given me by the women in my group. Their unusual sensitivity and awareness helped alleviate the growing pains that accompanied my developing consciousness as a woman and a feminist.

Of all those to whom I owe so much, perhaps no one has been more long-suffering and patient than my son Jeremy. He spent most of his childhood with either the first or second of "mommy's dissertations" competing with him for my attention and affection. Nevertheless he exhibited very little "sibling rivalry" and even managed to take pride in the work I was doing.

In my husband, Jeff, I have come closest to finding the model that I have been seeking most of my life. Through him I have learned the importance of being true to oneself, the value of moderation as a way of keeping all things in perspective, and, most important of all, that loving relationships and dedication to one's life's work are not necessarily incompatible.

Finally I should like to acknowledge the helpfulness and cooperation of all those who have assisted in a practical way. These include the librarians and archivists at the Sophia Smith Collection, Schlesinger Library, the Manuscript Room of the New York Public Library, the Massachusetts Historical Association, the Massachusetts State Library, Cornell University Library, the New-York Historical Society, and Houghton Library.

Preface

I feel very fortunate that publication of this book has given me the opportunity to regain contact with that time of my life when I was writing it, thinking it, and living it. It was in fact a consuming labor of love, and as I look back upon it now I am reminded of that me for whom the subject of women's opposition to women held so much meaning and fascination. Since that time, however, and as so often happens in women's lives, my own has changed direction more than once and coursed through paths so disparate that they would have been impossible to imagine in that far-off time. Looking back on the past from the vantage point of the present, I am gratified to discern within myself those strands of being, perceiving, and caring that enable me to experience at last a sense of continuity and wholeness.

My doctoral dissertation, on which this book is based, was a milestone, not just for me personally, but because it was one of the first dissertations written in the newly emerging field of women's history. In addition to riding the crest of the wave of feminist revival in the early 1970s, its subject resonated with efforts at that time to secure an Equal Rights Amendment (ERA) that would guarantee to women "equality of rights under the law." The struggle to secure passage of the ERA occurred in often similar circumstances and recapitulated many of the same arguments against woman suffrage that I discuss in this work. Opponents of the ERA predicted, while it was being debated in Congress, that most women would be against it once they realized it would sweep away the many laws that protected them on account of their sex. Raising the specter of losing the law's traditional bias toward women did in fact arouse women to opposition. The ERA passed both houses of Congress, but in a move similar to that of the antisuffragists, women organized themselves into groups whose avowed purpose was to oppose its ratification. Women were warned that they would have to pay alimony as well as men, that husbands would no longer be compelled to support their families, and that wives would have to go out to work. Echoing the sentiments of their predecessors, these latter-day "antis" believed that women could not have both equal rights and special privileges.

And similar to the antisuffrage movement, organized opposition to the Equal Rights Amendment was often headed by women in league with various right-wing organizations and interests. For example, one of the most active women's anti-ERA groups was headed by Phyllis Schlafly, founder of Stop ERA and long associated with right-wing causes.

Even the issue of states' rights, which became a clarion call in the battle over woman suffrage, was reincarnated in the anti-ERA movement, and in none other than Tennessee, the very state where the antisuffrage struggle reached its climax in 1919. The second time around, the fight was headed by State Senator Brown Ayres, whose chief reservation against the ERA, in line with all of those earlier diehard Southern antisuffragists, was that it would jeopardize the relation between state laws and the federal Constitution.

Unfortunately for all those who believed the passage of the ERA would presage the dawn of a new era, the wave had crested. In the Valhalla of the antisuffragists, there must have been great rejoicing, as they looked down on the stunning victory of the anti-ERA forces in blocking ratification in the requisite number of states.

Because the early 1970s was such a heady time, and because I feel that my dissertation was as much a product of the rapid changes taking place then as of my own intellectual and academic inclinations, I am including in this book almost all of the original acknowledgments, for I believe they are a period piece. I wish only to add mention of one other person, my sister-in-law Ellen Camhi. Her career in local, state, and national politics proves, contrary to the direst of antisuffrage predictions, that not only women themselves, but both their families and the larger community, are decided beneficiaries when women use their political power intelligently and disinterestedly.

Jane Jerome Camhi
Jerusalem 1992

Women Against Women

Introduction

The study of women in American history has undergone a renaissance. For the most part, however, efforts to reconstruct the woman's movement in this country have concentrated on the attempts of women reformers to elevate the position of women in society by securing for them the legal and political rights to which they were entitled. Inevitably the women who first articulated the claim to full equality with men, notably the right of women to vote, have emerged as heroines of this movement. There were many more women, however, whom one never hears about—the silent majority of American women who played no part in the suffrage struggle. What emerges from investigation is that, in fact, the majority was not so silent and that although most women may have appeared indifferent to the issue, many were overtly hostile.

It is perhaps not surprising that with few exceptions,[1] historians of the suffrage movement have tended to ignore the female opponents of suffrage, since the suffragists themselves did the same. The suffragists, aware that in the final analysis it was the men who held the power to change things, tended to depict the opposition as male power wielders (in a variety of guises) and to be almost blind to the resistance provided by women. Even as late as 1915, Carrie Chapman Catt could spur on her cohorts by making the following assertions:

> The forces arrayed against us are gigantic. The respectable ladies who pose as antis are not dangerous opponents. The real enemy is the "Vice Trust" which is at its old tricks, attacking our amendment submarine fashion under cover. It is the usual campaign of slander. To besmirch the character of our leaders, to misrepresent the motives of our movement, to belittle our cause, and especially to lie about woman suffrage in the Western states constitutes the plan of campaign.[2]

It was perhaps one of the greatest tactical blunders committed by the suffragists that they failed to recognize that their most vociferous opponents were among the supposed beneficiaries of all their efforts—namely, the women themselves. It is these women who are the concern of this study, together with an analysis of the reasons for their hostility, the peculiar form and content of that hostility, its mode of expression, and the ends it served.

Although the origins of feminism in general and suffragism in particular can be traced back to the first decades of the nineteenth century, the antisuffrage movement did not surface until the last two decades of the century. Beginning in the 1880s and gathering momentum throughout the 1890s, the antisuffrage movement reached its peak of power and influence between 1895 and 1907. Nevertheless, it retained sufficient force in 1919 and 1920 to offer substantial opposition to suffrage efforts to ratify the federal woman suffrage amendment. At its height the movement encompassed more than 25 state associations, some having numerous city and local branches, and a national association.[3]

The movement was organized, led, and staffed by women who went to lengths inconsistent with their goals in order to prevent the extension of suffrage to women. Common to all antisuffragists was the belief that the entry of women into public life (which was considered the inevitable consequence of the ballot) would bring in its wake disaster not only for women themselves but for all of society. Despite this belief, the antisuffragists were so intent on resisting the coming of woman suffrage that they leaped midstream into the battle, adopting all of the techniques they were so eager for womankind to avoid, including campaigning and even lobbying.

The women who led this movement were usually members of the social aristocracy. They were, for the most part, urban, wealthy, native born, Republican, and Protestant—members of established families either by birth or marriage, or both. They claimed to be favorably disposed to the gradual improvements in the status of women that had taken place over the century and, in this sense, did not consider themselves unsympathetic to women's rights as such. Nevertheless, on one issue they remained unanimously and steadfastly opposed—the granting of suffrage to women.

The pattern of antisuffrage resistance appears to have been the same everywhere. In the beginning it usually took the form of general public disapproval of suffrage claims, expressed in denunciations from the pulpit, ridicule by the press, or statements by prominent individuals deriding the movement and warning against its consequences. It was only as success for the suffrage movement began to appear likely that the Antis[4] saw the need for forming organizations to resist it. This was true, for example, in Massachusetts, which witnessed the earliest expression of organized antisuffrage activity, as well as in states that did not begin to organize in resistance until several years later.

There were certain regional variations in the style and manner of antisuffrage opposition. In the South, antisuffragism became the vehicle for the expression of a rigid states' rights doctrine that was overtly racist. In the Midwest and West, antisuffragism became intermingled with the battles between "wets" and "drys," and conservative and proper antisuffrage ladies found themselves unwitting political allies of the liquor interests, who feared that an enfranchised womanhood would ensure a state of permanent prohibition.

Antisuffrage activities were usually evoked in response to specific types of situations. For example, when a state constitutional convention was considering a woman suffrage amendment to the state constitution, antisuffrage forces would rise to the occasion. The same was true when a state legislature passed a bill submitting the woman suffrage question to the voters for approval. The third type of situation that spurred the Antis to great activity occurred after Congress passed the woman suffrage amendment and submitted it to the states for ratification. Certain states were crucial to a victory, and it was in these that the bittersweet battles were fought between suffrage and antisuffrage forces.

The antisuffrage movement had its male auxiliaries, which in 1912 formed a national Man-Suffrage Association to help further the aims of the Antis. The Antis also operated through front organizations, which were seemingly apolitical associations but in fact were devoted to the defeat of woman suffrage.

It is difficult to measure precisely the actual effectiveness of all of this activity since in the end the suffragists claimed the victory. Nevertheless, in some instances the Antis did achieve notable successes. By meeting the suffrage onslaught directly on a local level they managed to defeat their enemy in several critical legislative encounters; they thus delayed what historians in retrospect have tended to regard as inevitable—the enfranchisement of women.

Necessary to an understanding of the history of the antisuffrage movement is a description of the assumptions that underlay the position and of the arguments used to advance the cause. Just how the Antis hoped to accomplish their aims is outlined in a discussion of their strategy. The organization and structure of the movement can be seen by examining several of the most active antisuffrage organizations, including the National Association Opposed to Woman Suffrage. Some of the key figures in the movement are indicated throughout the various chapters and are described at greater length in the

Biographical Appendix. Ida Tarbell is singled out as a woman whose antisuffragist rhetoric belied her emancipated life-style and who therefore typified in her person some of the anomalies inherent in the movement. Following is an assessment of the impact of the movement as a whole, indicating what in fact it accomplished and how its accomplishments compared with its articulated goals. Finally, some explanation is offered for the antisuffrage movement, both as a historical phenomenon and a psychological anomaly.[5]

ONE

Antisuffrage Assumptions:
—Woman's Special Role
—Privilege and Power
—The Liability of
Being a Woman
—Separate, Not Equal

... in youth an adored darling and in mature years a loved wife.
—Freud, Letter to Martha Bernays

Let her life be a practical sermon.
—James McGrigor Allan, *Woman Suffrage Wrong in Principle, and Practice*

Antisuffrage rhetoric, although often repetitious and exaggerated, was not merely argumentative in nature. It often reflected, in fact, what was essentially a congruent philosophical position concerning the nature of man (and woman) and the meaning and purpose of the institutions developed to moderate, control, and inspire behavior appropriate to civilized human beings.

The arguments used by the Antis to support their position derived from basic philosophical assumptions. Therefore, it is necessary to begin by examining their views, particularly in the crucial areas that affected the relationship between the sexes. Beginning with woman's position in the family,

5

it is possible to follow the development of antisuffragist thought on the subject of woman as citizen-maker to her assumption of ultimate responsibility for the good and evil in man. The liabilities of being a woman in a world where emphasis on the natural distinctions between the sexes has traditionally worked to reinforce male superiority did not dismay the Antis. In fact, they proudly emphasized those characteristics that distinguished them from men, investing them with compensating and even superior qualities, to such an extent that only by maintaining distinctly separate spheres for men and women were they able to vindicate their deepest beliefs. The ultimate expression of their philosophy may be found in their views on government and what they considered woman's proper relationship to it.

The opponents of woman suffrage employed a wide variety of arguments in their efforts to influence the public to resist any extension of the elective franchise to women. The arguments, however, had two things in common. First, they were almost all predictive—intimating, if not explicitly detailing, the evil consequences that would ensue if woman suffrage were enacted. Second, they were usually imputative; that is, the arguments were presented in such a way that the suffrage question emerged as a mere symbol of what was assumed to be the real issue, the threat of the spread of feminist ideas. Most antisuffragists did not consciously intend to confuse the issue. If anything, their rhetoric belied the confusion in their own minds. However, whether conscious or not, it was one of the antisuffragists' most effective weapons.[1]

Obfuscating the issue by causing the advocates of suffrage to appear as feminists played upon contemporary uncertainties regarding the changing role of women. As a result, many who might not have taken issue with the justice or expedience of extending suffrage to women found themselves forced to take a stand either for or against what was made to appear to be two opposing value systems. The result was that the question of woman suffrage, which had over the years come to assume a symbolic significance for those in the suffrage movement, also began to assume a symbolic significance in the minds of the uncommitted and the unsure.

Woman's Special Role

A primary assumption of the Antis was that the family was the basic nexus, the self-governing unit upon which the state was built. Therefore, as a microcosm of the state, every well-regulated family had to have one head, for if authority were divided the outcome would be domestic anarchy.[2] To be preserved as a unit the family must be represented in the state by the voting power of its head, the man of the family.[3] The notion that there should be one head of the family and that this head should be the man even influenced the Antis' position on child custody. The Antis were in accord with the laws giving custody of children to the father in cases of disagreement and argued against granting equal custody to each parent. Again, their reasoning was based on the assumption that the head of the family should be a united head, and that exactly "equal custody" of anything was impossible by two persons since the power of decision must rest somewhere. For the Antis, "The man must be and is charged with the legal duty of support, and this is one great reason why, in case of disagreement, he, so to speak, is given the casting vote." Furthermore, they supported the fact that the force of law was on the side of keeping the family together, for they viewed the social value of the family as unexcelled in "perpetuating and properly training the race."[4]

The family, of course, existed within the home, and although man may have ruled as head of the family, it was assumed that in the home, woman reigned supreme.

> Woman is queen, indeed, but her empire is the domestic kingdom. The greatest political triumphs she would achieve in public life, fade into insignificance compared with the serene glory which radiates from the domestic shrine, and which she illumines and warms by her conjugal and motherly virtues.[5]

The home was woman's chief place and crowning glory, the arena in which her special qualities and talents could achieve their utmost expression. The Antis assumed that private interests and occupations must continue to absorb the great majority of women if society were to continue.[6] Women were urged to "specialize in the home," a vocation not confined to those who "by choice or accident have missed the highest privilege of womanhood," but appropriate for the great majority of women.[7] Within the home woman's role was indeed a lofty and important one.

> The business of women must be to work out a national ideal of domestic life and juvenile training. They must standardize the family life with their new understanding of the importance of the product of every separate family to the state.[8]

The office of woman was to be "a link among the days, to knit the generations each to each," for to her "has been committed the task of preserving the ideals of the race."[9]

When the Antis spoke of the "task of preserving the ideals of the race" they were not simply engaging in a rhetorical exercise, but had in mind specifically woman's assumption of responsibility for the raising of the nation's children.

> Though she may not teach from the portico, nor thunder from the forum, in her secret retirements she may form and send forth the sages that shall govern and renovate the world. Though she may not gird herself for bloody conflict, nor sound the trumpet of war, she may enwrap herself in the panoply of Heaven, and send the thrill of benevolence through a thousand youthful hearts.[10]

Woman's distinctive sphere was in building character, and in so doing, she was responsible for the nation's future leaders.

> Though woman is debarred from voting, she brings into the world, and rocks the cradle of the nation's future citizens. She rears and molds the character of those who are to be the future rulers and statesmen; the heroes and benefactors of the country. Surely this is glory enough for her.[11]

Thus, according to the Antis, woman builds the individual character by which society is reformed, and she does this not by compelling but by trying "to educate and civilize, to create in the children committed to her care an intelligent love for fair play, justice and self-control."[12]

In contrast to the suffragists who, according to the Antis, were clamoring for more laws, for more of the "man-element" in society,[13] the antisuffragists kept insisting that it was the "inner life and character, the mother's work," which everywhere needed strengthening.[14] The spirit nurtured by good women would make people want to obey the laws they already had.

The Antis were eager to assert that woman was the greatest influence on man in his earliest and most formative years. But their sense of involvement did not end there. They saw women fully responsible not only for the good they would produce in future citizens, but also for the evil that existed in their own world. By making themselves accountable for man's basic character, however, they were inadvertently depriving him of his autonomy. For by implication man was no longer considered responsible for his own weaknesses and shortcomings. These became attributable to his mother. Men were not responsible for "the evil of their upbringing." Their mothers should bear the heaviest burden of blame for failing to teach their children "the laws of the transmission of life in their sacredness and their beauty." Furthermore, the responsibility of women for the moral standards of men did not end in their boyhood, "for each sex is ultimately what the other demands of it to be." The mother's influence, particularly in matters concerning morals, was more important than the father's, "for the man who has talked of all things with his mother, to whom the sacredness of motherhood is indissolubly bound up with the great instinct of reproduction, will find it very hard to go far wrong." Women, through the training of their sons, "hold the future of the world in their keeping."[15]

In contrast to the Antis, feminists denied that mothers could be held accountable for the failings of their children under existing circumstances. The feminists implied, rather, that only when women were emancipated could they be indicted for the shortcomings of their progeny.[16]

That the Antis placed such faith in the mother role was due to their conviction that emotions and feelings could be controlled and cultivated. The province of sexual morality affords the best illustration of the application of this belief. Assuming that the "reproductive instinct" was normally stronger in men than in women, the Antis did not conclude that man was therefore responsible for all the sins of sex. This would have been true, they maintained, only if instinct and passion were beyond one's personal control. But men could be taught to control all the fundamental instincts of life: for example, they were capable of overcoming even the instinct of self-preservation by sacrificing themselves when necessary for women and children.[17]

> The anti-suffragist sees the evils of society as fundamentally resulting from the evil in individuals, and calls on women to check it at its sources. They emphasize the power of individual homes to turn out men and women, who, trained to self-control, will not necessitate control by law. Knowing well that the great training school for private morality is family life, the anti-suffragist seeks to preserve conditions making for sound family life, the sum total of private morality being public morality, the conscience of the people.[18]

Antisuffrage beliefs concerning woman's responsibility for the existing state of affairs were expressed most vehemently when countering the suffragist contention that men were not doing their job in running things and that, given the opportunity, women would purify politics. The antisuffrage position on both these points was firm. One the one hand, if American men were tyrannical, vicious, and unfit as legislators, this could only be because their

9

mothers misunderstood or did not fulfill their natural functions toward them. On the other hand, if women could not do their job of raising fit citizens, then they were obviously unqualified to assume even wider responsibilities.

From the Antis' perspective, the suffrage movement was diverting women's energies

> from the one point at which they can be exerted with unique effect—the training of individual character in childhood. . . . We see too little proof of the Suffragist's easy assumption that woman has made such a success within her own doors that "municipal housekeeping" should now have the benefit of her skill. The stern reformer who should rise up in our midst and ascribe municipal corruption to the failure of the home would be able to cite several facts. The need of the day, to Anti-suffragists, seems not more "mothering the community" but better mothering the individual boy and girl.[19]

If woman's work in the home were always properly performed, declared the Antis, "there would be far fewer bosses, ringsters and grafters in the world at large." Even more extravagant was their contention that when woman fails to perform the work nature has assigned her she "leaves the world depleted by just so much of moral strength and all the best educators and scientists declare, lowers the entire race in its affectional, social and moral achievements."[20]

The distinctive genius of woman, it was argued, did not lie in her logical or executive abilities, but in her sensibilities, which made her irreplaceable in the home where her influence over the lives of those around her was much greater than any she could possibly wield as a voter, where she would count as only one man.[21]

In the antisuffrage cosmology woman's influence did not stop in the home, but reached out through her lovingly indoctrinated citizen-sons to bring her message of love and fair play into the legislatures of the world. What was happening, in fact, was that woman's role was beginning to assume an almost mythic quality. It was only natural, therefore, that women who accepted the myths felt that they stood to lose considerably in the event of any basic rearrangement of the pyramid. The arguments used by the Antis reflected this basic fear.

Privilege and Power

The Antis argued that if women voted they would lose the power to mold the citizens of the future. Antisuffrage campaign material often included posters depicting the evil effects of woman suffrage on the domestic scene. In the antisuffrage litany, motherhood and participation in public life were always presented as mutually exclusive.

> It seems to me that it is a bigger feather in a woman's cap—a brighter jewel in her crown—to be the Mother of a George Washington than to be a member of Congress from the Thirty-second district.[22]

Woman suffrage, it was argued, would destroy the nonpartisan influence of intelligent and interested women who, under existing conditions, could bring the full force of their influence to bear upon legislation and thus exert a direct moral influence on men of all political parties and persuasions. This power would be lost once women gained the franchise because they would then divide into political parties and be able to influence only those men for whom they voted.[23] Furthermore, if women had the same rights and duties as men and yet "were forced perpetually to excuse ourselves from their performance," they would lose credibility as counselors of the political conscientiousness in others.[24]

A major fallacy in suffrage reasoning, according to the Antis, was the belief that women would have more power once they were enfranchised. The Antis maintained that just the opposite was true and that women actually had more power without the ballot. When the Antis spoke of power they usually meant woman's ability to influence, that is, her potential for effecting reform by means of moral example and social service activities.

> The influence of women standing apart from the ballot is immeasurable. Men look to her then (knowing that she has no selfish, political interests to further) as the embodiment of all that is truest and noblest. She has influence with all parties alike; if a voter she would have only the influence of her own party, even the woman's vote being divided against itself. We believe that it is of vital importance that our sex should have no political ends to serve![25]

Under existing conditions, the intelligent woman interested in public affairs could bring the full force of her influence to bear upon legislation. There was ample evidence of this in the many projects undertaken and laws secured by

11

the efforts of club women and social workers.[26] The Antis believed that if women exercised political functions, every act of every woman in public life would be viewed as relating to her personal and political future and not with reference to the good of the state.[27]

It was a great asset to women in public and philanthropic work that it could safely be assumed that they were working disinterestedly and with no axes to grind.[28]

> The voteless woman can go to any man, Republican or Democratic. She can ask for laws that create offices without suspicion that she wants to hold them. She cannot "trade" or "deal." She is known to be disinterested, and *it doesn't have to be proved*.[29]

Speaking from direct personal experience, Emily Bissell went on to testify to the tremendous power with the public that woman wielded due to the knowledge that her social service was aimed only at serving the community. (see Biographical Appendix.) "A woman working for any measure in a legislature has *an immense advantage over a man*." Despite antisuffragist avowals that their sex lacked political know-how, it is difficult to find a more astute assessment of political reality than Bissell's comment that "The vote is one thing. Legislation is another."[30]

Look at the record of what women have done without the vote, said the Antis, and this will demonstrate that women have accomplished more without the vote than with it. Comparing Chicago before and after, one Anti recounted that after suffrage, women achieved only covered markets, a court for boys 17-25, public wash houses, and abolition of garbage dumps. Whereas, before suffrage, the women of the city had established a kindergarten in the public schools, juvenile court and detention home, the small park and playground movement, vacation school, school extension, forestry department of the city government, city welfare exhibit, Saturday half-holiday, public comfort stations, the Legal Aid Society, and reform of the Illinois Industrial School.[31]

The Antis brought other evidence to bear including the following examples obtained from an article by Mary R. Beard. Beard, although an ardent suffragist, was still of the opinion that *without* the vote, women were a strong influence toward good legislation. For example, in Harvey W. Wiley's campaign for pure food laws, his strongest support came from women's organizations that inundated Congress with letters, telegrams, and petitions.[32]

This does not preclude the possibility that with the ballot, the job might have been easier. Nevertheless, the Antis were probably right that women in clubs were more of a power than individual women with a ballot.

Other examples were cited. The Consumers' League of New York helped the national food committee defeat a bad amendment to the Gould bill that required that all package goods be labeled as to amount of contents. Mrs. Albion Fellowes Bacon of Indiana secured the first tenement house laws, allegedly through personal initiative and moral persuasion. Finally, Frances Perkins of New York, representing the Consumers' League and supported by the Women's Trade Union League, in a fight for the 50-hour bill, effected legislation through her personal influence.

Evidently the Antis distinguished between political life and public life, and found forms of the latter perfectly compatible with their conception of true womanhood. As for public activities, it is noteworthy that even attempts to obtain legislative changes were considered legitimate avenues of activity.

> Let them [men] struggle with the vote. Let us aim at legislation. It takes less time, and gets greater results. I do not believe in the ballot as a sacred right. I consider it a more or less clumsy male expedient. I want direct results, and the ballot is the most indirect influence I know of compared to the direct influence women can bring to bear.[33]

The Antis viewed the ballot as the first step toward formally entering the male world of politics. Yet, as long as women operated from their traditional base, the Antis did not object to their functioning as political appointees. In fact, in England, the Antis even sanctioned the formation of a club by women for the purpose of promoting a male candidate.[34] The result, therefore, was an anomalous situation in which women functioned in a variety of ways that approximated the political (even manipulating varying degrees of power outside their traditional sphere) and yet went about denouncing the ballot because it represented *formal* entry into the world of male privilege and possible loss of female authority.

The Antis' insistence on their effectiveness without the ballot in the realm of legislation evokes a familiar anomaly. It was evidently permissible for women to operate *indirectly* on behalf of their various causes even in the male sphere of politics, but direct action would have been unladylike and contemptible. Furthermore, they seemed sincerely to believe that the influence of woman as a nonpartisan moral force was so widely recognized that politicians and commercial interests actually advocated woman suffrage as a

13

way of destroying the former. According to one Anti, the New York *World* came out for woman suffrage for the reason that only 10 percent of women had too much influence over the rest. These few, according to the *World*,

> have maintained at times a reign of terror over legislative bodies, in consequence of which half the country is now bedeviled by some form or other of harem government, and legislators are forever making ridiculous concessions to women agitators [i.e., the clubwomen, social workers, and others interested in social welfare].[35]

The Antis did not want to lose either the direct influence women were capable of wielding on public affairs by virtue of their nonpartisan moral approach, or their indirect power. The Antis sensed, even if vaguely at times, that the ballot would mean less indirect power, in terms of status and autonomy. Putting women into politics, they maintained, decreed that every question of social economy, art, or ethics "must be decided by a *majority*."[36] Once women voted, their power would be dissipated because they would be divided into political parties. Furthermore, then women would be able to influence only the men for whom they voted. In other words, political partisanship narrows a woman's sphere of influence. Woman suffrage would take the power out of the hands of women who without the vote exerted a strong moral influence toward good legislation and put the power gained through an increase in the electorate into the hands of bosses who could control the largest woman's vote.[37] These same good women would also lose out as they became increasingly dominated by political types. By political types, the Antis had in mind individuals such as Dr. Anna Howard Shaw, who proclaimed

> I believe in woman suffrage whether all women vote or no women vote; whether all women vote right or all women vote wrong; whether all women will love their husbands after they vote or forsake them; whether they will neglect their children or never have any children.

Fortunately, in the Antis' view, Shaw did not speak for the 24,000,000 women of voting age who were not members of NAWSA. The Antis

> . . . neither wish to be ruled by such women nor do they wish to have to wage an eternal fight not to be ruled by them and one thing or the other will be necessary if the ballot is forced upon women.[38]

The Antis argued that women themselves would be disadvantaged by admission into political life since they would be deprived of the by-products of chivalry. The Antis attributed to men a tendency to treat women fairly. They believed that as soon as the attention of lawmakers was called to injustice, laws were amended. They asked, justifiably, "Will women always be fair to women?"[39] The Antis assumed that men operated with reference to just and broad-minded principles that enabled them to demonstrate their concern for society as a whole, whereas the peculiar attribute of women—self-sacrifice—was directed toward that which was near and dear to them, home and family.

Another allegedly evil consequence of suffrage insofar as it affected women's standing was that they would lose their special privileges as well as the right to maintenance and protection in the home. The Antis contended that thus far women had experimented only with double suffrage, not equal suffrage, which meant favor to none "when women are stripped of legal and civil advantages and must take her place as man's rival in the struggle for existence; for, in the long run, woman cannot have equal rights and retain special privileges."[40] If the average woman were to vote, the Antis felt she also had to accept jury service and aid in the protection of life and property. Numerous handouts depicted the horrors attendant on jury duty for women. These included having to relinquish care of one's children to a nurse, exposure to lurid testimony at trials, and mingling with unsavory types. She had to relinquish her rights and exemptions under the law and in civil life if she were "to take her place as a responsible elector and compete with man as the provider and governor of the race. Such equality would be a brutal and retrogressive view of woman's rights."[41]

In addition to jeopardizing their sense of uniqueness, the Antis feared that equality would deprive them of access to their established avenues for realizing power and influence. They would not only become less effectual as a force for social change, but also would lose those special prerogatives to which they were entitled as mothers of the race.

Women stood to become seriously disadvantaged as individuals if they were put on a plane of legal equality with men.

The *obligation* of the husband to maintain his wife is of more value to women than all the so-called "equal rights" and "liberties" possibly could be. Women would purchase their freedom dearly if they surrendered this social and legal position, as man now *must* support his wife and also pay her debts even if she is rich and the husband is poor. The law protects the woman in property, conjugal and parental rights. Woman's dependence on the husband is her safeguard, the rock on which her ease and security rest. Self-support is more difficult for a woman than it is for a man by virtue of her physical inequality.[42]

The Antis also argued that all the special virtues of woman would be attenuated and ultimately corrupted by involvement in the world of politics, which would only enhance the bad qualities of women until the sex as a whole declined as a moral force. Women would lose their influence for good as the embodiment of the ideal that has sustained and uplifted Christian civilization.

With Christianity there came into the world a new example and a new thought. To woman's whole nature appealed that life of self-sacrifice, of love, and of willing service that has created a new heaven and a new earth. From the foot of the Cross there arose and went out into the world a womanhood that did not demand, or claim, or threaten, or arrogate; a womanhood renouncing, yielding, loving, and, therefore, conquering. For twenty centuries that has been the law of woman's life. It is sneered at and rejected today by the clamorous, but it has made of woman what we now find her. You see it in your mothers, your daughters, your wives. Do you wish to have that ideal changed? Woman has become to man not only a companion, but an inspiration. Out of the crucible of the centuries has come what we not only love but adore; before which, in certain hours, we bow with a reverence that links us unconsciously with the Divine. It is Christian civilization that is in the balance.[43]

This rhetoric, presented by a male traditionalist and quoted approvingly by an Anti as the ultimate argument in repudiating woman suffrage, raised two specters. If the highest Christian virtues of humility, modesty, and self-sacrifice were the special province of women, then who would embody them once women were emancipated? Christian civilization ostensibly stood to lose the standard-bearers of its values. Further, the only way that man could acquire the attributive benefits of those virtues without having to renounce, suffer, sacrifice, or deny was by arrogating them to his wife, by claiming that husband and wife were one, and that that one was the husband.

The housewife who voted would vitiate her purity by entering into the sphere of man.

The political arena is not the place for the highest development of all that is best in woman. Nothing but degradation can come from placing gentlewomen in the voting places to come in contact with all sorts and conditions of men.[44]

As solicitous of their self-image as of their actual status, the Antis feared that of the various classes of women, the worst would represent their sex in public life. Catharine Beecher, an early antisuffragist, had classified women into five categories: 1) rational and intelligent; 2) impulsive and enthusiastic; 3) busy and "easy" (who would vote as men advised); 4) superficial, unreflecting, and frolicsome (who are tools of the politicians); and 5) the lovers of notoriety (ambitious lovers of power who seek public office and money).[45] For someone of Beecher's sensibilities, notoriety was the last thing she would foist on her sex, which she felt must, above all, be kept out of public life. If the lovers of notoriety were to capture the limelight, then the image of all women would suffer and the virtues and accomplishments of the average woman would be diminished by comparison.

For most Antis the evils of woman's "preliminary dip into politics" were already visible. According to one Anti whose public life outside her home belied her position, women grow bitter, aggressive, and antagonistic and find their natural duties "flat, stale, and unprofitable." Speaking from platforms and being constantly in the public eye do not improve women who have better work to do along "civic, sanitary, and philanthropic lines, and in our homes" than to be as "our Western sisters are, out campaigning for candidates and engaged in struggles for political supremacy."[46]

For another Anti, the reason many women, indifferent to the suffrage question, joined the antisuffragist cause was disillusionment with suffragist tactics, particularly in introducing partisan politics and petty strife into women's clubs.[47] Whereas antisuffragist women derived their impression of what women in politics would be like from suffragist examples, antisuffragist men tended to view both sides as susceptible to the demoralizing effects of participation in politics.[48]

The Liabilities of Being a Woman

It was probably inevitable that the biological arguments used to buttress antifeminist thinking throughout the nineteenth century would eventually be brought to bear on the question of suffrage. Those "hopeful of preserving existing social relationships, employed medical and biological arguments to rationalize traditional sex roles."[49] This was truer in the nineteenth century than at any time before as the impact of science reached a new level, rationalizing and legitimizing almost every aspect of life.

Dr. Charles L. Dana, a late-nineteenth-century neurophysiologist who spoke of himself as "having had some experience with the anatomy and nervous system of women," lent his antifeminist view of women and his authoritative weight to the antisuffrage position.

There are some fundamental differences between the bony and the nervous structures of women and men. The brain stem of women is relatively larger; the brain mantle and basal ganglia are smaller; the upper half of the spinal cord is smaller, the lower half, which controls the pelvis and limbs, is much larger. These are structural differences which underlie definite differences in the two sexes. I do not say that they will prevent a woman from voting, but they will prevent her from ever becoming a man, and they point the way to the fact that woman's efficiency lies in a special field and not that of political initiative or of judicial authority in a community's organization. . . .

Besides, there are qualities in the nervous systems of woman that call for protection and make at least certain forms of aggressive and responsible life dangerous. About one-fourth of the insanity of civilized countries is due to serious blood disease, alcohol, and drugs. Men are three times more addicted to drugs and alcohol and ten times more the sufferers from blood infection and the accidents that come from an extradomicilliary life than women. Despite this, there are practically no more cases of insanity among men than among women. In fact women are rather more subject than men to the pure psychoses. *If women achieve the feministic ideal and live as men do, they would incur the risk of 25 per cent more insanity than they have now.* I am not saying that woman suffrage will make women crazy. I do say that woman suffrage would throw into the electorate a mass of voters of delicate nervous stability. We would . . . add to our voting and administrative forces the biological element of an unstable preciosity which might do injury to itself without promoting the community's good.[50]

Dana based his argument that women would incur a higher risk of insanity if they "live as men do" on the assumption that psychoses stem from congenital organic defects rather than from an inability to cope with a demanding environment. The environment, or society, was still considered a major source of variation despite the growing popularization of the germ-plasm theory in the 1880s.[51] This affected contemporary definitions of psychic abnormality, which was seen as deviation from a norm determined by the environment. The environment, or society, was the sine qua non to which the individual had to adjust for both to function efficiently.

The biological argument against woman suffrage went way beyond the ill effects it would have on women's health. Their unborn children would be affected, each successive generation weaker than the one before, resulting finally in race suicide. From the antisuffragist point of view it was also biologically retrogressive, "a backward step toward conditions where the work of man and woman were the same, because neither sex had evolved enough to see the wisdom of being specialists in their own line."[52]

For the Anti, suffrage was not a matter of live and let live so that only those women who wanted to would need to vote. They regarded the vote as an obligation as well as a privilege and felt that the life of woman was already sufficiently burdened with duties that only she could discharge. Why add to it one that her husband, brother, or son could discharge at least as well? Antisuffragist rhetoric indicated a sober regard for the responsibility of voting. Antis saw it as a task for which woman would systematically have to prepare herself, and not without both psychic and physical cost. Furthermore, class, race, and religious alliances would take their toll as women split into rival political groups. The energies of women who "already reach with sad frequency the breaking point of nerves and body" would become strained and dissipated.[53]

Finally, the Antis predicted that, in addition to moral and biological deterioration and civic decline, if woman suffrage were enacted, women would degenerate sexually. This ranged from atrophy of the reproductive organs as a result of disuse[54] to the debasement of motherhood, the supreme symbol of femininity, as singleness became a virtue. If women voted, there would be more who were not wives and mothers.

> When political rewards are held out as the price of services in public life, many women—and those of the brightest—will be tempted to forego marriage and motherhood for the sake of winning them.

Women would lose their femininity (and their instinctive desire to attract a mate) as they became increasingly unsexed, until civilization would be faced with either sex war or race extinction. "What will become of the morals of society when not to be married, not to be a mother, is the prerequisite for a woman's success in a chosen career?"[55] As women deserted their home duties to enter the "wider arena," men would be compelled to take up feminine occupations. The outcome would be a "race of masculine women and effeminate men and the mating of these would result in the procreation of a race of degenerates."[56]

Others argued that if women were permitted legally to do whatever some women wish, then they must also be permitted to be legislators, soldiers, and sailors, and even to wear men's clothes.[57] The Antis believed that the suffragists gloried in the fact that there were women blacksmiths, luggage masters, brakemen, undertakers, and even political "bosses" in Colorado.[58]

Loss of that essential femininity was bound to occur if women entered public life. Woman was physically and mentally designed for "home-keeping, child-bearing, a social, religious, and philanthropic life" and would be unable to preserve her femininity in politics if she "attends political meetings, serves on political committees, canvasses districts for votes, watches at the polls, serves on juries, and debates political questions or records and promises of political candidates."[59]

Although the Antis never wavered in their commitment to woman's infinite capacity for achieving good in others, they took a much more ambiguous view of womanhood itself. On the other hand, they could scarcely render sufficient praise on behalf of the woman who fulfilled her destined role in motherhood.

> She is the vessel of honor—too frail for rough usage, yet capable of the office of life-bearer, and as such to be guarded and built about with care and love. Everything related to this one essential difference is hers: first the family, next the house, the schools, the hospital, the charities, the college, the university—everything that opens the world to the young and that helps the downtrodden. Hers too, may be the cleanliness and sanitation of the city; and the housekeeping generally of the community. She alone can make men noble and purer, not by going down to struggle with them but by rewarding the best with her praise.[60]

On the other hand, there was no denying that the female sex was but a poor second when compared with the male.

> Woman's sex is a handicap to her—always was and always will be. From youth to old age every woman requires regular periods of mental and bodily rest—when these are denied, her life and health and the birthright of her children are sacrificed. The major part of two years' leave of absence from a profession or occupation is required by a woman to become a mother; she must become a mother on an average of over four times if the race is to survive![61]

The Antis perceived that women were weaker than men and assumed that less muscular power meant less ability to withstand exertion and nervous strain. Even the unsurpassed blessing of motherhood left its mark on women.

For even though it uniquely predisposed them to experience to the full one dimension of life, at the same time it handicapped them when it came to achieving in other areas. In other words, according to one version, the whole experience of the race has fitted the mother for unselfish devotion to her children to the point where to her they are and should be the very first, but this very element unfits her for political life when one must maintain a disinterested and objective viewpoint.[62] In essence, the peculiarities of woman's existence imprisoned her in her subjectivity. Woman was ultimately a loner, compelled to withstand all the great crises of her life alone. "The experience of all other women is of no use to her at the moment of her great trial. She is Eve, with her first born."[63]

As a result of this deeply personal approach to life, woman had a "lack of capacity for organizing" and an urgent desire to withdraw as soon as possible from "cooperative work," characteristics that could not help but disqualify her when it came to handling political affairs.

> It is the greatest power and the pressing danger of our woman's temperament that we cannot have difference of opinion and treat them impersonally as men do.[64]

Endowed with this frail vessel of a body, woman required protection, and so in the antisuffrage scheme of things, woman existed in a kind of feudal relationship to man.

> Woman in all her relations is bound to "honour and obey" those on whom she depends for protection and support.[65]

Woman's frailty not only precluded her entry into political life but handicapped her as a member of the work force, for the average woman had only one half the physical strength of the average man. This meant that when she competed with him on the open market, she would pay too high a price as far as her ultimate health and her hope of motherhood were concerned.[66] Furthermore, the Antis believed that woman's work (in the labor force) was not equal to man's.

> It is only the lighter trades that women can ply, and a needlewoman can hardly expect to be paid like an engine-driver or a stevedore.[67]

21

Since women were regarded as physically weaker than men, they were assumed to be feebler in all respects. Not only could women bear less physical strain, but the kinds of work they could engage in were limited.

Men, on the other hand, were endowed with all the attributes that women lacked. If, for example the "life-work" of women removed them from contact with political questions, then it was assumed that these would not only devolve upon men, but that they would constitute men's exclusive sphere. Since a woman's physical weakness and the fact of motherhood made her a person to be protected, then man's greater physical strength made him the protector and qualified him for the work of government. For the Antis, government, lawmaking, law enforcement, taxation, police, railroads, and international relationships "must still be the business of men."[68] In essence, the vote was seen as part of man's work. "Ballot-box, cartridge box, jury box, sentry box, all go together in his part of life."[69]

Separate, Not Equal

Basically, what it all signified was that women were different from men. The question was to what extent that difference would be treated as a liability or regarded as the sign of a special grace. Far from apologizing for the differences between the sexes, the Antis looked upon them as not only divinely inspired, but also as the crowning step in an evolutionary process. The growth of differences and specialization of forms that culminated in the masculine man and the feminine woman were a "necessary part of nature's economy."[70]

> Biology teaches her the tremendous value of sex. All the way from the one-celled amoeba up to man, the greater differentiation of sex is the mark of higher development. *Man and woman are not alike and are not meant to be alike.* They become more different the more they perfect their own development, and the development of the race.[71]

The Antis saw likenesses between the sexes steadily increasing as one descended the scale of animate life until species were reached that had no distinctive sex characteristics at all.[72] Inversely, this meant that the higher the form of life, the greater the sexual differentiation.

The better defined in any species are the differences of sex; the higher its rank in the scale of being, the greater its chance for still further progress. The inequalities which spring from sex are the dynamic force of evolution.[73]

Once sex differences had been acknowledged, extolled, and legitimized, the Antis were free to develop the implications. Beginning here, too, with a biological premise, that "specialization of function is the first law of progress," the Antis pointed out that the work of the world must be divided and that "sex forms a natural, ineradicable line of division. To interchange responsibilities would not be "working in the line of evolution."[74]

We believe that the emancipating process has now reached the limits fixed by the physical constitution of women, and by the fundamental differences which must always exist between their main occupations and those of men.[75]

The best illustration of the profound differences in capabilities that the Antis assumed to exist between the sexes is found in their views concerning the education of women. The purpose of higher education, according to them, was to train young women to serve their country and race so as to be the best influence on the shaping of character, "which has always been their special function."[76] If woman needed more liberty in intellectual directions, it was viewed as enabling her to do her own work more thoroughly, to teach her what had better be left to men to do, and to teach man how he might do it well. "She is the world's educator, he is the world's executive." Since character was the true business of life, education should be geared to obtaining it. The emphasis was always on meeting their responsibilities as women, and naturally their foremost responsibility was "care of the next generation."[77]

The college should teach people it is their positive duty to feel as they *ought* to feel and not otherwise; that any feeling that does not cost a little something in the remote marginal aspects of its domain, is, in all probability, wrong. Cheap and easy feeling is pretty certain to be classed in the domain of vice.[78]

Expressed in another way, it was hoped that higher education would not *unfit* women for their ultimate role as mothers. In an address to Radcliffe students in 1895, Dr. S. Weir Mitchell, a well-known author and nerve specialist, was not at all ambiguous in expressing this position.

I believe that, if the higher education or the college in any way, body or mind, unfits women to be good wives and mothers there had better be none of it.

Even more emphatically he insisted that if the result was that women crave merely what they call a career as finer and nobler than the life of the home, "then better close every college door in the land."[79]

The doctor did not intend to subject women to a life of subservience. He put himself on the line for independence as a human right.

> I want women to be free to be and to do what they like. . . . But with this freedom to choose, and this human right to select, I, personally, no more want them to be preachers, lawyers, or platform orators, than I want men to be seamstresses or nurses of children. *I want freedom within the noble limitations of sex.*[80]

Most antisuffragist perorations on the subject of education for women were usually lofty generalizations about preparing women for their future roles, but occasionally specifics were mentioned. Mitchell, for example, warned that all women, whether they married or not, would, in accordance with the natural life of woman, have at some time responsibility for households or for children not their own. Therefore, they must guard against becoming "sweet girl graduates" with a knowledge of romantic literature and Greek. Perhaps speaking from his own experience, he cautioned that it could reduce a gentleman to grief if his wife did not know how to run a house.

Higher education had to be sharply delineated as to its function and purpose because it was fraught with dangers for the unsuspecting woman. These dangers consisted primarily of damage to either the physical constitution or nervous system of women students. One of the popular authorities on the subject was Dr. Edward H. Clarke, who had been a professor at Harvard Medical School. In his book, *Sex in Education*, Clarke concentrated on both dangers. Drawing on clinical evidence from his patients, he explained that the active use of the brain required more blood than usual and that in the case of women this blood would be drawn from the nervous system and the reproductive organs. Not only would they then be unable to fulfill their ultimate function, but women who went to college were likely to suffer mental and physical breakdowns and possible sterility.[81]

The conclusion drawn from all this was that women should not receive the same form of education as men. This was a welcome idea to those who objected to coeducation on the grounds that it would make girls half boys and boys half girls.[82]

Others who rallied against coeducation also buttressed their position by appealing to the myth of biologically destined motherhood. Children might not be healthy if the brain of the mother as well as the father was severely taxed, wrote Goldwin Smith.[83]

Beginning in the 1870s and continuing into the twentieth century, writers and medical authorities testified to women's unfitness for higher coeducation.

> Woman is no more capable of enduring the same severe and protracted study with the other sex by day and by night through all the months and years of her early life than she is able to perform the same labors on the farm or in the shop.[84]

Mitchell, in his address to Radcliffe students, did not omit mention of this all-important subject. If his audience thought they could assume the man's standard as to what they did in the way of mental labor, it would be at their peril. He warned against those "special days" when to use the mind persistently was full of danger.

> Women have terrible consciences and decline to waste time as so many young men do and have done . . . hence women at college work harder than men; out of their eagerness arises disregard of physiological limitations. . . . Violating laws of health good for both sexes will make women suffer more than men. . . . I would rather be a healthy waiting maid than Professor Minerva with a yellow skin and a lazy liver.[85]

Finally, it appears as though women had everything to lose and nothing to gain by undertaking the rigors of a college education. Mitchell "never saw a professional woman who had not lost some charm." Then again, for many women, "learning won at college goes for nothing. With a man it has been a mind training for life work. For this class of women it is—shall I dare to say it—useless." The result, he predicted, was "neglect of duty, ungratified ambitions, discontent," for unlike the man who went out into larger life, the lot of woman "narrows to home functions" with the freedom of college life gone and the imposition of the restrictions and "simple duties" that it entails. The doctor concluded that "the best of the higher evolution of mind will never safely be reached until the woman accepts the irrevocable decree which made her woman and not man."[86]

The separateness of female and male spheres was an article of faith to the Antis. This included not only the areas in which it was considered appropriate for them to act, but also their concepts of masculinity and femininity.

25

If any man attempts woman's functions he will prove himself an inferior woman. If woman attempts man's functions, she will prove herself an inferior man. Some masculine women there are; some feminine men there are. Those are the monstrosities of nature.[87]

The theoretical underpinnings for the Antis' views of masculinity and femininity were supplied in part by Otto Weininger's *Sex and Character* (1903). Apparently unaware of the extremes to which he carried his bizarre views on sexuality, the Antis considered Weininger a leading authority on sex relations. Citing Weininger, Richard Barry, an antisuffragist polemicist and journalist, wrote that in the present civilization one will never find a man who is all masculine, nor a woman who is all feminine. What is usually called the normal man has about 85 percent masculine traits and 15 percent feminine ones, and the normal woman has 85 percent feminine traits and 15 percent masculine ones. Therefore, concluded Barry, the "perfect marriages" are formed when the 85 percent men marry the 85 percent women, and "havoc comes when an 85 percent man marries a 60 percent woman, or vice versa."[88]

In an attempt to demonstrate the perversity of the suffragists and discredit the movement as a whole, Barry went on to report that in an interview with Anna Howard Shaw, he asked her about this theory, to which she allegedly replied: "I think the ideal person would be 50% masculine and 50% feminine." Concluded Barry, "In that expression she unconsciously made an estimate of her own mentality and her own personality. As she is the President of the National Woman Suffrage Association, this seems an exceedingly significant sidelight."[89]

So not only was human nature either distinctly feminine or distinctly masculine, influencing the roles considered appropriate to each sex, but the spheres of the two sexes were essentially distinct.

Home is meant to be a restful place, not agitated by the turmoil of outside struggles. It is man's place to support and defend the family, and so to administer the state that the family shall flourish in peace. He is the outside worker. Woman is the one whose place it is to bear and rear the children who shall later be citizens of the state. As I have shown, she can, if she wishes, go into man's place in the world for a while. But man can never go into hers. (That proves she is superior, by the way.) He cannot create the home. He is too distracted by outside interests.[90]

There are obvious pitfalls in maintaining the idea that profound and unalterable differences exist between the sexes. For example, it becomes very difficult to avoid arriving at the conclusion that the sexes are constituted so differently that their interests are totally dissimilar. And if this is the case, then how can those of the weaker be said to be adequately represented by the stronger? In other words, how did the Antis handle the anomaly implicit in allowing for the worlds of men and women to be distinct and yet believe that when men went to the polls or participated in political life they did so at the behest of and in the interest of their wives, mothers, and sisters?

The more the Antis insisted on these differences, the more they ran the risk of backing themselves into a corner. For by opposing enfranchisement they were denying women the only logical means of protecting their own sphere against the competing interests of those who were supposed to look after both. The way they avoided this pitfall and remained logically consistent was by depicting the sexes as "different but complementary." The Antis alleged that antisuffragism was founded on the conception of cooperation between the sexes, and that men and women must be regarded as partners, not as competitors.[91]

> Men and women are held together in a common relation to the social organism, and as society develops, the interests of its members become more and more harmonious, but not identical. Equality means development of variety, rather than of similarity of function.[92]

The Antis' Rejection of Equality

It was inevitable that the Antis would not welcome the idea of true equality for the sexes. In fact, for most women, its connotations were undoubtedly confusing, if not actually threatening. The reason for this had to do partly with the context in which the notion of equality became a byword of feminism.

Embedded in the suffragist pantheon from earliest times was the concept of equality, which in its revolutionary context came to mean assuring the have-nots rights equal to those of the haves. In the case of the feminist movement, women responded to the idea that men had certain privileges that were denied women and therefore any move toward equality should involve evening the balance by bestowing on underprivileged women sufficient rights and privileges to make them equal to men. There were certain shortcomings inherent in this concept of equality, not the least of which was that it offered

27

women who wanted to change things only a male model.[93] Therefore, it is easy to see why, from the antisuffrage perspective, the feminist cry of equality meant making women not only equal to men, but also more like men. Inherent in the notion of equality was sameness, and this was abhorrent to the Antis. They feared that "the woman's suffrage movement is an imitation-of-man movement."[94]

> The suffrage ideal of womanhood is that of a woman putting on masculinity, assuming men's tasks, and laying aside as cumbering femininity a woman ready to bear out her views against man at the point of the ballot.[95]

The Antis had to tread a very fine line, however, if they wanted to reject equality and yet not lower their own self-esteem by appearing inferior as a sex. They accomplished this by disparaging equality in order to maintain their uniqueness. If something is unique, it is incapable of comparison, just as it is incapable of being equal. Here is how Mrs. Richard Watson Gilder, president of the New York State Association Opposed to Woman Suffrage, conceived of the equilibrium between superior and inferior.

> Nature has made man the superior in strength, grasp of intellect, in nervous energy; wisdom and power and glory are his, yet without us he is a vain shadow, for we, who seem so inferior, have the one gift, without which all his achievement goes for nought. We are the transmuters, the transmitters of all he has accomplished. Like a clear glass we hold it all and carry it on—a frail, half unconscious "vessel of the Lord," spiritually the equal of man.[96]

It is probably inevitable in any discussion of distinctions that they will become linked to certain value judgments. What is not clear is whether a subjective value judgment is the outcome of awareness of differences or whether emphasis on the differences is the result of a priori value judgments. If it is the former, and awareness of differences precedes the latter, then it seems that the greater these differences, the easier it is to develop the rationale of uniqueness. Since to be unique is to stand out either on a higher or lower plane than the undifferentiated mass, the chances are that one will sooner or later choose the higher position. Consequently, one acquires a vested interest in maintaining the distinctions in extremis. Once the subjective value judgment is reached it simply reinforces the need to emphasize the differences, and the cycle renews itself. The result is that equality becomes impossible both operationally and psychologically. Consequently, the Antis either extolled the areas in which they believed themselves superior, or else they referred to areas in which women were "unequal" only as it suited their purpose of remaining distinct.

In another section of the letter quoted above, Mrs. Gilder pointed out that the habits of mind and methods of action of women were different from men and that women were even irresponsible in matters not their own.

> When she talks of regulating wages, or conducting financial schemes, or government which must be backed by force, she seems like a child.

But, she concluded, take this away from men and they have nothing.

> Take away from men the task of protection and you cast them back two thousand years—you make them savages. Men love the struggle for mastery with one another: it makes them better, stronger, wiser; if they struggle with women it brutalizes them and degrades them while it robs women of their *especial superiority*.[97]

This scarcely veiled "white woman's burden" appears over and over again. Men "naturally relapse into barbarism when left too long alone." Gilder also felt that women could not engage in political life and all it entailed (learning who the candidates were and what they stood for, going to primaries, and sitting on juries) without giving up their *real* rights—keeping men "keyed to the more delicate harmonies of life."[98]

Rebuking her "socialist friends" for scoffing at the word *art*, Gilder said that for these people art was a sin against equality. But to her, of a higher order than equality was the art that woman brought to life.

> Art—all arts, and the greatest of all, the Art of Living—is in the hands of woman, and she is art herself. Though she is not conscious of it she is ever fashioning her work of art, the home.

Woman, in her role as mother, the one area exclusively reserved for woman, was elevated to almost metaphysical heights. She was "at once the altar, the divinity and the sacrifice." Borrowing from the Talmud, Gilder concluded with the expression that "God could not be everywhere, so he made mothers."[99]

What emerged is a sense of mission, a calling that devolved upon women and that only they were capable of undertaking. Also it was not limited to married women. Ida Tarbell, who decided at an early age to remain single, wrote

> . . . to hold one man that he reverts neither into savagery nor sloth—one state or the other being his natural condition—is the greatest school on earth.[100]

This denigration of man is difficult to understand since Tarbell knew many outstanding men, including her own father, who were anything but the depraved being suggested here. On the other hand, she believed single-mindedly in the infinite resourcefulness of her sex and perhaps in order to elevate the one she metaphorically had to downgrade the other.

It is ironic that the Antis, in denouncing suffragist ideology that saw the sexes in opposition and choosing rather to regard them as "opposite" and "complementary," by their mystical glorification of womanhood fell into the same trap. In order to give greater significance to woman's role as civilizer, they emphasized the awesome nature of the beast she had to grapple with and ended up in many cases with a view of man that was far from complimentary. Here, in what was intended as an attack on the suffragist, is more than a potshot at manhood.

> [The suffragist in action violates the] natural plan of women in the order of creation—the place of eternal superiority and supremacy. It is a movement *backward towards men and mastodons*, the miocene hipparion and eocene anchitherium—instead of forward, in the direction of woman, and the spiritual universe, and everlasting light.[101]

In summary, the Antis believed not only that equality was impossible to achieve but also that its effect would be demoralizing. They felt that it would result in a misconception of woman's true dignity and special mission and lead to personal struggle and rivalry between the sexes. They avoided the questions as much as possible, but when they did come to grips with it one of their basic fears was that equality would be equated with sameness.

> Equal rights do not imply that both sexes should engage promiscuously in the same pursuits, but rather that each sex should discharge those duties which are adapted to its physical constitution and are sanctioned by the canons of society. To some among the gentler sex the words "equal rights" have been, it is to be feared, synonymous with "similar rights." To debar women from certain pursuits is not to degrade her. To restrict her field of action to the gentler avocation of life is not to fetter her aspirations after the higher and the better. It is on the

contrary, *to secure to her not equal rights so called, but those supereminent rights which cannot fail to endow her with a sacred influence in her own and proper sphere.*[102]

Counting themselves progressive for applying evolutionary terminology to their cause, the Antis claimed to accept the "demands of specialization." But they mistook the biological definition of specialization for division of labor. Therefore, it was easy for them to view progress as "equal opportunity to men and women for expression along their *different* lines."[103]

"We are anti-suffragists," wrote Mrs. A. J. George, "because real political equality must mean a fair field with favor to none, and that is the last thing in the world women want." Women were entitled to special protection, she felt, because of their lower physical and nervous vitality, and to forfeit these rights and exemptions would be a "brutal and retrogressive" step.[104]

Dr. Viola Klein helps to explain this seemingly flagrant self-interest and apparent parasitism. Writing about women who were opposed to the women's rights movement, rather than about antisuffragists per se, Klein points out that then, as now, as long as men were paid higher wages for the same work, women had greater hope of raising their standard of living by marriage than by personal career. It is "still an easier and more profitable career for most women to marry than to work."[105] As long as women were in a state of "submission," they had a claim to protection, and their weaker social position was counterbalanced by certain privileges.[106]

This suggests that the sine qua non of the Antis' basic philosophy may not have been their insistence that woman's place was in the home, but rather their *need to maintain the distinction between the sexes*, to keep women out of men's sphere and vice versa. The elevation of woman's position within the home was extremely important, for it helped to reinforce the sexual boundary. If, on the other hand, the Antis had been primarily concerned with safeguarding the private domesticity of women, then it would be difficult to explain their justification of women's social activities. The latter obviously played a strategic party in the Antis' arguments against woman suffrage, where it was continually maintained that one of the greatest drawbacks of suffrage was that women would be less effective publicly if they were enfranchised. This means, as was suggested, that women would not only accomplish fewer reforms, but also *experience less power*, and explains why the boundary was so important—to ensure the continuation of their influence and power, *not* just to keep women prisoners of the home.[107] The Antis realized that the ballot offered women only a nominal gain in exchange for considerable losses.

The Antis believed that through her role as wife and mother, woman had proven herself capable of exerting a far-reaching and beneficial influence on society. Whereas conservatives in general saw woman's place in the home as essential for preserving the family as the basic unit of society, the Antis were equally concerned with maintaining a social order where the role and function of the sexes remained distinct. Only in this way could they ensure a preserve susceptible to feminine power and influence. In simplified form, woman's sphere should remain home and family, while man's involved the conduct of government and business. Any move of the sexes in either direction was regarded as a form of backsliding to an earlier stage in human development and as a direct threat to the position that civilized women had achieved. In an age when a minuscule proportion of married women worked and when it seemed highly unlikely that women would be invading the business world in any significant numbers, the changes felt from this direction, while present, were much less threatening than the prospect of women entering government. It was acknowledged that some women *had* to work, but the Antis found it hard to believe that any woman would choose to do so. Enfranchisement, on the other hand, especially if enacted by federal amendment, meant forcing *all* women to participate in the political process whether they wanted to or not. It now becomes necessary to turn to the antisuffrage view of government and woman's relationship to it in order to understand more fully the nature of their fears.

TWO

Antisuffrage Theories of Government: Women's Relation to Power

Manhood suffrage is the foundation of all our public policy.
   —Emily Bissell

It is simply and solely for the safe-guarding of the home and of woman as the centre of the home, that governments exist, that men labor and fight and strive and try to rule.

   —M. G. van Rensselaer

For the Antis the relationship of women to government was a particularly delicate area. They constantly had to walk a narrow line between, on the one hand, the idea that the interests and activities of women had nothing to do with the running of government and, on the other, that even without the vote, women had considerable influence on the way government was run. The success of the Antis in this delicate balancing act was due to three basic premises. The first, and most dubious of all, was that "though woman does not personally vote, she exercises the right of suffrage by proxy." That is, the sensible matron exerts so powerful an influence over her husband and sons that they will rarely fail to follow her counsel.[1]

Second, the Antis insisted that citizenship was not dependent on or identified with possession of the suffrage. In fact, they adopted a kind of Benthamite philosophy, maintaining that "citizenship lies in the participation of each individual in effort for the good of the community." Woman's contribution as a citizen derived from her special attributes as a sex.

> The quickness to feel, the willingness to lay aside prudential considerations in a right cause, which are among the peculiar excellencies of women, are in their right place when they are used to influence the more highly trained and developed judgment of men.[2]

In contrast to the suffragists, who believed that if woman's "quickness to feel" were translated into public action, the community would be better off, the Antis warned that "the risks of politics would be enormously increased, and what is now a national blessing, might easily become a national calamity."[3] This is the way they balanced it out between the sexes.

> Man has, in return for serving the state with his physical strength, or his wealth, or his intellect, been granted the privilege of voting on questions pertaining to affairs of state. And woman, in return for her services as child-trainer, and in consideration of the disabilities incident thereto, has been allowed immunity from further service; her rights as a citizen being taken care of for her by her male representatives.[4]

The third premise, derived in part from the other two, was that women did not constitute a separate class, but that "the women of every social group are represented in a well-ordered government, automatically and inevitably, by the men of that group."[5]

> Our democracy recognizes that rich and poor, ignorant and intelligent, native and foreign-born may have clashing interests, and it gives to each class the ballot to safeguard its own. But the interests of men and women do not clash, and their relations are so close that the men of each class may truly be said to represent the women of that class.[6]

All three strands are taken up and woven together in the following excerpt from a Minority Report made to the U.S. Senate in 1886.

> It is our fathers, brothers, husbands, and sons who represent us at the ballot-box. Our fathers and our brothers love us; our husbands are our choice and one with us; our sons are what *we make them*. We are content that they represent *us* in the cornfield, on the battle-field, and at the ballot-box, and we *them* in the school-room, at the fireside, and at the cradle, believing our representation even

at the ballot-box to be more full and impartial than it would be were the views of the few who wish suffrage adopted, contrary to the judgment of the many.

At the core of the Antis' position on government was the belief that ruling was man's work. The reason for this, they contended, was that only men were equipped with sufficient force to uphold the rule of law. Government "rests upon the political strength of the majority, which should be able in times of need to force minorities to obey their will."[7]

A government exists to secure the safety and best welfare of all who look to it for protection. The assumption that suffrage is a natural right is anti-republican, since the very essence of republicanism is that power is a trust to be exercised for the common weal. . . . To deny this is to imply that our government is a pure, unmitigated democracy, which may be interpreted in two ways—either as tantamount to no government, or as the absolute despotism of the ruling majority in all matters. This is not American republicanism certainly, since republicanism has always aimed to restrain the absolute power of majorities and protect minorities by constitutional provisions.[8]

It followed, therefore, that the state should place the responsibility of government upon those best equipped.[9] To the Antis, force meant brute physical strength, the capacity for which only males possessed.

. . . we would give them [women] their full share in the State of social effort and social mechanism; we look for their increasing activity in that higher State which rests on thought, conscience, and moral influence; but we protest against their admission to direct power in that State which *does* rest upon force—the State in its administrative, military and financial aspects.[10]

This male power to rule was also not capable of being shared with or transferred to women.

The power of men in the aggregate is the coercive force that energizes government. It is the basis of government, enforcing payment of taxes and obedience to law. It quells sedition, puts down rebellion, and makes law a rule of human conduct, and not merely a matter of suggestion, counsel or persuasion. *The organization of government itself creates no power; it is solely an organization of pre-existing power;* and up to the present time, the power so organized has been the fighting force of available manhood. *A grant of suffrage to women would extend to them a share in the directing of this power but it would not impart to them any power whatever that they do not now possess.*[11]

35

The author of this treatise, John C. Ten Eyck, went on to point out that the granting of man suffrage had its origins in recognition of the fact that men already possessed the power to obtain it by force. In other words, it was the "recognition, in the form of law, of a pre-existing condition, by reason of which the masses had the power and the will to determine the ends and methods of rule." Man suffrage guarantees the administrative and legislative officials of government that "a preponderance of the coercive power of manhood in the state can be relied upon to support them," and thus ensures the stability of government. In a situation where universal suffrage obtains, those in office have no assurance that a preponderance of the coercive force can be relied on to support the party in power because "success at the polls may be achieved by the great preponderance of woman's votes united with a minority of men's votes."[12]

Developing this idea even farther, Ten Eyck maintained that under universal suffrage a government's ability to enforce the policies it adopted would have to depend upon the organization of and maintenance of a standing army strong enough to coerce obedience to policies on the part of men within the state. In effect, Ten Eyck equated woman suffrage with female *dictation* of public policies, interpreted it as a shift in the balance of power to women, and then conjured up all the evils imaginable in the event of sex war, the creation of a mercenary army being only the first.[13]

This view of government was not limited to male antisuffragists. Emily Perkins Bissell felt that in America all suffrage was based on the power to bear arms for the state, if necessary.

> The vote expresses opinion. . . . But does expressing opinion ever really do anything. . . . The vote is nothing without determined continued effort to carry it out—and this effort is one more thing for our already overloaded shoulder.[14]

Another Anti, Elizabeth Jackson, described government as an organization for compelling one portion of the community to do the will of the other. In a democracy, she maintained, the minority is forced to obey the majority and the fundamental idea was compulsion. Jackson felt that the dream of an ideal democracy was illusory when one looked at government in action. In the city ward, for example,

> The machinery of government is a matter of stress and strain; of selfishness, cruelty, and hate, at the worst; at best, of conflicting interest, mutual incomprehension, and maddening friction.

Good government, by contrast, could mean only one of two things. It could mean a community where the majority was successful in imposing its will on the minority so that laws were "strictly enforced and scrupulously obeyed."[15] This, she added parenthetically, was a definition unfamiliar to the suffragists, who never used the argument that woman suffrage would produce a more tractable minority. The second meaning was one used largely by suffragists. It consisted of improving legislation along certain specific lines. Of course these laws would not necessarily be better enforced, but they would offer something different.

The antisuffragists, regardless of their personal opinions as to just what kind of women became suffragists, shared the view that the suffragists were defined by their belief that the ballot was woman's best means of social efficiency since the ballot would open the door to legislation.[16] Suffrage ideas, they felt, simply mirrored the general mania for uplift by legislation that characterized the period.[17] Woman suffrage was not a real reform, they argued, but only an experiment in legislation.[18] And legislation could not effect the necessary changes in human nature to bring about reform in society. The strengthening of each individual's moral fiber and the building of character were the only guarantees of an improvement in society. And these could be achieved only by the unremitting efforts of mature and well-intentioned women to instill in their children the necessary ingredients for proper moral growth. This training could not be given by enactment of laws, since "we cannot legislate the control of human passion." Law could prevent wrongdoing only by appeal to fear. In a free country it was impossible to enforce a law unless the will of the people (or public opinion) was behind it, therefore, women did not need the vote to protect themselves from evil men. All that was necessary was that all men be "self-controlled and pure in heart," and no law would be required. In fact, if all men were libertines, no law could be enforced against them.[19] Naturally, the Antis felt that it was ridiculous to imply that a society could legislate morality. In their view this represented an important distinction between the feminist, who

> . . . demands for men and women alike no restraint on sexual relations beyond the immediate desire of the two people most intimately concerned, while her milder sister, the suffragette, believes that women by voting can bring about in both sexes the control of human passion.[20]

Once they had reserved coercive force for the male sex, the Antis were generous in allotting to women the power to mold public opinion, which they believed had its source in social and domestic circles where the influence of woman was supreme. They regarded the vote as merely a tool of public opinion, which was controlled mainly by women. "In the last analysis it is she who is the arbiter; she whose wishes shape our destinies," and this was true because as a nonvoter, woman was above the fray.[21]

Male antisuffragists, although acknowledging the importance of public opinion, saw it as limited solely to the forming of policies, whereas enforcement and maintenance of government rested on male coercive power. Public opinion, they warned, cannot collect taxes, enforce contractual obligations, prevent or punish crimes, suppress riot or rebellion.

The female Antis, on the other hand, preferred to view public opinion as the keystone of government. Public opinion is the state, they said, since not merely the men who vote but everyone in the nation plays his or her part in molding public opinion. One can have a voice in government without the vote by either influencing a voter or forming public opinion. For the Antis, evidence of public opinion at work, that is, of woman's voice in making laws, was the fact that the interests of women were mirrored in the laws of certain states, especially man-suffrage states.[22]

Since they did not have to put their assumptions to the test, the Antis could also claim that whenever the majority of women would ask for the vote they would get it. The fact that they did not then have it was only further evidence that public opinion (i.e., the majority of women) was not in favor of it. Similarly, the vote merely registers public opinion, it does not make it.[23] What really counts is a community's predilection for good laws, and this depends not on government, but on civilization, in which public opinion is molded by many forces, of which home, church, newspaper, and public school are examples and in most of which women play a conspicuous, if not major, part.[24]

The business of state, on the other hand, was not only man's work but also his highest prerogative. To make and execute the laws of the country was equated with manhood. Therefore, men who favored the ballot for women "lowered their own dignity in the State and belittled their own importance as the true makers and enforcers of law."[25] From the lofty perspective of female Antis, governing was the one activity that "makes him a man, a being worthy to stand upon an equality with woman."[26]

Primaries, caucuses, conventions, courts, and legislatures were all involved in the simple casting of a ballot. These were man's work, however, and gave to man the inalienable quality that distinguished him from a mere brute. In other words, if politics were taken away, little would remain. Man's power to rule was what evened the balance between the sexes. Without it, man would be shorn of his manhood and the balance between the sexes destroyed. "What woman wants a man whose power of law-giving is no more than equal to her own?" She has her great gift from God to serve as mother of men, "the exemplar and expounder of all noble, moral and spiritual gifts." His birthright is equally inalienable. If he robs himself of it, "what would become of that mutual homage and respect which is the natural bond between the sexes? No, let him keep for himself something by which we may still reverence him, the horns of Moses, his manly power of law-giving!"[27]

Antisuffrage rhetoric on behalf of the male sex may sound patronizing, but it simply masked the basic anxiety that women addicted to the traditional mold were feeling as circumstances began to change for them. Recognizing implicitly that the future of the sexes was bound up together, it was logical for them to begin to concern themselves with how these changes would affect the male role as well.[28] That their efforts in this direction were somewhat limited was due to two factors. On the one hand, taking their cues from the suffragists, who devoted most of their energies to foreseeing changes in the female role, the Antis, like the suffragists, did not really question the basic patriarchal norms that expected the male to be provider, authority, stoic, protector, or lawmaker. On the other hand, since in the Antis' view all of these roles depended primarily on the male's greater physical strength, and since they believed that governments operated by rule of force, the question of how man could harness this brute force and yet not lose his manhood was crucial. By employing it to enforce the dictates of a civilized state, man's brute strength was transmuted into a special social virtue. Man the animal became man the governor.

According to the Antis' formula, not only was government the rule of force (and therefore man's work), but political life, in which the business of government was carried out, was "modified war." The attention they lavished on depicting the horrors of political life is understandable given their belief that suffrage meant more than voting. It meant entering the field of politics. "The vote is a symbol of government and leads at once into the atmosphere of politics."[29] One step will lead to another, they predicted, "first suffrage, then office, one barrier after another disappearing and then promiscuous

39

commingling," until both sexes are debased.[30] Even as early as 1879, Catharine Beecher protested the imposition of the responsibilities of civil government on her whole sex. "For with the gift of the ballot, comes the connected responsibility of framing wise laws to regulate finance, war, agriculture, commerce, mining, manufactures, and all the many fields of man's outdoor labor."[31]

The most concise statement of the Antis' position on political life was made by Elihu Root in a letter written May 3, 1915, to Alice Hill Chittenden, president of the New York State Anti-Suffrage Association.[32] Since Root at that time was residing officer of the New York Constitutional Convention, he was prevented from taking an active part in the campaign being waged by the Antis against woman suffrage. He did, however, express his support of their cause in this letter which, according to him, was a recapitulation of opinions he had expressed earlier at the 1894 Constitutional Convention. Disavowing any intention of relegating women to an inferior position, he was careful to point out that they were "different," not inferior. Evidently, in his mind this became a rather fine distinction.

> One question to be determined in the discussion of this subject is whether the nature of woman is such that her taking upon her the performance of the functions implied in suffrage will leave her in the possession and the exercise of her highest powers or will be an abandonment of those powers and an *entering upon a field in which, because of her differences from man, she is distinctly inferior.* [my italics]

For Root, suffrage would be a loss for women because suffrage implied not merely the casting of the ballot.

> Suffrage, if it means anything, means entering upon the field of political life, and politics is modified war. In politics there is struggle, strife, contention, bitterness, heart-burning, excitement, agitation, everything which is adverse to the true character of woman. Woman rules today by the sweet and noble influences of her character. Put woman into the arena of conflict and she abandons these great weapons which control the world, and she takes into her hands, feeble and nerveless for strife, weapons with which she is unfamiliar and which she is unable to wield. Woman in strife becomes hard, harsh, unlovable, repulsive; as far removed from that gentle creature to whom we all owe allegiance and to whom we confess submission, as the heaven is removed from the earth.

In closing, Root affirmed that the functions of men were by no means superior to those of women. What he was expressing was simply a variation of the theme that "the hand that rocks the cradle rules the world."

> The true government is in the family. The true throne is in the household. The highest exercise of power is that which forms the conscience, influences the will, controls the impulses of men, and there today woman is supreme and woman rules the world.

Others took up the theme that politics was an aggressive, warlike business, unfit for the finer sensibilities of women. Participation in political matters would not only impose cumbrous duties upon all women but would introduce them to the "bitter strife, the falsification and publicity often attendant upon political campaigns."[33] They insisted that an effectual vote was an organized vote and that this meant primaries and conventions, caucuses, and officeholding and endless work. In their view, politics to be effective involved "incessant organization and combination, continual perseverance against disappointment and betrayal, steadfast effort for small and hard-fought advance."[34] Political life was a notorious breeder of contention.

> In politics I do not think that women have any place. Neither physically nor temperamentally are they strong enough for the fray. The life is too public, too wearing, and too unfitted to the nature of women. It is bad enough for men . . . and it would be worse for women.[35]

The Antis were consistent in their view that man had an innate predisposition to aggression, and they believed that the suffragists were singularly naive in thinking that power relationships could occur in a noncompetitive atmosphere.

> Women fail to grasp the meaning of political power. And, where they do partially recognize existing facts, their whole campaign for suffrage is based on the supposition that we are past the age of violence, that wars, strikes, revolts and riots are not only things of the past, but that we are already in an age of triumphant arbitration.[36]

A look at the realities of political life probably only confirmed the Antis in their assumptions. Unfortunately for the suffragist cause, as increasing numbers of women were enfranchised and began to play a part in political life, they were as much caught up in the system as men. For every example of woman's benign influence at the polls cited by the suffragist, the Antis would point to the notoriety occasioned by the sight of women acting in the same way as their male counterparts.

> After the canvassing, heckling, button-holing, street-speaking, megaphoning, rioting and slugging which the country saw contributed by women to the last presidential campaign, no suffragist will ever tell us again that voting is "only casting a ballot on the way to market."[37]

It is no wonder that the Antis viewed as retrogressive any attempt to enfranchise women. Civilization in their terms had enabled women to escape the crushing burden and strife of doing battle in public. To allow them to enter political life was a throwback that would have deleterious influences on womanhood and eventually poison the whole system.

The Antis were much more realistic than the suffragists when it came to the question of woman's moral instincts. They realized, for example, that women were just as capable of aggression as men. Annie Nathan Meyer, one of the founders and a trustee of Barnard College, argued that the development of woman's character had not kept up with that of her intellect. The deterioration of women in public life, she felt, was evident in the wire-pulling, the unscrupulousness in attaining an end, the unfairness, the love of office, and the "insincerity which reveal themselves in the large organizations of women, with discouraging and startling resemblance to the methods of their weaker brethren." If women had lived for centuries in the same freedom and under the same temptations as men, they would have shown far less self-control and power of resistance. The assertion of sex superiority was not proven because there were fewer drunkards among women than men, for as women entered into industrial competition and into public life, "with its drain on the nervous strength," they simply assumed men's vices.[38]

Most antisuffragists shared Meyer's opinion, which might account for the fact that the Antis disdained and even derided the peace efforts of many of the leaders associated with the suffrage movement, who believed that once women could make their superior moral influence felt in public life, war would be eliminated.[39] In view of the fact that women's groups as a whole were largely pacifist in 1914, the Antis represented a distinct minority. While the Antis were willing to accept the idea that women might be men's moral superiors, they believed that woman's special virtue could operate only within the carefully circumscribed limits of the home and family. In the battlefield of politics this virtue had little chance for survival. Given the efforts of the suffragists on behalf of peace, the Antis viewed the outbreak of World War I as a setback for the suffragists and a vindication of the antisuffrage position that law and treaties were useless unless backed by physical force. They felt that what they had always maintained in national government had proved true in international relations—physical force was the fundamental basis of government and that only those who were capable of enforcing their decisions should be responsible for governing.[40]

The work that best reflects antisuffragist thinking on women and their relation to government is *Woman and the Republic* by Helen Kendrick Johnson. Johnson is a very difficult person to understand since she has left almost nothing in the way of memoirs or personal papers. Nevertheless, because her book was central to the movement—frequently cited and often borrowed from—and because she herself was extremely active within it, it is important to try to understand how she came to be involved.

Johnson was born in Hamilton, New York, in 1844 and died in 1917. She was an active author, editor, housewife, and antisuffragist, although she never achieved major recognition or prominence. In 1869 she married Rossiter Johnson, a sometime literary man and editor. They had six children, three girls and three boys, born between 1874 and 1888, of whom only one survived.[41]

Johnson edited several books of poems and songs, and was the author of *The Roddy Books, Raleigh Westgate,* and *Woman and the Republic.*[42] In addition to the latter, her other published works on women consisted of "Woman Suffrage and Social Evolution" (*American Woman's Journal,* June 1895) and *Home Training for Citizenship,* a series of seven articles that appeared in *The Examiner* in November and December 1900. She also wrote but did not publish various other works, among them "Woman's Place in Creation" and "The Aryan Ancestry of Christ."[43]

In 1893 and 1894, she edited the *American Woman's Journal.* She was a member of the New York State Association Opposed to Woman Suffrage, the National League for the Civic Education of Women, and the National Society for the Maintenance of American Institutions. In 1886 she founded the Meridian, a midday luncheon club apparently designed to attract women of high financial and social standing. The club held monthly meetings at a New York hotel. After lunch a paper, previously announced, would be read and the subject discussed according to parliamentary rules. Each year a different member acted as corresponding secretary, the only office of the club. Each member presided at one meeting when her turn came alphabetically, and each member presented a paper for discussion in alphabetical order. Alphabet ruled everything. If, for example a standing committee was desired, three members were named in alphabetical order. There was, as a result, "no aspiration to office, and no electioneering."[44] The club was still very active in 1917, the year of Johnson's death.

In 1908 Johnson founded and became the first president of The Guidon, an antisuffrage organization. Among her other varied activities she served as a member for several years of the board of managers of the Henry Street Settlement. This experience familiarized her with the work and management of the settlements and, as a result, she "conceived a distrust of them all." Some were used as forums where "very young men, half-educated and wholly satisfied, exploited socialistic theories, sometimes bordering on anarchism . . . she saw that they would become breeding-beds of atheism and disloyalty."[45]

Johnson regarded herself as always interested in everything that concerned women, yet she maintained that she did not become involved with the question of suffrage until 1893-94, the period in which she was editing *The American Woman's Journal*. In fact, she reported, she knew nothing about the subject when she began the job. Soon after, however, the New York State Constitutional Convention met at Albany and, she recalled in an interview, women contributors began flooding the office with articles favoring votes for women. With the need to exercise proper editorial judgment, her interest began to grow.

> Taking the matter which they submitted and examining it with what I tryed to make absolutely fair editorial eyes—that is, with eyes which endeavored to find the false and see the true—I discovered, working as I am sure I did, without prejudice, that most of the pro-suffrage arguments were illogical and otherwise unworthy. They remain thus to this day.[46]

Since she felt that she could not deny the suffragists space, she published their articles along with her rejoinders.[47]

By the time the Constitutional Convention was over, she "had become firmly convinced that the whole suffrage movement was unsound." As a result, she signed a protest opened by Mrs. Abraham Hewitt, wife of a former mayor of New York City, and then began her research that resulted in *Woman and the Republic*. Evidently she began by familiarizing herself with the suffrage position. She went through the then three existing volumes of *The History of Woman Suffrage* and "pondered the subject in all its legal, moral, and social aspects," until she became convinced that woman suffrage was founded on "demonstrable and radical errors; that it was neither due to women as a right, nor possible to them as an effective function. . . . nor necessary as an educative force."[48] It was then that she wrote *Woman and the Republic*, which was first published in 1897.

At some point, probably after the publication of the third edition of her book in 1913, she became an active member of antisuffrage organizations and even spoke on their behalf before legislative committees at Albany and Washington. She wrote pamphlets and newspaper articles and to a limited extent she even spoke before popular audiences.[49]

In the beginning of *Woman and the Republic*, Johnson declared that her main reason for writing the book was to defend the republic against suffrage charges that the United States was false to its democratic principles in excluding women from the franchise. "Manhood suffrage, and not womanhood suffrage is the final result of the evolution of a democracy." According to her interpretation of the progress of women in history, in proportion as aristocratic power lost its hold on Western Europe, women were exempted from services to the state and gained in *moral* influence.

> So it would seem that under a monarchical system, with a standing army and a hereditary nobility to support the throne, the royal mandate could be issued by a woman. Any Queen, as well as the one that Alice met in Wonderland, could say "Off with his head!" But when freedom grew, and the democratic idea began to prevail, and each individual man became a king, and each home a castle, the law given by God and not man came into exercise.

For Johnson, the early government of the colonies consisted of the "transported aristocracy of churchly power in the state." Women shared the undemocratic rule, such as voting for various offices when only property holders or other "duly qualified" colonists could vote. After 1789 under the Constitution the last vestiges of churchly political rule and property qualification disappeared and state after state inserted the word "male" into their constitutions, with the result that women no longer had a voice, but a more vital and enduring freedom was secured.[50]

Suffrage, seen this way, was not a natural right, and all Antis writing on the subject would have agreed. In Johnson's view, suffrage was also not a universal right, springing from the necessary conditions of an organized society, for individuals could not make a claim to suffrage on the grounds of their universal right as citizens. Once suffrage can be qualified, she concluded, it is deprived of its universality.

Believing strenuously in Jefferson's dictum that "the will of the majority is the natural law of every society and the only sure guardian of the rights of man," she predicted that if women had the power to create a numerical majority, when there was a majority of the law's natural and only defenders against them,

> they might soon precipitate a crisis that would lead to bloodshed, which they would be powerless either to prevent or allay. Would the majority of men submit to the minority of men associated with the non-combatants?

Johnson argued that in contrast to the suffragist who believed that the minority would submit until through argument and persuasion it could win over the majority, majority rule was made possible only by the rule of force. "Democratic government is at an end" she said, "when those who issue decrees are not identical with those who can enforce those decrees."

> Stability is one of the highest virtues that any government can possess, and perhaps the most necessary. It can have no stability if it issues decrees that it cannot enforce. The only way to avoid such decrees is, to make sure that behind every law and every policy adopted stands a power so great that no power in the land can overthrow it. The only such power possible consists of a majority of the men.

Johnson realized, of course, that her formula did not always guarantee *good* laws, but it did secure stability and avoid revolution. "The majority may blunder, but they are the only power that can correct their own blunders."[51]

Johnson was aware that if she stressed the fact that men were eligible to vote because they alone were considered potentially available to serve on juries, militia, fire department, army, or police, she would run the risk of having to admit that the vote was given to man as a *reward* for standing ready to give this service to the state. She tried to avoid this dilemma by making a rather fine distinction. In effect she built in a catch-22.

> . . . it is a recognition by the state that as he must stand ready to defend it, he should assist in establishing the laws which it may call upon him to enforce. As he has assisted to frame them, he cannot refuse to defend them.[52]

Woman's only relation to this defense was as beneficiary. Therefore, her relation to the laws with which that defense was associated must be one of advice, not control.

Although Johnson relegated woman to the role of adviser, she did not believe that her importance was in any way diminished. In keeping with the mainstream of antisuffragist sentiment, she insisted that

> woman's relation to the Republic is as important as man's. Woman deals with the beginnings of life; man, with the product made from those beginnings; and this fact marks the difference in their spheres and reveals woman's immense advantage in moral opportunity. It also suggests the incalculable loss in case her work is not done or ill done.[53]

In a postscript to the 1913 edition of her work, Johnson emphasized what she felt was the most general theme in her book, namely, that woman suffrage was inconsistent with true republican forms of government and belonged instead to its two greatest enemies—aristocratic government and socialism. She pointed out that in her first edition she had prophesied that the growth of woman suffrage and the ultimate destruction of "womanly ideals and womanly character" would come through socialism, and that her prophesy had been fulfilled. Describing the process by which Washington, California, Oregon, Arizona, and Kansas had adopted woman suffrage, she attributed its success in each case to the influence of "radical Socialism." Even the national government had not been spared the influence of this sinister and pervasive worldwide socialist conspiracy.

> The welfare lobby, at Washington—like the Woman's Trade Unions and a hundred other Socialistic-suffrage organizations—appear to believe that the government is a machine which, set in motion—will run on by itself and turn out money independently and continuously for pensions for "government motherhood," for the children of wives who are "economically independent," for salaried social workers, until—as one Socialist writer puts it—"everything that is now on top shall be on the bottom, and everything that is now on the bottom shall be on the top"—a most pious and unselfish programme![54]

And so, concluding on a note reminiscent of antisuffragism as a whole, Johnson closed ranks with the conservatives and sat back to await the destruction of the republic.

One of the by-products of the Antis' insistence on keeping women out of political life was their narrow definition of politics. They viewed politics as an extension of the activities of the male world. The heart of politics for them was concern with the business of tariffs, international trade, and international relations. Therefore it was but a short step from managing a business to governing a state. Home life, on the other hand, conjured up a different set of assumptions, and the activities associated with the home were regarded as strictly female. What is significant is that the two areas were seen as *wholly* distinct.

> The care of the sick and the insane; the treatment of the poor; the education of children; in all these matters, and others besides, they have made good their claim to larger and more extended powers. We rejoice in it. But when it comes to questions of national or foreign policy, or of grave constitutional change, then we maintain that the necessary and normal experience of women—speaking generally and in the mass—does not and can never provide them with such materials for sound judgment as are open to men.[55]

In the Antis' schedule of activities appropriate to each sex, those that were designated as matters of concern to women appear to have been regarded as somewhat less weighty than those within men's jurisdiction. Furthermore, in their insistence on maintaining the mutual exclusiveness of the male and female spheres, they failed to realize that the problems of women and men might be interrelated. For example, both suffragists and Antis agreed on the home as the fundamental socializing agent of western society. The usual suffrage position, however, was that in order to protect and preserve the home, the scope of woman's concern must be enlarged. American women needed suffrage to preserve the home. Furthermore, they held that the position of the family as the base of all social progress could be maintained only if the woman remained the central figure in the home. And this was possible only if woman had a full and equal voice and eligibility to shape public policies so that she had the power and influence she needed to preserve the integrity of the home.[56]

Therefore, suffragists urged that woman be given the ballot so that her work could become more effective. In other words, the suffragists regarded woman's actions on behalf of public health, pure foods, and social hygiene as legitimate and logical outgrowths of her interests and concerns within the home. Their view of what constituted political activity was more eclectic than that of the Antis. They enlarged the current definition of politics to include these extended activities of woman. Although usually overlooked, this represented an important contribution of the suffrage movement to the self-image of the American woman. After all, woman's foremost accomplishments in the nineteenth century took place outside the traditional definition of politics—in such activities as education, social work, and reform. The suffragists effectively enlarged the meaning of politics to include these areas.

In contrast, the Antis felt that it was important to keep charitable and educational administration out of politics. They believed that "education and municipal government should be taken out of the domain of party politics."[57] The Antis probably feared that suffrage insistence that the community be viewed as an extension of the home would obscure the distinction between the female and male spheres and turn that sanctuary for the female sex into a political arena.

Those who denigrated politics probably hoped to reduce its significance while elevating the social contributions made by women in their nonpolitical sphere. By limiting the male sphere to the mere business of running the nation, the Antis were able to claim for women a sphere accessible exclusively to female influence. Frequently when the Antis felt compelled to draw a comparison between suffragist views and their own, they discussed their differences in terms of more or less government. They believed, for example, that suffragism staked its faith on more government; that suffragists felt that in order to attack existing evils, women needed to organize for participation in lawmaking. To the Antis this was just another instance of suffragism's resemblance to socialism.[58]

In essence, the Antis seemed to have had an intuitive awareness that male domination has been expressed historically in Western society through male-controlled governments. Rather than take issue with the question of male domination, however, they chose to allow men full sovereignty within a narrowly prescribed realm of government, while claiming for themselves female supremacy in many of the areas outside of government.

THREE

Confronting
the Suffragists:
Deploying the Arguments
for Strategic Advantage

As the two sides became engaged in actual conflict, antisuffrage arguments became less theoretical and more pragmatic. Antisuffragists increasingly began to resort to the "facts" in an effort to reach even larger numbers of men and women. Since their immediate targets were the male legislators in both the state and national governments who were being barraged by suffragists to enact woman suffrage legislation on behalf of womankind, it is not surprising that the Antis began their attack by trying to persuade them that the suffragists were *not* representative of the majority of women.

> We believe that the great majority of women in this country are either against woman suffrage or entirely indifferent to it. The largest claim that the suffragists have made is, that one-tenth of the women have put themselves on record in their various organizations. The ninety per cent who have not should have some channel through which to express their opinions, and the associations formed in the different States have been organized with this end in view.[1]

That the Antis were probably sincere in this belief can be seen from the reasons they used to support it. Also it was almost impossible to disprove. They argued that if women had been exposed to the suffrage message for two generations and were still unresponsive, it was because the vast majority of women did not want the vote.[2] As the woman suffrage movement became more strident (and effective), however, it became apparent to the Antis that

51

silence on the issue might be interpreted as consent.[3] They began to realize that as long as women remained indifferent or inactive, they were indirectly acquiescing in the wishes of the vocal suffrage minority.

> Opposition to it has hitherto been passive, and to a great degree merely instinctive. No one has strongly felt the need to give her reasons against it. Therefore no one still uncertain upon the subject has had the chance to hear both sides and intelligently make up her mind, and few have even been prompted to think about it at all. But if the negative side is now faithfully presented, the current excitement, we feel, is likely in the end to do more to hurt than to help the "cause."[4]

The Antis justified their decision to violate their basic precepts and present their case before the public in order that their silence not be attributed to fear, indifference, or smallness of numbers.[5] Consistent with their basic philosophy, the Antis perceived themselves as operating only out of necessity, engaging in a preventive measure to ward off an imminent threat. Nowhere in their literature did they proclaim themselves the saviors of society, nor did they visualize themselves as part of a worldwide movement. In this sense their claims and their self-image were much less extravagant than those of the suffragists.

It undoubtedly worked to the advantage of the Antis, both in terms of morale and practical politics, to underscore the fact that the main opponents of woman suffrage were women and to urge that if women really wanted to vote, they would have it. For one thing, it enabled them to depict suffrage as the "only woman's movement which has been met by the organized opposition of women."[6] For another, it enabled them to claim that the weight of public opinion was on their side rather than just the self-interested forces that the suffragists consistently defined as the enemy.

> ... *chief opponents of woman suffrage are* not the special interests nor those men who take a narrow and prejudiced view of woman's relation to the state, but those *women* who have grave doubts whether their duty lies in service to the state by the ballot, or by a fulfillment of present responsibilities which bear no relation to the ballot.[7]

Furthermore, the novelty of the idea was not lost on the press, which began to perpetuate the notion by publicizing it. In 1897, the *Rochester Herald*, in a review of Johnson's *Woman and the Republic*, wrote

. . . for strange as it may appear, there is a well-defined movement among the fair sex to frown down the New-Woman idea, upon which a large proportion of the people look with feelings not unmixed with disgust.[8]

The *Indianapolis Journal*, reviewing the same book, wrote, "It is somewhat remarkable that the most vigorous arraignment of and attack upon the woman-suffrage movement should come from a woman."[9] And an unidentified Boston paper, in an article entitled "Women Actively Oppose the Suffrage Bill," claimed:

It is a unique and unprecedented thing on Beacon Hill to see a great throng of women at a committee hearing, who have come out to protest against having the franchise imposed upon them. Heretofore the remonstrants who have appeared at women's suffrage hearings have been men.[10]

It was inevitable that politicians and legislators reluctant to advance the cause of woman suffrage would find it to their advantage to stress the fact that women themselves were opposed to woman suffrage.

Although the Antis billed themselves as representing the "silent majority" of American women, they were certainly not representative. They came from families that had both money and power, and therefore they could not be construed as a cross section of society. As members of a native-born monied class, they shared all the prejudices of those who felt they had something to lose by the changes taking place in American society. They resented the immigrant and distrusted the poor and feared the swelling of the ranks of the electorate by what they regarded as an illiterate and ignorant vote. It was only natural that these class prejudices were reflected in their views concerning the types of women they felt ought *not* to vote and thus became part of their rationale for resisting the extension of suffrage.

Taking their cue perhaps from Catharine Beecher, who had classified women into five categories, the Antis were fond of visualizing womanhood as consisting of set types. Although these varied somewhat as to particulars, for the most part they constituted three basic categories—the better class, the indifferent, and the degenerate. It was only natural that the Antis considered themselves, and were in fact, a representative segment of the first category.[11] This was the handful of women who carried on church, philanthropic, and reform work when they were not devoting themselves to their domestic tasks. The Antis felt that this kind of woman was capable of developing an interest in and an understanding of political questions but was usually too preoccupied with her primary tasks to take the time to cast her ballot.[12]

The indifferent women constituted the vast majority and included the following subgroups—women of the shopkeeper, clerk, artisan, and prosperous laborer class; wage-earning women; immigrant women, and black women. The first sort were assumed to be overburdened with domestic duties and uninterested in questions outside of their limited sphere.[13] The working women were thought to be exposed to political affairs, but deemed uninterested in questions outside of their own narrow interests.[14] The Antis could not place immigrant women as a group or black women as a race in the third category reserved for what was variously designated the evil, wrong-minded, corrupt, and sordid women.[15] But they did cast them at the bottom of the heap of the indifferent. The Antis feared that the ignorance of immigrant women would make them subject to manipulation by their men, who would have no compunctions about selling not only their own votes, but those of their wives and daughters as well.[16] Sometimes, however, they were not too careful in distinguishing between the illiterate and the vicious.

> We must think of the tens of thousands of illiterate and vicious women in New York City, and just as carefully of the scores of thousands of ignorant negresses at the South. . . . Are we prepared to throw into political life all the women good and bad, intelligent and unintelligent, of the whole U.S., including the swarms which belong to Europe but have been adopted here? . . . Surely the well-trained, educated, intelligent boys of New York City, even though they be not more than ten years old, would make better voters than vicious tramps or stupid foreigners all but wholly ignorant of the English language.[17]

The third kind of woman—the degenerate—consisted of two general types, both considered beyond the pale of respectability and believed to far outnumber the first category of good women.[18] These were the prostitutes, manipulated by bosses, pimps, and saloon keepers, and who, it was feared, would vote because private (and sinister) interests would see to it that they did.[19] The following excerpt reflects this kind of thinking. Printed and reprinted by the Antis, this article appeared in the *San Francisco Examiner* the day after an election in which women voted.

> McDonough Brothers had several automobiles busy all day long hauling Barbary coast dance hall girls and the inmates of houses on Commercial street to the different booths, and always the women were supplied with a marked sample ballot.[20]

The Antis believed, on the other hand, that the great body of homemaking women would not vote, and they used this to buttress their argument that women, if enfranchised, would not purify politics. Arguing that the best women would remain at home, Senator Morgan of Alabama, in an 1887 Senate debate on woman suffrage, complained

> The effect would be to drive the ladies of the land, as they are termed, the well-bred and well-educated women, the women of nice sensibilities, within their home circles, there to remain, while the ruder of that sex would thrust themselves out on the hustings and at the ballot-box, and fight their way to the polls through Negroes and others who are not the best of company even at the polls, to say nothing of the disgrace of association with them. You would paralyze one-third at least of the women of this land by the very vulgarity of the overture made to them that they should go struggling to the polls in order to vote in common with the herd of men.[21]

The degenerate women, argued the Antis, were powerless without the vote, but once enfranchised, the ballot would become a weapon they would use against reform measures because they would want to ensure that their way of life was not interfered with.[22] Whether they went to the polls on their own behalf or because they were forced to, a higher percent of this sort of woman than of respectable women would vote, they predicted.

> Apathetic, ignorant, sordid women—poor or rich—as things now stand, are at worst a negative evil. But such women, with votes, become potential reinforcements to the forces of vice, and those forces are always prompt in rallying their re-enforcements.[23]

The other kind of degenerate or wrong-minded women were those who would devote their lives to public affairs, seeking conspicuous offices and "playing the role of bosses among the ignorant of their sex."[24] They would "employ the distinctive power of their sex in caucuses, in jury-boxes, and in legislative and congressional committees; thus adding another to the many deteriorating influences of public life." Thus the best of women would shun political life and the most unprincipled would have the field to themselves.[25]

Tallying up the score, the Antis felt that if women were enfranchised, the influence (and the interests) of the "better class of women" would be nullified. Woman suffrage would destroy the indirect power of the informed woman since the vote would give equal power to the uninformed. The forces lined up something like this. On one side were the *vote* of the informed man reinforced by the *influence* of the informed woman; on the other side was the *vote* of the uninformed man. Universal woman suffrage would destroy this situation. By distributing the power between women qualified for holding it as well as those not qualified, it would result in a face-off between, on the one side, the votes of informed men and women and on the other, those of the uninformed of both sexes.[26] Here is the most succinct statement reflecting the Antis' abhorrence of the possibility of changing the odds.

> To-day, without the vote, the women who are intelligent and interested in public affairs use their ability and influence for good measures. And the indifferent woman does not matter. The unscrupulous woman has no vote. . . . The state gets all the benefit of its best women, and none of the danger from its worst women. . . . We have now two against one, a fine majority, the good men and the good women against the unscrupulous men. Equal suffrage would make it two to two—the good men and the good women against the unscrupulous men and the unscrupulous women—a tie vote between good and evil instead of a safe majority for good.[27]

The Antis believed that their interests were threatened from yet another direction besides the imagined voting strength of ignorant and corruptible women. They realized only too well that an indifferent voter, to the extent that she or he was manipulable, was a potentially dangerous voter. They disputed the suffragist contention that casting a ballot took no time and argued that if that was all that men did, it was no wonder if government was mismanaged. The implication, as always, was that women would do better if they trained their sons to accept more fully the responsibility of government.[28] The Antis were also aware that many male voters fell far short of the ideal of an active and responsible citizenry and became pawns of those who used the game of politics for their own self-aggrandizement. One complaint was that Tammany leaders gave all their time to politics while the "reform" vote could rarely be got to the polls. Some Antis expressed the view that too few of the best men ran for office.[29]

The problem for the Antis, however, was that if they accused men of not doing their jobs, they would find themselves in agreement with the suffragists who maintained that since men were making such a mess of things, they might as well let women have a try at it. If, on the other hand, the Antis praised the way men carried out their political responsibilities, they ran the risk of appearing either totally naive or else unquestioningly supportive of the bowdlerization of the democratic process they held so dear. The Antis circumvented this dilemma by remaining avowedly aristocratic.

> Those of us who have had occasion to watch the work of the men who recognize a continuing responsibility to sustain good government, year in and year out, know that their problem is the "rousing" of the respectable, but indifferent voter. The problem has become harder as the number of elections has been increased by the primaries and by the extended use of the initiative-referendum.[30]

There was probably no better way for the Antis to enhance their own effectiveness than by pointing to the failures of their opponents. In this instance the record was on their side. From 1898 to 1909, according to Richard Barry, the suffragists suffered a total of 164 defeats—an average of one every 27 days, he was quick to point out.

> In that time not one single pro-suffrage law has been passed in this country. And every one of these 164 proposed woman suffrage laws was smothered in the committees of the various state legislatures.[31]

In later years, too, the Antis employed the same tactic. In 1917, Foxcroft pointed out that in the three preceding years suffrage amendments to state constitutions had been submitted to the voters at 14 state elections, defeated in 12, and adopted by narrow majorities only in Montana and Nevada, states whose combined population was less than that of the city of Boston, she made sure to inform her readers.[32]

The Antis were probably not too far off. From 1896 to 1910 the suffragists experienced their worst defeats in the campaign states.[33]

In their own lives the Antis were themselves beneficiaries of the many reforms that had been enacted on woman's behalf throughout the latter part of the nineteenth century. Since they were inheritors of these greater freedoms rather than pioneers in the battle to obtain them, many Antis tended, characteristically, to take them somewhat for granted. Others, however, were quick to see the advantage of using these advances to point to the fact that woman had already achieved *without suffrage* all the improvements in her status that only suffrage itself was supposed to confer. In fact, according to the Antis, the suffragists were in no way responsible for these reforms.

Beginning with higher education, proclaimed as the "special mark of her [woman's] progress in this era," the Antis pointed to the fact that the founders of higher education for women did not need aid from the suffragists, who merely "strove to break down the sex barriers in education" and directed their efforts to advocating coeducation, rather than "higher" education for women. Going beyond the opening of educational opportunities for women, the Antis alleged that favorable legislation such as married woman's property rights bills were enacted prior to the suffrage movement. Furthermore, they claimed, the professions were not opened to women as a result of suffrage demands, for women had studied medicine before the woman suffrage movement.[34]

Summing up the antisuffrage position, Helen K. Johnson argued that if the suffrage movement were disbanded, woman's gains would be unaffected: her philanthropies would be unharmed; her colleges would endure; the professions would continue to grant diplomas to qualified women; tradesmen would still employ women; good laws would not be repealed; literature would not suffer; and finally, there would be no more tendency than existed in her day to move to a state where women still had "freedom."[35]

In other words, the suffragists were unsuccessful in arousing public opinion to grant woman suffrage because women had already achieved a thorough reform in the laws and had more advantages and more respect than women anywhere else in the world.[36] And, as in other instances, the evolutionary principle was again borrowed. Viewing the past from the vantage point of their own relatively emancipated present, it was easy for the Antis to assume that all the changes that had occurred were part of an inevitable, ongoing, evolutionary process.

> the admitted limitations to the sphere of woman had arisen from conditions which natural growth and evolution were sure in the long run to dissipate, without any violent structural changes in society itself.[37]

The Antis felt that time was on their side.

> For is not time itself fighting our battles for us—bringing to pass, without the aid of Woman Suffrage, those conditions necessary for the best development of their sex for which the old-time Suffragists, with other women not Suffragists, strove so long and so courageously? Individual freedom, educational privileges, legal rights have all been gained without the ballot—women and women's organizations participate in public work and influence legislation. . . . What justification, then, remains in the demand for Woman Suffrage? . . . The right to participate in the mere machinery of politics, the only remaining ground for contention would seem a barren issue for which to contend.[38]

Of course the Antis did not address themselves to the question of why, if this issue of the suffrage was so "barren," it provoked such vehement opposition.

Just what were these advantages that women at the end of the nineteenth century were conscious of possessing? The Massachusetts Antis conveniently summarized those that pertained to the legal status of women in their state and circulated them as part of their propaganda. Women were not obliged to pay a poll tax,[39] perform jury duty or military duty. They were exempt from arrest in civil action until judgment was obtained against them. Women committing a misdemeanor in their husbands' presence were assumed to have been coerced and were prima facie excused. Alien women, by marrying citizens, or by their husbands' naturalization, became citizens.[40]

In New York State, the Antis also felt themselves to be the pampered objects of legislative concern. Mrs. Schuyler (M. G.) van Rensselaer, surveying the past in 1900, summarized the legal advantages and the customs of the courts in favor of greater "freedom, independence and security for women than for men."[41] All women of New York State could own property. A married woman was able to carry on a trade, business, or profession and keep her earnings. She might sue and be sued and make contracts as freely as an unmarried woman or man. She might sell or transfer her real or personal property. She was not liable for her husband's debts or obliged to contribute to his support (whereas her husband was obliged and liable for her). A woman was entitled to alimony even if she remarried. A woman in business could not be arrested in an action for a debt fraudulently contracted as a man might be. A husband's right to a portion of his wife's property began only after the birth of a living child and she did not need his consent to sell it during her lifetime and might even deprive him of it altogether by will. A married woman had equal rights in regard to children and her husband could not appoint a guardian without her written consent.

In addition to citing just how far-reaching and humane the laws were concerning women, the Antis also emphasized the positions of trust and responsibility to which women were appointed. In Massachusetts, beginning with the appointment of Clara Temple Leonard to the State Board of Health, Lunacy and Charity, trustees of hospitals and correctional institutions were often women.[42] In what was undoubtedly meant as a tribute to the progress women had made in a state that had not yet enfranchised them, antisuffragist Ellen Mudge Burrill pointed out that "There are plenty of positions already held by women who are doing *inconspicuous and unexciting work*."[43] Apparently from an antisuffragist perspective this did not present an incongruity. Working along from day to day in quiet obscurity was what was expected of women, even of those in public roles. Burrill also proudly indicated that the 18 State Boards employed a total of 45 women, all of whose work was *voluntary* and who were appointed by the governor and *working under laws passed by men in the Legislature.*[44]

The corollary of the Antis' belief that women had progressed considerably without benefit of woman suffrage was that man alone had been woman's chief benefactor. They repeatedly insisted that if women really wanted anything, they could rely on the generosity of male legislators to give it to them.

> The marvelous progress of the last half century has been brought about, not by one party nor by one movement, but by a combination of great forces working in legislation, education, science, invention, and practical religion. In this great world movement, men have done their full share always, and revision of the laws may be expected from them until the best interests of humanity are served.[45]

In fact, one of the key tenets of the antisuffragists was that of all the impediments to woman suffrage, the most important was "the long-continued indifference of the great mass of the people." Designed to undermine the suffragists' contention that their lack of success was due to a long-standing tradition of antifeminist prejudice, the Antis argued that public opinion was not opposed to advances for women. If anything, public opinion was in favor of advances, as evidenced by the contrast between its approval of all the legislative reforms that gave women equal opportunity in every detail of life and its obvious neutrality on the question of suffrage. The Antis attributed this indifference to the fact that from 1848 to 1910 every important legal restriction on women had been removed in most major states. One example cited was that in New York State the same legislators in Albany who removed property-holding restrictions from married woman and granted them full contractual and conjugal rights, placing them on a legal equality with men, "have turned a deaf ear to the annual demand for political equality." If public opinion were really in favor of woman suffrage, the "mere handful" of antisuffragists could not for one moment withstand the issue.

> Is it not absurd to say that the movement has been downed for sixty years by prejudice against women when everything else they could possibly ask for has been granted them unreservedly, and when all the efforts of the suffragists during that time have not even aroused resistance except spasmodically.[46]

Another ploy used regularly by the Antis as part of their tactics to defeat suffrage was to appeal to the historical record by asking what enfranchised women had done with the vote and what the vote had done to women. In the first category they were fond of pointing to those occasions where enfranchised women did not make full use of the ballot. For example, in Massachusetts, from 1879 when women were granted school suffrage, until 1888, the Antis used the smallness and irregularity of the vote against the suffragists.[47] Even as late as 1917, a popular antisuffragist pamphlet pointed out that "In Massachusetts, where women have had the school ballot since 1879, the proportion voting is still less than five per cent."[48]

In 1888, on the other hand, large numbers of Protestant women voted in an anti-Catholic election designed to eliminate Catholic influence in the public schools by ensuring that only Protestants were elected to the school board. The Protestant women's drive to save the schools from the menace of Catholicism (and the evils of foreign influence that it implied) was charged with a strong nativist element, which the Antis were quick to point out were instances of the emotional and unstable elements that women injected into politics. This argument was used as ammunition by the Antis until the 1895 election, when the woman suffrage referendum overshadowed even this issue.[49] Finally in 1895, when women went to the polls to decide on municipal suffrage in Massachusetts, the Antis were able to cite the very small number of women who voted as evidence that women did not desire the vote. (The Antis boycotted the polls rather than have to vote "no.") For almost the duration of the suffrage struggle, the Antis used the results of this referendum as one of their major weapons.[50]

As long as woman suffrage was an untried theory in the vast majority of states, the suffragists could remain unchallenged in their assertion that woman's vote would be cast for moral and human legislation to purify politics. Once gradual inroads were made, however, and increasing numbers of women became enfranchised, the opponents of women suffrage realized a strategic advantage by pointing to what women had *not* accomplished with the vote. It then became a common practice to call attention to all occasions when the changes envisioned by the suffragists did not materialize. In the end, the extravagant claims of the latter must have been a source of embarrassment to the cause, if not an actual handicap.[51]

Claiming that suffrage was a vastly overrated tool, the Antis, with little attention to consistency, enlarged upon the "pernicious effects of woman suffrage in the States where it now exists."[52] Frequently the Antis compared woman suffrage and man suffrage states, claiming that some of the most advanced protective legislation was enacted in man suffrage states.[53]

The Antis frequently used the first four states where women had been fully enfranchised since the 1890s (Colorado, Wyoming, Utah, Idaho) as illustrations of the ill effects of woman suffrage and the deterioration that occurred when women voted. For example, they pointed out that in Wyoming woman suffrage had been granted by one of the most corrupt legislatures the state ever had. They alleged that men knew that at the time *good* women were few and felt that they could manage the others. Colorado provided a much used example of what woman suffrage would mean in practice, since it was more highly developed than the three other western suffrage states and contained the one urban center where conditions approximated those in the East. By the second decade of the twentieth century, the Antis blamed Colorado's more than 20 years of woman suffrage for increases in the state's divorce rate, in the amount of juvenile delinquency, and in the number of wayward girls.[54]

In states where there was no organized opposition to woman suffrage, such as Utah, where women had been voting since 1896, the Antis concentrated their arguments almost exclusively on the actual experience of women as voters. In Utah the record of women actively engaged in politics had been a source of embarrassment to the suffragists. The suffragists had to live down the fact that from 1870 until 1887 Utah's women voters had voted to retain that menace to the sanctity of the monogamous family—plural marriage. The Antis referred to the situation in Utah as a "Turkish harem" and as evidence of the power of the priesthood over voting women.

> Utah answers the questions—the Elders command—the woman's religious fervor makes her obey, and her hero worship for the Elder weakens her judgment.[55]

As evidence of the fact that woman suffrage did not give women more self-respect, the Antis cited the fact that in Utah Martha Cannon was elected state senator against her husband, who was nominated for the same office on the Republican ticket. Evidently an interviewer for the *Salt Lake Herald*, speaking with Cannon while she was senator-elect, asked her among other questions if she was a strong believer in woman suffrage. The Antis delighted in quoting her reply.

Of course I am. It will help women to purify politics. Women are better than men. Slaves are better than their masters. . . . I believe in polygamy—a plural wife isn't half as much of a slave as a single wife. If her husband has four wives, she has three weeks of freedom every single month. Of course it is all over now, but I think the women of Utah think with me, that we were much better off with polygamy. Sixty per cent of the voters of Utah are women. We control the State. What am I going to do with my children while I am making laws for the State? The same thing I have done with them, when I have been practicing medicine. They have been left to themselves a good deal. Some day there will be a law compelling people to have no more than a certain amount of children, and then the mothers of this land can live as they ought to live.[56]

One antisuffragist, quoting Cannon, made sure to let the reader know that this was the character and opinion of the *highest* state official that woman suffrage had produced. She concluded, therefore, that it could only arouse disapproval and disgust and that women would not uplift the position of women, especially when they had full political power like men.[57]

As the Antis viewed the situation, not only had woman's position not improved since equal status, but it had actually worsened.

It has put lines in her face; sharpened her temper; given her a hawk-like expression, and lowered the whole tone of the public relationship of men and women. Women now stand in the cars; they are crowded away from ticket windows; men have ceased to remove their hats in elevators . . . it is a high price for women to pay for the right to vote.[58]

Another western state that served as an illustration of good women losing influence by entering politics was Nevada. This was particularly true, the Antis felt, in the area of divorce reform.

The easy divorce laws of that state, in force until three years ago [1913], were a national scandal. This was realized by certain women of the state, who in consequence brought their moral influence to bear upon the legislature for the repeal of these laws. Their efforts were successful and the laws were repealed. Woman suffrage was granted in Nevada last fall, and one of the very first acts of the legislature was to re-enact the easy divorce laws![59]

Despite the fact that easy divorce laws benefited women even more than men, as evidenced by the fact that most divorces were initiated by women, the Antis were definitely on the side of the conservative forces that opposed divorce. Sharing the latter's views that divorce promoted family instability, they

63

opposed any attempt to liberalize existing divorce laws. That divorce was demonstrably easier to obtain in the four woman suffrage states than in New York or Massachusetts was a point the Antis did not overlook. They pointed out, for example, that in Colorado it could be obtained for any one of eight causes; in Wyoming for any one of eleven; in Idaho for any of seven, and in Utah for any of six. New York State, by contrast, had only one legal cause for divorce.[60]

The antisuffragists were anything but consistent in their treatment of these western states; when they could not find the facts to fit their assumptions, they simply indicated that these states were disqualified as representative examples. Colorado, Wyoming, Utah, and Idaho were sparsely populated and rural, with few major cities and only a handful of electoral votes. Consequently, it was ridiculous to assume, they said, that what obtained for them should obtain for the more populous eastern states. They were fond of pointing out that New York City, with a population in 1900 of 3,437,202, had more than three times the population of the four woman suffrage states combined.

Since one of the major thrusts of the suffragist position was that politics was in such a deplorable state that only the woman's vote could restore it, it was inevitable that the Antis would meet this too on its own ground. When they were not pointing out that the men engaged in political life were only as good as the mothers who trained them, they were arguing that the existing system had much to recommend it. Extolling the legislative process in man suffrage states, the Antis went to great lengths to cite the large number of bills presented—some, in fact, offered by women who were able to petition the legislature—the referral of all bills to committees, and the system of giving a public hearing to each and reporting on it with action taken one way or another. This was often contrasted to those "Western States" where bills allegedly never saw the light because they were not even reported out of committee until the chairman consented. In Massachusetts, it was claimed, no bill was pigeonholed.[61]

Attempts to discredit suffragists were also part of the antisuffragist arsenal. These ranged from maligning the suffrage leaders as depraved and immoral beings who advocated repudiation of the Bible and the subversion of all decency to casting doubt on their loyalty as patriotic citizens.[62]

When World War I broke out, the Antis channeled their nativist tendencies into a jingoistic and belligerent Americanism that they directed against woman suffrage, decrying it as a vehicle of subversive and un-American activities.[63]

The September 30, 1917, edition of the New York *Evening Telegram* accused the suffragists of being unpatriotic and disloyal because they had paraded an auto through Herald Square with a large new flag streaming behind, while on the back of the car was a sign that read "Vote for Woman Suffrage." Calling it a camouflage, the paper accused the suffragists of using a United States flag for improper purpose.

> Suffrage is largely composed of pacifists. It is not back of the government, but throwing obstacles in its way. We protest the misuse of the United States flag by the suffragists.[64]

Since so many suffragists were active pacifists during the war years, it was impossible for the Antis to disprove the suffrage contention that war would be eliminated if woman had the vote.[65] Therefore, they chose instead the tactic of impugning the patriotism of any and all who worked for peace.

> And now, as to the genuineness of the patriotism of the suffragist. . . . Don't forget all the suffragists who, in the face of this fearful world cataclysm, argued that if women had the vote there would be no war. Don't forget that when our ships were being sunk, our citizens massacred at sea, our rights ignored, and our national dignity spurned, not one woman prominent among the suffragists declared herself for preparedness and against peace without honor. Don't forget that Jane Addams, Fola Follette, Crystal Eastman, and other prominent suffragists are still outspoken pacifists.[66]

Sometimes, however, these attacks backfired. In 1915, the Man-Suffrage Association was forced to withdraw from circulation a leaflet it had been distributing throughout New York State entitled "Woman Suffrage (Some Underlying Principles and Comments)." According to Carrie Chapman Catt, then president of the Empire State Campaign Committee, the leaflet said that "Woman suffrage should be repudiated because of the type and attitude of the leaders it has drawn to its cause." Evidently after naming the "leaders," among whom was Catt, it went on to say that "All are opposed to the doctrine that the family is the unit of society and the state."

Catt, in a letter to Everett Wheeler, president of the Man-Suffrage Association, demanded retraction, accusing him of seeking to defeat woman suffrage "by traducing the character of the women who are advocating it and by attempting to convey the impression that the leaders of the cause have immoral aims." Catt's letter must have made an impression, for Wheeler retracted the inflammatory remark and withdrew the leaflet from circulation.

65

Nevertheless, he did not give up entirely. In his reply to Catt, he said that regardless of the truth or falsity of the statement attributed to her, he could not keep from wondering whether she was in fact "opposed to the doctrine that the family is the unit of society and the State." Claiming that he had so often heard or seen this doctrine advocated by the antisuffragists and opposed by suffragists, he admitted that it seemed to him "the crucial difference between us." Finally, after denying that his organization ever intended to charge that Catt "held immoral views" or was "an enemy to home and family," he concluded:

> . . . as I see it, the most dangerous elements in our commonwealth are, 1. the Socialists; 2. the advocates of easy divorce; 3. the advocates of "the economic independence of women." These to the best of my knowledge without exception are suffragists. Can you name one exception?

Catt, in what was obviously intended as the last word on the subject, named the exceptions:

> (1) E. Belfort Bax is a socialist writer of reputation and fights woman suffrage as hard as you do. . . .
> 2) So far as I know there is no organized movement for easy divorce. The most conspicuous evidence of such movement is the Red Light District and by actual canvass it has been found to be unanimously on your side of this question.
> (3) I know several ladies who give their entire time to the propaganda of anti-suffrage and have found generous economic independence in so doing.

Catt concluded her letter with her version of "the most dangerous elements in this commonwealth: 1) Political bribery which invalidates the most sacred principles of our government. 2) Men who draw vast dividends from very underpaid labor. 3) White slavery which pollutes the health of the nation, robs the home of its self-respect."[67]

Accusing the suffragists of using their partial victories such as school suffrage as political stepping stones, the Antis questioned their sincerity and asked why those who advocated school suffrage did not instead work toward solving the problems in the public schools.[68] Discrediting the suffragists also took the form of insinuating that they were not representative of the "normal" woman for whom love should dictate active obedience. Denigrating them as "platform ladies" who fought for themselves first, and their sex afterward, they were sometimes cast as freaks.[69]

From the antisuffragist perspective, if the energy and money squandered to promote suffrage were expended on reforms that the suffragists foretold would accompany their voting, the reforms would have all been accomplished long ago.[70] They cited the Civic Federation, the Municipal Leagues, and the Women's Clubs, where women accomplished an enormous amount of work for the good of all, in contrast to the professional suffrage agitator who, they decried, was not out for service to the town, state, or country, but for herself.

Perhaps what most irritated the traditional type of woman was not that women were actually out there on platforms agitating for change but that they were willing to consider their own cause—that of women—as a priority. This went against the grain of womanly self-denial. What was admired in the male sex as initiative, independence, and self-esteem was looked upon in women as selfish and self-serving, bold and unwomanly. A short article in the January 1912 issue of *The Anti-Suffragist* singled out the dropping of the husbands' names on the visiting card or address of married women as the "most noticeable social innovation of the suffragists" and condemned it as "an assertion of separate and individual interests and bank account."

Elizabeth Cady Stanton's *Woman's Bible* was often cited as an example of that ultimate transgression, being true to oneself before all others. The following excerpt is a case in point:

> Though it is most commendable to serve our fellow-beings, yet woman's first duty is to herself, to develop all her own power and possibilities, that she may better guide and serve the next generation.

After calling this the "suffragist motto," *The Anti-Suffragist* wondered "what sort of a 'next generation' would evolve if all women considered their 'first duty' to be to themselves, and overlooked the fact that their strongest power and highest possibility is that of unselfish—and often unnoticed—service."[71]

As if woman suffrage by itself were not sufficiently worthy of contempt, the Antis often embellished its horrors by equating it with any one of the so-called radical isms. If not actually equated with feminism, bolshevism, or socialism, then it was the necessary harbinger of these and similar horrors. In the charged atmosphere of the years surrounding World War I, the Antis consciously resorted to a campaign designed to discredit the suffragists by playing upon popular fears of bolshevism and social revolution. Any instance in which a suffragist portrayed the goals of the movement as something broader than merely obtaining the ballot was seized upon by the Antis as an indication that suffragism was invariably linked with the social, educational, and economic demands of the whole feminist movement.[72]

Remarks such as the following by *Harper's Weekly* editor and feminist sympathizer Norman Hapgood were often cited by the Antis. "Suffrage is but an incident in the Feminist movement and the vote is only a symbol of women's new activity and new interest in the world." This seemingly innocuous statement was interpreted to signify that the vote was only a means to an end. "It is a wedge driven into the heart of our present social system, to shatter it and destroy it. Every feminist is a suffragist, not vice versa."[73]

Of all feminism's numerous demands, it is revealing that the one most often indicated by the Antis as illustrative of feminism's revolutionary implications was the plea for economic independence. "It is a feminist contention," wrote one Anti, "that every woman, married or single, should be allowed to choose the work in which she finds the most pleasure." This was too "individualistic," an outgrowth of the "radical suffragist" theory of "economic independence."[74]

Lily Rice Foxcroft, the author of these remarks, went on to denounce the suffragists for their contempt for the domestic round in which the average wife and mother was accustomed to finding her share of human satisfaction and claimed that women who denigrated domestic work were all in professional work and could use their earnings to provide "expert" care for their children. Indicting the suffrage movement as gauged to the talents and habits of the exceptional, rather than the average, woman, the author then listed ten "anti-heroines," examples of the worst produced by radical feminism, women who denigrated domestic drudgery and felt woman should be free to find fulfillment outside the home.[75]

Foxcroft was not the only Anti to oppose the idea of a wife having separate earnings. Helen K. Johnson feared it would place a valuation on woman's labor in the household and have the effect of making legislators regard marriage as a business partnership, placing wives in the role of hired servants of their husbands.[76] It was no wonder these upper-middle-class women were outraged, for the richer their husbands, the fewer the wives' duties in proportion to their husbands' income, and the lower the proportionate value that could be placed on their labor. All too often, woman did appear to be a luxury, the symbol of conspicuous consumption. In this situation it was impossible to measure her importance to the well-being of the family in terms of dollars and cents.

Mrs. A. J. George argued that votes for women was merely the political aspect of feminism, that cult

> which looks forward to a social revolution based on the economic and social independence of the woman. We are Anti-Suffragists because we are coming to see that on a basis of economic independence for woman rests all woman suffrage doctrine. Economic independence for married women—and this is a married woman's question—is impossible, as long as the self-governing group of the family is taken as the unit of the State.[77]

The feminist theory of economic independence, while never too widely accepted, received considerable notoriety with the publication of Charlotte Perkins Gilman's *The Home* and *Women and Economics*. Gilman offered a perspective on marriage that was anything but complimentary. In her view, for example, woman's subordinate role in society and her dependent position in the home were due to her economic dependence, which turned woman into a "parasite." Because women's work in the home and for the family was not valued in terms of money, their work outside the home was poorly paid. The way to increase the value of woman's work, she argued, was to professionalize it both inside and outside the home. Thus she advocated not only the entry of all women into a state of economic self-sufficiency but also freeing women from the inefficient drudgery of individual housework and child care by providing state-supported institutionalized home and child care. It was no wonder the Antis feared that "Feminism is all for the individual and not at all for the race."

> The whole point of view of feminism is concerned with the woman—not with the adult male or the human child. Whether wages for wives are asked, whether maintained wifehood is regarded as parasitism or selfhood, whether woman should be economically independent on the one hand or insist on more liberal maintenance and fresh privileges on the other hand, or whether a woman shall refuse to complicate her existence at all by any relations with the male, the whole burden and song of feminism is the individual self.[78]

The trouble with economic independence, in the antisuffrage view, was not only that it would destroy the existing division of labor whereby the wife depended on the husband for her support and he on her for the care of their home and the happiness of their children, but also that it was the first step in the direction of socialism.[79] Mrs. Richard Watson Gilder argued that "closely allied to woman suffrage is socialism, a belief in the sanctity of the individual,

69

making both men and women independent."[80] Alice George, professional lobbyist for the Antis, denounced the notion of economic independence of the married woman and her coresponsibility for maintenance of the children because it would "put marriage on a business basis. . . . This is the socialistic view. It must be the view of every suffragist who has the intellectual honesty and perception of the feminist."[81]

It is a curious fact that George was herself a *paid* retainer of the Massachusetts Association Opposed to the Further Extension of Suffrage to Women despite her husband's objections to her speaking before legislative committees. Although she was militantly committed to the belief that women were subject to men and should stay out of politics, she heeded his protests for only two years. From 1904 on she appeared at practically every hearing in Boston and many in Washington, D.C. Apparently she was a former suffragist who abandoned the movement because she believed women could do better public service without the ballot (see Biographical Appendix).

Numerous articles and handouts circulated by the Antis attested to the importance they placed in creating the impression that woman suffrage was a crucial part of a worldwide socialist conspiracy.[82] In 1911 the *Fifteenth Annual Report* of the Illinois Association Opposed to Woman Suffrage contained an elaborate explanation of the relationship between the two doctrines. In this account, woman suffrage was imported to the United States from Europe, "an offshoot of the rising agitation for Communism and Socialism," and was introduced into New York in 1848 at the first Women's Rights convention in Seneca Falls. Since then, the report continued, it "has been agitated in the East by a growing number of radicals often with atheistic tendencies." In the latter part of the nineteenth century, it was taken up by Populism, a party with socialistic tendencies and thus became a political issue in the West. When Populism died, it left a remnant of woman suffrage that merged with a new infusion of European socialism and with Mormonism and "gained an ascendancy in five of our least organized and least civilized Western States." According to the report, this did not alarm the more conservative East, but when California joined them in 1911, "energetic opposition was aroused."[83] In short, the Antis believed that woman suffrage could not succeed without the aid of socialism.[84]

One of the strongest allegations that woman suffrage was a tool of socialism was made by Annie Bock of Los Angeles. Bock, formerly secretary of the California Political Equality League and of the College Equal Suffrage League, and at one time actively engaged in bringing suffrage to California, had renounced her allegiance to woman suffrage because she had discovered that "women in politics are no better than men." Suffrage in her view had proved to be a failure. Accordingly, in 1913, she prepared an address opposing a federal woman suffrage amendment. It was presented to the U.S. Senate Committee on Woman Suffrage during the 63rd Congress. Included in her remarks was the observation that "the majority of women wanting suffrage (outside of Socialist women) are the dupes of the Socialists." Furthermore, she insisted that

> The gravest, most awful thing that the home, the church, the nation must confront in giving the ballot to women is socialism. Woman suffrage is one of the clever suggestions of modern socialism. It is the Socialist's most important tenet.[85]

The Antis devoted strenuous efforts to exploiting the nation's fear of socialism by publicizing the participation of socialist groups in suffrage parades and the appearance of socialist speakers at suffrage rallies. For example, in Tennessee between 1914 and 1916, the suffragists held May Day celebrations, consisting of parades, public speeches, pageants, and adoption of resolutions, endorsing, among others, a federal woman suffrage amendment. Evidently these were well attended and even supported by the WCTU.[86] An article in the New York *Evening Telegram* alleged that "the Woman Suffrage Party of New York State has appealed for funds to help out the suppressed socialistic paper *The Masses* and has declined to participate in Red Cross work because 'Suffrage comes first.' "[87]

Delighting in any opportunity to cite voting figures, *The Woman's Protest* called attention to the fact that *The New York Call*, a leading socialist paper, claimed that 45 percent of the women's vote in the city election in Los Angeles in December 1911 was cast for "Harriman, the Socialist candidate for Mayor." The article concluded, "so far as Los Angeles can be taken as a criterion, the women have certainly overthrown speculation as to their natural conservatism."[88]

The careers of Martha Moore Avery and David Goldstein also helped the Antis in their fight to link the perils of socialism with suffragism. As former socialists converted to antisuffragism and, in the case of Goldstein, Catholicism, they reached a wide audience of diverse conservative interests, publishing their message in the form of exposés of how the socialist menace lurked in the extension of suffrage to women.[89]

Drawings and cartoons issued by the Antis alluded to the connection between woman suffrage and socialism. One pen and ink drawing depicted a man driving a roadster labeled "Good Government" toward the brink of a cliff. A nearby road sign implanted in a flower bed named "Fair Promises" read "Antisuffrage Warning: Danger! Turn to the Right." The message was obvious. If the driver failed to turn he would go over the edge into the Woman Suffrage abyss where lurked the rocks of "Feminism," "Socialism" and "Fanatical Legislation." The reverse side of this drawing was devoted to "Facts and Figures about Woman Suffrage" and called attention to the coincidence that in 1848 not only was socialism formulated by Karl Marx, but "Votes for Women" were first demanded at Seneca Falls. Other alleged facts were that in 1912, the Men's League for Woman Suffrage was organized by socialists and in the same year at a parade in Washington, a socialist banner read "One Million Socialists Vote and Work for Woman Suffrage!"; in 1913 Anna Howard Shaw, while president of NAWSA declared, "We welcome every socialist vote"; and finally, in 1914 socialists in a suffrage parade carried a sign reading "Antis, train your cameras here—you're seeing red."[90]

Sometimes the Antis lumped together all the subversive "isms," as on the masthead of the *Woman Patriot*, which began publishing in 1918 as "a national newspaper for Home Defense against Woman Suffrage, Feminism and Socialism." Another example of this polyglot approach is reflected in the title page of a publication issued by the New York State Association Opposed to Woman Suffrage, which read

"To Men Who Think," Will You Help Make the Country Safe Against Pacifist Doctrines, Socialist Government, Feminist Teachings, "A Little Book of Facts—Not Fancies."

The tenor of this pamphlet was that woman suffrage had always been allied with radicalism, and could not be considered apart from pacifism, socialism and feminism, as evidenced by the following facts:

1) "Jane Addams, Fola LaFollette, Elizabeth Freeman, Crystal Eastman and Lillian Wald, who are all workers and speakers for Woman Suffrage, are leading Pacifists."

2) "The famous Ford Peace Party was manned by prominent suffragists."

3) The Reverend Anna Howard Shaw said at a meeting in Rome, New York, in June 1915, "Preparedness for war is an incentive to war," while on another occasion she said, "We welcome every Socialist vote."

4) Morris Hilquit, recently nominated for mayor of New York by the socialists on a "non-conscription platform," has been a frequent speaker for suffrage, and at a suffrage meeting held in New York on March 11, 1912, said, "Patriotism is the last resort of the rascal."

5) Prominent suffragists made fund appeals for *The Masses*, the "revolutionary socialistic magazine that has recently been forbidden the mails because of its anti-conscription cartoons and articles."

6) Max Eastman, editor of *The Masses*, was one of the organizers and first secretary of the New York State Men's League for Woman Suffrage and praised Jeannette Rankin at a socialist meeting for voting against war.

7) Beatrice Forbes Robertson Hale, in her book *What Women Want*, said: "Suffrage is an essential branch of the tree of Feminism." In the chapter entitled "New Man," she wrote:

At present, in the whole world there are only a few new men. Their numbers are increasing yearly, but still far short of the new woman. Every male instinct of domination and sovereignty has to be bred out of the individual before you can attain the status of the new man and be a fit mate for the new woman . . . the new man has to unlearn these deep-rooted habits and instincts of sex. The important fact for women to realize is that this nation . . . is the nation where the new type of man is most rapidly developing.

All of this, concluded the author of the pamphlet, accounted for the fact that the nation was becoming effeminized.[91]

Summing up all of the tendencies considered repugnant by the Antis, Helen K. Johnson saw the suffrage movement as allied with coeducation against woman's higher education in colleges of her own; with "isms" as against tried principles; with prohibition as against temperance; with Mormonism as against separation of church and state; with socialism as against representative government; with radical labor movements as against the best-organized and unorganized efforts of wage-earning men and women; with "economic independence" and the cooperative household as against family life and the home.[92]

Although the various strategies employed by the Antis often seem to have been designed as a matter of expediency, they were for the most part the natural outcome of the Antis' basic assumptions concerning woman and her role in society. Thus, even though they were elaborated in the heat of what the Antis viewed as a struggle for survival, they nevertheless retained a certain internal consistency that made the Antis worthy opponents of the suffragists.

Furthermore, even when the Antis did not have the full facts at their disposal, their presumptions seemed to have as much validity as any made by the suffragists. Thus the Antis could maintain that as the suffrage movement represented only a tiny fraction of American womanhood, the vast majority of women were opposed to it. It was only natural that they would draw attention to the record of suffrage defeats in order to try to prove their point. From here it was but a small step to the position that most of the opponents of suffrage were women.

Sharing the same nativist and class biases as the suffragists, the Antis too feared that the country faced the threat of being overwhelmed by an alien and uneducated electorate. The suffragists hoped to offset this influence by enfranchising women, believing that the better class of women outnumbered the undesirable elements, whereas the Antis, somewhat more realistically, it seems, argued that the "better class" of women was only a small fraction of American womanhood and that it would not only be outnumbered at the polls, but that their nonpartisan influence would be nullified once they took part in the political process. Again the Antis were able to substantiate their claims by pointing to the small proportion of women who actually used the ballot where it was available and by drawing attention to the negligible, if not negative, effects produced by the ballot. It was decidedly to their advantage strategically to indicate just how suffragist claims for the ballot failed to materialize.

As far as their insistence that the status of women had advanced remarkably without benefit of suffrage, most women probably would have agreed. Women had not only achieved new opportunities in education and the professions but their legal status had undergone a radical change in the second half of the nineteenth century. Furthermore, one could point to numerous social and civic organizations and charitable and health institutions where women had prominent and responsible positions. It was easy to maintain that if women wanted anything, they had but to ask for it and that man, if not out of chivalry, then in his role as benefactor and protector, could not help but respond.

Only in one area did the Antis seem to be operating out of unreasoning fear and hysteria. Their view of suffragism as an arm of a worldwide socialist conspiracy was a reaction out of all proportion to the facts. And it was here that they were most bitterly aggressive and vindictive. Yet again, given their basic view of the family as the nexus of civilized life, it becomes easy to see how a movement that emphasized the relationship between the individual and the state, seemingly at the expense of the family as mediating institution, conjured up a sinister and threatening alternative to patriarchal norms in which the Antis had so much invested.

FOUR

Organization and Tactics: The Antis Mobilize Within the States

Antisuffrage women, through their various organizations, operated on both state and local levels as well as nationally in order to impede the progress of women suffrage, if not to eliminate it. Of all the battle sites, however, the most critical were the floors of the state legislatures. There the chief battles between suffragists and antisuffragists were waged, from the first tentative encounters to the final attempts of the Antis to forestall ratification of the Nineteenth Amendment.

Organizational Structure

The oldest and most active of the various state organizations was the Massachusetts association, which at the height of its popularity in 1907 claimed a membership of 12,500, with more than 34 branch committees and a large standing committee.[1] Furthermore, the Massachusetts association was instrumental in helping to lay the groundwork for the establishment of sister organizations in other states. Fortunately, much is known about the development of the antisuffrage movement in Massachusetts. Since it played such a central role and provided a model of antisuffrage organizational and tactical maneuvering, it is useful to summarize the key developments in the formation of the antisuffrage movement in Massachusetts.[2]

On May 15, 1895, a letter signed by ten women representing some of Boston's most socially prominent families was sent to a carefully selected list of women. The letter invited them to become members of a Standing

Committee for the purpose of forming an organization to resist suffrage pressure on the legislature by working to defeat a forthcoming referendum that would grant municipal suffrage to women.[3]

On May 21, a Standing Committee of 100 women met in Boston and elected an eleven-member Executive Committee, all of whom were women, and a male treasurer. Thus the oldest and most active organization opposed to the extension of suffrage to women was established on a formal footing—the Massachusetts Association Opposed to the Further Extension of Suffrage to Women (MAOFESW). Full power was given to the Executive Committee to "carry on active work and to control the finances." The aim of the association, formed by women who believed that "a more systematic resistance should be made to the appeals and claims of Woman Suffragists," was to increase "public interest in the great question of the extension of Suffrage to women" and stimulate "public opinion in opposition to it."[4]

The first actual business of the association was the formulation of a three-point plan of action for increasing membership. This included: initiating and sustaining correspondence throughout the state in order to acquire the names of women in sympathy with its aims, with membership open to women 21 years and over; holding parlor meetings to solicit interest at the homes of members of the Standing Committee for which the association would furnish speakers; and circulating pamphlets and leaflets prepared by "Massachusetts and New York writers."[5]

The expression of antisuffrage sentiment in Massachusetts did not have to await the formal organization of MAOFESW. As early as 1868, a remonstrance from 195 women of Lancaster protesting against suffrage was presented to the Massachusetts legislature. But it was really not until 1870, with the formation of the Massachusetts Woman Suffrage Association and the increasing regularity of its efforts to secure an amendment to the Massachusetts constitution, that the Antis began to raise their voices regularly and frequently. In 1870, the Massachusetts legislature had established a joint Senate-House Committee on "Female Suffrage." Then in 1879, the legislature made the taxpaying women of the state eligible to vote for school committee members.[6]

The growing pace of suffrage success intensified the activities of the Antis, who recognized the need for more systematic and organized resistance. George G. Crocker, Massachusetts state senator from Boston, has been credited with formulating the idea of establishing a woman's organization to direct the antisuffrage opposition.[7] As indicated above, from the antisuffrage point of view, this would prove to be a valuable strategy. For not only did it make it possible for men to claim that women themselves did not desire the ballot, but it also gave male antisuffragists the opportunity to work through women in their opposition and thus avoid being accused of resisting woman suffrage merely from an antifeminist bias.[8]

The first meeting of women committed to resisting the extension of suffrage to women took place in 1882 as the Antis prepared to circulate remonstrances against an impending attempt to win municipal suffrage. The suffrage proposition was defeated in the Massachusetts senate, and the antisuffrage women, buoyed up by their success, met and formed a permanent committee of thirteen to work for the cause. Thus was established the Boston Committee, the working nucleus of the organization that would formally emerge in 1895 as the MAOFESW.

The women who conducted the antisuffrage campaign in Massachusetts were for the most part members of the social elite. All of the original thirteen who joined forces in 1882 were from wealthy families, well educated, and with both leisure time and money to devote to the cause. Only two were single, the other eleven married to prominent men. Most of these women were involved outside the home in charitable or reform work. When this informal group metamorphosed into the MAOFESW in 1895, the members as well as the officers continued to be drawn from the same element.[9]

Despite the fact that during these early years the activities of the Antis were cloaked in secrecy (members' names were not made public and in hearings and newspapers the organization was referred to mysteriously as "an informal ladies group")[10] and that the association was only informally organized, the Antis realized some important successes. They not only facilitated the efforts of legislators who wished to defeat the woman suffrage petitions submitted each year, but also convinced much of the press that only a small band of unrepresentative women was demanding suffrage against the will of the majority.

Between 1890 and 1893, municipal suffrage was defeated in the Massachusetts legislature on four occasions.[11] In 1894, however, a municipal suffrage bill almost passed, and in that same year the legislature began to favor the idea of a referendum on the issue. A referendum would enable the legislators to avoid responsibility for defeating the suffrage bills and thus not jeopardize their own position. Submitting the question to the voters and allowing them to defeat woman suffrage at the polls would not only remove the onus of complicity from individual legislators, but would also provide those opposed to woman suffrage with a much clearer mandate to continue their campaign.

In 1895, despite objections by both suffragists and female Antis,[12] the House and Senate passed a bill submitting the question of municipal suffrage to a referendum that would give women who were eligible to vote for school committees an opportunity to vote on the issue.

Needless to say, the embryonic antisuffrage organization was not oblivious to the changing circumstances (both the *narrow* defeat of municipal suffrage by the legislature a year earlier and the decision by the legislature now to submit the question to a referendum). It was in response to the latter situation that the Antis felt the time had come to organize themselves systematically and that they sent out the letter that resulted in the establishment of the MAOFESW. With the drawing up of a formal constitution, the initiation of a membership campaign, and the beginnings of a real treasury, the MAOFESW was finally established on firm ground and could undertake its immediate objective of defeating the referendum.

The election, which was monitored by many areas outside of Massachusetts, saw only 297,011 men and women voting. Of the 273,946 ballots cast by men, 186,976 were no votes and 86,970 were yes. Of the 612,000 women eligible to vote, only 42,676 registered, of whom only 23,065 voted. The vote was 22,204 yes to 861 no.[13] The Antis claimed that the results showed that the majority of women were apathetic and did not desire suffrage and that the men were opposed. As indicated, the results of this and other elections would be used by the Antis for strategic advantage in the years to come.

The period from 1896 to 1907 has been characterized as one of ascendancy among the Antis in Massachusetts. As a result of the outcome of the 1895 election and the activities of the new formal antisuffrage association, suffragists were forced to assume a defensive posture.

Now that the 1895 election was behind them, the Antis felt the need both to elaborate their ideological position and to provide an even more definite form of organization. In 1897 the Executive Committee of the MAOFESW appointed a committee to frame the association's bylaws. In these they refined their philosophy and described their strategy. The stated purpose of the association, according to the bylaws, was "to oppose the further extension of political duties to women," based on the belief that

... the ballot is not necessary to equality of position or of influence; that nature has established the basis for the present division of labor between men and women; and that the general suffrage of women would involve a dangerous political change and social readjustment. The Association is in full sympathy with the highest ideals of educational and professional opportunities for women, and it claims that these can best be attained without the ballot.[14]

The association considered that its effort fell into three categories: legislative, educative, and constructive. Legislative activity involved presenting the views of the opponents of woman suffrage to members of the legislature by sending them literature, speaking before special legislative committees, employing counsel to oppose suffragist petitions, and keeping legislators informed of the antisuffrage opinions of their constituents. Educational work meant increasing general interest in the subject, stimulating public opinion "to an opposition based on intelligent conviction" by means of articles in newspapers and magazines, addressing audiences, and "distribution of these articles and addresses in printed leaflets and pamphlets." Constructive work involved extending the organization throughout the state by increasing membership, "as it is most important that the latent antisuffrage sentiment of the State, in order to be effective, should make itself felt through a strong and formal organization." Obviously, the Antis were by no means self-effacing women, unsure of their talents and interested in keeping women confined to the home.

To facilitate enrollment, the Antis made it relatively effortless to become a member of the association. All one had to do was "pledge herself as in sympathy with its creed and work." There was no fee required for membership, although donations were encouraged. Furthermore, the bylaws guaranteed that, "In joining, no publicity is incurred, as the names of members are kept on file for reference only." The bylaws also included directions on how to organize and form a committee. The recommended procedure was personally to invite a small number of women to a member's home to listen to a speaker sent by the Executive Committee. If three or more guests became interested, a Branch Committee was formed of not fewer than three or more than seven. It was further advised that,

> When practicable, it is wise to have a representative from every church in the community on this committee, as thereby the communication with the whole people is more easily established.[15]

These Branch Committees were to meet regularly (monthly or bimonthly) and file reports with the Executive Committee on what they had accomplished. Eventually the branch should call a larger meeting of women of the community, excluding the "pronounced suffragists," and try to urge those present to become members.

The bylaws urged that "All unnecessary friction with suffragists" be avoided and that public debates be eschewed since all they would do was "excite ill feeling, and to make few converts for either side." Workers were exhorted to push "steadily and quietly, without malice toward those who differ from us" and to seek converts "from every walk in life—the professional woman, the bread-winning woman, as well as the so-called woman of leisure."[16]

This was a period of growth and expansion for the Massachusetts antisuffrage association. Massachusetts Antis were active both within the state, where they initiated a major lobbying campaign to defeat the suffrage effort, and in other states, where they directed their efforts and propaganda to counteract the suffragists whenever the question came up before a legislature or appeared on a ballot. They also used their organizational talents to help establish formal antisuffrage associations in other states and financed speakers and organizers as occasions warranted.[17] By 1908, Massachusetts Antis were better organized and more numerous than ever and stronger than at any time in the past. In fact, it has even been suggested that the antisuffrage forces by that date were as strong as the suffrage proponents.[18] In almost every case, when a woman suffrage amendment was to be voted on by a state, the Massachusetts association could be counted on to send literature and/or speakers and money to work for the cause.[19]

By 1910, partly as a result of the efforts of the Massachusetts association, permanent antisuffrage committees had been established in New Hampshire, Vermont, Maine, Rhode Island, Washington, D.C., and Maryland. In 1914, under the leadership of the MAOFESW, the New England Anti-Suffrage League was established to help coordinate antisuffrage activities in the area.[20]

One of the major difficulties in arriving at a clear picture of the extent of the antisuffrage organization is that there are few exact figures available. When the MAOFESW, for example, listed 43 branches in operation, this could have ranged from 129 members (since the minimum stipulated was three) to 301 (the maximum of seven). Furthermore, none of the antisuffrage operations in the other states was as well organized or as extensive as the MAOFESW. In some states the Antis were organized only into a committee, as in Wisconsin, or into an auxiliary, as in South Dakota. In the latter, for example, it appears that the resistance was centered in one or two major cities and operated only sporadically in order to meet a current crisis. Some of the state associations did not have a permanent headquarters, and in several states the city branches were more important than the state organization as centers of most organized activity.

This appears to have been the case in New York State where, despite the existence of a state association, most of the organized resistance emanated from Albany and New York City. In New York State, the antisuffrage movement got under way in 1894 when suffragists, taking advantage of a Constitutional Convention that year, petitioned that the word "male" be removed from the constitution's qualifications for voters. According to an antisuffrage account, "Immediately a numerous and powerful body of women appeared in the field to oppose this movement."[21] It was reported that petitions signed by thousands of well-known and responsible women were sent in by a group that called itself the Albany Anti-Suffrage Association, while New York City witnessed action by "a very large contingent of the best known and most influential women in the city."[22]

The foremost representative of the antisuffrage position at the Constitutional Convention of 1894 was Francis M. Scott of New York City, who addressed a committee of the convention on behalf of the Antis on June 14. Not until the present year, he noted, had agitation for the extension of suffrage in New York made sufficient headway to appear really dangerous. Justifying his role as spokesman for the Antis, Scott noted that the genteel women opposed to suffrage had refrained from imitating the methods of the suffragists. They had held no meetings, made no speeches, and conducted no campaign, but had merely circulated a protest and sent out literature to each member of the convention.

Resorting to the rhetoric of extremism, Scott denounced the proposed amendment as a revolutionary innovation that would sap the foundations and overthrow the existing structure of society. Assuming that women would use the franchise to vote as a body, if a question appealed to sentiment or emotion, all women would cast their vote on one side of the issue. Furthermore, since women always outnumbered men and since many of man's avocations were itinerant in character, the voting women would always largely outnumber the voting men. Consequently, he lamented, men would be forced to abdicate their position and turn over to women the power of making laws.[23]

It should be pointed out that in the early years of the antisuffrage movement apologists for the cause frequently argued that once enfranchised, women would vote as a body. Since New York and Massachusetts had the largest number of women in excess of men it was only natural for antisuffragists in those states to assume that woman suffrage would mean that women would not only outnumber men at the polls but would also outvote them. It was this fear, in fact, that gave rise to the paranoia reflected in the writings of the Antis on the subject of women and government; namely, that government that depended on the ability of those who made the laws to enforce them (or on the majority to impose its will on the minority) would come to an end with woman suffrage.

As the antisuffrage movement became more sophisticated, however, and as the Antis were able to observe that where women were enfranchised woman's vote counted for very little, they began to realize that in actual practice women did not influence major policy issues by voting together as a sex. In fact, the Antis increasingly scoffed at the suffrage contention that an enfranchised womanhood would use the suffrage to provide the country with a much needed moral transfusion. This could never happen, because woman's interests were more closely tied to her socioeconomic status than to her sex. That the antisuffrage arguments continued to reflect a certain ambivalence on this subject was due to the fact that the Antis were under constant pressure to refute the suffragists' exaggerated claims.[24]

In their heyday, however, the Antis were not as inconsistent on this subject as their adversaries claimed. They were able to reconcile their two seemingly contradictory positions—that woman suffrage was vastly overrated and that woman suffrage would usher in the end of the republic—by arguing that either way, the outcome would be negative. Men and women might vote according to individual preference, along general lines of thought having nothing to do with sex, in which case the net result would be simply to "double the vote, delay the count and vastly increase the expense without affecting the outcome." Or, they predicted, men and women would divide along sex lines, "leading to diverse and warring policies destructive of family harmony, the home life and the orderly administration of public affairs."[25]

While it is impossible to measure exactly just how instrumental the New York Antis were in influencing the 1894 Constitutional Convention, in the end it was an antisuffrage victory. The convention refused to strike the word "male" from the constitution, and the Antis, assuming their efforts were no longer needed, disbanded. In March of the next year, however, suffragists in the state won a large majority in a vote in the Assembly on a resolution for a constitutional amendment. According to the antisuffrage account, the suffragists had worked so quietly that it was not until the resolution had passed the Assembly and reached the Senate's judicial committee that the Antis awoke to the threat.[26] By that time it was too late for concerted action. This may have accounted for the fact that the resolution passed the Senate. However, the resolution was never acted on due to a clerical error that caused it to be invalidated.[27]

On April 8, the New York Antis, realizing that vigilance was the better part of valor, set up a formal organization known as the New York State Association Opposed to the Extension of Suffrage to Women, with a standing committee of over 100 of the "best known" women in New York and with a membership supposedly of 20,000.[28]

In the West, up to this time, antisuffragists had engaged in only sporadic efforts. In 1886, for example, a group of Chicagoans began sending protests to Congress to counteract the activities of the National Woman Suffrage Association in Washington. Members of this group also addressed the Illinois legislature and the legislatures of various other western states and initiated correspondence with "well known" women in many states, "thus bringing influence to bear privately upon public men."[29] By 1896, the Illinois Association Opposed to Woman Suffrage was founded in Chicago. Its work consisted mainly of circulating literature to the press, to legislative bodies, and to leading men and women in the western states; it did not appear to be as active in resisting suffrage on the floors of the legislature as either the Massachusetts or New York associations. In 1900 the Illinois Association described its aim:

> . . . to encourage a free, intelligent, and impersonal discussion of the subject of Woman Suffrage and to set forth the arguments which lead many women to believe that possession of the ballot would be neither a benefit nor help to woman but, on the contrary, would weaken her power and direct her attention from the absorbing and important duties which devolve upon her as the mother of the race and the conservator of the moral and spiritual interests of society.[30]

The foremost spokeswoman for the association was Caroline F. Corbin (see Biographical Appendix). Largely through her efforts, the association issued numerous bulletins, designed primarily to warn the public against the ubiquitous threat of socialism. In fact, if any single theme characterized the association it was the need to forestall the advent of socialism by impeding the progress of woman suffrage.

> It is a very serious fact that the doctrine of the industrial and political equality of women is an offshoot from that Social Democracy which unswervingly insists

that women shall be units and factors in the State equally with men, that both men and women shall thus be absolved from all domestic obligations, the rearing of children becoming the charge of the state.[31]

Antisuffrage resistance had begun rather modestly, with the presentation of antisuffrage petitions at legislative hearings, the reading by antisuffrage members of the legislature of antisuffrage testimonials, and the mailing of antisuffrage pamphlets and leaflets to all legislators.[32] During the 1880s there was great reluctance on the part of the Antis to appear personally at legislative hearings. In fact, members' names were not even made public, and the Antis employed paid solicitors rather than gather names themselves on antisuffrage petitions. As the movement gained strength, however, their tactics became more direct. They not only employed counsel to present their case, but even began to appear themselves as remonstrants before all-male legislative committees.[33] In New York State, for example, Mrs. Francis M. Scott, whose husband represented the Antis in 1894, appeared herself the next year to address the Senate Judiciary Committee.[34] The Antis were aware that the outspoken objection by women to woman suffrage was one of their most effective devices. Nevertheless, they continued to avow that this was "a necessity most repugnant to all their instincts and habits."

We deplore the necessity for the semi public position that we must take in order to preserve for ourselves the right to live apart from public life.[35]

Eventually, however, the Antis even employed female lobbyists, such as MAOFESW's Alice George, who not only presented the antisuffrage case before the Massachusetts legislature, but also appeared before other state legislatures, as well as in Congress.

As late as 1902, the MAOFESW, recognizing the importance of having remonstrants appear before the legislatures in person, was still bemoaning the distastefulness of legislative work. In the *Annual Report* of that year, the MAOFESW exhorted its members to keep up the distasteful work "until we have the sentiment of the state so fully with us that we can afford to be represented only by a petition or by counsel."

Both sides of the suffrage struggle were aware of the strategic importance of establishing a beachhead in the individual states. For the suffragists, the more states that enacted woman suffrage legislation, the sooner their chance of convincing Congress that suffrage for women was inevitable and that it should move with the times and enact a federal amendment enfranchising women in all the states.[36] Suffragists feared that setbacks in the states, particularly in the key populous eastern ones, would be interpreted by Congress as evidence of the lack of a clear mandate to proceed with a federal woman suffrage amendment and result in interminable delays.[37] Looking at it from the other side, the Antis, who were just as attuned to the necessity of courting public opinion, saw antisuffrage victories in the states as their mainstay against federal enactment of a woman suffrage amendment.

For the suffragists, enfranchisement by state action was no easier to achieve than winning the necessary two-thirds vote in both houses of Congress. In fact, in most states a constitutional change was required that would strike out the word "male."[38] According to Catt, thousands of voters did not know what a constitution or an amendment was and were persuaded that striking out the word "male" would take the vote away from men and give it to women.[39]

State provisions for suffrage varied according to the difficulties they imposed in the way of amending their constitutions. Some states required that amendments pass two successive legislatures before being submitted to the voters; others provided that their constitutions be amended only once in ten years; and some required a majority of all votes cast at the election. Massachusetts was one of the few states that did not require a constitutional change in order to enfranchise its women. Massachusetts legislators had the power to grant suffrage to women as long as it passed two consecutive sessions of the legislature, and the legislature met annually. The fact that there were so few obstacles in the way of enfranchisement may have accounted for the fact that from 1889 on the suffragists never missed a year petitioning the legislature. It may also have explained their opponents' keeping a continuously watchful eye on the legislature, and thus account in part for the strength and effectiveness of the Massachusetts Antis.

Within the individual states, antisuffrage operations were for the most part defensive. They were concerned mainly with opposing campaigns to get legislatures to submit suffrage amendments to the voters, opposing efforts to get state constitutional conventions to write woman suffrage into state constitutions, or opposing attempts to get state party conventions to include woman suffrage. During the 52 years between 1868, when the Fourteenth Amendment wrote the word "male" into the U.S. Constitution, thus eliminating women from the electorate, and 1920, when the Nineteenth Amendment was ratified, the suffragists conducted 480 campaigns to get legislatures to submit suffrage amendments to voters, 47 to get state constitutional conventions to write woman suffrage into state constitutions, and 277 campaigns to get state party conventions to include a woman suffrage plank, in addition to 56 campaigns of referenda to male voters.[40]

In addition to state and local groups, the Antis operated through a national antisuffrage organization. There too Massachusetts took the lead, inviting seven other state associations to a convention in New York in November 1911. At that meeting a constitution was drafted, officers selected, and the decision made to publish a national periodical, later named *The Woman's Protest*.[41]

The National Association was formed to bring together under one committee representatives from the various state associations to secure cooperation in organizing new state associations and forming public opinion by distributing literature and providing information through *The Woman's Protest* of the progress of the antisuffrage movement throughout the country. It hoped to "arouse the indifferent women to a realization of the danger of having this additional burden thrust upon them by a minority" so that they would awaken from their apathy on this subject and express their opinion.[42]

Although the objectives of the National Association encompassed all that was dear to the conservative heart,[43] their view of womanhood tried to incorporate a progressive outlook.

We who are opposed to woman suffrage believe that women do not yet realize the enormous opportunities that have been given to them in the past forty years, and that they have not yet been able to adapt themselves to new conditions and to all the work which is now within their power. By throwing women into the arena of active politics and the holding of elective offices, with all that it implies, we are confident that neither women themselves nor the State will be benefitted, but we earnestly believe that the serious purposes, ability and experience to be found among women in many walks of life should be used for the benefit of the community and that women of judgment and energy should be appointed on such educational, charitable, sanitary, and reformatory boards, commissions and committees as the safest methods of utilizing their capacities and interest in the public welfare.[44]

If nothing else, one could say that the Antis were at least trying to cover all their bets. For example, they made sure to indicate that their opposition to the entry of women into public life did not extend to appointed offices. Many of the leading Antis held such offices, in most cases by virtue of their social standing and connections (see Biographical Appendix). Therefore it is hardly surprising that they objected to altering the system in such a way that women seeking public office would be elected on the basis of their personal credentials and experience.

Antisuffrage Ammunition

In addition to appearing before legislative committees, lobbying, and campaigning in state elections, a great deal of antisuffrage energy went into the production and dissemination of vast amounts of printed matter. These fell into three basic categories—periodicals, books and pamphlets, and ephemeral materials such as campaign fliers, advertisements, and various handouts.

The earliest periodical produced by the Antis, and in the end the longest-lived, was the *Remonstrance*, published in Boston by the MAOFESW from 1890 to 1920. Beginning as an annual, it became a four-page quarterly in 1908 when *The Anti-Suffragist* began publishing. The *Remonstrance*, although an organ of the female Antis, was edited by Frank Foxcroft, who was employed as a regular secretary by the MAOFESW. As a paid retainer of the Antis, Foxcroft was not typical of the many men who served the antisuffrage cause. Nevertheless, he was from an old Yankee family, had graduated from Williams College, and had served as associate editor of the *Boston Journal* and as a freelance writer before becoming associated with the Antis. He was one of the most prolific antisuffrage writers, helped attract other men to the cause, and appeared at innumerable legislative hearings. As chairman of the No License Committee of Cambridge, he was of great value to the Antis in refuting suffrage charges that the Antis were "tools of the liquor interests."[45]

In 1895 the *Remonstrance* took on the character of a national paper, changing its heading to indicate that it expressed

... the views of such Remonstrants in Massachusetts, Maine, New York, Illinois and other states, who believe that the great majority of their sex do not want the ballot, and that to force it upon them would not only be an injustice to women, but would lessen their influence for good.[46]

Designed primarily for legislators, congressmen, and newspapers, the *Remonstrance* was mailed nationwide to apprise them of the antisuffrage position. The paper reported on British as well as American antisuffrage activities, information on the former culled from the *London Anti-Suffrage Review*. The *Remonstrance* brought to the attention of its readers news of antisuffrage activities at legislative hearings and committee meetings and particularly those occasions on which the Antis scored in the popular press. Its editors enjoyed calling attention to the more extreme statements of the suffragists, citing them out of context and then emphasizing their absurdity or their extremism. For example, it cited an interview in *Pearson's Magazine* (February 1910) between Richard Barry and Carrie Chapman Catt. Catt, asked what would become of the 80 percent of American women "who are now home-loving and home-keeping" and who would not want to leave their homes to gain the fuller knowledge of industrial, economic, and political life necessary in order to vote effectively, allegedly replied:

> I believe that the time will come, and that comparatively soon, when every American woman who does not earn her own living will be considered a prostitute.[47]

On another occasion, citing Mrs. Oliver H. P. Belmont—in antisuffrage eyes "a leader of American suffragists" and "financier of the movement"—the *Remonstrance* reported there was in her view one way women could get the ballot all over the world in 18 months: have every woman take an oath not to marry until woman suffrage was granted.[48]

In July 1908 a second important antisuffrage periodical, the eight-page *The Anti-Suffragist*, began publication as a quarterly. Sponsored by the Albany, New York, Association Opposed to Woman Suffrage and edited by Mrs. Winslow Crannell, its credo was expressed in the first issue:

> The aim of this paper is to put before its readers, in concise form, the various arguments against the ballot for women; to disseminate a knowledge of such facts in the case as can be substantiated; to make public such ideas as may seem to the editor to be of weight or worthy of consideration; in short to be the mouthpiece of a no longer silent majority; and we trust that we are not in error in thinking that interest in this question is widespread enough to make the publication of such a paper desirable.[49]

The Anti-Suffragist continued publishing until April 1912, when it was superseded by the new monthly publication of the National Association Opposed to Woman Suffrage, *Woman's Protest*. Beginning with twelve pages and later enlarged to sixteen, *Woman's Protest* was published in New York until 1918. It was a bellwether of antisuffrage sentiment, reporting on the progress of the state campaigns, pointing up the relationship between suffragism and socialism, descrying militant tactics, quoting well-known women on why they objected to woman suffrage, and drawing up tables comparing the laws of suffrage and nonsuffrage states in order to "prove" that women's vote brought no legal benefit to women. In 1918 *Woman's Protest* merged with the weekly *Anti Suffrage Notes* (published by the Cambridge, Massachusetts, Anti Suffrage Association) into the *Woman Patriot*.

Published in Washington, D.C., under the auspices of Mrs. J. W. Wadsworth, successor to Mrs. Arthur M. Dodge as head of the National Association Opposed to Woman Suffrage and wife of the U.S. senator from New York, the *Woman Patriot* prided itself on serving as a national newspaper for "Home Defense against Woman Suffrage, Feminism, and Socialism." Partially financed by the Wadsworths,[50] and edited by Minnie Bronson and Charlotte Rowe, two active Antis from New York, the *Woman Patriot* continued to reflect the sentiments of the national antisuffrage association until the latter's dissolution in 1920. During the 1920s, the *Woman Patriot*, in keeping with the superpatriotism and ultraconservatism of its adherents, carried on a campaign to vilify the efforts of social feminists and liberal women's organizations in America.[51]

One other antisuffrage periodical surfaced during the years of the movement's greatest activity. Inside the cover of the 1913 edition of Helen K. Johnson's *Woman and the Republic* appeared an advertisement for *The Reply, An Anti-Suffrage Magazine*, edited by Helen S. Harman-Brown, with offices in New York City and New Canaan, Connecticut. Published by the Connecticut Antis throughout 1913 and 1914, *The Reply* explained the reason for its existence in the first issue. According to the editors, *The Reply* arose in response to changes taking place within the suffrage movement, particularly the growing tendency of American suffragists to adopt the militant stance of English suffragists.

> The impression seems general that Anti-Suffragists have done nothing in the past, and are doing nothing to show their opposition to what they feel to be a grave national danger—a most mistaken impression. The need for activity was not considered great before the formation of the following quartette—Fashion, Militancy, Socialism and Woman Suffrage. . . . To-day, however, the woman-who-does-not-want-to-vote—and she is the overwhelming majority—cannot fold her hands helplessly, and say "The vote for women is coming, I cannot help it." Every woman who does NOT WANT TO VOTE has only to say so, loudly enough to be heard. . . . Earnest women there are on both sides, however mistaken we believe our adversaries to be, but to-day Anti-Suffragists must come out into the limelight and give a reason "for the faith that is in them." This

Magazine published in Connecticut and the organ of that State Association, stands as an exponent of that Faith.[52]

A second category of antisuffrage publications was the large number of pamphlets and books written by members and supporters of the movement. Between 1883 and 1895, the Boston Committee (that became the MAOFESW in 1895) had the field to themselves as they published and republished numerous pamphlets. These were usually handled by Houghton Mifflin Co., probably through the liaison provided by Elizabeth Houghton, daughter of the publisher and an active Anti.[53] Beginning in 1895, pamphlets issued by other associations began to appear.

This category included printed versions of addresses and lectures given by Antis on various occasions, briefs submitted to legislative committees, reprints of sympathetic articles that appeared in magazines and newspapers, personal testimony by individual Antis as to why they opposed woman suffrage, and scholarly monographs by learned men demonstrating the unsoundness of woman suffrage from the perspective of their particular fields. There was practically no subject that did not lend itself to treatment in an antisuffrage diatribe. All that was needed was the occasion, and the Antis responded with pen in hand. Sometime during the first decade of the twentieth century the MAOFESW issued a bound volume of more than 60 of their pamphlets under the title *Why Women Do Not Want the Ballot.* Omitted from this volume were two pamphlets written in the mid-1880s that expressed antiforeign and anti-Catholic prejudices—Mrs. A. D. T. Whitney's "Law of Woman Life" and Henry Martyn Dexter's "Common Sense as to Woman Suffrage."[54] These were probably omitted as part of a conscious attempt to diminish their ultraconservative image in an effort to win Catholic and working-class women to their cause.

The third group, consisting primarily of campaign materials, was diverse and imaginative. It included postcards bearing the antisuffrage message in the form of a poem or picture, baseball schedule books interleaving between the batting averages reasons why woman suffrage should be defeated, antisuffrage calendars with a different antisuffrage message for each month, cartoons, posters, graphs, fliers, and even an occasional play.[55] The Antis even had their own song, "The Anti-Suffrage Rose," available in sheet music, with words and music by Phil Hanna and dedicated to the Women's Anti-Suffrage Association.

Suffragists say, Happen what may
They'll win the coming fight
'Twixt you and me, I don't agree
We're going to show them who's right!

Jonquils they wear, Cannot compare
With the Anti-Suffrage Rose,
Token of love and a gift from above,
Loveliest flow'r that grows.

Chorus:

Red, Red, Anti-Suffrage Rose
You're the flow'r that's best of all!
You're better far, than Jonquils are,
We are going to prove it in the Fall.

Sweetest flow'r in all the world,
Everybody knows, You're the emblem of
the Anti Suffrage Cause!
You lovely, red, red, rose!

Second verse:

Work for the "cause," No time to pause,
Tell all the men you know,
Why should a few, Rule over you?
Suffrage is ev'ry man's foe.

Beautiful flower, Sign of the hour,
If the Jonquil wants to fight,
You cannot fall, You're the Queen of them all,
Emblem of Truth and Right.

The Antis offered one collection of cartoons and verse for sale. Entitled "Ruthless Rhymes of Martial Militants," the pictures and verses were done by Nelson Harding, cartoonist of the *Brooklyn Daily Eagle*. The following were typical fare:

Notice how the weeping sky
Makes poor little Jenny cry!
Jenny is an Arsonette
And she got her matches wet!

93

Or:

Rock-a-bye baby, thy cradle is frail
Mother's a militant, locked up in jail.
Grandma's another, and so is Aunt Sue,
Off fighting "bobbies," and nurse is there too!

The Antis also prepared a series of black and white glossy photos with elaborate captions, which were probably sent to newspapers. One entitled "Handicapped" showed a storefront polling place as three women were approaching it, one wheeling a carriage. The caption read:

The woman voter who has a child is handicapped by the necessity of pushing or carrying it to the polling place. Probably this is one of the reasons why so many suffragists favor the limitation of families, or what Colonel Roosevelt calls "race suicide," and "professional motherhood," so that women might be "free" to exercise their "equality" with men.

Several photos tried to establish the idea that suffragists worked for saloon-owning candidates. In an attempt to depict the evils of "double suffrage," one photo showed a woman walking down a street where two elderly men were standing and talking, a third standing by himself, and a fourth walking past the woman. The caption read:

Election day is the one day when any man may speak to any woman on the street. This picture shows a woman voter being accosted by a male "worker" on the way to the Hull House polling place April 6.[56]

"Front" Organizations

One of the more intriguing aspects of the antisuffrage movement is that antisuffrage activity occurred in organizations ostensibly devoted to civic and cultural affairs, but that operated in fact as decoys. Under cover of such harmless subterfuges as noonday luncheon clubs, antisuffrage women came together to renew their zeal and further their objectives.

These "front" organizations appeared to be of two kinds. Some, such as the Massachusetts Public Interests League, the Maryland League for State Defense, and the American Constitutional League, usually were established by or grew out of existing antisuffrage associations in an effort to pursue a particular goal.

For example, the MAOFESW founded the Massachusetts Public Interests League in order to identify the antisuffrage cause with civic issues.[57] The Maryland League for State Defense was simply a new name for the former Men's Anti-Suffrage League of Maryland,[58] and was organized to prevent state ratification of the Susan B. Anthony Amendment.

The American Constitutional league, established in Washington, D.C., with Charles S. Fairchild, former secretary of the treasury under Cleveland, as president, seems to have been organized to fight ratification of the federal woman suffrage amendment. Listing its sole object, "to uphold and defend the Constitution of the United States against *all* foreign and *domestic* enemies," it claimed to be nonpartisan and offered to defend any state in maintaining its constitutional rights to local self-government. Apparently, however, the league feared the domestic enemy more than the foreign one, though it is difficult to tell whether the black vote or the suffragists themselves were the greater threat. In the first issue of the league's "Constitutional Bulletin," the leaders of woman suffrage were referred to as "female political profiteers," "woman bosses who demand office and political reward for themselves." It alleged that since the suffragists were unable to deliver the women's vote in Congress, they had resorted to "deliberate deception to mislead Southern Senators" on the number of white women in the South.[59]

One of the league's major objectives was to counter the suffrage argument that southern whites need not fear the woman vote since the number of white women in the South was greater than the total black population. It claimed that the suffragists in their figures included every white baby girl in the border states as a "white woman of the South." According to their own figures, purportedly derived from the "Official U.S. Census Figures of White and Negro Men and Women in the Southern States," the league cited a southern white male population of 3,650,298 and white female population of 3,401,622, for a total white population of 7,051,920; and a black male population of 1,850,713 and a female of 1,858,150, for a total black population of 3,708,863. Yet, in analyzing these figures, the league pointed out that "while the white *men* outnumber the white women by a quarter of a million, the negro *women* outnumber the negro men." Thus, the article concluded, "the negro could *more than double* negro political power with women voting—while the whites could not come within 250,000 votes of doubling *white* representation, even *if every white woman in the South* were willing to be *crowded into the polling places with negroes of both sexes*."[60]

This reasoning is so incredibly fallacious that it is no wonder the Antis were often ridiculed by the very opposition whose arguments they were working so hard to refute. One further ploy of the league was to allege that experience indicated that every election in which white women had participated in the North and West had proved that the majority of women eligible did not vote. On the other hand, they warned, one could be sure the black woman would use the vote, either to demonstrate her "equality" with a white man or woman or because political profiteers of both sexes had seen to it.[61]

The other kind of "front" organization seems to have been designed by individuals who preferred to express their antisuffrage leanings through nonpolitical and less overt means than participation in an antisuffrage organization. Among these were the National League for the Civic Education of Women, which numbered among its officers many individuals known for their antisuffrage activities, as well as many socialites. Organized in the spring of 1908 under the presidency of Mrs. Richard Watson Gilder "with the object of studying civic questions from an antisuffrage point of view," plans were made to incorporate it as a national body with branches organized in every state.[62]

In 1909 Mrs. Gilbert E. Jones, founder and chairman of the league, elaborated the organization's objective. It was obvious, she felt, that women had shown themselves singularly credulous in accepting the statements of suffrage leaders, rarely bothering to investigate them. Therefore, the National League was organized "to give women of the country the best possible means of obtaining information bearing on their rights, responsibilities and economic position in the community." Jones felt that if women had studied the fundamental principles of government, "Woman Suffrage could not have gained the headway that it has and many of them would very clearly see how the movement is strongly allied with Socialism."[63]

Through semicovert and nonpolitical means the league was earnestly devoted to promoting the antisuffrage cause. The league issued an invitation to anyone interested to call at its office "whether suffragist, 'anti,' or suffragette," offering to supply each one with "whatever brand of literature or information she wants." It claimed that its clipping bureau followed "The history of the suffragist as well as the antisuffragist movement, and there is literature on both kinds on the bookshelves."[64]

The league not only kept members informed of new articles expressing antisuffrage sentiments[65] but also arranged both lectures and informal talks before select private audiences at which members spoke on behalf of antisuffrage.[66] The College Committee of the League donated edifying antisuffrage books to college and university libraries.

Another organization in this category was the Guidon Club, founded by Helen Kendrick Johnson. Johnson founded the club as "an Anti-Suffrage, Educational Study Club, for Progressive, Patriotic and Studious Women." Established in 1908, it operated for a time as an informal study class, beginning with "a study of primitive life, tracing the sources from which the ideals of Empires and Republics sprang, and the growth of the destructive spirit of State Socialism." Originally, weekly meetings were held, at which a fifteen-minute historical paper was presented "followed by the presentation of some live theme of discussion on a phase of the woman suffrage problem." Each member of the class drew a paper with a number on it and discussion was carried on in the order of the numbers drawn, with each speaker rising while speaking. The size of the group was purposely kept small (only 12 members were on the original roll), although by the end of 1908 a branch had been formed. The Constitution of the Guidon Club described the objectives of the organization:

Whereas, "No question is settled until it is settled right," and whereas, American women have always aided, and desire to aid more directly in shaping the ideals of our civic as well as our social life, we of this movement, deeply convinced that those who have long been crying "Votes for women" have been following a false lead, have organized to assist the opposition to woman suffrage.

We have chosen as a name The Guidon, from the small ensign which, while it does not flaunt itself, is never absent from the fore-front of a marching column. Its business is to point out the straight line.

The Suffrage movement at this hour is beginning visibly to resolve itself into the elements from which it originally sprang. We believe that sooner or later its irrelevance as a feature of American life will be clearly shown, yet it seems desirable to point out the evils of the situation, as we see it. It is unpatriotic to leave to the correction of a bitter experience, those civic wrongs that may arise from perverted ideals, if we can do anything to warn or ward. The freedom and gallantry of American life make this a question for which we, as woman citizens are peculiarly responsible.

Object: An intelligent opposition to Woman Suffrage, based on a study of woman's right relation to the Republic, to social life, and to the home.

Organization: The Club to consist of small circles for study, discussion and speaking.[67]

The New York State Association Opposed to Woman Suffrage was proud of the Guidon Club and of the League for the Civic Education of Women and called special attention to them at the association's annual meeting of the Standing Committee in December 1908. They were called "two very significant movements, indicating the interest of thinking women in New York State in the work of opposing woman suffrage."[68]

This similarity of aims must have caused some confusion in the public mind for, five years later, Johnson, in a letter to the editor of *The Woman's Protest*, felt called upon to clarify a misunderstanding "to the effect that The Guidon Club was in some way affiliated with New York State Association Opposed to Woman Suffrage." She went on to say that although a few women were members of both, "The Guidon Club, is, and has always been, an entirely independent organization." The error arose because when it was formed a connection with the New York State association was contemplated, "but the clause in the constitution providing for it was not made effective."

> The two bodies, while harmonious and working to the same general end, have distinct fields and distinct methods of operation. The Guidon Club was founded when the suffrage movement began openly to merge with Socialism, and its intent was to study and to oppose that ominous phase of the question. This matter should be fully understood in justice to the older members of The Guidon Club, who know that there was never a connection, and to the new, enlarged membership of men and women that has joined an independent body, and of whom some have asked for explanation, which I know you wish to give.
>
> For myself, I earnestly hope that many anti-suffrage organizations and many periodicals will arise to meet other crises of this all-important work—the most momentous that has ever been laid upon the women of this land, who must refound a society whose destructive, irreligious, Socialistic trend is now evident to all.[69]

The relationship between the New York State association and the Guidon Club, while never formalized, was nevertheless a close one. In 1915, Alice Hill Chittenden, president of the New York State association, wrote to Johnson:

> I was very much interested in your letter in the *Times* on Sunday. I wish the Guidon Club would have it printed and sent to all the ministers in Greater New York, as far as possible, through the state. The ministers are so far astray on this whole question, they really need more information than any other group of men. Hoping the Guidon Club will take this up.[70]

In 1912, when the major party platforms incorporated recommendations to the state legislatures to submit the question of woman suffrage to the popular vote, the Guidon Club broadened its activities to include political action. When the New York State Legislature passed a resolution favoring a woman suffrage referendum, the Guidon enlarged its membership, admitting men, and prepared a campaign aimed directly at the voters.[71] In 1913 the club presented a bill in Albany, requesting that the "present favorable status" of women be retained.

> If what is called "equal suffrage" is to be granted to the women of this State we ask, as a matter of simple justice, that the voters at the same time make them equal with men in all respects before the law. Therefore, we propose this for an additional amendment to the Constitution to be submitted to the people:
>
> At any election if there shall be submitted to the people an amendment to Section 1 of the Constitution which shall propose to omit the words "every male citizen" and substitute therefor the words "every citizen regardless of sex," then, in conjunction therewith, and not otherwise, these words shall be added following "regardless of sex": "there shall be no law that shall discriminate, either in favor of or against either men or women considered as classes."[72]

The Man-Suffrage Association

Although the antisuffrage movement was organized, staffed, and run primarily by women, it was inevitable that men too would play a role, even if not an obvious one. Since antisuffragism was organized essentially for the preservation of the status quo and since most of the leading Antis were married to, or daughters of, men with vested interests in maintaining the existing order, it was only a matter of time before the latter lent their business expertise and political acumen in support of the women.[73] In fact, almost from the beginning, in Massachusetts, male associates of the antisuffragists played an important role, functioning behind the scenes as an unofficial male advisory board. In 1895, when the Antis reorganized with a more elaborate structure to meet the threat of the impending municipal suffrage referendum, they saw to it that their informal male advisory board transformed itself into a male antisuffrage organization, and in September 1895, the Man-Suffrage Association was established.[74]

A list of the officers and members reads like a *Who's Who* of Boston society. Many of the members were Republicans, some of whom were prominent in the leadership of the party. The association established a headquarters in Boston and devoted itself to campaigning for a large no vote in the forthcoming referendum on municipal suffrage.

After the defeat of the referendum in the 1895 election, the Man Suffrage Association dissolved its formal organization. Nevertheless, its leaders continued to meet informally, and somewhat secretly, and to provide the antisuffragists with legislative counsel, advice on how to conduct their campaign and hearings, and money.[75] By 1907, this informal core of male advisers reconstituted itself into a formal committee to continue to provide moral support and financial aid to the women. Eventually, however, even this committee structure was not considered effective enough, and in 1911 a regularly constituted men's organization known as the Massachusetts Anti Suffrage League was established.[76]

The Massachusetts Anti Suffrage League established its headquarters on Beacon Street in Boston, hired a treasurer and counsel, and established a joint committee with the women to plan campaigns, give advice, and share expenses. Probably in order to distinguish itself as a separate woman's organization, the MAOFESW changed its name to the Women's Anti-Suffrage Association of Massachusetts.[77] In 1915, a national men's committee, calling itself the Man-Suffrage Association Opposed to Political Suffrage for Women was established, with headquarters in Boston.[78] Its purpose was to show legislative committees and the people

> that giving of political suffrage generally would draw attention and interest of women from home duties which they alone can discharge, would bring selfish and artful women into prominence, entice them by holding out political prizes, and would encourage freak legislation. "We call ourselves the Home Rule Party."[79]

The Antis devoted considerable time, energy, and money to building an organization to stanch the flow of suffragism. Their successes during this period probably helped to forestall the advent of woman suffrage. The Antis, however, did not have to work alone. In addition to the backing of their male "auxiliaries," they were often sustained by support received from other elements who were hostile to the idea of woman suffrage. Furthermore, as the suffrage struggle wore on, the Antis realized it was to their advantage to win the support of specific segments of the population. Just who these various allies were and how they interacted with the Antis is the subject of the next chapter.

FIVE

Antisuffrage Allies

It is one of the ironies of the woman suffrage movement that despite all the rhetoric of the suffragists on behalf of their oppressed sex and all their arguments that, given equal opportunity with men, women would prove themselves as capable, the suffragists failed to recognize that their most organized and effective foes were women themselves. It was characteristic of those who worked the longest and hardest for woman suffrage to see the forces behind the opposition as liquor, big business, the church—in short, as almost anything except women. As a result, when the antisuffragists do figure as a force in suffragist writings they are usually depicted as malicious and misguided men who would resort to anything to discredit the suffrage movement. Only rarely are the Antis portrayed as women, and at such times they are dismissed as deviants from the path of true womanhood.

Suffragists and Prohibition

Since the suffragists were unwilling or unable to realize that the most consistent opposition to their efforts was the unremitting resistance of other women, whom, then, did they conceive to be their enemy? The major foe, from the suffrage perspective, was the liquor interests, including the brewers, the hard liquor distillers, and the middlemen. According to Carrie Chapman Catt, the United States Brewers' Association, the Wholesale Distillers' Association, and the Retail Dealers' Association masterminded the liquor trade's influence over United States politics. In her view, a trail led from the women's antisuffrage organizations to the liquor camp traveled by men appointed by the Antis. She alleged that whenever a woman suffrage amendment was submitted, particularly in the midwestern states, one could find evidence of the Brewers' Association at work, ordering defeat of the amendment and sending out its henchmen to do its dirty work. This included removing pro-amendment posters or covering them with opposition ones, instigating the foreign-born by representing to them that woman suffrage meant prohibition, distributing copies of the *Remonstrance* by "saloon men," and mobilizing non-English-speaking foreign men, who in some states were allowed to vote on receipt of their first papers, to mob the polls, voting no. In suffrage eyes some power enlisted these men, voted them, and paid them, and whatever that power was, it had either commanded the political parties to do its bidding, or the political parties had called it to their aid.[1]

Even as late as 1919, Catt was still issuing directives to the presidents of suffrage associations in states that had ratified the federal suffrage amendment, warning them that "In most states opposition to suffrage is co-extensive to the opposition to prohibition." As evidence she cited the situation in Texas, where immediately after ratification, the impeached governor and his followers organized an antisuffrage association with the intention of electing an antisuffrage legislature that would repeal ratification by turning it into a "wet" versus "dry" fight.[2]

The suffragists viewed the liquor trade as the natural enemy because of its resistance to prohibition and its fear that an emancipated womanhood would provide the necessary vote to institutionalize prohibition. Press reports of the Brewers Convention of 1881 included an account of adoption of an antisuffrage resolution to the effect that brewers would welcome prohibition as far less dangerous to the trade than woman suffrage because prohibition could be repealed at any time, whereas woman suffrage would ensure the permanence of prohibition.[3]

On one level the fears of the liquor interests were understandable, given the sentiments of large numbers of women and the growing support of the WCTU for the suffrage movement.[4] Nevertheless, temperance did not mean the same thing as prohibition, and even though many women supported the latter, the majority would probably have settled for some form of temperance. Furthermore, the woman suffrage states were not dry (as the Antis always hastened to point out). Therefore, it is all the more difficult to understand why the brewers seemed to revel in their hysteria and persist in viewing any advance in the position of women as a direct threat to their interests. They felt that only a matter of weeks after woman suffrage would be enacted, local option elections would enable women to vote in prohibition.[5] This response to the rhetoric of the battle rather than to the facts may have been a strategic device, enabling the brewers to appear as merely defending their jobs and families against a hostile and fanatical mass of women dedicated to their destruction. In any event it was inevitable that sooner or later they would find themselves political bedfellows of the Antis.

The Antis and the Liquor Interests

Just what the relationship was between the Antis and the liquor interests is difficult to ascertain. The suffragists were quick to see the advantage of embarrassing the Antis by implying that since they and the brewers had similar interests at stake, they were probably in collusion as well.[6]

If, in the public mind, suffrage meant prohibition, then opposition to suffrage probably conjured up opposition to prohibition. In 1913 Inez Milholland of the National Suffrage Association stated that the National Brewer's Association endorsed the antisuffrage organizations and contributed to their treasury. Although this was denied by the Brewers' Association, the Antis were discredited because they and the liquor interests worked for a common cause.[7]

It is virtually impossible to assess the actual role of the liquor interests in the woman suffrage struggle from the accounts given by either side. Both the Antis and the suffragists held distorted views of the "enemy," the suffragists seeing liquor interests behind every move, the Antis discounting their role entirely and assuming that resistance to suffrage, in whatever form, was a spontaneous expression of public opinion.[8]

The Antis were forced to come to terms with what they called the "liquor lie" and in so doing found the opportunity to retaliate as well. For one thing, the Antis pointed out not only that woman suffrage did not necessarily imply prohibition, but that male suffrage states were the first to adopt it. For example, in 1916, the Antis delighted in showing that the only two suffrage victories in the previous three years had occurred in the "two wettest States in the Union"—Montana and Nevada.[9]

A letter from Mrs. Arthur M. Dodge, president of the National Association Opposed to Woman Suffrage, replying to a suffrage statement linking antisuffragists and liquor interests in Michigan, concluded by dismissing as comical the suffragist claim that the liquor interests were their opponents in prohibition states.

It would seem that if the liquor interests cannot save themselves from being put out of business, they surely cannot prevent woman suffrage. . . . That they [suffragists] stoop to innuendo and misrepresentation about their sister women who oppose them, and try to link the names of some of the best women in every State with the liquor interests, without any justification whatever, should be a reflection on them, not us.[10]

Antisuffrage reasoning was not always so consistent. In a "Prohibition Map of the U.S.," drawn up in October 1912, the Antis tried to make the point that although the six states then having full woman suffrage (Colorado, Wyoming, Utah, Idaho, Washington, and California) had not voted for prohibition, not one of the states that voted for prohibition was a suffrage state.[11] What they failed to point out was that there were many other male suffrage states that had not voted for prohibition, such as New York, Pennsylvania, New Jersey, and Nevada. Furthermore, it is not clear that any of these so-called prohibition states had enacted statewide prohibition, rather than being simply under license law in various local areas.

In their attempts to show that suffrage would not ensure prohibition, the Antis often cited remarks made by suffragists that were obviously meant as disclaimers of any association with or sympathy for prohibition. These were uttered, it seems, in an effort to court the liquor interests, regarded by the suffragists as their chief obstacle, and to bid for the votes of drinking men.[12] It is not surprising that the Antis took advantage of this situation by arguing that it showed that the suffragists had no intention of ever outlawing drink.[13] However, their position does suggest that in the antisuffrage scale of values the only justification for woman suffrage was as a deterrent to vice or to serve some other socially useful function, and that if it did not fulfill this function, it served no worthwhile purpose.

Despite all their protestations to the contrary, however, there seems to be sufficient reason to believe that the liquor interests did support antisuffrage activities,[14] and that the antisuffragists unofficially, and perhaps even unwittingly at times, worked hand in glove with liquor interests and against woman suffrage.[15]

The United States Brewers' Association was organized quietly in 1862, primarily for political protection of the trade. At its 1867 convention the association warned political parties it would declare war on all candidates favorably disposed to the "total abstinence cause." It is uncertain when the decision was made to include woman suffrage as an indirect menace to the liquor cause, but in 1867, during the Kansas campaign, the local liquor men were conspicuous workers against the woman suffrage amendment.[16] From the suffrage perspective, the liquor trade exercised a dominant, if behind-the-scenes, influence over United States politics for a generation.[17] In the Midwest and West the evidence certainly began to mount up. For example, on January 14, 1914, H. T. Fox, secretary of the United States Brewers' Association, wrote the Fred Miller Brewing Company of Milwaukee in answer to an inquiry as to what was being done "in regard to woman suffrage and the spring elections in Illinois."

> In regard to the matter of woman suffrage, we are trying to keep from having any connection with it whatever. We are, however, in a position to establish channels of communication with the leaders of the Anti-Suffrage Movement for our friends in any State where suffrage is an issue.[18]

Copies of the *Remonstrance* found their way into the hands of liquor dealers for distribution. Liquor organs such as the *National Forum*, published in Butte, Montana, and the *Liberal Advocate* of Columbus, Ohio, ran articles sent out by the Antis. In Stark County, Ohio, streetcars carried ads for a liquor amendment in 1914 that urged readers to "see the card on the opposite side of the car." On the opposite side was the women's antisuffrage ad, asking for votes against the suffrage amendment. In Warren, Ohio, literature issued by both Antis and liquor interests was folded in the same package and left on doorsteps by professional bill distributors. In Macomb County, Michigan, the Retail Liquor Dealers' Association sent advertising copy for the Michigan Association Opposed to Woman Suffrage to newspapers under their own cover letter. In some states posters issued by women's antisuffrage associations even hung inside saloons.[19]

Then in 1917, in an effort to offset a pending presidential suffrage bill, "wets" in the Ohio legislature introduced a bill for submission of a full suffrage amendment, hoping by this move to obscure the issue and effect the ultimate rejection of the presidential suffrage bill. The suffragists felt that after fifty years of trying, the time for a state amendment had gone by. They saw woman suffrage coming by way of a federal amendment and were unwilling to dissipate their energies on what they regarded as a futile gesture. Preferring instead to speed ratification of a federal amendment, they opposed this full suffrage bill. As a result, the Ohio legislature was treated to the spectacle of suffragists resisting enfranchisement and women Antis and wet men occupying seats in a bloc, pleading for submission of the bill.[20]

Since close association often begins to breed similarities, it was only a matter of time before the arguments of the liquor interests began to resemble those of the Antis. Opposing prohibition on the same grounds that the Antis resisted enfranchisement, the harried liquor interests decried the efforts of a minority to exert control over the majority. They argued that prohibition would result in a decline in public and personal morality, alleging that whenever it had been enacted there had been an increase in the amount of whiskey drinking and drunkenness, much in the same way as the Antis made similar claims on behalf of woman suffrage. And, finally, they argued, in line with the antisuffrage dictum that morality cannot be legislated, a man could not be made temperate by legislation. Only education, better conditions, greater comforts, and moral persuasion diminish drunkenness and cure the habits that destroy.[21]

While the Antis and the liquor interests may have developed a common rhetoric in an effort to pursue a common goal, their basic political philosophies had little in common. Nowhere is this better illustrated than in the efforts of the liquor people to demonstrate their avowed liberalism. Even their opposition to suffragism was couched in these terms, for they depicted themselves not only as fighting for their very survival but also as the standard-bearers of sanity and liberalism in a war against the fanatical parochialism of the suffragists. It was not uncommon to see liquor organs pick up the gauntlet for the underdog, pleading for tolerance for far-out religious sects, engaging in antitrust diatribes against such megamonopolies as the Bell Telephone Company, deriding the "narrow fanatic," and urging that the problems of beggars and organ grinders on the streets of the cities could be solved by a massive welfare system that would take from "the bounteous blessing of those who are perfect in mental and bodily health" and give to the poor.[22]

In suffragist eyes, the long arm of the liquor industry extended way beyond the confines of the trade. They saw evidence of liquor money at work manipulating politics, in collusion with big business, and in a host of lesser ways. In short, NAWSA regarded as an antisuffrage, and therefore hostile, force all those whose interests seemed to lie in denying the vote to women. As far as outright power was concerned, as well as reasonable motive, suffragists viewed the political machines, i.e., the traditional party bosses and leaders of the dominant Republican and Democratic parties, as a threat second only to that of the liquor industry.[23]

From the suffrage perspective, the same men who conducted the antiprohibition campaign directed the antisuffrage contests in the legislatures, constitutional conventions and referenda campaigns. To finance these efforts, suffragists believed that they took money from funds placed in the hands of political committees organized by the liquor interests to fight prohibition. According to Catt, in states reported strong for woman suffrage and prohibition, the attitudes of congressmen and state legislators on both questions were reported to the national political committees of the liquor interests with equal care.[24]

Suffragists alleged that the liquor interests would first "fix" the committee to which a suffrage bill was referred. They believed that this was done in nearly three-fourths of the suffrage legislative campaigns, with the explanation given the suffragists that an overworked committee or crowded legislative calendar prevented the bill from being considered. Then if the suffrage bill was likely to be reported out by the committee, work was begun on the legislators. When the legislative campaign was confined to the Senate, the liquor lobbyist would concentrate his efforts on the key men, trading votes, instilling fear of party defeat, promising help in coming campaigns, and giving presents to their wives. In the end, if all this failed, allegedly they would resort to intimidation, threats, and bribery. Sometimes liquor counsel were nominated as representatives and elected by unsuspecting voters.[25]

Regardless of the accuracy of the suffrage allegations, major party leaders did have every reason to oppose woman suffrage. First of all, they could not be certain how women would vote. In the four states in which women had been enfranchised the longest (Wyoming, Colorado, Idaho, and Utah), two of the states were Democratic and two Republican. Therefore, there seemed to be no apparent advantage in enfranchising women.[26] On the other hand, there must have appeared to be considerable disadvantage. Believing, as did much of the public, that women would vote as a bloc, they must have feared the unleashed fury of a disciplined force of voting women reputedly unsusceptible to bribery and dedicated, among other things, to a reform campaign directed at purifying contemporary politics. No wonder they doubted that they could control the woman voter sufficiently to serve their interests.

In 1918, during a Senate investigation of the brewing and liquor industries, evidence of their widespread influence was made available for the first time. Secured on subpoena, the material garnered indicated that the industry often worked through various front organizations. For example, every state with a prohibition or a woman suffrage campaign had its Home Rule Societies, Personal Liberty Leagues, Traveling Men's or Merchants' Leagues, or Men's

107

Anti Suffrage Associations. In addition, druggists, tobacco manufacturers and dealers, and hotel men were organized opponents of both movements. The brewers themselves set up allied organizations with auxiliaries in each state to help provide revenue for the campaigns.[27] The evidence also indicated that the liquor industry financed political campaigns throughout the country in amounts from $4 million to $10 million a year.

The Antis and Business

Business interests were the hardest to link with opposition to woman suffrage. This was true in part because there was no organized protest by the National Association of Manufacturers, the United States Chamber of Commerce, or *The Wall Street Journal*. Nevertheless, the suffragists continually referred to the antisuffrage activity of railroad, oil, and general manufacturing lobbies whenever suffrage was up for legislative action or referendum. Evidently, during a congressional investigation of Swift and Company, it became apparent that even the meat packers secretly contributed to the Antis. In Nebraska, an appeal to the public to vote against a woman suffrage referendum in 1914 carried the signatures of nine railroad and municipal transit executives, seven bankers and other businessmen, and two Episcopalian ministers. In Texas, the Businessmen's Association distributed articles to newspapers on numerous subjects including opposition to woman suffrage. (The association included a number of brewers, Gulf Refining Company, Swift & Company, Santa Fe Railroad, American Express Company, and Southeastern States Portland Cement Company.) The association supported a National Farmers Union, some of whose funds were also supplied by railroads. The union also issued material opposed to woman suffrage. Finally, if this were not enough to indicate collusion, the personal links are a dead giveaway. Two directors of the National Association Opposed to Woman Suffrage were wives of directors of railroads (see Biographical Appendix). The board of the Man-Suffrage Association included J. P. Morgan's son-in-law, as well as four other railroad directors. And "the moving spirit of the Man Suffrage Association, considered by the suffragists to be the evil genius of the opposition, was Everett P. Wheeler, who made his livelihood as a corporation counsel."[28]

In the United States Senate, those who led the fight against woman suffrage appear to have been spokesmen for the business interests. Senator Wadsworth of New York, for example, continued to vote against woman suffrage even after his own state had enfranchised its women and despite the fact that the New York State legislature twice called on him by resolution to vote for it. In 1918 he resisted a plea by the National Republican Committee to vote for the federal woman suffrage amendment.[29] Despite this overwhelming mandate, he chose to go on record against woman suffrage even when it seemed to be no longer feasible politically. Just what his motives were is difficult to determine. But one thing is apparent—through his family and business connections he was linked personally with some of the major antisuffrage interests. Furthermore, in the Senate he had voted against such democratic measures as an income tax, direct primary, taxation of war profits, and an investigation of Wall Street.[30] Senator Weeks, also a staunch opponent of woman suffrage and leader of the Republican machine in Massachusetts, voted against direct election of senators, income tax, taxation of war profits, and establishment of a Federal Trade Commission.[31]

These and other northern antisuffrage senators who remained opposed until the very end were joined in their opposition to woman suffrage by a large majority of southern Democrats. The suffragists alleged that for the latter, fear of the Negro woman vote was only a pretext and that the real motive lay in the fact that the cotton industry employed thousands of woman and children at very low rates.[32]

Other than the railroads and farmers, both of whose interests coincided with those of the liquor industry, it would seem that many of the large manufacturers, such as the textile industry, had little reason to oppose prohibition and every reason to resist woman suffrage. In fact, beginning around 1913, as court decisions began to be increasingly friendly to temperance, many manufacturers joined the prohibition forces. Some may have done so out of a genuine belief that with liquor outlawed, their workers, particularly on Monday mornings, would operate more efficiently. At any rate, these same individuals remained steadfast in their opposition to woman suffrage.

In Massachusetts, many officers and active members of the Man-Suffrage Association were closely connected with the textile interests. Eben Draper, for example, a founding member of the association, belonged to the family that owned the Hopedale Cotton Mills, offenders in "weaver's fines."[33] As a regular contributor, his family helped finance the MAOFESW. In 1902 the nominating committee of MAOFESW chose Mrs. Draper as vice president "in view of the great influence of Mr. Draper, and the very generous contributions given by the family."[34] Needless to say, she was elected. Draper himself, a power in Republican circles (he was governor of the state from 1900 to 1903), was elected chairman of the Republican State Committee in 1892 through the efforts of the Arkwright Club, of which he was a member. The club, representing textile interests in the state, fought bills to limit working hours for women and children and opposed all democratic measures such as the Australian ballot, removal of the poll tax, initiative, and referendum. Interestingly, Draper's uncle, Ebenezer Draper, had in the 1870s been a staunch supporter of woman suffrage and of the *Woman's Journal*.[35]

Liquor interests, party bosses, and big business all had one thing in common—the belief that enactment of woman suffrage would result in a shift of power between their established interests and the force of enfranchised womanhood. In the case of the foreign born and the Catholic church, the motivation was much less obvious.

Suffragists, Antis, and the Foreign Born

Fear of the foreign born obsessed the suffragists, who believed that wherever the former lived together in large numbers they were natural dupes of the party machine and the liquor interests. Throughout Anthony's *History of Woman Suffrage* recurs the theme that in state after state as referenda on woman suffrage took place, the foreign born were organized to vote against it. The suffragists maintained that the latter were misled by the brewers into believing that woman suffrage would herald in prohibition. Russians, Poles, and Scandinavians in the Dakotas, the Chinese in California, the Mexicans in Colorado, they felt, were all being manipulated to vote against it.

Of all the foreign associations, the deadliest from the suffrage viewpoint was the German-American Alliance. Assisted financially by the brewers, the alliance had a membership in the millions, organizing committees throughout large sections of the Midwest, and in 1914 headquarters and a lobby in Washington. Apparently, in return for the support of the brewers, the alliance committee in each state received instructions from the liquor campaign managers on whom to vote for at each election. In Texas, Missouri, Iowa, North Dakota, Nebraska, Wisconsin, and Michigan, "This organized German-liquor vote was hurled into woman suffrage referendum campaigns . . . making a well-nigh all-controlling political power in these States."[36]

110

While all this may have been true, the foreign born had little reason of their own to pursue an alliance with the Antis. They were not motivated to participate in an all-out battle with the forces of woman suffrage. Their main interest was in preserving their way of life, which often included a certain amount of alcohol. Therefore, they may have let themselves be persuaded to join forces with the brewers in voting against suffrage. There seems to be no evidence that the Antis worked *directly* with the alliance or with any other association of this kind. The only connection between these two segments of the opposition was through the liquor industry, and possibly through the Catholic church in its relationship to various ethnic groups.

The Catholic Church, Suffrage, and the Birth Control Question

In contrast to their lack of a real alliance with the foreign born, the Antis actually went out of their way to court Catholic opposition. For a long time, however, the Antis had been too blinded by their nativist fears of foreigners and papists to realize that the Catholic church, with its traditional antifeminist bias[37] and its fear of suffragist anti-Catholicism, offered them a potential ally. The church resisted woman suffrage for ideological rather than strictly political reasons. Unlike liquor, bossism, and big business, the church did not feel as directly threatened by a loss of power, except during the Know-Nothing periods, when it was on the defensive. Although it may have feared that in the long run woman suffrage presented a challenge to its authority, its most consistent reaction derived from its traditional views concerning the separateness of the female and male spheres. The church both desired "to prevent a moral deterioration which suffrage could bring" and "feared the development of a political structure and social climate deleterious to Catholicism."[38] In general, the opposition conformed to the established pattern that saw the more hierarchical and ritualistic churches opposing woman suffrage and the democratically organized ones more receptive.[39]

Catholic opposition was based on the view that traditionally constituted society was "a system designed by God, revealed by a Pauline interpretation of scripture and/or the natural law, re-inforced by biological differences, and supported by a historical tradition which proclaimed the political supremacy of man." In this view any move by either sex on the domain of the other was unnatural and "a threat to the universal order."[40] The Catholic press and clergy warned the public of the dangers of such a move. In 1900, NAWSA could list only six Catholic clergymen in the United States who supported woman suffrage.[41] In fact, as late as 1915, the Church-Work Committee of NAWSA singled out as one of the suffragists' most important tasks "the organization of the Catholic women, that they will make their demands so emphatic the church will see the wisdom of supporting the movement."[42]

In the years after 1885, the growth of the birth control movement added a new element to Catholic fears and to Catholic opposition. Catholics were warned that married women could be active in politics only as a result of limiting their families. Apparently Margaret Sanger believed that woman suffrage would lead to legal changes in states that prohibited birth control and therefore publicly endorsed woman suffrage. Furthermore, some suffrage leaders openly supported her crusade. The situation was compounded in 1915, when the National Birth Control League was organized by women who were primarily active in suffrage and feminist endeavors.[43]

Although the church was unalterably opposed to woman suffrage, for a number of years it did not express its opposition officially. Instead, eminent Catholic laymen and prelates used their influence as individuals to fight woman suffrage. For example, when the first male antisuffrage petition was submitted to the Massachusetts state legislature in 1885, it included the names of John Boyle O'Reilly, editor of the Catholic newspaper, the Boston *Pilot*, and the Reverend Joshua P. Bodfish, chancellor of the archdiocese of Boston.[44] An antisuffrage pamphlet published in 1886 included one of Bodfish's sermons and an appeal by O'Reilly.[45] When the Man-Suffrage Association was formed in 1895, its supporters included Bodfish, Charles F. Donnelly, friend and legal counselor to Archbishop Williams, and the young congressman John T. Fitzgerald.[46]

In effect, what happened was that while individual Catholics indulged their private hostility to woman suffrage, the church maintained a kind of public neutrality. In Massachusetts, the clergy definitely veered away from openly endorsing the MAOFESW.[47] Nevertheless, by 1912, the *Catholic Encyclopedia* could write:

> The opposition expressed by many women to the introduction of woman suffrage, as for instance, the New York Association Opposed to Woman Suffrage, should be regarded by Catholics, as, at least, the voice of common sense.[48]

For a long time the Antis seemed oblivious to the possibility of an alliance with the church. For one thing, most Antis were caught up in the Know-Nothing revival of the 1880s and 1890s and, fearing the immigrant vote, which was largely Irish-Catholic, were unaware that the latter were just as opposed to woman suffrage as they were. Furthermore, they could not have known that even if the franchise were bestowed, most Catholic immigrant women would not exercise it. This was demonstrated in the Boston School Committee election of 1888. Protestant women, realizing that the school committee franchise they had received in 1879 could be a valuable weapon in protecting the public schools from Catholic influence, came out in full force to vote for committee members of their choosing. The Catholic women, contrary to expectations, did not vote, thereby validating the nativist tendencies of suffragists, who believed that extension of full suffrage to women would provide a barrier against increased Catholic influence.

This was further demonstrated in the Massachusetts municipal suffrage election of 1895 in which of 612,000 women eligible to vote, only 23,065 voted (22,204 for and 861 against), with Catholic women again not voting. The results of the election reinforced the suffragist-nativist alliance by confirming their view that native-born Protestants would outvote foreign-born Catholics.[49] The outcome of the campaign also alerted many Catholics to the necessity of the vote for women. Nevertheless, the church itself, as well as the majority of Catholic laymen, remained markedly antisuffrage.

Despite the evidence of considerable Catholic support for the antisuffrage position, most Antis continued to remain unaware that most Catholics opposed woman suffrage. Ironically it was only in the next decade, as some Catholics increasingly saw the possibilities for an enfranchised Catholic womanhood, that growing numbers of Catholic women began to speak out against woman suffrage. By 1905 the Antis were becoming aware of the general Catholic attitude.[50] In 1913, in Massachusetts, they began lecturing to Catholic women's clubs and even selected a Catholic woman for the Executive Committee. They held rallies before Catholic men's groups such as the Knights of Columbus and the Ancient Order of Hibernians. This affinity became even more pronounced as Antis and Catholics found themselves mutually compatible on the subjects of birth control and socialism. The antisuffrage role in the birth control controversy was to call attention to what they regarded as the sinister relationship between woman suffrage and birth control. During the 1915 Massachusetts woman suffrage campaign, the MAOFESW distributed material warning against this association. Furthermore, the MAOFESW charged that planned parenthood was being taught young factory girls by socialists and suffragists. By around 1917, the Antis had adopted a "social purity" policy to check birth control.[51]

By this time, the Antis were making considerable use of Catholic opponents. They invited Cardinal Gibbons of Baltimore to address their annual meeting in Washington in 1916, and although he could not attend, his prepared speech was read to the Antis and later reprinted as one of their pamphlets. In addition, the Antis cited passages from the *Catholic Encyclopedia* expressing antifeminist and antisuffrage sentiments. They also quoted other eminent Catholic prelates, such as John Cardinal Farley, Rt. Rev. John S. Foley of Detroit, Archbishop Moeller of Cincinnati, Archbishop Messmer of Milwaukee, and Cardinal O'Connell of Boston.[52] The *Anti-Suffragist* of June 1909 contained a short notice that the pope in a recent speech had taken a stand against women in politics.[53]

The antisuffragists also tried to gain the support of other churches and church groups. It was a major thorn in their side that the Protestant churches tended increasingly to sympathize with the suffragists. Nevertheless, this had not always been the case. Throughout the 1880s and 90s, the more hierarchical the church organization and the more formal its ritual, the greater was its opposition to woman suffrage, while the democratically organized churches with little dogma tended to be more receptive. By the turn of the century, however, more and more Protestant clergymen and churches were endorsing woman suffrage. As a result, the Antis found it necessary to intensify their campaign through Protestant organizations and were especially active just prior to the 1915 election in Massachusetts.[54]

The antisuffragists were fortunate to enlist in support of their cause Methodist Bishop John H. Vincent, founder of Chautauqua. Through the Chautauqua Society's summer session and home education program, housewives and other women who wanted to "improve" themselves were exposed to what was a basically traditional viewpoint concerning woman's place, if not to outright antisuffrage propaganda. Vincent had all the more authority since he spoke as a convert to antisuffragism, claiming to have been a public defender of woman suffrage in his younger days.

Vincent's basic objection was that woman suffrage would disrupt the existing relationship between the sexes "by virtue of which each sex depends upon and is exalted by the other." It would "make man less a man, and woman less a woman." He attributed to women enormous power without the vote, claiming that "Woman now makes man what he is." Naturally, if one starts from this assumption, there are only two possible conclusions that can be drawn. On the one hand, if women use their power wisely, any additional power would be superfluous; on the other, if they abuse their opportunity, they are not worthy of any additional responsibility. Vincent arrived at both conclusions, joining the many female Antis who at one and the same time exalted woman to a position of supreme power and simultaneously attributed to her ultimate responsibility for all the evils of society.[55]

Antisuffrage and the Working Woman

Finally, after a long history of disinterest in the working woman, the Antis began to realize that they too represented a power to be reckoned with. What is striking about the antisuffrage approach, however, is their incredible naiveté concerning the female labor force. The Antis regarded the typical working woman as either a professional or semiprofessional forcing her way into a male-dominated field, "compelled in a life and death struggle, to knock at the gates of all trades and professions, and to force her way into them against determined opposition from tradition and prejudice";[56] or else they viewed the mass of wage-earning women as mostly young girls living at home who joined the work force to spend fourteen hours a day in a factory just to make some extra money for fancy clothes.[57] The assumptions in either case were not those that would endear them to the masses of working women. That they achieved a hearing at all was due to the fact that the great majority of working women probably shared the same goal as the Antis—to obtain sufficient economic security to enable them to remain at home. In this connection, it is noteworthy how few, if any, of the radical women trade union leaders were in favor of suffrage.

The foremost spokeswoman for the antisuffrage position on women and labor was Minnie Bronson, who claimed authority in this area as a result of having served on two occasions as a special agent of the United States Bureau of Labor. From 1907 to 1909, she conducted an investigation of the conditions of labor of woman and children for the bureau, and then in 1910 in this same capacity she reported on the strike of shirtwaist makers.[58]

In 1910, the MAOFESW published Bronson's "The Wage-Earning Woman and the State," a pamphlet designed to counter the suffragists' argument that the ballot would lead to fairer treatment of women in industry and to better protective legislation. Supporting her position by referring to the 1909-10 shirtwaist strike in New York City, Bronson contested the notion advanced by a "noted suffragist" that if the women engaged in that industry had had the ballot, such a strike would have been unnecessary. According to Bronson, not only were 40 percent of the strikers men, but 60 percent of the remainder were under twenty-one years of age, while 25 percent of all women workers of voting age had not been in the country long enough to gain residence.[59]

Consistent with the Antis' strategy of comparing suffrage and nonsuffrage states, Bronson devoted the major part of her essay to demonstrating that there were more and better laws for the protection of women wage earners in the nonsuffrage stages. Furthermore, in her view, the laws for safeguarding wage-earning women were better and more comprehensive than those for the protection of wage-earning men. She was probably right on both counts. Men had had the ballot for years and yet when it came to improving their working conditions, the only effective means was to organize and try to create change through labor unions. Furthermore, the four states that had the longest history of woman suffrage, Utah, Idaho, Wyoming, and Colorado, had a minimum of women engaged in the work force—by the Antis' own reckoning, fewer than 4,000, compared with over 600,000 in factories in three eastern states.[60] Therefore, the need for such legislation was relatively nonexistent in the woman suffrage states. If men and women were to be on an equal footing before the law, said the Antis, then the law should not discriminate between them. "Equality means *no privileges for anybody.*"[61] Of course, equality could also mean elevating the lower to the higher and procuring the *benefits* of the privileged for the disadvantaged.

One of the most controversial issues in the appeal to working women was the question of the wage differential for female and male workers. The suffragists had gone out on a limb by arguing that the ballot would provide women with the means of bringing their wages into line with those paid to men. As all Antis who took up the cudgels on this issue pointed out, variation in the wages paid to male and female workers was due to the operation of the law of supply and demand. It remained to indicate just how neither the wages paid to woman nor remedial legislation on her behalf depended on her political status. According to antisuffragist Mrs. George A. Caswell,

> What can the ballot in the hands of women do that it has not done for men? It is more than a year since a shop girl wrote to the New York Times to ask how when Messrs. Mitchell and Gompers reported 500,000 voting men out of employment, working women could hope to gain anything from the suffrage. Her question has never been answered.[62]

Since a minimum wage law had not yet been enacted, the Antis maintained that the price of labor could not be made a legislative matter, or even if it could, it would not be able to be enforced. There was not a factory in existence in New York State, said one Anti, that did not have a long roll of names of girls who were begging to be employed.

> How are these girls to regulate their pay if they can vote? Are not the unemployed men already too numerous in our streets to-day? They can vote, and they are generally willing to be employed at any wages that may be offered.[63]

One of the major shortcomings of the Antis' position on the working woman and the reason for their failure to gain the support of a significant constituency among the female labor force was the inconsistency in their approach to the question. Ostensibly directing their appeal to the working woman, they made the mistake of at the same time trying to win the support of the working man. Thus, while they kept insisting that working women would gain nothing by the ballot except the added burden of having to vote and the possibility of losing their virtue, they were also warning working men that women in industry meant job competition.

> Everywhere the wage is regulated by demand and supply; and as women enter the field as competitors with men, the result is always that instead of wages being increased for women, they are lowered for men.[64]

The Antis believed that women edged men out of jobs by their willingness to work for less money. They tended to view the majority of the female work force as entering the shop or factory merely to span the interval between school and marriage and not as involved in a struggle to gain a livelihood. The latter, they believed, was furnished to most women by their fathers or brothers. Therefore, the money they earned was merely for "extra clothing or trinkets." Consequently, the working woman could "accept prices for labor that no man who has to provide for a family could accept."[65]

That the Antis failed to endear themselves to the masses of working women was also due to their belief that if a wage differential existed between the salaries of male and female workers, it was probably justified.

> Women often earn less than men because they produce less, and what they produce is usually valued in the market at a lower rate, perhaps because of its smaller quantity, sometimes because of its inferior quality.

Even in the teaching profession, where wages were notoriously unequal, the Antis felt that the larger supply of women workers intensified the competition among women, while the "temporary and intermittent character of their work due to their tendency to marry, and the disability resulting from a less degree of physical vitality" offered an explanation for what "at first sight seems wholly unjust."[66]

One male antisuffragist argued that the New York State law establishing equality of wage between men and women teachers of equal grade created an "obvious inequality" between a woman teacher and the wife of a teacher who, together with him and their children, depended on his salary for support. He felt that the only means for a wife to establish economic equality between herself and the female teacher was to turn over her home and children to the care of another and become economically independent herself. What the author was saying, in effect, was that it was but a short step from the concept of equal pay for equal work to the realization of feminist goals.[67]

One could conclude, following this line of reasoning, that women really should not work at all, because when they worked for less pay than a man (which according to the Antis was the only fair way), they were competing with and taking jobs away from the working man whose legal (and moral) responsibility was to provide for the woman in the home so that she could perform her real job of wife and mother.[68]

Most Antis were able to sanction the idea of a female labor force only as long as they could view women workers as a provisional or reserve unit in the "great army of labor."

> It is for the good of the State that this should be so, and whatever tends to prolong the period of woman's labor at occupations in which she is the competitor of man, and especially at purely mechanical materialistic occupations, lessens therefore her chances for a happy marriage, and directly decreases the number and value of those homes from which flow the purest streams of morals and refinement, the highest ideals of civic courage and worth.[69]

Furthermore, every effort to make of woman an independent laborer and gain for her "industrial equality" reeked of socialism. It was a movement away from marriage and homemaking, "because the contract of marriage, written and unwritten, is that civil and industrial labor shall devolve upon the man, as a consideration for the labors of home-keeping and maternity."[70]

That the Antis were unable to win much support among women workers was also due to their tendency to regard them as a potential reservoir of housemaids and cooks. It was a crying shame, they felt, that so many able-bodied women preferred to work for a pittance in a sweatshop, living under dangerous and unsanitary conditions, rather than enter domestic service.[71]

If the Antis were suspect in the eyes of working women, it might have had something to do with the fact that despite their argument that women could improve their working conditions only by organized effort through trade unions, the Antis were noticeably absent from the ranks of the Women's Trade Union League. Since the Antis often were married to men whose interests depended on cheap labor and nonunion shops, this is not surprising. Nevertheless, many of the workers for the league were also active in the suffrage movement.

As has been shown, the Antis were not alone in their opposition to woman suffrage. They found considerable support among numerous men representing diverse interest groups. Since these interests were often powerful and well organized, it was not surprising that the suffragists regarded them as their major foe and chief obstacle to securing a federal amendment. On the other hand, what the suffragists failed to realize, or at least underestimated, was the function served by the Antis. They provided a rallying point for all the enemies of suffrage. The liquor industry, big business, and politicians, all of whom were afraid of woman suffrage, were able to operate more effectively by virtue of the legitimate cover the Antis provided for them. That an alliance was inevitable between the Antis and these three major interests seems likely, given their common economic background and social class. In contrast, the Antis had almost nothing in common with the Catholic church, the foreign born, or the wage-earning woman. As far as the church was concerned, the Antis managed to overcome their general antipathy sufficiently to develop a reasonably effective alliance. They never really reached out to the foreign born and were ineffectual when they tried to appeal to the working woman. Although the Antis realized that they needed their support, they seemed incapable of appealing to their interest sufficiently to arouse any significant support. The history of the working woman took place essentially outside of the suffrage struggle.

SIX

The Antis in Congress
and the Fight
over Ratification:
The States' Rights Issue

Despite the fact that the antisuffrage organization had grown considerably in the decade between 1896 and 1906, the years prior to the outbreak of World War I saw a gathering of suffrage strength. Inspired by accounts of English militants and encouraged by the support of organized labor, the suffragists attempted to seize the initiative once again. In Massachusetts in 1909 they petitioned the legislature for a constitutional amendment, and, though defeated, won the largest prosuffrage vote in the House in over a decade. Furthermore, many crucial segments of the public were now swinging toward the side of the suffragists and showing increasing hostility toward the Antis. In Massachusetts, several important dailies that had formerly supported the Antis changed sides and actively supported the suffragists.[1]

The Federation of Women's Clubs, which had managed to stay uncommitted for so long, finally endorsed woman suffrage. Suffrage political power had begun to make itself felt at the polls as suffragists worked to weed out undesirables when they came up for election.[2] It was probably inevitable, therefore, that the Massachusetts legislature would find it in its own interest to submit the question of woman suffrage to a vote. The Antis, too, recognized that it was only a matter of time before an attempt was made to assay public sentiment on the woman suffrage question. They decided, however, to oppose any type of suffrage referendum as long as possible.[3] The suffragists, with growing resolution, preferred that a constitutional amendment be submitted to the public so that its sentiment could be expressed formally and bindingly at the polls, rather than by a referendum or straw vote, even though the latter would have enabled women to vote on the issue.[4]

In 1914, and again in 1915, a proposed woman suffrage amendment passed both houses of the Massachusetts legislature by the necessary two-thirds, thus completing all steps necessary for it to be placed on the ballot that year.[5] For the suffragists, this reversal of fortune represented their first real victory in twenty years.

Both Antis and suffragists viewed the outcome of the impending election as crucial, so both sides prepared for a vigorous campaign. Throughout the summer, Antis held meetings and rallies, organized a school to drill speakers, and followed men to the ball parks and racetracks dispensing leaflets, fliers, and scorecards bearing the antisuffrage message. The Antis derived their financial support largely from their own members, who represented the "conservative wealth" of the state. Combined donations from three antisuffrage groups (the Women's, the Men's, and the Public Interests League) amounted to $48,910. An additional $12,390 was raised through fairs, dances, and other social functions, for a total of $61,300.[6] The suffragists raised $106,967, of which $40,000 came from personal contributions.

In the fall of 1915, as election day drew closer, the number of antisuffrage meetings and rallies rose considerably. Even street corner gatherings became part of the antisuffrage tactics. At the peak of their activity, the Antis' Boston headquarters employed 50 typists. On election day, all of this activity again returned ample dividends. Despite growing support from press and pulpit for the suffrage side, the latter was defeated 295,939 to 162,492.[7] Furthermore, on the same day, suffrage was also defeated in Pennsylvania and New York, while a month earlier it had been defeated in New Jersey.

Of these four states, however, the Antis could claim the greatest victory in Massachusetts. There the suffragists suffered their worst defeat, with only 35.5 percent of the total vote cast in favor of woman suffrage.[8] The suffragists attributed this to the fact that Massachusetts had been the origin and home of the antisuffrage movement for 30 years, but it must also not be forgotten that it was in Massachusetts that the Antis waged their strongest campaign. Their phenomenal organization and activity had certainly paid off.[9]

This was a momentous victory for the Antis. It enabled them to interpret the election results as a vote of confidence by the Massachusetts public for the antisuffrage position.

At least 90% of the women—either by open opposition, or by a marked indifference to the subject—showed that they did not believe in woman suffrage.

Their victory was due to a deep-seated aversion to woman suffrage. Massachusetts men discovered that nine out of ten women did not want the vote and believed that creation of a large body of stay-at-home voters would result in bad government. "They grew disgusted with the temperament, the notions, and the methods typical of the few women who clamored for the vote."[10]

For the suffragists, defeat meant a change of tactics, and they turned to Congress to concentrate their efforts on winning a federal amendment. But on the basis of these suffrage defeats it was now possible for Congress to postpone indefinitely action on a federal amendment, claiming that the outcome of these recent and decisive state elections was indicative of public opinion.

In 1916, the Massachusetts Antis, their strength in excess of 40,000, optimistic about their gains within the state, and aware that the legislature was unsympathetic to woman suffrage, were free to concentrate on suffrage campaigns outside the state. Nevertheless, despite their recent victories and their renewed efforts, discerning Antis should have been able to see the handwriting on the wall. Time was running out. Almost all of the major Boston newspapers now actively supported woman suffrage. And an even greater threat existed in the continuous development of suffrage support within the churches. Perhaps most significant in Massachusetts was the fact that the Catholics were abandoning the Antis.[11] Outside Massachusetts, woman suffrage was being adopted by Washington, California, Oregon, and Illinois,[12] and then in 1917 New York State adopted woman suffrage.

By the end of 1917 the tide had turned in favor of the suffragists. Even the solid South had been breached that year when the Arkansas legislature granted women the "primary vote." In New York City a margin of more than 100,000 votes carried suffrage.[13] What this meant was that the Antis were in no position to rest on their laurels. If they were going to forestall the suffrage onslaught they would have to meet the suffragists on their own ground. Therefore, as the latter began to focus their attention on Congress, the Antis were forced to establish a second front by massing their forces to prevent Congress from passing a federal amendment.

Antisuffrage activity in Congress was not a new phenomenon. In fact, as early as 1869, in the wake of the disillusionment that rocked suffrage expectations while the Fourteenth and Fifteenth amendments were being considered, a suffrage spokesman, George W. Julian, submitted a joint resolution in Congress proposing a Sixteenth constitutional amendment by which women would be enfranchised.[14] This action elicited the first antisuffrage petition sent to Congress by women. Organized by Madeleine Vinton Dahlgren, widow of Admiral Dahlgren, Mrs. Sherman, wife of General William T. Sherman, and Almira Lincoln Phelps, sister of Emma Willard, their protest allegedly bore the names of 15,000 women.[15] Presented in 1873,[16] it read:

> To the Congress of the United States, protesting against an Extension of Suffrage to Women: We the undersigned, do hereby appeal to your honorable body, and desire respectfully to enter our protest against an extension of Suffrage to Women; and in the firm belief that our petition represents the sober convictions of the majority of women of the country.
>
> Although we shrink from the notoriety of the public eye, yet we are too deeply and painfully impressed by the grave perils which threaten our peace and happiness in these proposed changes in our civil and political rights, longer to remain silent.[17]

In 1878, when the issue of a federal woman suffrage amendment was again brought before Congress, Dahlgren appeared as a representative of the "silent women" of the nation to testify against it.[18] From then until 1900 there was little organized antisuffrage activity in Congress.[19] Then in 1900, on the occasion of Susan B. Anthony's eightieth birthday, the suffragists made a special appeal to Congress to celebrate the event by voting on a federal amendment. At that meeting a small number of Antis appeared and addressed both the Senate Committee on Woman Suffrage and the House Judiciary Committee.[20] From then on, whenever the suffragists appeared before congressional committees, the Antis were sure to send letters supporting their position. When the National Anti Suffrage Association was formed in 1910 and the Massachusetts Antis assumed the leadership, they ensured that each state association direct its protest against a federal amendment to Congress.[21] In 1912 a few women from the District Association Opposed to Woman Suffrage appeared at a hearing and "said a few words of protest."[22]

When in 1913 certain suffragists established the Congressional Union to agitate solely for a federal woman suffrage amendment, and the National Suffrage Association began to pressure Congress to establish a Special House Committee on Woman Suffrage, the Antis again intensified their efforts before

Congress.[23] These included the dissemination of pamphlets to all the legislators and testimony of George before the Senate's Woman Suffrage Committee. Her arguments elaborated on the ideas presented in the pamphlets: the small school committee vote; the 1895 Massachusetts election results; the ignorant and foreign vote; the relationship between woman suffrage and feminism and socialism; and the black woman vote.[24]

The House of Representatives, unlike the Senate, did not have a separate woman suffrage committee. Hearings on woman suffrage took place before the House Judiciary Committee. In 1913, when it was proposed to establish a standing House committee on Woman Suffrage, three members of the MAOFESW headed a large delegation to Washington to oppose its creation, and apparently their efforts met with success since a House Woman Suffrage Committee was not established until December 13, 1917.

By 1917, all of the local Massachusetts antisuffrage branches had organized special committees to influence Congress. Then in 1917 George went to Washington to testify before the Senate. The following year Mrs. Edward Ford of Boston testified before the House, stressing points similar to those of George—the results of the 1915 elections, the connection between suffragism and pacifism, and the sex antagonism stirred up by the suffragists.[25] The efforts of the Antis were more easily coordinated at this time due to the establishment in Washington of the headquarters of the National Anti Suffrage Association.

The Antis did not limit themselves to courting members of Congress. They also realized the necessity of gaining a favorable hearing in the upper echelons of the major parties. And so, in what was basically a defensive posture against suffrage demands for more positive action, the Antis became involved in national politics to the extent of making a stand at party conventions. As early as 1897, the New York and Massachusetts Antis joined forces and sent Mrs. Winslow Crannell of Albany to appear before the Committee on Resolutions of the Republican National Convention in St. Louis. The Antis were elated with the outcome. They reported that as a result of her efforts, "a more general approval of woman's work was substituted for the more special woman suffrage resolution originally offered to the committee." The two associations agreed to have her go to the Democratic Convention in Chicago, where the results proved even more favorable, "no recognition whatever being given to the suffragists."[26]

In 1912, the year that the Progressive Party adopted an equal suffrage plank, George appeared at the Republican National Convention in Chicago

125

and actually prevented the suffragists from getting a hearing before the platform committee.[27]

Despite all these efforts, however, public sentiment was growing in favor of woman suffrage. Working women began increasingly to identify with the aims of the suffragists—an alliance that was formalized by the establishment of the Equality League of Self-Supporting Women, later called the Women's Political Union. Growing public awareness of the role of the liquor interests in working against women suffrage began to arouse many who were formerly indifferent to side with the suffragists in order to resist what was generally regarded as the pernicious influence of the liquor industry. And with the entry of the country into World War I, the public could no longer remain indifferent to the fact that women were shouldering every kind of public responsibility in order to promote the war effort and yet were deprived of political responsibility.

This change in public sentiment was reflected in Congress when on January 10, 1918, the House, with an even two-thirds majority, passed the woman suffrage amendment. But on October 1, the Senate vote fell two short of the number needed to pass.[28] During the fall elections that year two antisuffrage senators—John W. Weeks of Massachusetts and Willard Saulsbury of Delaware, well-entrenched machine leaders of the Republican and Democratic parties, respectively—were defeated, due in part to the efforts of the suffragists.[29] Furthermore, South Dakota, Michigan, and Oklahoma were added to the suffrage ranks, bringing the number of states where women would vote in the next presidential election to 20, and representing a total of 237 electoral votes. The Antis did not remain inactive while these events were taking place, but continued to work to defeat woman suffrage whenever it came up for election within the individual states.

New York was the first major state with a large, active antisuffrage constituency that enfranchised its women. Those who wondered how women who had resisted enfranchisement so vigorously would act once it was foisted on them did not have long to wait. First of all, the newly enfranchised Antis adopted a resolution demanding that the equal suffrage amendment to the state constitution be resubmitted to the electorate. They claimed that the "alien pacifist and Socialist vote in New York City" was responsible for carrying the measure and that women themselves should have a chance to decide their status.[30]

The Antis may have dreamed of reversing the historical process and revoking the grant of suffrage to women, but suffragists in the state did not seem to regard the Antis as a serious threat. Referring to the Antis' potential voting strength, the suffragists could not refrain from adopting a sardonic, yet condescending, tone.

> Think of the benefits accruing to a state when this organized body of intelligent conservative women, having no mean training in the ways and wiles of the body politic, dedicates itself to the duties of citizenship.[31]

Sometime after January 10, 1918, when the House of Representatives passed the federal woman suffrage amendment, New York Antis organized the New York Women Voters' Anti-Suffrage Party to use the voting power of its members to prevent enactment of the federal amendment.[32] Apparently New York Antis did not let their scruples stand in the way of their politics. They must have known that even if they obtained a reversal of the law in New York State, a federal amendment would have contravened all their efforts. Nevertheless, in an attempt to maintain for the states the right to change, the New York Antis continued to work for the possibility of change.

In Congress, the amendment that had failed to pass the Senate in October 1918 was again brought before that body during the lame duck session on February 10, 1919. The amendment lost again, this time by only one vote. The 66th Congress convened on May 20, 1919, after six more state legislatures had given the presidential vote to women (Iowa, Minnesota, Missouri, Ohio, Wisconsin, and Maine). On that day, the House repassed the amendment by 304 to 89, a margin of 42 over the necessary two-thirds majority.[33]

On June 3, the amendment came before the Senate and on June 4, after two days of debate, the Senate voted to accept the woman suffrage amendment. But the battle was not over. The Antis were not about to give up, and as the discerning might have noted, the debates in the Senate during the previous six months had been potent indicators of the struggle to come. In their unremitting efforts within the Senate to obstruct the passing of a woman suffrage amendment, the Antis had been perfecting their latest weapon, an old-fashioned missile in modern dress that they had honed to perfection until it was finally ready to be launched against ratification—the states' rights argument. Even as far back as the September 1918 Senate debates, the Antis were worrying less about preserving their femininity and the home and concentrating more on political issues such as states' rights.[34]

The issue of states' rights may have helped to unite all the opponents of votes for women, but it served to divide the suffragists. Many southern women who favored suffrage became increasingly concerned at the prospect of achieving enfranchisement by means of a *federal* amendment. They feared that a federal amendment would be used to justify federal interference with the states' traditional right to control elections and determine *who* should vote. In short, a federal amendment seemed to pose a threat to states' rights and white supremacy. In Louisiana, Kate M. Gordon, an organizer of the Equal Rights Association Club and the Louisiana Woman Suffrage Association, believed that the race problem made it necessary for southern women to control the suffrage movement in the South. Accordingly, in 1912 she took the initiative in creating a sectional suffrage organization.[35]

There was little agreement, however, on how the suffragists should respond if the states failed to enfranchise their women. Apparently Gordon wanted a *new* suffrage organization that would unite all the state and local organizations and seek enfranchisement exclusively by the state means. She prevailed, and the Southern States Woman Suffrage Conference (SSWSC), was formed. The states' rightist leaders of SSWSC, though they claimed they sought "political equality," hoped to enfranchise all white women and exclude all blacks. Gordon felt that intelligent white women should be able to use the same means to protect themselves from black women as southern white men used to protect themselves from black men. A federal amendment, in her view, would open the door to Negro domination, especially in states such as Mississippi or South Carolina where blacks were in an absolute majority. Furthermore, she warned, white supremacy would be threatened in any area where black voting strength was great enough to hold the balance of power between two or more parties.[36]

For about two years, 1913 and 1914, the states' rights position among southern suffragists was in its heyday. But beginning in 1915, when it became increasingly apparent that state legislatures could not be counted on to enact woman suffrage, there was a steady decline among southern suffragists for this approach. A rift gradually developed between states' rightists and moderates in SSWSC. Gordon, however, did not give up; instead, she put all her hope in securing a Democratic party plank calling for woman suffrage by state action. In 1916 she appeared before the platform committee of the Democratic Convention. As it happened, she was one of four speakers to address the committee concerning woman suffrage. Mrs. Arthur M. Dodge, representing the National Association Opposed to Woman Suffrage, opposed any political action that would recognize woman suffrage as an issue; Gordon, representing the SSWSC, favored a plank calling for woman suffrage by state action; Carrie Chapman Catt led a NAWSA delegation demanding a statement that the Democratic Party favored woman suffrage; and Alice Paul, leader of the National Woman's Party, demanded woman suffrage immediately by federal amendment.[37]

The party plank that was finally adopted represented a victory for Gordon. It stated, "We favor the extension of the franchise to the women of this country, State by State, on the same terms as to men." Unfortunately for Gordon and her adherents, the national party platform was not a mandate for state action by party members, and when in 1918 a woman suffrage amendment to the Louisiana state constitution was submitted to the voters, it was defeated. During that same year SSWSC activities came to an end. Disappearance of the SSWSC, however, did not eliminate the states' rights sentiments of many southern suffragists. Even after the defeat of woman suffrage in her state, Gordon was unwilling to promise not to work against a federal amendment. Then in June 1919, when a federal amendment passed Congress and went to the states for ratification, Gordon and her cohorts joined forces with the Antis and worked to prevent ratification in Louisiana and Mississippi.[38] Apparently their efforts in these states were successful. Nevertheless, all was negated when Tennessee became the thirty-sixth state to ratify the Nineteenth Amendment.

In January 1919, the American Constitutional League, claiming to represent both suffragists and antisuffragists, had submitted a brief to the Senate, opposing a constitutional amendment that would *compel* the states to adopt woman suffrage. Viewing the amendment as arrogating to the federal government the right to prohibit the states from denying to women the right to vote, the brief presented the following arguments: 1) The regulation of the right and duty of voting should be left to each state and should not be controlled by federal constitutional amendment, for such a situation would contravene the existing meaning of the constitution. 2) The question of woman suffrage was of less importance than the right of each state to regulate the suffrage. 3) The question ought not to be submitted during the period of world reconstruction. 4) Woman suffrage should not be given as a reward for public service, but if it were, women's role in wartime would *not* qualify them, for "have they furnished one useful suggestion for the reconstruction era?"[39] 5) And finally, a federal amendment would be final and would prevent the possibility of a change by the people of each state.[40]

The states' rights philosophy of the American Constitutional League appealed to all those who feared that with the enfranchisement of women, the local power structure would be overturned. It was only natural therefore that the South, with its paranoia and fear of blacks, would become an ardent upholder of this position. In fact, according to Carrie Catt, the first antisuffrage organization of importance to be established in the South was formed in Alabama with the slogan "Home Rule, States Rights, and White Supremacy."[41] Also, as indicated above, the league was specifically concerned with demonstrating that black political power would be doubled if the southern woman were enfranchised.[42]

The spectre of the black woman vote was not a new phenomenon. In 1887 the Senate had witnessed a debate on woman suffrage in which various southern senators, reacting against a "wholesale and indiscriminate extension of the electorate," zeroed in especially on the black woman. According to Senator Beck of Kentucky, one mistake had already been made, when the ignorant "colored men of the South" had been enfranchised. It was going to take years not only to dispel their ignorance but also to turn them into intelligent voters. The colored woman, he argued, was even more ignorant, never having had the advantages of communication with the outside world.

No one perhaps in a hundred of them can read or write. . . . Take them from their washtubs and their household work and they are absolutely ignorant of the new duties of voting citizens. . . . Why, sir, a rich corporation or a body of men of wealth could buy them up for fifty cents a piece, and they would vote, without knowing what they were doing, for the side that paid most.[43]

During the battle over ratification, the Antis would continue to exploit southern prejudice by identifying women suffrage with racial equality. In a leaflet entitled "That Deadly Parallel," they quoted the Fifteenth Amendment and the proposed woman suffrage amendment in parallel columns in order to link woman suffrage with Negro suffrage. Another leaflet warned that woman suffrage meant reopening the Negro question, the loss of states' rights, and all the reconstruction horrors with "female carpet-baggers as bad as their male prototypes."[44]

By July 1920, when only one more state was needed for ratification, the National Association of Colored Women's Clubs at a convention in Tuskegee, Alabama, adopted a recommendation that the Antis quickly turned to their advantage. The recommendation proposed that with enfranchisement around the corner, black women should prepare themselves by studying civics, laws of parliamentary usage, and current political questions "both local and national, in order to fit themselves for the exercise of the franchise."[45] The

Antis were to cite this recommendation as evidence of the threat of black women's domination of southern politics.

The most blatantly racist leaflet in the antisuffrage propaganda campaign was entitled "How Many of These Will Your County and State Produce Under Federal Suffrage?" Designed to raise the threat of blacks holding public office, the leaflet showed a photograph of several black women, under which was written "Majorities Win at the Polls" and the following explanation:

> Suffragists of Ward 2, Chicago, advertised for a candidate for alderman. From several applicants, they selected Al Russell, saloon keeper, as the best vote-getter. The hand-picked suffragist candidate for alderman was defeated on April 6, 1915, by a negro candidate, whose workers are shown above.[46]

This leaflet was used whenever a decision was pending, in order to stir up local fears. The implication was obvious: enfranchise women and blacks would soon be running things.

George Robinson Lockwood, an antisuffrage spokesman and a native Southerner, was the author of a pamphlet distributed by the Antis and entitled "Woman Suffrage a Menace to the South—A Protest Against Its Imposition Through Federal Authority." For Lockwood it was a moot point, however, whether woman suffrage were to be imposed by state or federal authority. As far as the South was concerned, he felt it should not be imposed at all, especially in "any State in which there is a considerable negro population." He warned that if woman suffrage was inflicted on the South, "the bars will have been lowered." Recalling the one time when Negro suffrage was imposed on the South (by federal amendment), and "its Anglo-Saxon civilization, nearly wrecked," he exhorted Southerners to be proud not only of their Civil War record, but also to remember that "their greatest glory is the fact that they saved themselves from negroism after the war." This menace, he warned, was only *scotched*, however, and each year was growing in strength.

> . . . through sleepless vigilance only can their revival be prevented, for each year the negroes of the South will be better able to meet the "grandfather" and other tests, and pay the poll taxes through which so many of them are now disenfranchised.

The black man, said Lockwood, realized that he did not suffer merely because he did not vote and "many amongst them who could meet the voter's tests do not attempt to do so." The black woman, however, would be harder to

131

eliminate as a voter, because her right to vote would be a novelty and she would be urged by her preachers (who are more influential with the women than the men) to exercise her rights. Furthermore, black women were better educated than the men (an argument at odds with that of Senator Beck in 1887), and "through the urging of their 'pastors' will put aside the dollar or two for their poll tax, which the men will not pay for the privilege of voting."[47]

Lockwood was not above implying that history might repeat itself if woman suffrage were imposed on the South by a federal amendment and "some of the bitterness of the early post-bellum days" revived.

> I do not intend to intimate that a second effort at secession is possible, or even thinkable; but the brutal or reckless indifference of the people of some of the States to the deep convictions and anxious problems of the people of other States may be a serious obstacle to that thorough union which we all so much desire.

Of all Lockwood's arguments, however, none was more convoluted than his effort to link woman suffrage, black suffrage, and prohibition. He maintained that most of the advocates of woman suffrage in the South were women, many of whom were prohibitionists. But these women seemed unaware that prohibition had grown in the South solely through men who voted in prohibition in order to keep liquor away from blacks. Therefore, it was to be expected that the latter would overthrow prohibition at the first opportunity, an opportunity that would not be long in coming once women (including black women) were enfranchised.[48]

The states' rights issue was not always couched in such blatant white supremacist terms. Many staunch advocates of "home rule" were concerned mainly with the problem of how the constitution ought to have been interpreted.[49] The traditionalists went back for their interpretation to the original ground on which suffrage was left to the individual states, maintaining that to deprive the states of such regulation would endanger important local interests and that the federal government was not competent to decide justly the particular issues concerning suffrage. This, they maintained, was a matter for local governments.[50] The suffragists, in contrast, felt that no constitutional provisions would be violated and argued that votes for women were proper under the Constitution when interpreted in the light of the Declaration of Independence.[51] The most reasoned elaboration of the view that a federal woman suffrage amendment would violate inherent rights reserved to the states was prepared by Henry St. George Tucker, a Virginian who had been a member of Congress and at one time president of the American Bar Association. His *Woman's Suffrage by Constitutional Amendment* was presented originally as five lectures in the Storrs Lecture Course at Yale Law School in 1916 under the title "Local Self-Government."

In the introduction to his book, Tucker, while disavowing the wish to take sides, clearly indicated his biases. Believing that through local self-government the American citizen achieved "the greatest power and greatest opportunity for individual liberty," he regarded the woman suffrage amendment as an attempt to break down the equilibrium between the state and federal governments—an "awful example" of a breach in the proper relationship of governmental powers. Nevertheless, he claimed to be avoiding the question of the "right of women to vote."[52]

Tucker's arguments took shape around five basic propositions. The first was that to deprive the states of the right of determining suffrage was a violation of the United States Constitution. To illustrate this he enumerated various sections of the Constitution that would be affected if a woman suffrage amendment were enacted. Specifically these concerned the provisions that left to each state the way it designated its electors (both for state and national offices), the right of citizens not to be denied the vote on account of race, and the direct election of senators. As Tucker saw it, the only organic change in the Constitution by amendment during the 126 years of its existence was in the postwar amendments (the Thirteenth, Fourteenth, and Fifteenth), and these "were the result of revolution." Only these three took from the states powers originally given to or allowed to remain with them.[53] But, he argued, if the woman suffrage amendment were adopted, women would be allowed to vote not only in state elections for state legislators and other officers, but also for congressional representatives and senators and presidential electors. Therefore, the addition of women as voters altered the basic intent of the Constitution. In short, the United States had no authority to interfere with the discretion of the states in determining what classes of persons possessed the qualifications for electors.

A second pivotal theme in Tucker's analysis was that a federal woman suffrage amendment would destroy the balance of power between the federal and state governments.[54] The proposed amendment was further evidence of a growing trend toward centralization, which would break down the proper relations between the states and the federal government. Other examples of this alarming tendency were the proposed prohibition amendment[55] and the attempts by Congress to control child labor by making it subject to interstate commerce regulation. He described the latter as an example of the "lust for power" by Congress, a bold attempt at "spoilation and robbery of the States," which would ultimately destroy competition.[56]

Tucker's third proposition was that a federal woman suffrage amendment would be subversive of the right of local self-government and of local interests. The right of suffrage was a state privilege that would be interfered with by the other states if woman suffrage were imposed on one quarter of the states by the three-fourths needed to ratify an amendment. Since local conditions varied so greatly, it would be damaging to impose a solution that might work in one area to a different situation elsewhere. Specifically, if the argument were valid that women in the cities needed the ballot in order to improve their conditions as factory workers, this was no reason to impose suffrage on women living in a small village in another state where none of the women was a factory operative. By the same token, it would be unjust to force on states that were plagued with the problem of illiteracy (such as those in the Northeast, with their large immigrant populations, and those in the South, with their large black populations) a policy that they felt would endanger their civilization.[57] The proposed amendment would invade the domain of local self-government and deprive a state that did not ratify the amendment of a right it possessed before its adoption.

A fourth assumption central to Tucker's thesis was that the woman suffrage amendment would deprive the citizen of his liberty. For whenever a power that rightfully belonged to a state was transferred to the federal government, the result was a diminution of the power of the citizen of that state. Tucker measured power in terms of the relation one bore to the total number of voters. The smaller the number of voters, the greater the influence of the individual voter. A man would obviously have less power to influence if he were voting on a national issue where his vote was only one in several million, whereas in his city ward his influence could be as one to several hundred. Although Tucker did not mention it, given his assumptions, he also must have feared that man's power would be doubly diluted if women were added to the electorate. By the same token, man's power in the home, that ultimate bastion of local self-government, would be further reduced by 50 percent if his wife were also enfranchised.

Tucker believed that local self-government was the most perfect principle "for securing the liberty of the citizen." What he meant by liberty, however, was freedom for man in his patriarchal role to occupy a dominant position over as wide an area as possible, while having at his disposal the means to exert the necessary authority. It was recognition of "the trusteeship of man as the defender of the home and the guardian of its sacred precincts."[58] In other words, man's power should be greatest where he had the opportunity to exert the most control. And, since he was undoubtedly master in his home, he should have as much political influence as possible to be able to exercise his authority and responsibility for the home and neighborhood.

> The important relationship of the man to his family, and the duty which he owes them, as well as his relations to the government, as the provider of the school, makes it necessary that he should be armed with the greatest power in making this system respond to the demands which an enlightened and Christian society has a right to expect.[59]

It is ironic that Tucker, in his argument that a federal woman suffrage amendment would weaken local self-government and consequently man's mastery over his domain, used the same argument advanced by the suffragists—namely, that since woman was responsible for the education and moral development of the child, she should also have the power necessary to enable her to fulfill her responsibility.

The fifth, and in some ways most provocative of Tucker's propositions, was that the numerous similarities between the Fifteenth Amendment (granting blacks the vote) and the woman suffrage amendment should warn the public against duplicating the mistakes of the former. One was that the movement for a woman suffrage amendment, as in the case of the Fifteenth, was started prematurely and without the backing of popular approval.[60]

Tucker was not engaging in wishful thinking when he described the opposition obtaining in one-fourth of the states. At the time of his writing, only eleven states had granted the full right of suffrage, while many states had recently defeated it with populations far exceeding those of the suffrage states. The aggregate population of the former was less than 8 million, less than one-twelfth of the population of the United States, whereas that of New York, Pennsylvania, Massachusetts, and New Jersey was 23 million, or nearly one-fourth the total United States population. Tucker recognized that one of the suffragists' main reasons for resorting to a federal amendment was that they could not get satisfaction in certain state legislatures.[61]

All that needs to be done is to look at the history of the Fifteenth Amendment, Tucker pointed out, to see how useless is adoption of an amendment that does not have the sanction of popular approval behind it.

Even though once ratified, an amendment becomes binding on *all* states, its adoption against the protest of one-quarter of the states (which states might constitute a majority of the people of the United States) might lead to results as effective in evading it as those which followed the adoption of the Fifteenth Amendment.[62]

In Tucker's view, the resentment engendered by the passage of the Fifteenth Amendment accounted for the ubiquitous attempts to evade it. Furthermore, evasion of its provisions was justified to save American civilization. Similarly, he felt, many believed that adoption of a woman suffrage amendment "would tend to destroy the home as Americans have known it and have been taught to love and admire it—the foundation of American ideals."[63] If passed by Congress in its present session, warned Tucker, and sent to the states and ratified within the next twelve months, it would create considerable resentment, especially in Pennsylvania, New York, New Jersey, and Massachusetts, which had only recently rejected it.

The Fifteenth Amendment, said Tucker, showed the futility of attempting to enforce a policy believed to be hostile to the best interest of any considerable portion of the country and destructive of their civilization. As a result, the people of many states felt justified in evading the amendment "because by it they were prevented from excluding from the right of suffrage those whose domination, in their ignorant condition, might result not only in the destruction of their property, but of their liberty itself."[64]

Tucker's analogy was for the most part well thought out and supported by data from a variety of sources, including U.S. Census figures, Congressional Reports, interpretations of the Constitution, Supreme Court decisions, and the works of jurists and historians. Nevertheless, his bias was unmistakable, and was nowhere more in evidence than where his analogy revealed his deep-seated fears. He obviously felt that those who had evaded the Fifteenth Amendment had faced such an imminent threat that they were justified in so doing. Apparently he felt that the effects of a woman suffrage amendment would justify similar behavior. What he failed to point out, however, was that the evasions of the Fifteenth Amendment took place primarily in the South, where many whites were disfranchised. Why he assumed that men would be similarly incapable of exercising any effective action if women were enfranchised he did not say.

Similarities between the two amendments besides the fact that they did not have the sanction of popular approval, said Tucker, were that none of the major parties came out for black suffrage or woman suffrage in their platforms, nor did either receive the support of the president. (At the time Tucker was writing this was true for woman suffrage.) He warned that forcing suffrage by means of party legislation, as the Fifteenth Amendment was forced through after the Civil War, would lead to the failure of the party, and possibly even to revolution and the destruction of the institutions of the country.[65]

Nevertheless, despite these overwhelming liabilities, three things, presumably missing in the case of woman suffrage, contributed to the passage of the Fifteenth Amendment—gratitude, apprehension, and politics: gratitude to blacks who fought the battles of the Union; fear that the so-called rebel element in the South would control the blacks; and desire to perpetuate the dominant party in power (to Tucker, this was the most important of the three). Tucker's underlying fear that enactment of a federal woman suffrage amendment would mean the end of the values and way of life that he had known probably blinded him to the fact that similar conditions might in fact also expedite passage of a woman suffrage amendment. There was undoubtedly a considerable feeling of gratitude abounding for the role women were playing in the war effort; there was a rampant fear on the part of many native-born voters that they would be overwhelmed at the polls by sinister foreign elements unless they doubled their voting strength by enfranchising their women; and Woodrow Wilson, constantly reminded by the suffragists, must have been aware that the party that was responsible for taking the nation into war to guarantee democracy abroad had better look to its freedoms at home if it wanted to stay in power.

On June 4, 1919, when the woman suffrage amendment was carried by the Senate, it still had to face ratification by thirty-six states. At once the Antis mobilized to prevent state ratification and called on members and friends to join the Maryland League for State Defense being organized in Baltimore.

As the ratification battle raged, strategists from both sides concentrated their efforts on securing the commitment of the minimum number of states necessary either for or against ratification. The Antis needed thirteen states to hold out against it. The suffragists realized that one of these would have to be secured in order for them to gain the necessary thirty-six. Finally, by the summer of 1920, only one more state was needed for ratification. Suffrage hopes hinged on Connecticut, Vermont, Delaware, and Tennessee. Connecticut and Vermont refused, but prospects for winning in Delaware seemed particularly promising since the state Republican and Democratic committees and the Republican governor were prosuffrage. Furthermore, the national committees of both parties threw their weight behind ratification in

Delaware. With a suffrage victory imminent, the opposition joined forces, and lobbyists representing breweries, railroads, and other business interests descended on the state capital at Dover.[66] The upper house voted to ratify the amendment, but on June 2, the lower house voted to refuse the bill. The suffragists turned toward Tennessee, their final hope, and the antisuffragists massed their forces for their last major stand.

Conflict over the suffrage issue had not surfaced in Tennessee until late in the struggle. It was only in 1912 that the first expressions of antisuffrage sentiment began to be heard. From then until 1916 the most common vehicle in that state for expressing antisuffrage opinions was letters to the editors of local papers, deriding suffragist claims to equality, proclaiming loyalty to traditional values, and predicting dire consequences if suffrage were introduced.[67] Letters in the southern press added a sectional twist by associating woman suffrage with abolition and denouncing it as alien to the South.

> This business does not sound like the Southern women to me, but rather of the frozen North, where everything is equal, where a colored man can call upon the white girls and marry them if they agree. Suffrage never originated in the South. . . . No, we do not want suffrage. Many of our men are not so depraved as some would make us believe. They will make laws to protect us and stand by us until the end.[68]

Cartoons, editorials, and sermons also served to express the inchoate reaction to the threat of suffragism. Yet by 1913, as the woman suffrage movement in Tennessee began to gather momentum, the Antis realized the need for more organized activity. In October two women publicly debated the woman suffrage question in Knoxville. Representing the antisuffrage position was Mrs. Annie Riley Hale who, a few days after the debate, issued a call inviting "all persons, men and women, who are interested in opposing the enfranchisement of women in Tennessee . . . to attend a meeting for the purpose of forming an anti-suffrage society." Subsequently a meeting was held at which Hale stated that she was against woman suffrage because it was opposed to the laws of nature and to "Woman's higher self" and was responsible for the "modern unrest among women."[69]

The meeting was less than successful, however; it took another three years for the Antis to organize. In 1916, Mrs. Arthur M. Dodge of New York, president of the National Association Opposed to Woman Suffrage, came to Tennessee in response to a "recent invitation signed by a number of the leading women of Nashville."[70] While in Nashville she made a long speech against woman suffrage, which incorporated most of the standard antisuffrage arguments: woman's vote would not purify politics, nor could it achieve "what the vote of man fails to accomplish"; woman's work was to train children and to develop high ideals in the younger generation, a duty far more important than influencing legislatures; the best laws regarding women and children were made in male suffrage states; and women have achieved more without the vote.[71] A few days later, at a meeting attended by forty-four women, the Tennessee Chapter of the National Association Opposed to Woman Suffrage was organized with Mrs. John J. Vertrees as its first chairman.[72]

On May 3, 1916, the Tennessee chapter held a second meeting and decided that its program should be discussions of "subjects of vital interest to the cause of antisuffrage" and selected for consideration such topics as "Feminism and Socialism," "Woman's Suffrage, a Menace to Social Reform," "Taxation and Suffrage," "Suffrage, Not a Natural Right," "What Suffrage Means to the Farmer," "Child Labor and Legislation," "The Wage-Earning Woman and the State," and "Woman Will Not Gain by Suffrage."[73]

It was inevitable that the antisuffrage movement in the South would not only become clothed in the rhetoric of the South's position on states' rights but would also manifest much of the racism inherent in the position. At a May 16 meeting the Antis discussed the effect of equal suffrage on the South and on the legal status of married women and concluded that men had been "just and wise in making laws for the benefit of women" and that woman suffrage would be dangerous to the South because of the large number of black women in that area. At this time, the Tennessee antisuffrage association claimed to have more than 200 members.[74] During that year Mrs. Vertrees resigned as chairman and was succeeded by Josephine A. Pearson, who led the Antis until after ratification of the Nineteenth Amendment.

Little more is known of their activities after this time since the Antis ceased reporting their meetings to newspapers.[75] Evidently the Tennessee chapter carried on little organized activity between 1917 and 1919. Nevertheless, the Tennessee Antis maintained their organization and demonstrated their capacity for action in 1919, when they put all their effort into opposing ratification of the Nineteenth Amendment by the General Assembly of Tennessee.

For the suffragists, one of the problems in Tennessee was that the state constitution specified that the legislature was not to act on any federal amendment unless it had been elected *after* the amendment was submitted. As it turned out, the Tennessee legislature had been elected in 1918. Although a U.S. Supreme Court decision on June 1, 1920, had ruled that a similar restriction in Ohio (requiring that a federal amendment be submitted to a referendum before it could be ratified) was unconstitutional because it conflicted with constitutional provisions empowering state legislatures to ratify amendments, there still remained considerable confusion, and many persons opposed ratification in Tennessee because of it. By the time the Tennessee session had been called, a flood of suffrage opponents had arrived in Memphis.[76]

The Tennessee antisuffrage association was reorganized as the Tennessee Division of the Southern Women's League for the Rejection of the Susan B. Anthony Amendment, with Josephine Pearson as president. The Southern Women's League, commonly called the Southern Women's Rejection League, had been organized in Montgomery, Alabama, in December 1919 and soon had divisions in North Carolina, Mississippi, Virginia, Maryland, Georgia, Florida, Texas, and South Carolina. It strongly opposed the federal amendment and maintained that if women were to be enfranchised, it should be through state legislation.[77] The Tennessee Division of the Southern Women's Rejection League led the fight against ratification.[78]

The Tennessee legislature convened August 9, and the next day resolutions to ratify were introduced in both houses. The Antis were active. Judge Joseph C. Higgins, president of the Tennessee Constitutional League, told the press that if the legislature ratified, the league "would be constrained to go into the courts and inhibit the Secretary of State from certifying."[79] On August 12, the Senate and House committees on constitutional amendments held a joint hearing. Both suffragists and Antis spoke. Charlotte Rowe of New York, a lawyer and an active Anti, explained the attitude of the Antis.

> We feel that if you men are good enough to work for us, die for us, live for us, you are good enough to vote for us . . . to give woman the ballot is only to break up the home and the beginning of socialism.[80]

On August 13, the Senate by a vote of 25 to 4 adopted a resolution to ratify after a vigorous debate in which the opposition was led by senators H. M. Candler and J. D. Summers. Summers was opposed because he did not want to force woman suffrage on states that did not want it. Candler was in the Senate "representing the mothers who are at home rocking the cradle and not representing the low neck and high skirt variety." He predicted that if the amendment was ratified, "Tennessee would have negroes down here to represent her in the Legislature." The legislators, he said, were allowing themselves to be dictated to "by an old woman . . . whose name is Catt."

> Mrs. Catt is nothing more than an anarchist. I heard her say in an address before an audience in New York that she would be glad to see the day come when negro men could marry white women without being socially ostracized. This is the kind of woman that is trying to dictate to us. They would drag the womanhood of Tennessee down to the level of the negro woman.[81]

On August 18, the House debated the issue, following a committee report urging ratification. On the same day Tennessee Antis published "An Appeal to the Citizens of Nashville," urging citizens to become involved in "the most important issue that has confronted the South since the Civil War by wearing either red roses or ribbons. . . . In the name of millions of Southern women, we appeal to the unquestioned chivalry of the South."[82] Despite continuous pressure on members of the legislature, the house adopted the ratification resolution by a majority of 50 to 46.[83] On the next day, the *Nashville Tennessean*, a prosuffrage daily, commented:

> The people do not yet realize the many kinds of opposition that suddenly developed after the action of the senate. Probably the most formidable lobby that ever gathered at Nashville was assembled to defeat this measure, and every weapon in the arsenal of the skilled and unscrupulous lobbyist was fully employed in the fight.[84]

The article went on to warn the winners to stay on their guard, for given the desperate character of the opposition, it would probably use any advantage that became available.

The Antis were not through. At a mass meeting held in Nashville on August 19 "to Save the South from the Susan B. Anthony Amendment," the same old arguments were expressed and resolutions adopted demanding rejection of the woman suffrage amendment. In the House, Speaker Seth Walker, an antisuffragist fearing that the majority was still in favor of woman suffrage, delayed bringing up the reconsideration motion. But on August 21, R. K. Riddick tried to force the issue in order to dispose of the motion and complete Tennessee's ratification. The opponents had foreseen this and, believing they lacked sufficient votes to reverse the House's action of August 18, many left Tennessee late at night on August 20 and went to Decatur, Alabama, to prevent a quorum. According to the *Tennessean*, this "red rose brigade" included 34 refugee legislators.[85] And so, as predicted, when Riddick moved that the House take up reconsideration of the ratification resolution, Walker ruled it out of order because there was no quorum. Furthermore, he reported that an injunction had been obtained that morning from Judge E. F. Langford at the Chancery Court at Nashville, restraining the governor, the secretary of state, and the speaker from signing the declaration that would have formalized Tennessee's ratification. The House voted on Walker's ruling, and by 49 to 8 refused to sustain him. Then by a vote of 49 to 0 the house voted *not* to reconsider. The ratification resolution went to the governor, who had the injunction dissolved and mailed the certificate of ratification to the secretary of state. On August 26, United States Secretary of State Bainbridge Colby signed the proclamation certifying final adoption of the Nineteenth Amendment.

The Antis still did not consider themselves defeated. In Nashville, their headquarters issued this statement:

> The fact that Secretary of State Colby this morning issued a proclamation that the Woman Suffrage Amendment had been adopted by the necessary thirty-six states will not cause any cessation of the fight in this state both in the courts and in the legislature against the validity of Tennessee's alleged ratification.[86]

The Antis held several mass meetings to condemn ratification and then on August 31 made a last stand in the Tennessee House of Representatives. Due to the absence of some of the suffrage supporters, the Antis had a majority and the house adopted a motion to expunge from the House journal the action taken on August 21 relative to reconsideration of the ratification. The House then voted 47 to 24 *not* to concur and requested the governor to report this to the United States secretary of state. The attempt was futile since Colby followed the established policy that ratification of an amendment may not be rescinded, and ignored the matter.[87] Furthermore, Connecticut and Vermont, which earlier had refused to ratify, ratified immediately after Tennessee, making a total of thirty-eight states.

In Massachusetts, after efforts to use the initiative and referendum to repeal ratification had failed in July, the MAOFESW had been forced to close its offices. So in that state the last hope of the Antis was that the United States Supreme Court would declare the amendment unconstitutional. The last issue of the *Remonstrance*, published in the fall, expressed the hope that the amendment could be beaten through the courts. Others still looked for legal redress and hoped women would register and vote a conservative ticket. In 1921, the Massachusetts Antis opposed a petition from the New England League of Women Voters that women be given equal rights with men to hold office, but their opposition was ineffective. In 1922, antisuffrage hopes were crushed finally when on February 27, the Supreme Court in *Leser v. Garnett* ruled that the Nineteenth Amendment was the law of the land.[88]

SEVEN

Ida Tarbell:
The Making of an Anti

Not all Antis were as vitriolic in their denunciations of suffrage as many of the women cited in preceding chapters. Some women, with just as much faith that their sex and the world would be better off without suffrage, concentrated their efforts on trying to demonstrate this instead of attempting to discredit the suffragists.

The most reasoned exponent of this position was Ida Tarbell. In many ways Tarbell was not typical of the women who made a name for themselves as organizers and leaders of the antisuffrage movement. She was from a frontier family rather than a moneyed urban background. She seemed to take much less for granted concerning her future prospects and life-style than did the Antis who grew up in the lap of luxury and looked forward to a fulfillment of their personal lives in marriage and motherhood. Her career and accomplishments resulted from her own initiative and ambition. By "making it" in a man's world, she achieved all the freedom and worldly success that the most ardent feminist could desire. In contrast to most Antis who had careers, Tarbell did not use her personal life as an illustration of the terrible cost involved when a woman forsook marriage and motherhood for a career. She was in this sense less consistent than the career Anti who posed herself as an exception. If anything, Tarbell seemed oblivious to the fact that her own life-style was incompatible with her views of womanhood. The Antis, however, extolled her for what she said, not for what she did, and to the extent that they shared the same views on woman's place in the world, Tarbell allowed herself to become a spokeswoman for the antisuffrage cause.

Tarbell presents an anomaly. Yet in neither her autobiography nor her other reflective works did she intimate that there was any inconsistency between her life and her beliefs. She did, however, leave a number of clues as to how she arrived at her position and consequently became an antisuffragist.

Ida Minerva Tarbell, the eldest of three surviving children, was born on a farm in Erie County, Pennsylvania, on November 5, 1857. Her mother, Esther Ann (McCullough) Tarbell, had been a schoolteacher before her marriage. Her father, Franklin Sumner Tarbell, had put himself through the Jamestown (N.Y.) Academy by working as a flatboat captain and a carpenter. During the year that Ida was born he went to Iowa, hoping to buy a farm, but his plans were upset by the financial panic of 1857 and he was forced to "teach his way back" to his farm. In 1859, oil was discovered in Titusville, and her father, using his knowledge of carpentry, became the first manufacturer of wooden tanks for oil. Eventually the family moved to Titusville, and it was there that Ida spent the greater part of her youth.

Though they always managed to live in relative comfort, her father's dependence for a livelihood on the new and unpredictable oil industry and his rugged individualism tended to imbue the household with a pioneering spirit. Another contributing factor was the willingness of both parents to suspend the realization of present comfort of the sake of their family's future security.

In her autobiography, *All in a Day's Work*, Tarbell's description of her parents indicates that their roles were clearly defined, at least in her mind. Although she apparently had great respect for both, she alluded more frequently to her mother. Writing about her mother after she herself was eighty years old, she still maintained profound respect for her endurance, in the face not only of unusual circumstances but especially in surviving on a routine day-to-day basis. She admired her mother's acceptance of her nursing tasks "as her part," a role she was continually being called upon to fill; and she remembered her "wisdom in dealing with hard situations." From her maternal grandmother she learned as gospel that "a married woman's place is at home," a place her mother unquestioningly occupied.[1]

It was in adolescence that she discovered evolution and its implications for Christian revelation. The study of geology made her realize the vastness of the universe and that the world was not made in six days. It was after reading an article by Herbert Spencer in 1872 that she rejected the notion of personal immortality, but she decided to postpone rejecting Christianity until she could find a better substitute. "It cost me curious little compromises, compromises that I had to argue myself into." To this period she attributed the birth of doubt and uncertainty, the knowledge that "nothing was ever again to be final," that she would always have to ask, "How can I accept without knowing more?" Gradually, however, evolution began to replace religion, and with the gift of a microscope she experienced her first and greatest intellectual passion.[2]

Despite the distance of many years, Tarbell recalled her parents' desire to give her advantages, but her determination to go to college she owed chiefly "to the active crusade going on in those days for what we called woman's rights." "Ours was a yeasty time," she wrote, speaking about her youth in the 1870s. Every tradition and philosophy was attacked and remodeled. Her father was hard hit by the attack on his conception of individualism in a democracy, as the Standard Oil monopoly began to spread over the surrounding country and most independent oilmen were either absorbed or went down in the struggle to resist. Her father survived, independently, though never happily. As a result of the Standard Oil conspiracy fight, she learned to hate privilege and was "ready for a future platform of social and economic justice if I should ever awake to my need of one."[3]

Her mother too was caught up in the changing times, "facing a little reluctantly a readjustment of her status in the home and in society." She thought of her mother as a potential "Woman's Righter."

> Had she never married, I feel sure she would have sought to "vindicate her sex" by seeking a higher education, possibly a profession. The fight would have delighted her.

Tarbell recalled crusaders for women's rights being welcomed at her home.

> I remember best Mary Livermore and Frances Willard—not that either touched me, saw me; of this neglect I was acutely conscious. . . . Men were nicer than women to me, I mentally noted.

She noted also that she had been aware of the differences that had split the woman suffrage movement into the American Woman Suffrage Association and the National Woman Suffrage Association in 1869 and of the sordidness and notoriety associated with the Beecher-Tilton scandal.

> The reverberations of the conflict inside the suffrage party, together with what I picked up about the Beecher trial (I read the testimony word by word in our newspapers), did not increase my regard for my sex.[4]

As far as the claims of the woman's movement were concerned, she felt that women did not have an exclusive monopoly on subjection, for there were not only "down-trodden women" but also "henpecked men." The chief unfairness, as far as women were concerned, was that "women who must do the spending were obliged to ask for money or depend on charging."[5]

The result of this awareness was that she believed there were two "rights" worth going after—"the right to an education, and the right to earn my living—education and *economic independence.*" Believing that the only way for her to achieve the latter was by teaching, she decided she would go to college and become a biologist. When she was ready to enter in 1876, she chose nearby Allegheny College, which appealed to her pioneering spirit by claiming to provide an opportunity for a serious young woman "interested in the advancement of her sex." She carried with her a sense of "purpose," an outline for the future, which consciously omitted marriage as a possible choice.

> I would never marry. It would interfere with my plan; it would fetter my freedom. I didn't quite know what Freedom meant; certainly I was far from realizing that it exists only in the spirit, never in human relations, never in human activities—that the road to it is as often as not what men call bondage. But above all I must be free; and to be free I must be a spinster. When I was fourteen I was praying God on my knees to keep me from marriage. I suspect that it was only an echo of the strident feminine cry filling the air at that moment, the cry that woman was a slave in a man-made world.[6]

Tarbell's decision to remain single was not as simple as indicated here. On the contrary, she seemed to have conflicting views on the subject. In *The Business of Being a Woman* she started out by depicting "false mating" as the "greatest obstacle to woman carrying her business of life to a satisfactory completion." She felt that women suffered from this. Later on in the book, however, in analyzing what she regarded as a growing penchant for celibacy, she implied that the only way to fulfill oneself as an individual was to remain single:

> Four hundred years ago a woman sought celibacy as an escape from sin; service and righteousness were her aim. To-day she adopts it to escape inferiority and servitude; superiority and freedom her aim.[7]

Tarbell's ambivalence may have reflected a deep-seated grudge against the women's rights movement for instilling in young women the idea that man and marriage were a trap.[8] She said that those who had opted for marriage instead of a career or "life work" after college were treated as apostates to the cause. Since she started out by believing in the cause, it is possible that in later years she felt that by having accepted the feminist message, she had forfeited her own chances of marital happiness.[9]

So far, Ida Tarbell emerges as a woman whose views on three basic issues differed sharply from most Antis, namely, the value she placed on *economic independence* (an idea repugnant to most Antis, according to their rhetoric), the value she placed on her *freedom*, and her decision to remain *single* in order to achieve the first two.

Allegheny College had begun to admit women in 1870 and in the six years before Tarbell arrived had graduated ten women. The year she began, two seniors and two juniors were the only other female students on campus. Tarbell was the only woman in a freshman class of "forty hostile or indifferent boys." During her four years there, an increasing number of women entered Allegheny. And, while at first Tarbell felt like an intruder in a male preserve, gradually the taboos yielded. "They swept masculine prohibitions out of the way—took possession, made a different kind of institution of it, less scholastic, gayer, easier going."[10] It is difficult to tell whether Tarbell approved of this "feminization" of her school. She does not give the impression of having been a gay, easygoing, nonscholastic type and probably found it difficult to sanction the changes wrought by women students. Though she managed to leave college thinking that possibly some day she *might* marry, she remained sufficiently obsessed by the threat of entangling alliances to resent the whole notion of "pinning," a custom that was then in vogue.

Her first job after graduation for $500 a year and "board yourself" was as preceptress of the Poland (Ohio) Union Seminary. In Poland life was made tolerable by her friendship with Clara Walker, the daughter of a local banker. Tarbell admired sensible clothes for women and apparently also admired Clara for having revolted against lacing, high heels, and long skirts and for having "substituted for them an admirable uniform of independence." Tarbell approved of Amelia Bloomer's influence on woman's dress and was impatient of woman's acquiescence to fashion in place of common sense.

We owe it to Amelia Bloomer that we can without public ridicule wear short skirts and stout boots, be as sensible as our feminine natures permit—which is not saying much for us when it comes to fashions.[11]

It was in surrounding Mahoning County that she first glimpsed the devastating process of a farm country giving way to industry. She lamented the

. . . destruction of beauty, the breaking down of standards of conduct, the growth of the love of money for money's sake, the grist of social problems

149

facing the countryside from the inflow of foreigners and the instability of work.
. . . I gathered a few impressions which I realize now helped shape my future
interest and thinking.

And it was during her stay in Poland that another realization took place, one
that was to influence profoundly both her intellectual career and her
perspective on the woman question.

And it was on one of these chance drives that I first saw what women can do
in moments of frenzied protest against situations which they cannot control, *first
had my faith challenged in the universally peaceful nature of my sex*. I learned the
meaning of Maenads, Furies, as we came upon a maddened, threatening crowd
rushing towards the offices of the mills which had been shut down without
warning. It was led by big robust shrieking women, their hair flying, their
clothes disheveled. It was a look into a world of which I knew nothing.[12]

After two years of Poland, Tarbell was ready to reconsider whether she
really wanted to continue with teaching as a career. As for her first love,
biology, laboratories that employed women were unknown in 1882. And with
the country entering a new depression and the oil business "in a serious state,"
she could not ask her family to finance her graduate studies.

But my home was wide open. I think it was this fact that is at the bottom of my
strong convictions that the home is an essential link in the security of men and
women. After one has gone forth on his own there frequently comes a time
when he is shelterless so far as his own resources go. To have a refuge of which
he is sure is one of the most heartening and stabilizing experiences in a life.[13]

Home was also where she was living when she began her career as a
journalist on the staff of the *Chautauquan*, a monthly magazine that served as
a teaching supplement for the Chautauqua movement's home study courses.
And although she appreciated knowing that her home always existed for her,
home was not where she stayed. In 1891, after eight years on the
Chautauquan, she decided to go to Paris. Desiring above all else to write a
novel, she planned to obtain just enough work to support herself while she
devoted most of her time and energy to her book.

I did not consider the possibility of getting a regular job; I did not want one.
I wanted freedom, and I had an idea that there was no freedom in belonging to
things, no freedom in security. It took time to convince myself that I dared go
on my own. But finally I succeeded.

Her friends, however, were not as easily convinced. They told her, "remember you are past thirty. Women don't make new places for themselves after thirty!"[14]

It was not as if she had supreme confidence in herself as a writer. Her only published writing at that time consisted of articles written for the *Chautauquan*, which amplified and commented upon the material in the assigned textbooks. In fact, when she told the editor of her magazine that she was going, he asked her how she planned to support herself. She told him by writing. "You're not a writer. You'll starve," he said.

> He had touched the weakest point in my venture: I was not a writer, and I knew it. I knew I never should be one in the high sense which I then and still more now give to that word. I had neither the endowment nor the passion nor the ambition to be a writer. I was rather a student, wanted to understand things quite regardless of how I could use that understanding if I reached it. There was much selfishness in my wanting to know for the sake of knowing, much of a dead scholar in me; and that dead scholar has always hung, more or less a weight about my neck.[15]

And so, despite the skepticism of her friends, the prophecy of her editor, and her own existential misgivings about her ability, she left for Paris and a career of "self-directed, freelance journalism." Even if she were not a writer, she believed she had the necessary qualifications for journalism.

> I did have a certain sense of what mattered in a subject and a strong conviction that it was my sense of what mattered, and not somebody else's that would give my work freshness and strength if it was to have any.[16]

Tarbell's realism about herself as a writer was probably kindled shortly before her decision to go to Paris. She had been working on a novel on the surrender of the independents to Standard Oil, a story she was to write later as *The History of the Standard Oil Company*. She abandoned the novel, she said, for the sake of "a more fundamental research." Her new plan was to write a science of society. This too never got beyond a few chapters, but the nature of the assignment confronted her with a new intellectual problem, which was to remain one of her basic concerns until the end of her life—what was woman's true role in society?

> . . . I had concluded I could not construct society as it was until I knew more about woman. I suspected she had played a larger part in shaping society than

151

she realized or perhaps was willing to admit. I was questioning the argument that this is entirely a man-made world. I had found too many woman-made parts in it to accept the characterization at its face value. My science of society would not be honest, I concluded if the only part a woman was allowed to play in it was that of doormat, toy, and tool. I was troubled, too, by the argument that woman must be given suffrage if society was to be improved. Man had made a mess of the world, I was told; woman must take his tools and straighten things up. I did not feel the confidence of my courageous friends. "Why should we expect them to do better with the vote than men have done?" I asked. "Because they are women," I was told. But they were human beings, like men, and they were human beings with no experience of the tools they wanted to use; and I had enough sense of the past to believe that experience counted, and that it would be wise for all men and women to consult it when they tried new ventures.

There had been women in public life in the past. What had they done? I had to satisfy myself before I went further with my science of society or joined the suffragists. It was humiliating not to be able to make up my mind quickly about the matter, as most of the women I knew did. What was the matter with me, I asked myself, that I could not be quickly sure? Why must I persist in the slow, tiresome practice of knowing more about things before I had an opinion? Suppose everybody did that. What chance for intuition, vision, emotion, action?[17]

This passage contains the key to Tarbell's position on several basic issues related to the woman question. It reflects her belief that women deserved more credit than they received for their contribution to civilization. But it also indicates a certain ambivalence. She felt woman was more than just a "doormat, toy, and tool," but she was nevertheless not quite sure that women had anything special to offer. In fact, with men's tools, namely, the ballot, they would be unequal to men for they lacked the experience of voting. Where she supposed men gained theirs, she did not say. Yet she assumed that women would ignore all experience when they went about utilizing their vote. It seems as though she was not too sure that most women exercised good enough judgment, at least in matters outside their usual sphere. Furthermore, there is something disingenuous in her protestations concerning her inability to make up her mind quickly. In fact, she seemed to value the slow, deliberate, rational, and unemotional approach to controversial questions more than a hasty, spontaneous, irrational, and emotional response. She was asking not what was the matter with herself but with most women that they reacted to the question of suffrage this way. She was implying that she was glad she was not typical, that she was an exception to ordinary women.[18]

The earliest product of this newly awakened interest consisted of a series of short studies on the women of the French Revolution, which she submitted to the editor of *The Chautauquan*. Published were those on Madame de Staël, Marie Antoinette, and Madame Roland. Of the three, Tarbell was particularly fascinated with Roland and she made up her mind to learn more. "She probably would teach me what sort of contribution might be expected from a woman in public life."[19] This fascination with Madame Roland also influenced her decision to go to Paris.

Tarbell's first published book was a biography of Madame Roland, and it was while working on the book that she developed the rationale for her position on the role of women in public life.

> I had undertaken the study of this woman in order to clear up my mind about the quality of service that women could give and had given in public life, particularly in times of stress. I had hoped to come out with some definite conclusions, to be able to say: "The woman at this point will be a steady, intuitive, dependable force. She will never lend herself to purely emotional or political approaches to great social problems; she knows too much of human beings. Her business has always been handling human beings. Building families has been her job in society. You can depend upon her to tell you whom to trust, whom to follow, whom to discard. These intuitions of hers about people are born of centuries of intimate first-hand dealing with human beings from babyhood on—they are among the world's greatest values. And she will be no party to violence. . . . She has been the world's greatest sufferer from these things, and she has suffered them in order that she might protect *that thing which is her business in the world, the bearing and the rearing of children*. She has a great inarticulate wisdom born of her experience in the world. That is the thing women will give.[20]

It appears as if she wanted to believe that women, by virtue of their nurturing role, possessed certain inherent eminent characteristics that would make a significant difference in public life. But given her choice of subject, as well as her method of approach, she was destined to be disappointed.

> I had found . . . new proof of that eternal and necessary natural law that the woman backs up her man. Madame Roland had been Royalist, Republican, Revolutionist, according to the man she loved. She had served her man with unyielding conviction, would not temper or cooperate, intolerant, inflexible.[21]

Responding, it seems, to the suffragist claim that women, if enfranchised, would inject a lofty nonpartisan element into public life, Tarbell wondered, "what woman in America seeking the vote as a sure cure for injustice and corruption would listen to such a message?" The implications of that message were unmistakable: a woman is subordinate to her man; she has no convictions of her own, deriving them instead from the man she loves; and she gives herself wholly and unquestioningly to her lover (if she is a *real* woman). No, a suffragist with any degree of feminist leanings would have found it difficult if not impossible to listen to this message.

There was still another lesson that Tarbell learned from this situation, and eventually elevated into a principle, that sex complicated politics. "Sex does complicate all the relations of life, politics included, in proportion to the intimacy allowed." In other words, woman was constituted in such a way that when an important public crisis arose, she would go with her man. Tarbell recognized, of course, that there would be exceptions, such as the "so called 'sexless' woman who will follow only their own 'views'. . . but they are a negligible quantity, and precious few of them are to be as fully trusted as they themselves suppose!"[22]

Tarbell's sad conclusion was that Roland, instead of opposing violence, had been eager to use revolutionary force to accomplish her ends. She was nothing more than a "revolutionary tool and victim." Thus Tarbell ended up by losing faith not only in woman's capability to play a constructive role in public life, but also in the revolutionary process as well. For her, revolution left behind the same proportion of good and evil it started with.[23]

But what Tarbell failed to realize was that Roland, like any other exceptional person in history, was not an ordinary representative of her sex. She was as much lover, activist, and visionary as she was woman. The characteristic of sex in this instance was secondary to other more salient aspects of her personality. Perhaps if Tarbell had ever wondered what historians might try to make of her own life, she would have realized that one could hardly generalize about the turn-of-the-century woman by resurrecting Ida Tarbell.

In Paris, Tarbell made the acquaintance of Madame Marillier, great-granddaughter of Roland, and was invited to visit Le Clos, her ancestral home where Roland had lived before becoming a public figure.

> I knew from her letters before me she [Roland] could and did fill the role of a local Providence. She filled her time as I saw my friend Madame Marillier filling hers, busy from morning until night with the affairs of the estate, visiting the people, prescribing remedies for man and beast, vegetables and vines, arranging a marriage for this pair, making an invalid more comfortable, taking care of some peasant's wayward son, climbing up the steep hillside to early mass to set a good

example, discharging naturally and intelligently that responsibility to the family, the estate, the dependent countryside, which the Frenchwoman seems to accept as her contribution to the state. It makes her something steady, wise, superior, a strong factor in the economic, social, and religious stability of France.[24]

Tarbell was so taken by this vision of what life must have been like for Madame Roland at Le Clos that she assumed that the years spent there were her "happiest and most useful days." Yet this idyllic vision of endless toil on a country estate as woman's finest hour reflected a profound and unconscious nostalgia. It also contained a distortion, for Madame Marillier was anything but a provincial shepherdess tending her flock in bucolic serenity. Other than the two weeks each year spent at Le Clos, she lived in Paris, where she presided over a salon of brilliant men, and into whose circle Tarbell considered herself privileged to be admitted.

In 1894, after having successfully managed to survive for three years in France, Ida Tarbell packed up her manuscript on Roland to take home to edit. Unsettled and dissatisfied because she had not yet found the answer, she began to wonder if she would ever settle the question about woman in society—"the point or position where she can best serve it."[25] Apparently by the time *The Business of Being a Woman* was published in 1912 she had found the answer.

Between 1894 and the outbreak of World War I Tarbell forged a successful career for herself as a journalist. In Paris she had met expenses by writing articles for *Scribner's*. Her work came to the attention of S. S. McClure, who published her articles on Pasteur, Zola, Daudet, and Dumas in his new magazine. She worked for *McClure's Magazine* until 1906, when she withdrew from the staff along with Lincoln Steffens, Ray Stannard Baker, and John S. Phillips, and, together with Finley Peter Dunne and William Allan White, purchased *The American Magazine*. During this period she published *Madame Roland* (1896), *Napoleon: with a Sketch of Josephine* (1895), *Life of Abraham Lincoln* (1897), *The History of the Standard Oil Company* (1903), *He Knew Lincoln* (1907), *Father Abraham* (1909), *The Business of Being a Woman* (1912), *The Ways of Woman* (1915), and numerous articles.

Despite her successes in what was ostensibly a man-made world, Tarbell's view of women remained consistent throughout her career. In 1916, on the basis of her systematic study of the tariff system, President Wilson asked her to become a member of his Tariff Commission. She refused because of personal obligations, *unfitness*, *lack of experience*, and a sense of hopelessness about the service the commission might render. She felt it would not stand a chance in Congress "when a wool or iron and steel or sugar lobby appeared. A Tariff Commission was hamstrung from the start." But in addition to these pragmatic reasons, she reiterated her views on women and public life. She said that Wilson offered her the position not just for her work on the tariff but because

> he was looking about for women to whom he could give recognition. He was an outspoken advocate of suffrage and wanted to use women when he thought them qualified.

Evidently Jane Addams pleaded with her to accept "for the sake of women," but Tarbell remained firm.

> I did not feel that women were served merely by an appointment to office. . . . The cause of women is not to be advanced by putting them into positions for which they are untrained.

It is surprising that Tarbell considered herself "untrained." But did she really? In her autobiography she included an excerpt of a letter from Wilson when he learned of her refusal, which she allowed "I am not too modest to print."

> As a matter of fact, she has written more good sense, good plain common sense, about the tariff than any man I know of, and is a student of industrial conditions in this country of the most serious and sensible sort.[26]

It is ironic that there was probably no greater praise he could have given her than to underscore how her sensibleness on the subject of the tariff exceeded that of any man.

In early April 1917, after the United States had entered World War I, Tarbell was appointed a member of the Woman's Committee of the Council of National Defense. The head of the committee was Dr. Anna Howard Shaw. According to Tarbell, the administration called the Woman's Committee into existence to have an "official group to which it could refer the zealous and importuning women who wanted to 'help' the various organizations already mobilizing women for action." In addition, considerable rivalry had developed among these groups and it was hoped the committee would galvanize their energies into a constructive war effort. On the committee were the presidents of leading women's groups: National Suffrage Association, Women's Federation of Clubs, National Women's Council, the Colonial Dames, the

National League for Women's Service. Everybody on the committee represented an organization or publication except, according to Tarbell, herself. Heading the Council of National Defense was Walter Gifford (eventually president of American Telephone and Telegraph Corporation). According to Tarbell, it bothered Shaw "that we had to go to men for orders."

> She felt we ought to be able to decide for ourselves what women should do, or at least she, the head of the committee, should sit on the Council of National Defense. I think Dr. Anna never quite forgave the Administration for subjecting us to the directions of man, whose exclusive authority in world affairs she had so long disputed.[27]

It is unfortunate that Tarbell did not express her own feelings on this subject. Was she, who prided herself on her manlike competence, perfectly willing to sit back and leave "world affairs" to the menfolk? Or did the fact that she set so much store on compliments that likened her to a man indicate that she actually valued male qualities more and yet doubted whether she was, in fact, man's equal in certain things?

Despite the fact that her relationship with Shaw was anything but smooth during that period, Tarbell tried to be fair in giving credit. She attributed the organizational strength of the committee to both Shaw and Carrie Chapman Catt, who "were the most experienced and successful organizers of women in the country." Tarbell had hoped that the Woman's Committee would turn into a permanent federal agency in the Department of the Interior. She envisioned it under a woman assistant secretary and to be used as a kind of extension service to inform women in remote areas what the departments of government were doing to improve their lives. Apparently, Secretary of Interior Franklin Lane was interested in the idea, but the Woman's Committee was not.

> Dr. Anna pooh-poohed it. It was too limited a recognition. What she wanted was a representative in the Cabinet, and she was unwilling to take anything else.
> It is possible that Dr. Anna did not want to encourage ideas concerning women from a woman as lukewarm as I had always been in the matter of suffrage. She wanted a committee as actively interested in pushing ahead the cause of votes for women as it was in defense work, in protecting women and children. From her point of view the cause was as vital as protecting women in the industries, indeed essential to that problem.[28]

Tarbell tried to understand Shaw's feelings toward her and apparently continued to have great respect for her despite their obvious differences.

> Dr. Anna's attitude toward me was quite understandable. She was familiar with and resented, as she told me quite frankly, certain activities of mine which had conflicted with both her convictions and her arguments—activities which had been a surprise and a regret to many of those whose opinions I valued highly.[29]

These differences, from Tarbell's perspective, involved first their divergent conceptions of what women had done in the world. Tarbell resented the attempts of "militant suffragists" to belittle the work that woman had done and to picture her as a meek and prostrate "doormat."[30] In fact, her decision to do a series in *The American Magazine* on leading American women from the Revolution to the Civil War probably owed a great deal to this attitude.

In addition to the fact that she was "lukewarm" on the suffrage question and diametrically opposed to the suffragists on the subject of woman's contribution to civilization, Tarbell felt there was a third reason she was persona non grata to her suffragist colleagues—her book, *The Business of Being a Woman*.

> That title was like a red rag to many of my militant friends. The idea that woman had a business assigned by nature and society which was of more importance than public life disturbed them; even if it was so, they did not want it emphasized.[31]

Even more important, however, was what in her view distinguished her from the suffragists.

> Feeling as I did, I could not fight for suffrage *although I did not fight against it.* Moreover, I believed that it would come because in the minds of most people democracy is a piece of machinery, its motive power the ballot. The majority of the advocates for women's suffrage saw regeneration, a new world through laws and systems; but I saw democracy as a spiritual faith. I did not deny that it must be interpreted in laws and systems, but their work deepens, broadens, only as the spirit grows.[32]

Concluding her autobiography, which she wrote at the age of eighty while still at work, Tarbell was obviously proud of a life well lived. She was not troubled by an awareness of any lack of consistency in her viewpoint. Somehow she managed to effect a reconciliation between her views on woman and her perception of her own life. She recounted that Madame Curie, when asked what a woman's contribution to a better world should be, replied,

> . . . that it began at home, then spread to those immediately connected, her immediate friends, then the community in which she lived; and if the work proved to meet a need of the world at large it spread there. But the important thing was the beginning, and that beginning, Madame Curie insisted, was in the home, the center of small things. Work backed by such a faith makes life endurable. I doubt if I could have come into my eighties with anything like the confidence I feel in the ultimate victory of freedom, the ultimate victory of man's self-respect, if I had not groped my way through work into some such faith.

All was part of a consistent whole. She had taken on self-support at the start so that she might be free "to find answers to questions which puzzled me." And although she never stopped searching for the answers, she assumed in the end that the basic question of what was the most fruitful life for woman remained unanswered.[33]

Tarbell's fascination with this question throughout her life suggests that its resolution was of more than academic concern to her. Although she never articulated it in terms of her own personal choices, her life was a testimony to the ambivalence she must have felt. To all outward appearances she was the model of emancipated womanhood, a prototypical feminist. She was economically independent, successful in her career, unfettered by domestic responsibility, self-directed, independent of the need to affirm her self-esteem by dependence on a man, sure enough about herself to tout conventional opinion, and accepted and acclaimed by many of the outstanding figures of her day. And yet, almost as if to atone for her success in the male world, she spilled a considerable amount of ink writing books and articles to promote the idea that a woman's place was in the home. At the close of her life, however, she regarded the question as unanswered, the only indication that she experienced any ambivalence in the discrepancy between her own life and the ideal life she posited for most women.

If she had claimed to have found the answer, she would have been forced to grapple with the question of how her own life stacked up in the balance. To affirm her own autonomous and successful existence she would have had to deny many of her fundamental beliefs. On the other hand, if she had endorsed the creed that woman's place was in the home she would have nullified the validity of her own life. She avoided this dilemma by claiming that she had not found the answer, professing, that is, that she was unwilling to take sides. Did her viewpoint, in fact, offer an alternative to the extreme positions taken by both feminists and Antis? Perhaps one way to find out is to examine the works she devoted exclusively to this question.

The American Woman

Women need the ennobling influence of the past. They need to understand their integral part in human progress. To slur this over, ignore, or deny it, cripples their powers. It sets them at the foolish effort of enlarging their lives by doing the things man does—not because they are certain that as human beings with a definite task they need—or society needs—those particular services or operations from them, but because they conceive that this alone will prove them equal.
  —*The Business of Being a Woman*

Ida Tarbell's reputation as a journalist, her renowned common sense and intelligence, and her intellectual commitment to the woman question suggest a person who would have been a welcome asset to any cause she undertook. She had all the makings necessary to become an ally of either the Antis or the suffragists. In the end, however, it was the Antis who could boast of her support.

Tarbell was intellectually, if not emotionally, in sympathy with the Antis, and though it appears that she never became *actively* involved on an organizational level, her works on women served to buttress the antisuffrage position. In her autobiography she never mentioned her affiliation with the Antis, yet from at least as early as 1908 she considered herself on their side. In a 1908 issue of *The Anti-Suffragist*, an article discrediting rumors that the suffragists had converted Tarbell to their cause claimed that she had assured the Antis of her allegiance. It included a letter from Tarbell to *The Sun*, in which she disavowed any association with the suffragists.

Sir: My attention has just been called to an article in this morning's Sun headed "A Secret Suffrage Council." The writer errs in including my name among the members of this body. I am not enrolled in the council nor have I any idea of joining any body which is actually engaged in working for Woman Suffrage. I am not in sympathy with the idea of immediate universal Woman Suffrage. *Moreover I am enrolled in the Anti-Suffrage Association*. Ida M. Tarbell.[34]

What she meant by being "enrolled in the Anti-Suffrage Association" is not clear. There is evidence, however, that she lent her name to the New York State Association Opposed to Woman Suffrage, for her name appears on the letterhead of that organization as a member of the Executive Committee.[35]

Of all Ida Tarbell's works on women, probably none was more controversial than *The Business of Being a Woman* (1912), chapters of which appeared in *The American Magazine*. The title of this work, as well as its deliberate attempt to provide a theoretical cushion for the notion that a woman's place was in the home, provoked immediate reactions from both sides. In the July 1912 issue of *The Woman's Protest* the headline of a story on Tarbell read, " 'The Masculine Mind' of Miss Tarbell Excites Suffragists. They Attack Her Writings on 'The Business of Being a Woman,' but Unwittingly Pay her a Nice Compliment." The story went on to discuss suffragist Rheta Dorr's comment that Tarbell had a "masculine mind." *The Woman's Protest* was in agreement.

> It is indeed unusual to find in a woman such highly developed judgment, sound observation and straight logic on matters outside the home as Miss Tarbell exhibits. It is just the possession of these rare qualities (which Mrs. Dorr terms "masculine") which give Miss Tarbell her intelligent and broad view of matters affecting the nation as a whole.

For the author of the article, if all women possessed Tarbell's "masculine mind," there would be "fewer objections to suffrage, just as there would be fewer suffragists." But "one swallow does not make a summer" and it was only "through exceptional ability and circumstances" that Tarbell was able to reach her "sane and statesman-like conclusions." In the view of this one Anti, Tarbell had enough of the masculine quality of judgment *not* to undervalue the "business of being a woman."[36]

Following this article, and in sharp contrast to it, appeared an excerpt from a letter to the editor of *The New York Times* written by suffragist Harriet Burton Laidlaw, in which she referred to "the business of being a woman" as a "degenerate and shameful phrase."

> There are just two cases, salient cases, of the business of being a woman, and that is, the Oriental harem . . . and the tolerated house of prostitution in our great cities and throughout our great country. . . . I submit to you that that is the business of being a woman.[37]

On the day after this appeared, Mrs. William Forse Scott, chairman of the Publications Committee of the New York State Association Opposed to Woman Suffrage, replied to Laidlaw. Her letter to the editor was printed in full following Laidlaw's. After pointing out how mistaken Laidlaw's interpretation of the phrase was, Scott began a critique of the suffrage movement as a whole. The agitators "persist in discussing the exceptional woman . . . while they relegate to a secondary importance the normal type." But the great question is "how to decrease the number of exceptions." One should focus on the "normal" woman, who is daughter, wife, and mother.

> The woman who has not carried a child close to her heart, guarding her thoughts and acts in loving care of the new life which she creates for the world's use, and for which she is opening the gates of human experience, has never known the true, high "business of being a woman."[38]

Tarbell's views on the proper role for women, which realized their full expression in *The Business of Being a Woman*, had already been more than hinted at in her series on "The American Woman" in *The American Magazine*. The series consisted of six articles that represented not only Tarbell's bird's-eye view of women in American history, but are also important contributions to women's history. Tarbell began with the effect of the Revolutionary War as a leavening agent on the political consciousness of women. "It was inevitable that she break with the notion that the duty of her sex was first to please, then to obey and finally to endure humbly and cheerfully." Once the revolution was over, the first step taken in the advancement of women—a movement that characterized the nineteenth century, which she called "The Woman's Century"—was the demand for new education.[39] In the wake of the American Revolution women realized that for democracy to work, the young must be trained, and they regarded as their first obligation "to fit their children for citizenship."[40]

The establishment of educational institutions for women in the first forty years of the Woman's Century was a revolutionary achievement. But from Tarbell's perspective its impulse had come not from a desire for advancement on the part of women but from their unselfish passion to rise to the need of the new democracy. "There was practically no question of 'rights' in it. To give better service was what they were after."[41]

During this early stage, she pointed out, men in particular were very cautious and even those who backed all the educational enterprises for women had no sympathy for innovations that gave woman the same education as men or fitted her for occupations formerly closed to her. Education, as contemporaries saw it, was to "fit, not unfit, her for the normal woman's life" and was not to lead her to "undertake good works not suited to her condition."[42] This was a recurrent theme of anniversary addresses before the advanced female seminaries of the 1830s and 40s. It was also not that different from those of the 1890s and later, as evidenced by such homiletic exercises as the address of Dr. Weir Mitchell to the girls of Radcliffe.

The second great event that triggered a large-scale response from women was the Civil War.

Nothing had occurred since the birth of the Republic which demonstrated so well the seriousness with which women took their personal relation to the government.[43]

Even the "non-progressives," said Tarbell, responded immediately to the call to action as nurses. In the end, this also meant advances for women, for one of the effects of their participation in the war was a revolution in popular feeling regarding women. They had proven themselves capable of more than most people expected. Advances in their status occurred not as a result of woman's desire for self-determination but as a result of the fact that they were needed.

It was a tremendous lesson in one eternal fact which had always been too generally overlooked by the advocates of Woman's Rights, that *you get new privileges in the world because it is necessary for the good not of yourself but of the whole that you have them.*[44]

Tarbell's favorite exemplar of this theory in action was Dorothea Dix, whom Tarbell greatly admired both as a reformer and as a person.

Throughout her life, indeed, she set herself firmly against the exploitation of her career. She was by taste and judgment strongly opposed to notoriety of any kind. Service was its own reward, she held. She probably was made more emphatic on this point by the growing tendency among women who were interested in the movement for "rights" to exploit indiscriminately any unusual activity of women. She was too intelligent and too experienced not to realize both the vulgarity of the practice and its danger to the real development of women who found themselves in unaccustomed occupations.[45]

It is inevitable that anyone writing a history of women in America has at some point to deal with the question of the women's rights movement. Tarbell tackled it in her usual matter-of-fact fashion, trying very hard to look at it objectively, although in the end her bias was unmistakable. The movement, she wrote, was an open *declaration of war on man* as the conscious enslaver of woman. The most significant feature of the Declaration of Sentiments (1848) was "the way in which it hurls the gauntlet at man. The Declaration was really a call to war on man," making of him a "deliberate oppressor, a conscious conspirator, woman his slave." The framers did not recognize that the question was a human question, that the wrongs were other than the deliberate and conscious intent to enslave, and that woman herself was a partner to her position.[46]

Tarbell felt that the framers also lost sight of several other factors. For one, she pointed out that universal male suffrage itself was still in the experimental stage. Second, men had already begun to attack the civil laws affecting women. And third, from the beginning men had called for the political education of women as essential to their role in a democracy, as evidenced by the fact that the greatest advancements for women were in education.

Perhaps even more disturbing to Tarbell was the inference one could draw from the women's rights platform that the business of being a woman was of less importance than the business of being a man. Women assume that having a profession, mingling with the crowd, and getting into politics (the same as men) will cure their inferiority of position and power. They do not believe that a man's life may not be altogether satisfactory.[47]

Tarbell was extremely ambivalent about the women who led the movement for equal rights. On the one hand, she was greatly impressed by the breadth of vision and revolutionary ardor of many of the movement's leaders, but on the other hand, she relied heavily on the glib contemporary characterization of feminists as maladjusted females.

A group of remarkable women were drawn into the movement—*all of them because of some peculiar thwarting personal experience* which led them to understand and sympathize with the general spirit of the Declaration, though probably very few accepted or understood all of its sentiments.

The zealous feminist of the 1840s and 50s was a tragic figure to Tarbell.

. . . driven by a great unrest, sacrificing old ideals to attain new, losing herself in a frantic and frequently blind struggle, often putting back her cause by the

164

sad illustration she was of the price that must be paid to attain a result. *It was, and is, common to speak slightingly of her, but it is uncomprehending.*

Tarbell's view of the feminists may have been ambivalent, but it was also original. For despite her deep convictions about woman's place she always managed to steer clear of the "official" antisuffrage party line. This independence of thought is greatly in evidence in her treatment of the gains women had made.

> Certainly no woman who to-day takes it as a matter of course that she should study what she chooses, go and come as she will, support herself unquestioned by trade, profession or art, work in public or private, handle her own property, share her children on equal terms with her husband, receive a respectful attention on platform or before legislature, live freely in the world, should think with anything but reverence of these splendid early disturbers of convention and peace, *for they were an essential element in the achievement.*[48]

Apparently Tarbell was too much aware of the extent to which she herself was a beneficiary of these advances in woman's condition to take these changes for granted. At any rate, she diverged here from those Antis who dismissed the need for suffrage on the grounds that women had achieved all their gains without it.

Tarbell never underestimated the power of women; therefore it is no wonder that she was the first (and only) historian of the woman's movement to place in proper perspective female resistance to the movement, to attempt an interpretation of it, and to point out that on this subject the feminists experienced a blind spot. In the period between 1848 and 1861 the vast majority of American women were "unsympathetic and often contemptuous" of woman suffrage.

> The most discouraging thing they [suffragists] had to face was the attitude of their own sex. . . . To the vast majority it was all an incomprehensible performance which amused, bewildered or shocked them.[49]

Her interpretation of this phenomenon derived in part from her basic assumptions concerning woman's role—"whatever her civil and political position, her educational disadvantages, her social humiliation," she was "by no means the nonentity as a class that exclusive reading of the suffrage literature of the time would lead one to suppose." The American woman of 1840 and 1850 still retained the executive ability and the fine moral and social feeling that characterized her forebears in the revolutionary period. "She was a real person, one of genuine achievement." And a real person, according to Tarbell, was one who recognized the importance of her role as a contributor to the overall good of society. This kind of woman could never be dissatisfied with her lot; therefore, it was only natural that she would be unreceptive to the ideas of the feminists and shun the movement for woman's rights.

> . . . the American woman of the '40's and '50's failed to be swept into the Woman's Rights movement in any general fashion [because] . . . she was too occupied with preserving and developing the great traditions of life she had inherited and accepted. She was firmly convinced that these traditions were the best the world had so far developed, not merely for women, but for society. She did not deny that women had not the full opportunity they should have, but, as she saw it, no more did men. She saw civil and educational and social changes going on about her. She feared their coming too fast rather than too slow, and as men do, in all ages, she held to the great traditions, honoring them and viewing with watchful and generally suspicious eye all sweeping movement for change.[50]

For Tarbell the underlying principle that influenced the actions of most American women in the 1840s and 50s and continued to influence them at the turn of the century was "the spirit of progress" without compromising "true womanly nature."

> The conviction that the Woman's Rights movement somehow, few of them could have explained how, violated this rule, that kept a great body of women out of the movement—the fear that they were going to lose something of their womanliness.[51]

Despite her own misgivings, Tarbell was not one to underestimate the influence of religion on the American woman. She believed that women were strengthened in their belief about themselves and in their resistance to the new views about women by their acceptance of what the Bible had to say about women.

> They got from the church the reason of things as they found them—the reason for their submission to masculine authority—the explanation of their place in society, their program of activities. From it they got, too, their vision.[52]

But before most women were able wholeheartedly to accept the Bible as their touchstone, they needed an interpretation that was compatible with their

166

estimation of themselves and that would, if anything, serve to enhance their position.

Evidently it was not just Elizabeth Cady Stanton and the feminists who were unable to reconcile biblical teachings with their views. The accepted literal interpretations, according to Tarbell, caused most women more or less of a struggle. But for the majority of women the problem was solved by Sarah Josepha Hale. Hale, who through *Godey's Lady's Book* reached more than 150,000 subscribers, "felt keenly the need of squaring up those features of the movement for emancipation which she had accepted, with Biblical teachings." Her argument is found in the preface to her magnum opus, *Woman's Record*, an encyclopedia of more than 800 women and their achievements drawn from both ancient and modern times.[53]

Basing her view of woman's place in the world on the Scriptures, Hale arrived at the conclusion that woman is the superior of man and was intended to be so by the Creator. Her argument was that the first chapter of Genesis indicated that more care and preparation went into forming woman than man. Furthermore, woman was "the last work of creation"—"The crown of all"—and, as Tarbell pointed out, according to the theory of evolution "the last is best!" Hale argued that St. Paul's injunction that woman remain covered and man uncovered in the churches also taught the superiority of women, for "Is it not the privilege of the superior to remain covered in the presence of the inferior?" Moreover, in the affair of the apple, Hale found woman much less blameworthy than man. For Eve confessed and took her punishment, whereas Adam threw the blame on her, and "like a felon he was condemned to hard labor for life on the ground cursed for his sake." Eve was to suffer for her children and be subject to her husband, but she was not "cast down by [the] fall—like man." According to Hale, "to her was confided by the Creator's express declaration the mission of disinterested affection—her 'desire' was to be to her husband." However, woman was not subject to man for his pleasure, but for his elevation. Hale's conclusion, based on this argument, was that "woman is God's appointed agent of morality."[54]

Tarbell felt that the implications of Hale's message were plain to all women.

Anything that leads her away from this mission, that leads her to aspire to intellectual, professional or industrial equality with man is to obscure her real and higher calling—to weaken her powers and to debase rather than elevate her.

The impact of this message on the vast body of women was, in Tarbell's view, another explanation for woman's resistance to change. But underlying both these reasons—fear that in some way the new ideas would undermine their gentility and womanliness, and their inability to accept any view that seemed to be in opposition to biblical teachings—and working most powerfully against the woman's movement, was "a fundamental conviction of the *worthwhileness* of the woman's life."

> To bear and to rear, to feel the dependence of man and child—the necessity for themselves—to know that upon them depended the health, the character, the happiness, the future of certain human beings—to see themselves laying and preserving the foundations of so imposing a thing as a family . . . to feel themselves through this family, perpetuating and perfecting church, society, republic—this was their destiny—this was worth while. They might not have been able to state it, but all their instincts and experiences convinced them of the supreme and eternal value of their place in the world. They *dared* not tamper with it.
>
> Their opposition, badly and even cruelly expressed, had at bottom, as an opposition always has, the principles of preservation. It was not bigotry or vanity or a petty notion of their own spheres which kept the majority of the women of the '40's from lending themselves to the Woman's Rights movement. It was a fear to destroy a greater thing which they possessed. The fear of change is not an irrational thing—the fear of change is founded on the risk of losing what you have, on the certainty of losing much temporarily at least. . . .
>
> All the sentiments in the revolting women's program seemed trivial, cold, profitless beside the realities of life as they dreamed it and struggled to realize it. It was the woman's life which barred the way most effectually to the growth of the cause of Woman's Rights.[55]

It is unfortunate that Tarbell did not project her insights ahead fifty years and try to place in perspective the antisuffrage movement of her own day. In none of her works written prior to ratification of the Nineteenth Amendment did she even allude to it. Certainly this was not because it was too contemporaneous to be treated historically, for her history of the Standard Oil Company pioneered the study of recent history. Perhaps the reason she avoided treating the opposition of her own day was that she feared that women in her time no longer had the same faith in themselves or the greatness of stature of their forebears. At one point she even wrote that "The women of the American Revolutionary Period certainly challenge sharply the women of to-day, both by their intelligent understanding of political issues and by their sympathetic cooperation in the struggle."[56] On the other hand, she may have written *The Business of Being a Woman* as an apology for her antisuffrage contemporaries (and for herself), since she was continually trying to demonstrate that not all resistance to change was bad. If anxiety had caused the women of her own day to become conservative rather than preservative, Tarbell wanted her readers to know why. In fact, she tried to show that the line between the two was tenuous. In *The Business of Being a Woman,* she wrote that while woman fears changes as disturbers of her plans and her ideals. But the changes persist and eventually win over her husband and children while she remains where she was.[57]

The Business of Being a Woman

> For the normal woman the fulfillment of life is the making of the thing we best describe as a home.
> —*The Business of Being a Woman*

If the title *The Business of Being a Woman* was a "red rag" to the suffragists, they must have been even more enraged by the contents. The central figure of the book was "Uneasy Woman," modern emancipated woman who was freer than ever before, yet never more dissatisfied with her lot.

> . . . a spirit not at home with itself, and certainly not convinced that it is going in any particular direction or that it is committed to any particular worthwhile task.[58]

The notion that true womanhood might not be compatible with emancipated womanhood disturbed Tarbell greatly.

> Is [the business of being a woman] incompatible with free and joyous development of one's talents? Is there no place in it for economic independence? Has it no essential relation to the world's movements? Is it an episode which drains the forces and leaves a dreary wreck behind? Is it something that cannot be organized into a profession of dignity, and opportunity for service and for happiness?

More than one hundred and fifty pages later Tarbell resolved the dilemma, but at the same time gave herself away, implying that she had decided on the answer before she had even begun. Her book, she said, was founded on the proposition that

. . . the Uneasy Woman of to-day is to a large degree the result of the belittlement of her natural task and that her chief need is to dignify, make scientific, professionalize, that task.[59]

The task itself involved taking responsibility for three areas that only women were equipped to handle. The first was responsibility for the household economy. Woman as consumer could direct the family's wants and enforce simplicity and thrift, making of the home a most effective school for imparting the principles of "scientific household management."[60]

Second, equipped with the necessary education and liberty to teach her children the meaning of democracy, she was a crucial factor in their education. But unfortunately, modern woman had lost respect for her task and believed that the tools she had acquired to perform it were more important than the purpose for which she was to use them.

> She has found out that with education and freedom, pursuits of all sorts are open to her, and by following these pursuits she can preserve her personal liberty, avoid the grave responsibility, the almost inevitable sorrows and anxieties, which belong to family life . . . the beauty and joy of free individual life have dulled the sober sense of national obligation.[61]

This provides an inkling of the conflict that she apparently never resolved in her own life. She certainly had the education and freedom to engage in a variety of pursuits. By making the preservation of her personal liberty her chief goal she avoided the "inevitable sorrows and anxieties, which belong to family life." She must have wondered whether her own free, individual life prevented her from fulfilling her obligation to the nation.

This belief that everyone has an obligation to society not only underlay her conception of woman's role but also informed her basic view of life. Women (and she must have included herself in this category) owed society a return for their freedom, their means, their education.

> Nature has made them the guardians of childhood. Can they decently shirk the obligation any more than a man can decently shirk his duty as a citizen? Indeed, the case of the woman unresponsive to her duty toward youth is parallel to that of the man unresponsive to his duty toward public affairs. One is as profitless and parasitical as the other.[62]

What did this make Tarbell?

Unfortunately she had to deal not only with the question of moral responsibility vis-à-vis her own life, but also with the question of peace of mind. Failure to fulfill one's function in the scheme under which one lived, she wrote, always produced unrest. "Content of mind is usually in proportion to the service one renders in an undertaking he believes worthwhile."[63] Beneath the worldly veneer and the homespun philosophy, was Ida Tarbell "content of mind"? She never said directly. She probably would have considered it an indulgence to devote herself to idle speculation on this matter.[64] In any event, she seemed to believe that everything she did was worthwhile.

The third area of woman's responsibility was to provide moral training for her children. Here Tarbell's position was identical to the mainstream of antisuffrage thought. Whether for good or ill, a child is the product of its mother's training. Therefore, if mankind was not living up to expectations, look to the mothers.

> If a child is anchored to basic principles, it is because his home is built on them. If he understands integrity as a man, it is usually because a woman has done her work well. If she has not done it well, it is probable that he will be a disturbance and a menace when he is turned over to society.

Tarbell went as far as one could go with this idea, by suggesting that if woman did not do her job and instead turned her child over to the mass educational process to do it for her, it was not just the individual child who suffered. Might not this be related to the "general lowering of our commercial and political morality?" After all, she pointed out, the corruption in the American cities and the use of government in the interest of private business that have from time to time discredited the democratic system have all occurred under the regime of the emancipated woman, the woman who substituted dreams of personal ambition for the early democratic ideal.[65]

Women should not shrink from their great task—preparation of the citizen—for this very role brings them into the mainstream of public life. Furthermore, woman has the tools to provide the necessary training: education, freedom of movement and expression, ability to organize, discuss problems, and work for whatever changes are essential.[66]

All of this training of the future citizen took place, naturally, in the home, that great social laboratory "where all the problems are of primary, not secondary, importance, since they all deal directly with human life." At the head of this social laboratory was the woman, whose task was to create the atmosphere necessary for the development of affection and the growth of spirit and intellect. Thus, woman's responsibility for this socialization process involved more than just housekeeping.

> Housekeeping is only the shell of a Woman's Business. Women lose themselves in it as men lose themselves in shopkeeping, farming, editing. Knowing nothing but your work is one of the commonest human mistakes.[67]

With perceptive insight, Tarbell concluded that knowing nothing but one's own work was not only a common occurrence but often a deliberate mistake. Though without having resolved it for herself, Tarbell graphically explored the nature of this discontent. Many women say that they would be "women" if they could be guaranteed economic freedom, opportunity for self-expressive work, and political recognition. They do not see in woman's life a satisfying and permanent end. According to Tarbell, they claim such a life fails because it is antagonistic to personal ambition, makes dependents out of them, leaves them in middle life without an occupation, keeps them out of the great movements of their day, and gives them no part in the solutions of ethical and economic problems that affect them and their children. They want fuller participation in life, and, by life, they mean "the movements of the market place, of politics, and of government."[68]

Tarbell could not help but agree that if there were something to this contention, then modern woman had every right to be "uneasy."

> If the cultivation of individual tastes and talents to a useful, productive point is out of question in the woman's business, if it is not a part of it, something is weak in the scheme. Something is weak if the woman is or feels that she is not paying her way. Both are not only individual rights; they are individual duties.

Tarbell conceded that woman was also right to be dissatisfied if after twenty-five years she was left in middle life with "her forces spent, without interests, obligations . . . without important tasks."[69]

The answer lay not in denigrating woman's role, but in emphasizing its broader significance, its organic relationship to the social institutions of which all women were a part. Perhaps nothing better illustrates this than Tarbell's views on how even something as seemingly unimportant as "a woman and her raiment" related to the larger good. Instruction in the principles of dress, she said, could teach girls "the importance of the common and universal things of life," for these everyday processes were expressions of the great underlying truths of life. The matter of dress was bound up with the whole grist of social and economic problems—the cost of living, woman's wages, wasteful industries, the "social evil."[70] Thus, with the proper knowledge of such a simple matter as dress, women could exert control over the textile industry, certain aspects of the economy, labor, and public morals.

The Antis loved this book. They referred to it often, making Tarbell an apologist and spokeswoman of their cause, and quoted passages that illustrated their basic philosophy. In "The True Function of the Normal Woman," Mrs. Horace A. Davis used the following excerpt to demonstrate the mutual exclusivity of men's and women's work.

> Human society may be likened to two great circles, one revolving within the other. In the inner circle rules the woman. Here she breeds and trains the material for the outer circle, which exists only by and for her. That accident may throw her into this outer circle is, of course, true, but it is not her natural habitat. Nor is she fitted by Nature to live and circulate freely there. . . . What it all amounts to is that the labor of the world is naturally divided between the two different beings that people the world. It is unfair to the woman that she be asked to do the work of the outer circle. The man can do that satisfactorily if she does her part; that is, if she prepares him the material. Certainly he can never come into the inner circle and do her work.[71]

Tarbell's didactic works on women were important not only as artillery in the war against feminism, but also for what they reveal about the author. In *The Business of Being a Woman*, she devised an elaborate explanation of why women failed to reach the first rank. She said that women believed that in order to succeed, they had to suppress their natural emotions and meet the world with a nonresilient "man-like" surface. Necessity also abetted this tendency by forcing woman to encase herself in unnatural armor so that contact with all aspects of life would not result in a tremendous drain on woman's sympathy.

> For the normal, healthy woman this means the suppression of what is strongest in her nature, that power which differentiates her chiefly from man, her power of emotion, her "affectability" as the scientists call it.

Therefore, woman must overcome her own nature if she is to do her work. She must sacrifice "the most wonderful part of her endowment . . . this superior affectability crushed, leaves her atrophied." Atrophied woman was not only cold but also "self-centered and intensely personal."

> Let a woman make success in a trade or profession her exclusive and sufficient ambition, and the result, though it may be brilliant, is repellent.

Did Tarbell feel that she was brilliant and unattractive? She circumvented this too, believing somehow that her impersonality and her ability to keep in perspective the value of woman's role made her an exception—neither brilliant nor unattractive. For her the usual woman who wanted to do a man's business believed it was better than woman's and consequently devoted herself totally to the task.

> Her work is her child. She gives it the same exclusive passionate attention. She is as fiercely jealous of interference in it as she would be if it were a child. She resents suggestions and change. It is hers, a personal thing to which she clings as if it were a living being. That attitude is the chief reason why working with women in the development of great undertakings is as difficult as cooperating with them in the rearing of a family. It is also a reason why they rarely rise to the first rank. They cannot get away from their undertakings sufficiently to see the big truths and movements which are always impersonal.[72]

Tarbell believed that in every profession there were scores of successful women, but "almost never a *great* woman." She stressed that woman's greatness lay *outside* of professional life. The world is full, she wrote,

> . . . of women who understand, are familiar with the big sacrifices, appreciative of the fine things, far-seeing prophetic. Why does this greatness so rarely find expression in their professional undertakings?[73]

If woman's "greatness" lay outside of professional life, then this would explain why a professional woman—even Tarbell herself—though successful, could never be great.

At some point in her career it was inevitable that the incongruity between Tarbell's life and her position on women would catch up with her. Tarbell's nemesis came in the form of her boss, John S. Phillips at *The American Magazine*. Apparently Phillips wanted the magazine to stand for an open and progressive attitude toward the liberal movements of the day and found it anomalous that a member of his staff and a regular contributor to the magazine should be publicly identified with the opposition to woman suffrage. He asked Tarbell to explain her position, and this she attempted to do by writing Phillips a personal letter.

Tarbell took great pains with the letter. She seemed to have been hurt by Phillips's allegation that her position was illiberal and contradictory and that it in some way reflected on her "mind and character." Apparently he had gone even farther and accused her of not supporting woman suffrage out of vanity since she had earlier allowed her name to be used by the Antis and probably therefore did not want to acknowledge that she had been wrong. Tarbell, though wounded, admitted that there might have been "at least a suspicion of truth in all that you say." She said she found it difficult to explain "myself, even to myself, and I do not often try." Nevertheless, she felt duty bound to try to analyze her position even though she felt "pretty sure in advance that it is not going to satisfy *you*."

> "Come across" you say and I really don't know that I can. There is in feminine nature a strange barrier against complete self-revelation. The woman never admits all even to herself. This is probably a protective device of nature, intensified by social conditions. At all events the impersonal and experienced of us rarely get entirely away from it. I don't know that I can even on a subject which has come to be as purely objective to me as suffrage, but I'll try.

Although more retrospective than introspective, Tarbell did try. She went back to the beginnings when she was "born to the idea."

> I grew up among people who believed in women's suffrage as much as they did in the abolition of slavery, the observance of the Sabbath, or the beneficence of the protective tariff. It was part of the creed I learned as a child—a part of the liberal program of the day. Elizabeth Cady Stanton and Susan B. Anthony were grouped in my young girl's mind with William Lloyd Garrison and General Grant and Abraham Lincoln and George M. Curtis and Horace Greeley and Carl Schurz.[74]

She said she grew up with the idea that suffrage was one of the great "rights" that woman was born into the world for the express purpose of acquiring. Her contribution to the cause was going to be "to go to a man's college and fit myself for a man's work." College, however, changed things for her, not because she ever discussed suffrage there, but because she learned that there were other things in the world beside "causes" and "rights" and "reforms" and "revolutions." Furthermore, this realization coincided with a lull in the movement during the late 1870s; by the time it rose again in the late 1880s she was out of college, involved in editorial work, and devoted to examining ideas she had grown up believing in, one of which was suffrage.

By this time, however, she said she had come to have "a very profound feeling that sound education and real cultivation depend almost solely on women." Time had only intensified her conviction that women's civilizing work existed apart from public life. Interested in biographical study, she proposed to examine the "character of the contributions made by women who had played bit parts in the past in public affairs" in order to throw light on the question. But her study of women in the French Revolution "took from me all the enthusiasm I had ever felt for women in public life." The effect of her study, she admitted, was "decidedly reactionary."

> Radical and conservative, Royalist and democrat, aristocrat and proletarist, I had the same revulsion against them all.

Tarbell was capable of enough self-criticism to admit that it was possible that she had not been quite fair to any of them. Nevertheless, she held firm to the conclusion that women would complicate public life by "their intensity and implacability."[75]

Her studies only confirmed her view that the suffrage argument that women would interject a higher moral quality into politics was unfounded. "Women take on the political morality of their times, rising and falling with it as men do." The only way women can make politics better "is to send a large number of boys into public life whose principles are sound and whose courage and faith are high."[76]

Tarbell realized that for the most part her judgment had remained over the years where it had been at the end of her French Revolutionary studies, but she did not want it thought that she was getting too old "to understand or sympathize with the aspirations of a growing world."[77] She insisted, therefore, that she had been open to later developments in the arguments favoring suffrage. If she thought women in industry could improve their conditions by the ballot, she would drop everything and fight for it. She was not unswayed by the fact that women like Jane Addams and Florence Kelley contended that women could get what they needed more easily with the vote, but she held fast to the belief that the complications of politics would make their cause harder. As for the suffrage contention that the ballot would serve to educate women, Tarbell still maintained that education came from life and that motherhood was the greatest life experience anyone could have.

Of all the arguments made on behalf of suffrage, Tarbell admitted she was most influenced by one she had heard Phillips himself make—that suffrage would break down the barriers that separated women from women. It is here that Tarbell's real vision of sisterhood emerges, a vision that was in many ways in advance of her day, transcending even the class boundaries so often invoked by the suffragists.

> It would be something which would give the poverty-stricken helpless, cringing woman a sense of being somebody—of possessing something in common with those more fortunate women she sees from afar and must but too often dimly hate for their happiness, their ease, their fullness of opportunity. . . . It is not only she, the unfortunate, who would get from a ballot a new sense of her value as a human being which she so terribly needs. The fortunate who would get a new sense of the value of other human beings which she quite as much needs.

Tarbell acknowledged that perhaps Phillips was right that "women may discover women, in this operation," although she felt that it had not done much to bridge the gap among men.[78]

Tarbell's sense of justice was deeply attuned to women who felt they were being deprived of a "right" in being denied the ballot, even though she herself did not view the vote as a right. She was also sympathetic to women who felt that with the ballot they would be more fully in the stream of life. But she admitted that she was faced with a dilemma since there seemed to be "more women who don't want the vote." The result, she said, was her equivocation. "For my part, while I am not willing to work for the ballot, I am not willing to work against it." This was a difficult position for Tarbell and one she felt constantly called on to justify. Nevertheless, out of this need grew not only her basic philosophy of life but also her platform for change. She believed that she lived in an era in which the possibilities for enlarging the scope of life existed for everyone, not just "the favored few." She believed with her Progressive contemporaries that "the things which have so largely defeated life for the many are unnecessary." These ogres, in her mind, were poverty, war, and privilege. But unlike her Progressive colleagues she did not have faith that men or women could legislate them out of the world.

> Poverty and war and privilege are the children of greed and selfishness and unbridled natures. Nothing but the slow processes of education will put an end to them and believing this how can I fight for that which I do not feel I need—for that which I believe will hamper the direct use of the tools which will do the work.

In this she resembled her antisuffrage sisters. To her, the most dangerous fallacy of her time was the belief that "we can be saved morally, economically, socially by laws and systems." She felt suffrage was the least of tools, especially for women who had others much stronger. In the end she confessed to Phillips that she suspected that the reason she felt as she did about suffrage "is a kind of instinct—it is not logic or argument, I mistrust it—do not want it."[79]

We do not know whether this letter satisfied Phillips or if it in any way altered their relationship. Tarbell closed by wanting to know if she had "come across." Although she certainly raised more questions about herself than she answered, she came across to a later generation of women as one with an unshaken faith in women's place and value in the world.

EIGHT

Impact

In the long run the Antis were unable to prevent the extension of suffrage to women. As a result, they have tended to be ignored by history, for the Antis were losers, and history tends to relegate losers to obscurity. Furthermore, in the period after ratification of the Nineteenth Amendment and following the First World War, antisuffrage was not a very popular cause. Self-determination increasingly came to be regarded as a legitimate objective, both for nations and for individuals. And the process continues.

It is practically impossible to arrive at an accurate estimation of the importance of the Antis in the eyes of their contemporaries. Their public image varied from place to place and in proportion to the intensity and effectiveness of their actions. Accounts of their exploits in the press often reflected the sympathies of the particular newspaper. In the suffragist journals, reactions to the Antis were obviously biased; at times they were considered inconsequential, and yet on occasion they were pictured as a real threat.[1]

Nevertheless, during the period in which the Antis were active they had considerable impact on the way the suffrage issue was to be decided. The Antis certainly had an effect on the suffragists themselves, judging from the latter's reaction to them. Further, the Antis did influence public opinion, as can be seen by the remarks of legislators, political candidates, and journalists. And by offering resistance to woman suffrage at elections, legislative hearings, and committee meetings, the Antis often blocked direct attempts to introduce woman suffrage, thus contributing to its delay.

It is unclear when the suffragists first became aware of the existence of an organized opposition. Apparently, the acceleration of antisuffrage activities in 1896 and their increasing effectiveness throughout the following decade resulted in more than occasional suffrage complaints.[2] As early as 1885, suffragists in Massachusetts were aware of the presence of antisuffrage remonstrants at the legislative hearings. Appearing to welcome the Antis as opposition, though in fact ridiculing them, *The Woman's Journal* contained the following comment:

The annual hearing of remonstrants promotes woman suffrage in many ways. It excites discussion: it generally finishes the conversion of some waverers to the right side, and it invariably makes the friends of suffrage indignant and stirs them up to redoubled zeal. Last, but not least, it brings forth a crop of argumentative papers or set speeches against woman suffrage which are an arsenal of weapons for the suffragists during the following year.[3]

It was after 1910, however, that the suffragists really came to grips with the Antis, meeting their onslaught with everything from ridicule to pitched battle. But although the suffragists were consistently provoked to react, they failed to realize the true nature of their opposition.

Ridicule is an ancient weapon which, used effectively, can prove devastating. There is no precise way of determining just how the Antis or, for that matter, public opinion were affected by the suffragists' use of it. From 1914 to 1916 the *Nashville Tennessean*, a prosuffrage newspaper, carried a number of rhymes. The first was in response to the position that voting was unwomanly and would "unsex" woman.

It doesn't unsex her to toil in a factory
Minding the looms from dawn until night;
To deal with a schoolful of children refractory
Doesn't unsex her in anyone's sight;
Work in a store when her back aches unhumanly—
Doesn't unsex her at all you will note,
But think how exceedingly rough and unwomanly
Woman would be if she happened to vote.[4]

The following poem is a satire of some of the common antisuffrage objections, many of which by this time were becoming well known. It was entitled "Why We Oppose Women Travelling in Railway Trains."

Because travelling in trains is not a natural right.
Because our great-grandmothers never asked to travel in trains.
Because woman's place is in the home and not the train.
Because it is unnecessary; there is no point reached by train that cannot be reached by foot.
Because it will double the work of conductors, engineers, and brakemen who are already overburdened.
Because men smoke and play cards in trains.
Is there any reason to believe that women will behave better?[5]

The suffragists often drew attention to the inconsistencies they saw in the Antis' arguments. Following is " 'Our Own Twelve Anti-Suffrage Reasons' Why Woman Should Not be Enfranchised."

Because no woman will leave her domestic duties to vote.
Because no woman who votes will attend to her domestic duties.
Because it will make dissension between husband and wife.
Because every wife will vote exactly as her husband does.
Because bad women will corrupt our politics.
Because bad politics will corrupt our women.
Because women have no power of organization.
Because women will form themselves into a woman's party.
Because men and women are so different that they must have different duties.
Because men and women are so much alike that men with one vote can express themselves and us, too.
Because woman can not use force.
Because the militants can and do use force.[6]

The suffragists applied their talent for ridicule in a more direct fashion, by aiming at a specific target. "Anti-Suffrage Periscope Detected Showing Which Way the Wind Blows" is a scathing piece directed at the male antisuffragists, the "aunty men." It made fun of the

. . . pathetic little wail of men antisuffragists, who want President Wilson to "call off" Dr. Anna Howard Shaw and Mrs. Carrie Chapman Catt. The pitiful voice of Everett P. Wheeler utters the cry . . . imploring the President to make Mrs. Catt and Dr. Shaw stop all their political activities because they are in the service of the government as members of the Woman's Committee of the Council of National Defense. . . . What about the fact that Nature, Providence and Elihu Root, not to mention Mr. Wheeler himself have established the fact that men can govern and women can't. And now two unenfranchised ladies have terrors for them with which only executive authority can cope.[7]

The longer the battle was waged, the more vindictive became the tone of the blows struck by both sides. The World War I period saw numerous attempts on the part of the Antis to slander suffrage leaders by impugning their patriotism. Carrie Chapman Catt, president of NAWSA at that time, particularly was singled out in what was apparently an effort to discredit the movement as a whole.

In a bulletin published by the Antis in 1917, Catt's patriotism was questioned because of various alleged actions, attitudes, or associations. Among other things, she was accused of having brought Rosika Schwimmer, a Hungarian pacifist and conscientious objector, to the United States, and of having been influenced by her; of having been associated with the Woman's Peace Party, and of being somehow linked with the radical International Workers of the World (IWW). All of this she categorically denied in a lengthy open letter to Margaret C. Robinson, chairman of the press committee of the Cambridge, Massachusetts Anti-Suffrage Association. Catt reminded the Antis that when it had become clear that war was imminent, she had "called an authoritative meeting" of the presidents of the state branches of the NAWSA, at which "that body not only declared its loyalty to the country in the event of war, but offered its machinery of organization for helpful patriotic service." She called the effort to link her by implication with the IWW "untruthful and malicious." She went farther, placing the onus on the Antis themselves by calling attention to the antisuffrage stance of the IWW and its leadership. She went on to point out that "One of your well-known co-workers, Annie Riley Hale, was arrested recently after a seditious speech. The most vigorous opponent of Woman Suffrage in the world, and consequently an ally of yours, is The Kaiser of Germany."[8]

The tone of Catt's reply was certainly not indifferent. She was evidently deeply affected by the allegations and went into considerable detail to disassociate herself from the "undesirables," whom she mentioned by name. In 1917, in the climate of intense patriotism produced by the entry of the United States into World War I, most persons accused of a lack of patriotism were quick to defend themselves. Nevertheless, the nature of Catt's response seems to indicate that she was as intent on preserving the integrity of the suffrage organization from antisuffrage attack as she was in defending her own reputation. In any event, the extent of her involvement with the Antis on this issue only served to dignify the opposition, in contrast to the suffragists' more typical efforts to belittle it.

Only a month later, Catt again entered the fray. In a press release entitled "Mrs. Catt Quotes John Hay Against Antis' Contention That to Believe in Peace is to Be a Traitor to Country," she implicated the father of a leading Anti in the peace movement. John Hay, a former secretary of state, was the father of Mrs. James W. Wadsworth, Jr., president of the National Association Opposed to Woman Suffrage. Catt, still responding to inferences about her loyalty because she had worked for peace prior to war, pointed out that Hay had drafted a peace treaty while the United States was at war with Spain. He believed, said Catt, that the war with Spain was a necessary and righteous war, but he detested war and believed in peace. "If I am a traitor, so was he."[9]

The antisuffrage bombardment against Catt continued into 1918. Still charged with being a pacifist and therefore disloyal to the United States, she was forced onto the defensive once again by the Antis. In a news release entitled "Wanted—More Patriots Like Mrs. Carrie Chapman Catt," she continued to iterate that she had pledged NAWSA's forces to the government as early as February 1917 and that the National Suffrage Association was probably the first organization of women to line up behind the president for patriotic service. She also pointed out that she was a member of the Woman's Committee of the Council of National Defense and of the Council of National Unity.[10]

Although the suffragists seemed at first not to fully appreciate the threat posed by the Antis, they eventually grew apprehensive about the effect the Antis were having on public opinion, and devoted considerable time and effort to refuting the arguments and preparing their own suffragist counter-propaganda. One of the Antis' favorite arguments was that if women were enfranchised, the good women would stay at home while the less reputable went to the polls. The suffragists tried to meet this argument by referring, wherever possible, to the actual record. In this connection, certain correspondence between Mary Sumner Boyd, head of the Data Department of NAWSA, and Frederick Whitin of New York City is revealing. Boyd wrote to Whitin:

> It is hard for a sensible person to realize how deep an impression the anti-suffragists make on the public with their bad-woman's vote objection to woman suffrage . . . the lines I rather wanted to follow in the case of immoral woman were to compare the number of women in the business of prostitution with the number of men, directly and openly, profiting by this business, together with the number of men who frequent prostitutes. Thus the volume—though not, of course, in either case the exact figures—of the "bad man" vote would be placed over against the volume of the "bad woman" vote.[11]

In response, Whitin pointed out that the number of professional prostitutes (those whose sole source of income was from sex relations) varied. For example, when the police were active and the vice resorts were closed the number was only between 2,500 and 5,000; when the town was open there were between 10,000 and 15,000.

With a total electorate of about one million as we would have with equal suffrage, it would only be in the closest elections that the vote of the prostitute, did she vote, would be a factor, and it seems to me that our anti-suffrage friends have overlooked the fact that the prostitute class would be very largely among the non-voters, not the least because she would not have sufficient permanence of residence.

If this was true of New York City, it was equally true of all other cities, he concluded, "for there are probably more professional prostitutes in New York in proportion to its voting population than in any other city in this country."[12]

The "bad woman" vote was always a sensitive subject for the suffragists. They were constantly pressured to indicate that whenever women voted, it was the "better woman" who voted and therefore her vote that made the difference. The suffragists elicited statements from sympathetic politicians supporting their position. For example, a Fred W. Eckert of Berkeley, California, in "Effects of Woman's Suffrage on the Political Situation in the City of Chicago," averred that wards in which the highest percentage of women voted were those of skilled workers, homeowners, medium-salaried office and professional workers, in other words, the middle class.[13]

Responding to antisuffrage attempts to embroider incidents of women involved in election frauds, the suffragists insisted that election polls had been transformed into respectable places. There was no danger of insult to a woman at the polls where neighbors and friends voted and elections were conducted locally. The suffragists maintained that "red light" women were confined to a few precincts, and unless a woman lived in a precinct that included a red-light district, she need never see a prostitute at an election. Furthermore, as for the assertion that by granting women the right to vote, to the vote of every criminal man would be added that of a criminal woman, the suffrage reply was that the vicious and criminal class among women was comparably very small.[14]

The suffragists also came out in full force in response to the position that the ballot would not benefit the working woman. Perhaps the most widely circulated suffragist pamphlet on this subject was "The Wage-Earning Woman and the State: a Reply to Miss Minnie Bronson," by Edith Abbott of Hull House and Sophonisba P. Breckinridge, assistant professor of social economy at the University of Chicago.[15] Basically, their position was opposed to Bronson's view that woman suffrage would *not* lead to fairer treatment of woman in industry or to better protective laws. They claimed that Bronson was a paid representative of the Antis, and they tried to discredit her by showing that she was unqualified to speak about women in industry. They maintained that for the suffragists the ballot was not the *only* redress for woman's wrongs, but was the *most direct* means to reform. The suffragists were concerned not with "laws on our statute books," which were unjust to the working woman, but about the absence of adequate protective legislation. When some women obtained the vote, conditions for all would improve. Statutes had been enacted in industrial states for over seventy-five years through the efforts of workingmen to bring about by legislation a larger measure of justice than by bargaining with individual employers; these represented the results of the struggle by workingmen with votes to improve their condition and were not to be compared with special provisions designed to protect the health of women.

In response to Bronson's assertion that protective legislation for women was found on statute books of some states where women did not vote, they argued that most protective legislation had been achieved through the efforts of the suffragists. In reply to her point that in a few states where women did vote similar laws and had not yet been passed, they emphasized that Colorado, Wyoming, Idaho, and Utah were mining and agricultural states with few factory women; Massachusetts alone had 152,713 factory women, compared with 681 in Idaho, and New York had 136,788, compared with 501 in Wyoming. Furthermore, in states where voteless women had secured these laws, they had never been given the means of enforcing them.

There was no reason for night work for women to be prohibited in suffrage states and most laws of manufacturing states were not needed in the suffrage states. They objected to Bronson's inference that when a woman had the same right to vote as a man "she must give as many hours of toil per day as he." And they refuted the contention that the suffrage states of Wyoming and Utah provided for equal pay for equal work of teachers due to the law of supply and demand. Finally, they concluded, Bronson had been deliberately misleading by refusing to note the good laws passed since women obtained the vote.

In the same vein as the Abbott-Breckinridge retort was "The Truth About Wage-Earning Women and the State, A Reply to Miss Minnie Bronson," by Florence Kelley and Pauline and Josephine Goldmark.[16] Using arguments similar to those of Abbott and Breckenridge, they attempted to show that political equality for women would not deprive them of the extension of protective legislation.

"Normal Women Not Neurotic" was the eye-catching title of a pamphlet by Dr. Frederick Peterson, enlisted by the suffragists to counter the antisuffrage belief that there existed a biologically determined gap between the sexes. Peterson's remarks were designed to refute Professor William T. Sedgwick, an antisuffrage polemicist who had been interviewed by *The New York Times* on feminism and woman suffrage.[17]

> If the revolutionary views of Mr. George on feminist intentions as set forth in *The Atlantic Monthly* should ever in some distant future take such shape as to be the actual menace to the world that Professor Sedgwick apprehends, then, no doubt, the race will rise up to protect itself.

He went on to assert that Sedgwick made too much of the differences between men and women. How could a biologist, he wondered, overlook essential points in which men and women were exactly alike—in human nature, the possession of individuality, and the potential ability to perform most kinds of the world's work? Individual capacity varies, but differences in capacity between men and women were no greater than between various groups or classes of men alone.[18]

During the summer of 1915, Catt and her supporters planned an elaborate piece of guerrilla theater called "a woman's day at home" to counter the Antis' belief that "a woman's place was in the home." It was designed to show that woman's work was so involved with industry, business, public service, and education "that all the comforts inside the home may be said to depend on the work she does outside it."

> For a long time we have all been trying to meet anti-suffrage insistence that woman's place was in the home by citing these selfsame facts from the economic history of our times. But the antis couldn't seem to take it in. They shut their eyes to the facts, gazed sentimentally into space and repeated "Woman's place is in the home." So we carried our project on to the antis. We called their bluff! We let it be known that we had under consideration the idea of applying their precept literally *for just one day!*

Catt went on to explain that the Antis had hastened to condemn women for the proposal to abide by their precept, quoting an anonymous Anti who said that for women to stay in their homes for even one day would be to "prove the limit of lawlessness to which suffragists are prepared to go, in order to gain their ends." Yet, Catt pointed out, this was exactly what Antis urged as woman's excuse for being—one sphere only, the home, was her legitimate concern. As a result, anyone forced to leave it did so with a sense of public condemnation, having to face the accusation that she was "a usurper, and a betrayer of home and society."[19]

The suffragist position, reminded Catt, was to emphasize the dignity of woman's labor outside the home, its extent, its responsibility, its involvement in production, manufacturing, and distribution, so that it would never again be possible to lose sight of woman's great contribution to industry, business, education, or morals in her work *outside* the home. All of this, she pointed out, was assiduously denied by the Antis.

On August 24, the Empire State Campaign Committee held a conference and passed the following resolution:

> Whereas, the proposal that woman agree to stay at home for just one day has shown, through the protests of employers, business men, factory men, public service men, and anti-suffragists themselves, that to apply the time-honored precept that woman's place is in the home would mean the essential stoppage of the entire machinery of life, emperil public health, call a halt on education, cripple industry, cut off important public utility services, shut down stores and factories;

> And whereas, it is the sense of this meeting that the irrelevancy, the unfairness, and the crass stupidity of maintaining that woman's place is in the home have already been made obvious and already it has been demonstrated to the satisfaction of the public that *there can be no home except as woman takes her place outside as well as inside it.*[20]

Therefore, resolved the suffragists, it was advisable to postpone the agitation for a woman's day at home. And so plans for what would have been the first woman's strike in American history came to an end. One wonders why the suffragists backed down. The project seemed an excellent way not only to illustrate the justice of their position but also to strike a telling blow at the Antis. The very reason offered by the suffragists—that it would effectively immobilize society if women were to remain at home—was what they allegedly hoped to demonstrate by such a strike. Did they not believe their own rhetoric? Were they afraid they would not be able to muster sufficient support among working women? Were they threatened by the establishment or by the men in their lives? Did the war in Europe make a difference? Or did they identify so thoroughly with the system they planned to disrupt even for only one day that they did not have the heart to go through with it for fear that it would not be in their own self-interest?

It seems that they did not take themselves seriously enough. In the end they called their own bluff, for prophesying what would happen if woman's role were withdrawn from public life and then being told by the very forces they hoped to persuade that this was indeed likely to occur were two different things. It appears as if their utterances were designed more for their own sense of self-esteem and to relieve their minds by countering antisuffrage assumptions than really to try to make an impression on the public mind.

Without the strike, women in New York State had to wait two more years before they were enfranchised. One wonders what would have been the outcome if the suffragists had gone through with this display of woman power.

Suffragist response to provocation by the Antis was also embodied in pamphlets designed expressly to counteract prevailing antisuffrage arguments. One of the more elaborate published by NAWSA was "Twenty-five Answers to Antis." It contained twenty-five five-minute speeches that were delivered at a meeting in New York City on March 11, 1912, by a host of suffrage leaders. The title of each speech was intended to portray a specific antisuffrage argument.[21]

The National American Woman Suffrage Association also published a pamphlet, "Objections Answered," listing thirty-four reasons offered by the Antis why women should not be enfranchised and their rebuttals.[22] Following are some typical examples.

As to the contention that women were represented already by their husbands, the suffrage reply was that this representation bore no proportion to numbers, since a bachelor counted for just as much as a man with a wife, a widowed mother, unmarried sisters, and daughters. As to men and women being different, the suffragists maintained that men and women were *too* different and man could not put himself in woman's place. As to the contention that women would lose their influence over their children, the suffragists pointed out that a mother had no legal rights over her child in most states; the suffragists had been trying to secure joint guardianship legislation, but thus far had obtained it in only fourteen states and the District of Columbia.

The Antis argued that woman suffrage would double the ignorant vote; the suffrage response was that more girls graduated from high school than boys. Against the Antis' contention that woman suffrage would double the foreign vote, the suffragists replied that in the United States there were more than three times as many native-born women as foreign-born men and women put together. Replying to the notion that women in large numbers were organized against suffrage, the suffrage answer was the organized opposition among women to suffrage was very small compared with the organized movement of women in its favor.[23]

As to the Antis' argument that if women voted, they would have to hold office, the suffragists pointed out that women already served as officials. Some of the women most prominent in opposing equal suffrage had been holders of public office. For example, the late president of MAOFESW, Mrs. J. Elliot Cabot, was for years a member of the school board of Brookline and an overseer of the poor. Yet the association in its documents objected to equal suffrage on the grounds that "suffrage involves the holding of office, and office-holding is incompatible with the duties of most women." Furthermore, according to the suffragists, suffrage did not involve officeholding by the majority of women, but only by a few, and there were always some women of character and ability who could give the necessary time. "Women, as a class, have more leisure than men." In the enfranchised states there had been no rush of women into office and those that women did hold were mainly educational and charitable. In Wyoming, women have had full suffrage thirty-nine years, they maintained, and yet no woman had ever been a member of the legislature, while neither Colorado, Utah, nor Idaho have ever had more than three women in the legislature at one time.

Whereas the Antis insisted that if women voted, they ought to fight and do police duty, the suffragists pointed out that old, infirm, lame, blind men voted, and that some woman risked her life whenever a soldier was born. Against the argument that women were too emotional and sentimental to be trusted with the ballot, they maintained that sentiment was involved in many of the decisions made by men and was a necessary part of life. Government would not be damaged by increasing the supply. As to the Antis' contention that the smallness of woman's school vote showed that they would not use the full ballot, the suffragists replied that the size of men's vote was in proportion to the size of the election, very large at presidential ones and very small at school elections. In Kansas, women got school suffrage in 1861 and the vote was small, but in 1887 when they achieved municipal suffrage, it became larger. Furthermore, the school vote disproved the fear that only the so-called bad women would rush to the polls.

Responding to the Antis' insistence that there were too many voters already, the suffragists felt this meant too many of the wrong kind; if just an increase in number were bad, then every woman who becomes the mother of half a dozen sons would harm the country. And as to the Antis' argument that when the majority of women ask for it, they will get it, the suffragists pointed out that "Every improvement in the condition of women thus far has been secured not by a general demand from the majority of women, but by the arguments, entreaties and 'continual coming' of a persistent few. In each case the advocates of progress have had to contend not merely with the conservatism of men, but with the indifference of women, and often with active opposition from some of them." They argued that human nature was conservative and it was fully as conservative in women as in men. The persons who took a strong interest in any reform were generally few and regarded with disfavor, even by those the proposed reform was to benefit. Not one of the changes made during the previous half century in laws relating to women (all of which were subsequently approved) could have been made if it were necessary to wait until the majority asked for them. "In the light of history, the indifference of most women and the opposition of a few must be taken as a matter of course. It has no more rational significance now than it has had in regard to each previous step of women's progress."[24]

By 1917 the suffragists realized that the biggest threat to a federal amendment was the growing states' rights sentiment that was being fanned by the Antis. The suffragists tried to meet this in a variety of ways. One was the publication of a book compiled by Carrie Chapman Catt entitled *Woman Suffrage by Federal Amendment*.[25] Among the most interesting essays contained in the book was one by Henry Wade Rogers, judge of the United States Circuit Court of Appeals in New York City and professor in the Yale University School of Law. Entitled "Federal Action and States Rights," this article was an attempt to refute Henry St. George Tucker's *Woman's Suffrage by Constitutional Amendment* by arguing that woman suffrage by federal amendment would not be a departure from the original thought of the makers of the Constitution. Picking up where Rogers left off, Catt zeroed in on some of the points raised by Tucker. If the states felt that provisions for amending the Constitution were "unfair, undemocratic or even unsatisfactory," it was curious that "no movement to change the provision has ever developed." In her view, "states rights" was "either a theory to be invoked whenever necessary to conceal an unreasoning hostility to a measure or that those who advance it are guilty of extremely muddy thinking."[26]

According to Catt, even if *all* the state constitutions were amended to enfranchise women, the word "male" would still stand in the Constitution and men and women would still be unequal,

. . . since the National Constitution can impose a penalty upon a state which denies the vote to men, but none upon the state which discriminates against women.[27]

In other words, the only way to put teeth into the law was to build in the power to enforce it, as in the case of male suffrage.

Taking up the argument that a federal woman suffrage amendment would confer the vote on black women and thus interfere with white supremacy in the South, Catt pointed out that "No larger number of negro women can be enfranchised by Federal Amendment than will be enfranchised by State Amendment." Appealing to the racism of southern women, Catt argued that if the franchise were obtained by federal amendment, it would "come by the votes of white men in Congress and legislatures." Whereas if women were enfranchised by state constitutional amendments, "they will be forced to appeal to voting negroes to elevate them to their own political status." It seemed that behind the objection against black women lay a "hope and belief that Southern women will remain disenfranchised forevermore." From here Catt went on to demonstrate that woman suffrage in the South would mean the strengthening of white supremacy. Furthermore, for those who had a "sly dread of female supremacy," she hastened to assure them of the excess of white males over white females. When the "grandfather clause" in southern constitutions is removed and blacks readmitted to the polls, there would be no greater guarantee of white supremacy than adding the votes of the South's white womanhood.[28]

Ridicule, personal attacks, and preparation of counterpropaganda were not the only indications that the suffragists were affected by the tactics of their opponents. They were on occasion even influenced to modify their own tactics.

On October 9, 1915, Catt, directing the Empire State Campaign Committee, wrote a letter "to the Speakers in the New York campaign." Warning that campaigns were lost in the last week by speakers losing their heads, she urged them not to make statements they could not prove.

Do not state that the liquor interests are fighting us; we have seen no sign of it. Do not say the Catholic Church is opposed; it is not. Do not promise what women will do with the vote. Plead for justice, progress, and right and let the rest go.

Among points she directed the speakers to stress were the following:

191

The anti-suffragists have widely advertised the statement that woman suffrage will double the cost of elections. An inquiry has been directed to the Secretary of each one of the Suffrage states with the result that unanimously they reply that woman suffrage has not caused additional state taxation nor an appreciable increase in the cost of elections.

. . . The anti-suffragists are putting up posters with a new slogan—"Safety First." Announce that our slogan is "Justice First." They have it also on match boxes and printed matter.

. . . The main defense of the opposition is that women don't want the vote. But a million women want it.[29]

Many years later, Catt was still willing to give credit to the Antis for having influenced her to change not only her tactics but also her mind.

When I first began to work for woman suffrage in the East, the anti-suffragists were as thick as blackberries in summer, but they were a little afraid to speak out for themselves and usually got men to do it for them. I heard Cabot Lodge, Lyman Abbott, and other men, half in politics and half out, speak quite often, and when they spoke, they made their chief point that suffrage—the vote—was not a right and that no citizen of the United States held it because it was a right.

This was usually followed by the statement that for this reason women could not claim the *right* to vote. According to Catt, they influenced many "Eastern people" with this argument, herself included. Deciding to study the question, she reported, she had come to the conclusion that the Antis were right and therefore subsequently when arguing for woman suffrage she had emphasized that the vote was not a right but a permission.[30]

The Antis' impact on the suffragists can also be seen in the skirmishes that occurred between the two forces. Perhaps the most critical juncture for the suffragists was in 1919 and 1920 as they were eagerly waiting for the necessary thirty-six states to ratify the woman suffrage amendment. The Antis, turning all their efforts to preventing ratification, needed thirteen states to hold out against it. They would have no difficulty holding the South, but they were also counting on Kentucky, Tennessee, New Jersey, Connecticut, Vermont, and New Hampshire. But New Jersey and Kentucky ratified by January 1920, giving the suffragists thirty-five states; only one more was needed. In the remaining states, however, opposition was very strong and their governors were opposed to passage.[31]

On July 9, Catt, then president of NAWSA, sent a telegram to Governor William D. Stephens of California, asking him to "wire endorsement of woman suffrage to Governor Roberts of Tennessee . . . to offset anti-suffrage propaganda from a Californian who signs herself Annie Bock and defames California in astounding terms."[32]

Governor Roberts had also been urged by Wilson to support ratification. On August 7, Roberts issued a formal announcement of a special ratification session of the state legislature and called for ratification of the woman suffrage amendment.[33] In the ensuing special session of the Tennessee legislature, the woman suffrage bill passed the Senate and reached the House August 26, where it lacked two votes needed to win. In what turned out to be an ironic reversal for the Antis, the bill finally passed the House, the decisive vote coming from twenty-four-year old Harry Barns who, in accordance with antisuffrage precepts on mother-son relationships, listened to a plea from his mother and dutifully cast his ballot in favor of suffrage.

Catt advised the suffragists to distribute as much literature as possible throughout the summer.

> The anti-suffragists will flood Tennessee with the most outrageous literature it has ever been your lot to read. It will contain outright lies, innuendoes and near truths, which are more damaging than lies. It will be extremely harmful and the "nigger question" will be put forth. . . . Therefore, I entreat you to begin at once with a campaign of literature even though you think it is not needed.[34]

She then advised them to reach legislators and leading politicians before the Antis got to them.

Suffragists were not the only ones to react to the organized antisuffrage movement. The Antis were also persuasive in influencing individuals who could shape public opinion.

In an editorial entitled "Woman Suffrage," in *The Boston Saturday Evening Gazette*, the editor, Dr. Philip Woolf, wrote:

> A very potent argument against woman suffrage is that women are opposed to it. . . . There is no reason why a woman should not vote except that she does not wish to vote, and has not the capacity for voting reasonably.
> . . . even now she catches her breath in surprise when she is told that she is her own superior self and the equal of man at the same time.
> . . . the womanly woman is thoroughly satisfied with her social position, and if we may judge by the Massachusetts Assn. Opposed to the Extension of Suffrage to Women, she is actively opposed to changing her condition. The

most telling and philosophic book against suffrage has been written by a woman, and it has been practically demonstrated than ninety-six women out of every hundred have not the slightest inclination to voice, rather indignantly protest against the business.

. . . with her new opportunities the modern woman is showing less and less interest for suffrage. With greater liberty of action, greater knowledge and wider experience, she has learned and accepted the truth that equality between the sexes is an impossibility, is in defiance of nature and of civilization, and she has turned from politics to the fields that have been opened to her in the arts and sciences.

It is not clear just what was the source of Woolf's exposure to the antisuffrage position, but apparently it amply reinforced his inherent antifeminist bias. He went on to side with the "younger" women, "who are fully in sympathy with the times" and who did not see voting or politics as the way to advance their sex. He felt that the more intelligent the woman, the greater her indifference, and alleged that older women still retained their crude original aspirations based on the foolish arguments heard a few years before. Qualifying the antisuffrage vision of a golden present, Woolf did not feel that women had achieved utopia. He thought that many discriminations still existed, especially lack of equal pay for equal work. But this could be overcome only if women would shelve the question of the vote once and for all and concentrate on really important changes. The woman of advanced thought did not want to be burdened with suffrage, he said. She asked "Why should we try to make man and woman alike?" The suffrage cause was dying, he concluded.[35]

A letter to the editor of *The Boston Herald* discussed the refusal of the Massachusetts House of Representatives by a vote of 116 to 60 to substitute a license suffrage bill for an adverse report made by the Committee on Election Laws. The result was due in part to the "success of the movement for organization among the women opposed to women suffrage." The writer also referred to the "serious energy" of a "large body of thoughtful women in Mass., and also in New York State," which was already bearing fruit in the West. In Illinois an antisuffrage association had been formally organized within the last six months. Apparently well informed as to suffrage politics, the writer pointed out that Iowa was the newest goal of the National Woman Suffrage Association but that their activities had roused antisuffrage women to active opposition. Antisuffrage speakers (all Iowa women) spoke at the legislative hearings in Des Moines and the outcome of the House vote was fifty opposed and forty-seven for. Iowa women, concluded the letter, had been activated by the work of suffragists from outside the state and, as a result, were organizing an antisuffrage association.[36] The Antis' claim that they represented the majority of women was not lost on at least one legislator. Massachusetts Representative L. M. Haskins wrote to antisuffragist Helen Mansfield.

> My views on Woman Suffrage would be of small value to the Society more than to indicate my status as a member of the House of Representatives.
>
> I desire to subserve the interests of the majority of my constituents. For that reason *at least* I feel I should vote to defeat any Bill for such purpose—making such defeat more pronounced.
>
> This must not be construed however to [be] the endorsement of any argument as to the inaptitude of woman to all political questions vide—this very Bill. I find both sides manifesting a very lively interest and persistent persuasion [*sic*].[37]

Haskins had been solicited as part of an antisuffrage campaign to contact personally every legislator in the state and ascertain his position on woman suffrage. Haskins evidently had no ideological commitment to either side and seemed quite willing to be persuaded to vote against woman suffrage in the belief that the majority of his constituents were of that opinion.

It is not surprising that the period of antisuffrage ascendancy (1896-1907) occurred when the suffragist forces were making their slowest headway.[38] The suffragist explanation of events was that between 1896 and 1910 Congress interpreted the *inaction* of the country as a cue for inaction in the Senate and House.[39] But this was exactly what the Antis had hoped to achieve. Their most persistent strategy over the years was to convince legislators and politicians that women were unwilling to participate in the action necessary to obtain the suffrage because they did not want it.

In 1910, Theodore Roosevelt wrote a letter to the president of the National Norwegian Woman Suffrage Association.

> Mrs. Roosevelt and I have always believed in the suffrage for women, although we have not thought that the question was as yet of great practical importance in America; for we believe that the best and most serious minded women of our country should feel the need of the suffrage before it thus becomes of practical importance in our own land.
>
> The prime duty of the average woman is to be a good wife and mother just as the prime duty of the average man is to be a good husband and father, a good and efficient home-maker. Whenever this woman, the good woman, the woman who is really the most important citizen in all the State, feels that to the

vital and exhausting duties which she already performs, she can with wisdom and profit add yet another duty, that of the suffrage, why, I shall be most glad to see her assume it; but I wish to be certain that this is her real feeling, and that it represents not a passing emotion, but the sober thought of the great majority of those women for whom one has a respect and regard such as can be accorded to no other people in the nation.[40]

In the supercharged election year of 1912, all of the presidential candidates were approached by the suffragists for their opinion. Taft, who was hoping for reelection, was unwilling to commit himself. His explanation echoed that of Roosevelt's two years before.

I don't think we ought to take as radical a step as that without being certain that when we do it it will meet the approval of all those or substantially all of those in whose interest the franchise is extended because if it does not meet their views and they don't avail themselves of the opportunity to exercise the influence which that would give them, then we should be in a bad way because we might lose a substantial proportion of the votes of those that would be for better things. Therefore I am willing to wait until there shall be a substantial, not unanimous, but a substantial, call from that sex before the suffrage is extended.[41]

In effect, Taft wanted a mandate from women that they were in favor of suffrage. By avoiding specifics and not indicating what he thought was a "substantial" call he played right into the antisuffrage position. The Antis enjoyed their most successful results by impressing politicians with the idea that the suffragists were not representative of womanhood as a whole.

The most positive indication of the Antis' direct impact on the course of suffrage history is their role in influencing various election campaigns. Even the suffragists themselves testified to the effectiveness of the Antis in these campaigns. In 1893-94, a Constitutional Convention was held in New York State. The suffragists sent appeals throughout the state and held gatherings and meetings in order to obtain passage of a woman suffrage amendment. Then, according to Elizabeth Cady Stanton,

Strange to say, some of the leading ladies formed a strong party against the proposed amendment and their own enfranchisement. They were called the "Antis." This opposing organization adopted the same plan for the campaign as those in favor of the amendment. They issued appeals, circulated petitions, and had hearings before the Convention.

Despite the efforts of the suffragists, recalled Stanton, the Committee on Suffrage of the Constitutional Convention refused even to submit the proposed amendment to a vote of the people, though half a million people signed the petition. "Joseph H. Choate and Elihu Root did their uttermost to defeat the amendment and succeeded."[42]

The impact of the Antis on the decisions taken in Massachusetts regarding woman suffrage has already been noted. In 1913, however, another indication of antisuffrage effectiveness occurred in Massachusetts. As a result of the failure of governors of twenty states to recognize the validity of documents signed by woman notaries, the Massachusetts legislature passed a constitutional amendment allowing women to hold this position. But it was rejected by voters 181,343 to 154,691. Evidently Antis both worked for and were encouraged by its defeat.[43]

It is extraordinary that the suffragists never went beneath the surface in an effort to analyze the forces of resistance. They assumed almost always that the leadership and impetus came from men, whether referring to those conspiratorial forces that controlled politics or to the Antis themselves.[44] Even as astute an observer as Stanton attributed the success of the Antis in New York state to their male colleagues. Catt remarked that although the strongest suffrage organizations were in the East (where the movement began and where the initiative and insistence that enfranchised blacks began), "yet in Massachusetts, New York, New Jersey, Pennsylvania, Ohio, Indiana, Illinois and Iowa, where the woman suffrage appeal was continual during these forty years, no suffrage referendum was secured."[45] It was not coincidental that these very states witnessed the highest levels of antisuffrage activity.

NINE

Retrospect on Feminism and Antisuffrage Thought: Some Explanatory Hypotheses

One of the most difficult questions concerning the Antis is why they did what they did. There were so many possible solutions in the event women were enfranchised that could have been posed *within* the system of social values acceptable to them. For example, they could have used the club organization for becoming informed, taken turns voting while they cared for each other's children, or accompanied each other to the polls to mitigate against exposure to unwholesome influences. Since these solutions seem fairly obvious, one can only suppose that they had strong reasons for resisting them. There is no single or simple answer. In fact, trying to understand their motivation leads to a bewildering array of possible explanations. These do lend themselves to categorization, however, and can be approached in four ways.

The Psychological Approach

The psychological explanations tend to offer an insight into the Antis primarily in terms of the interactions of power and personality. The core of this approach is the assumption that if an individual is deprived of freedom, he or she will seek power as an outlet. The theoretical underpinnings of this view were expressed as early as 1869 by John Stuart Mill in his essay "Subjection of Women." Concerned with the existing inequality in the social relations between the sexes, Mill explored both the effects of this imbalance on women, and its implications for society.

When human beings have to depend on others for their sense of self-esteem, that is, when their self-definition derives from how others view them, power becomes increasingly important as a means of bending others to their will.

> An active and energetic mind, if denied liberty, will seek for power: refused the command of itself, it will assert its personality by attempting to control others. . . . The love of power and the love of liberty are in eternal antagonism. Where there is least liberty, the passion for power is the most ardent and unscrupulous.

For Mill, power could not be anything but a corrupting influence on the way people ran their lives. It reduced men to brutishness and made women slaves to acquisitiveness.

> The law, not determining her rights, but theoretically allowing her none at all, practically declares that the measure of what she has a right to is what she can contrive to get.

Therefore, women will do the utmost to acquire and retain that which they think will give them security, wealth, and status, such as excessively cultivating beauty and dress, or else in compensating themselves by meddling in their husbands' affairs. Unfortunately, Mill concluded, "Her power often gives her what she has no right to, but does not enable her to assert her own rights."[1]

Looking at the Antis from Mill's perspective, they begin to emerge as personalities thwarted in their self-development by a system that denied them worthy outlets for their active faculties and also as collaborators in perpetuating that very system, because it offered them power as a compensation for their loss of freedom.

More recently, Ronald Sampson has also concerned himself with the nature of dominance-submission relationships, particularly as they are reflected in the dynamics between men and women. In *The Psychology of Power*, Sampson proves himself an ardent disciple of Mill. Concerned primarily with the psychoanalytic implications of power relationships for the individual, Sampson focuses on the harmful effects of the deprivation of liberty. He feels that one cannot yield to power without experiencing psychic tension as the resentment is driven underground. In agreement with Mill, he believes that the dammed-up energies will seek some other outlet, and in the absence of freedom, that outlet will be the quest for power. When healthy emotions are denied an outlet in one direction, they find substitute expression. The woman, therefore, who is denied by birth the normal freedom permitted to males, will seek power as a surrogate. In other words, the development of power is a necessary compensation to maintain the balance of the existing psychic structure.

> . . . women, denied the rewards of psychic freedom, develop a strong interest in preserving such opportunities for psychic power as they have been able to forge for themselves.

In Sampson's view, however, Mill did not go far enough. He discerned the relationship between woman's subordinate social role and the depth of female craving for power, but he did not realize that the most common outlet for woman's power was her relationship to her children.[2]

For example, one might argue that in their role as mothers, women release their pent-up frustrations, manipulating their children the way they themselves were manipulated. Perhaps there is no clearer evidence of the extent to which women have always taken for granted and benefited from the power structure than the fact that they have been instrumental in perpetuating its sexist aspects. Thus, a woman, whose self-esteem was at best vicarious, would have found it to her advantage to inculcate in her son the notion of male superiority. In this way she would vicariously enhance her own sense of worth as the mother of someone who was superior to at least one half the human race.[3] Since motherhood is the one arena in which women have always been free to re-create themselves, it is no wonder that most women wish to retain their prerogative inviolate. From here it is but a short step to the glorification of their role as mothers and the denunciation of all that threatens it.

With so much psychic compensation invested in their role as mothers, it is understandable that women have not only been reluctant to complain of their condition, but have actually supported the existing pattern of woman's subordination and obedience to male authority. Mill's explanation for women's acquiescence was that they stood in fear of retaliation if they adopted insurrection as a means of changing things and that most women had been socialized to conceive of their primary role as submission.[4] For Sampson these explanations might have accounted for women's indifference to pleas for equality, but they do not explain "why are women's fear and resistance often as strong as men's or stronger, if they feel the existing relation to be genuinely threatened."[5]

Sampson went beyond Mill in his understanding that when individuals have never lived other than in fetters, they are not able to recognize the fetters for what they are. "You learn to adjust your wants to the goad in order to preserve the precious illusion of freedom."[6]

In summary, for Mill and Sampson, women have as much or more invested in maintaining the power structure than men because, for women, power is the substitute for psychic freedom; and one of the essentials of a healthy personality is to preserve the illusion of that freedom. If one accepts this hypothesis, it is necessary to assume that the drive for power is probably present in most women. Naturally, however, it takes diverse forms. In the suffragists it was expressed by their desire for a share of the pie. In the Antis it meant maintaining the illusions of dominance, their position in the home and their role vis-à-vis their children.

Not all who have studied the antisuffragists agree that they had such healthy personalities. In fact, if anything, one might assume that antifeminism or antisuffragism in women was a form of psychopathology. Could an Anti have been a "normal" woman? William O'Neill tends to regard the Antis' emotionality as an aberration, particularly in view of their rhetoric that contended that suffrage would make little or no difference in the feminine condition. Thus he finds it difficult to account for the fact that they invested so much emotional energy in resisting what they alleged to be inconsequential.

> Anti-suffrage emotionality is less easily understood, particularly among the considerable body of Antis who were themselves a part of the woman movement and subscribed in a general way to the benevolent goals of social feminism. Perhaps they suffered from deep personality disorders or status conflicts, but until we know more about them little can be added to what has already been said.

As far as O'Neill is concerned, the suffragists, too, were aberrant in their way. In his summary of the qualities he feels characterized the typical feminist, O'Neill seems to imply that for them to have been anything but abnormal would have been a contradiction in terms.

> By and large, feminists were complicated people; had they been otherwise, they would not have become feminists. When woman's role was defined entirely in domestic terms, these women who rejected domesticity almost had to be neurotic.[7]

Viewing both the suffragists and the Antis from O'Neill's perspective, one cannot resist the opinion that although he regards both groups as aberrant, he believes the Antis were probably the better adjusted of the two, just as he believes that social feminists were "better balanced than hard-core suffragists." Assuming, as does O'Neill, that the Antis were cut from the same cloth as the suffragists (both being largely urban middle- and upper-class women), with the simple difference that the Antis were "more addicted to Victorian formulas than feminists," one might speculate that they may have had fewer difficulties in adjusting to the prevailing female stereotype.[8]

Nevertheless, the contradictions engendered by their role in combating feminism must have provoked serious conflicts in many of the individuals involved. For others, the dynamics of their new role as activists may have offered them release from the frustration of sitting idly by at a time when their traditional role and status were being questioned and even undermined. In these cases, resistance might have been therapeutic. Perhaps the antisuffrage movement offered women a legitimate and healthy outlet for their drive to power.

Viola Klein, although primarily a sociologist, has also been concerned with how women as members of an "out-group" have internalized society's attitudes toward them. By "out-group," Klein means that women are distinguished from the dominant (male) strata by virtue of their physical characteristics, historical tradition, and social role. Furthermore, as in the case of other groups in a similar position, women have been subjected to preconceived opinions and collective judgments instead of being treated on their own merits. The general effect of this stereotyping is to inhibit the development of individualism, resulting in an "incalculable amount of restrictions, discouragement, ill-feeling and frustration."[9]

Furthermore, Klein feels that the fact that women occupied an inferior social status had to have an impact on their mental and characterological development. Citing the German sociologist Georg Simmel, Klein points out that one of the features that distinguishes women from men is the fact that the elite (man) never doubts that it was born an elite and takes its qualities for granted. It sets the prevailing standards and has sufficient prestige to enforce them on other groups. Women, on the other hand, are almost never free from the consciousness of their subordinate status.

If we express the historic relation between the sexes crudely in terms of master and slave, it is part of the master's privilege not to have to think continuously of the fact that he is the master, while the position of the slave carries with it the constant reminder of his being a slave. It cannot be overlooked that the woman forgets far less often the fact of being a woman than the man of being a man. Innumerable times the man seems to think purely objectively, without his masculinity entering his consciousness at all. On the other hand, it seems as if the women would never completely lose the more or less vague feeling of being a woman.[10]

Sex-role stereotyping, which is endemic to our culture, underwent a revival in the late nineteenth century, when Freud and his contemporaries began to use the prevailing biological views of women to buttress their definitions of the characteristically feminine personality types. According to Klein, however, Freud's identification of masculinity with an absolute cultural norm was his greatest disservice to women.

On the one hand, it resulted in a "mystifying over-estimation" of women by virtue of those qualities that could not be explained by male criteria. At the same time, it resulted in contempt for humans who failed to live up to the norm, in other words, for those women (or men) whose life-style challenged the prevailing stereotype. Both of these tendencies are apparent in the Antis. Their position was basically an affirmation of womanhood. In its more moderate form, it reflected the belief that women had in fact contributed a major share to civilization by virtue of the qualities they shared as women, that is, the nonmale aspects of their personality. In its extreme form, it involved the elevation of those traits that were uniquely feminine into a pantheon of special female graces. This provides an important clue as to why women were capable of such bitter opposition to suffrage. In men, the claim to equality challenged masculine feelings of power and superiority, but

it attacked in women, those symbols which they had developed as substitute gratifications for their lack of real power, and which were no less close to their heart than the feeling of superiority was to man's.[11]

It is difficult to determine just what was the impact of women's inferior social status. For some women the contradictions between what woman was and what it was felt she ought to be may have resulted in guilt or confusion. At any rate, some women really believed that women were not as capable of exercising the ballot as men and on this basis resisted the extension of suffrage. These women had internalized the prevailing myths of female inferiority and out of their own sense of powerlessness and limited self-esteem came to the conclusion that women should not be enfranchised.

Psychologists are finding increasing evidence not only that "the predominant cultural views of women are indeed disparaging," but also that in populations of college students, women as well as men regard men more highly. "It would be surprising," writes Sheri Naditch, "if the cultural stereotypes of female inferiority were *not* attended to in some way by women, perhaps eventuating in relatively low levels of self-esteem based on the social definition of their circumstances."[12]

The vulnerability of woman's self-esteem is confirmed by increasing evidence that female identity is perceived interpersonally, that is, the self is appraised through the reflections of the opinions of others.[13] For women, success is defined almost exclusively in terms of interpersonal success, first "popularity," then love.[14] This kind of "success" is subjective by definition and in the hands of others. It seems reasonable to assume, therefore, that the typical woman develops a vulnerable sense of self-esteem, almost completely dependent on the judgments of others.

It is difficult to say to just what extent a vulnerable sense of self-esteem may have contributed to the psychological makeup of an Anti, yet there is evidence that this was at least a contributing factor. Antisuffrage journalist Richard Barry, after interviewing Josephine Daskam Dodge Bacon, quoted her in "Why Women Oppose Woman's Suffrage."

> No. I do not believe in woman suffrage. Why? Because a woman can no more do a man's work than a man can do a woman's. There has never been a first-class woman writer, statesman, general or executive. I write second-class stuff myself. All women writers are second-class the minute you compare their work with that of the best *workmen*. But while there have been no really great women writers . . . no really great generals . . . no really great painters . . . there *have* been a large number of good mothers.
>
> And while women have repeatedly been great mothers I defy you to mention a man who has ever been a really first-class mother.
>
> Therefore, I conclude it is possible for women to achieve greatness as mothers and in no other way, and I do not believe Nature intended us to enter a field of effort where the laws of our being declare us outsiders.[15]

Mrs. Richard Watson Gilder, president of the New York State Association Opposed to Woman Suffrage, in a letter signed only H. de K. G., spoke of the "unable worm," houseless and weak, which is soon destroyed. Woman without the art of homemaking, she felt, was not only vulnerable, she was nothing.[16]

205

Apparently some Antis believed that it was a fairly general phenomenon that women did not have faith in other women. Mrs. Augustine H. Parker, an antisuffrage essayist, contended that because most women "are unconvinced by the feminists' protestations, few women care to be represented by other women." This was only natural, she thought, since "women do not, as a rule, employ other women to take care of their business affairs." As evidence she pointed to the fact that one half of the stock of the Pennsylvania Railroad was owned by women who could have elected several women directors if they wished, and yet the board was composed entirely of men.[17]

What at first may seem a strictly fanciful model for understanding the Antis emerges from Albert Memmi's study of colonialism, *The Colonizer and the Colonized*. Racism serves the same function in colonialism as sexism does in a patriarchal system. That is, in the same way that "racism sums up and symbolizes the fundamental relation which unites colonialist and colonized," sexism functions to unite male and female. The analogy is even more striking if one looks at the three major ideological components that according to Memmi constitute colonial racism: a gulf between the culture of the colonialist and the colonized; exploitation of these differences for the benefit of the colonialist; and the use of these supposed differences as standards of fact.[18]

The colonialist stresses those things that keep him separate, just as does the male in a patriarchy. And once the behavioral feature that characterizes the colonialist (or male) and contrasts him with the colonized (or female) has been isolated, this gap must be kept from being filled.

> The colonialist removes the factor from history, time, and therefore possible evolution. What is actually a sociological point becomes labeled as being biological or, preferably, metaphysical. It is attached to the colonized's basic nature.

If the colonizer (colonialist) wants to be the master, it is not enough for him to be so in fact, "he must also believe in its legitimacy." Furthermore, in order for that legitimacy to be complete, it is not enough for the colonized to be a slave, "he must also accept his role."[19] In the history of the relationship between the sexes, women until quite recently also have accepted their role, thus helping to legitimize the condition of male supremacy.

One of the devices that maintain the subordination of women and prevent the formation of a shared community of interest between the sexes is the prevalence of stereotypes that conform to mankind's needs. So, too, in the cases of the colonizer and the colonized. Another similarity is that the traits ascribed to the weaker are in both cases often incompatible with one another. Both women and colonized are simultaneously regarded as inferior and wicked, lazy and backward, without desires (frigid) and gluttonous (insatiable).

> The humanity of the colonized, rejected by the colonizer, becomes opaque. It is useless, he asserts, to try to forecast the colonized's actions ("They are unpredictable!" "With them, you never know"). It seems to him that strange and disturbing impulsiveness controls the colonized. The colonized must indeed be very strange, if he remains so mysterious after years of living with the colonizer.[20]

Another mark of the colonized's depersonalization is the "mark of the plural." Just as Viola Klein pointed out in the case of women as an out-group, the colonized does not exist as an individual. Neither women nor colonized are free to choose between being colonized or not being colonized.

One of the most compelling similarities between the plight of the colonized and that of all women is that they have been removed from history and from the community. As Memmi indicates, "Colonization usurps any free role in either war or peace." The colonizer "pushed the colonized out of the historical and social, cultural and technical current."[21] While Memmi feels that the colonizer did so in order to subdue and exploit, and it is certainly not clear that male domination involved such vindictive motives, nevertheless the dynamics in both situations were such that the success of the one depended on the failure of the other. If one looks at the culture, society, and technology of both women and colonized, one sees how seriously damaged they are. And the same holds true of women as of the colonized—one has no idea what they would have been without colonization (or subjection), but one can see what has happened to both as a result.

There are also remarkable similarities between the *experiences suffered* by the colonized and by women in general. For many women, as for the colonized, their first ambition was to assimilate, to "become equal to that splendid model and resemble him to the point of disappearing in him." Memmi points out that when the colonized rebelled, the rebels were laughed at because of their insistence on wearing khaki uniforms. They hoped to be considered soldiers, and by this tactic, "They laid claim to and wore the dress of history."[22] By the same token, women suffered ridicule when they first expressed belief in their autonomy by donning the female facsimile of male dress, namely bloomers.[23]

Considered incapable of governing, both women and colonized were kept away from power. And in both cases, long absence from autonomous government resulted in the loss of interest in and feeling for the control and skills that it requires.

As a result of colonization, says Memmi, the colonized almost never experiences nationality and citizenship, except privately. This social and historic mutilation (the absence of self-assurance or pride of citizenship) is perpetuated by the educational system where references to the community and nation are always in terms of the colonizing nation.[24] In what schools or textbooks could American women have derived any pride of citizenship in learning about the history of their country? Everything takes place outside of the experience of the oppressed. They are nonentities or exist only with reference to others. Neither women nor the colonized recognize that they had a past. They have no history, no leaders, no heroes.

Faced with little hope of changing this situation, says Memmi, the only alternative is to live isolated from one's age. The young colonized will fall back on traditional values. This usually results in an internal catastrophe.

> He will remain glued to that family which offers him warmth and tenderness but which simultaneously absorbs, clutches and emasculates him.[25]

In the historical experience of women, the Antis emerge as the young women who fall back on traditional values, with one important difference from the colonized. As domesticity engulfed them and removed them from the mainstream of civilization, they attempted to find comfort in the only way of life they ever knew by postulating that it was the highest kind of life for all women. Instinctively they rebelled against assimilation, against becoming "equal" to the male model and resembling man to the point of disappearing in him. This would have deprived them of what was uniquely their own. Psychologically wedded to the system, they sought to secure their way of life by enveloping it in a self-perpetuating mystique.

The Antis' similarity to the colonized who reject assimilation is further evident if one compares the assimilationist and the feminist. At the very moment when the colonized tries to combat his sense of powerlessness by trying to assimilate (becoming equal to the colonizer), he rejects himself.

> Rejection of self and love of another are common to all candidates for assimilation. Moreover, the two components of this attempt at liberation are

closely tied. Love of the colonizer is subtended by a complex of feelings ranging from shame to self-hate.[26]

To most women, the strident feminists who were trying to become more equal to men must have seemed to be denying their true selves. Given the lack of alternatives for women in the late nineteenth century, women's attempts to imitate the male value system must have enhanced the notion that liberation in feminist terms could be accomplished only by systematic self-denial.

Memmi argues that the colonial condition cannot be changed except by doing away with the colonial relationship. The relationship demands that there be both the colonizer and the colonized; therefore, if one or the other is eliminated the basic relationship is altered. Assimilation and colonization are contradictory, for if all the colonized were assimilated, the colonizers would have no one left to exploit. On the other hand, when assimilation does occur, the colonized is even further removed from being in touch with his culture. The Antis did not want to lose what they believed were the civilizing effects of female culture. They believed in themselves. They were the exponents of a female subculture.

According to Memmi, in order for recovery of self to occur, a conscious rejection of assimilation is necessary. If imitating the colonizer requires self-denial, then it would seem as if rejection of the colonizer is the "indispensable prelude to self-discovery." Memmi treats the two as mutually exclusive. "After having been rejected for so long by the colonizer, the day has come when it is the colonized who must refuse the colonizer."[27] So, too, the Anti had to "refuse" the male.

And just as the colonized, excluded from the universality common to all men, begins to assert his differences, the Anti also had to assert hers. Both ran the same risks. By taking up the challenge of exclusion, the colonized and the Antis accepted being separate and different, *but* their individuality was that which was limited and defined by the colonizer. Thus both the colonized and the Antis drew pride from their differences, but they were differences that had been formulated by the dominant group. Therefore, rejection of the colonizer's values and system was based on the conviction that everything that belonged to the colonizer was *not* appropriate for the colonized. According to Memmi, this is just what the colonizer has always told the colonized. Therefore, the rebellious colonized takes the first step toward liberation by accepting and glorifying an image of himself that emphasizes the apparent differences between himself and the colonizer. In the same way, the Antis took their first steps toward a new definition of womanhood by unhesitatingly fostering those uniquely feminine qualities that they had been taught differentiated them from the male element in society.

In Memmi's view, before and during the revolt, the colonized always considers the colonizer either as a model or as an antithesis. He continues to struggle against him, and whereas formerly he was torn between what he was and what he wanted to be, now he is torn between what he wanted to be and what he is making of himself.[28] The Antis consciously chose *not* to consider man as "model," but they failed to realize the implications of treating man as "antithesis." As a result, they were unaware that their conception of womanhood had its origins in a sexist etiology that allowed women little room for self-definition on their own terms. This lack of awareness was common to almost all women, suffragists and Antis alike. And without this consciousness, it is impossible to write the next chapter of the story of women's liberation.

The Ideological Approach

A second approach involves viewing the antisuffrage position on women as the logical outcome of the Antis' conservative social philosophy—their family-centered worldview, their opposition to individualism and belief that advancement of the individual at the expense of the group would be disastrous, their similarity to other moral conservatives such as the opponents of divorce, and their adherence to the domestic mythology that characterized the woman's movement in its later conservative stages.

According to Aileen Kraditor, the Antis' social philosophy was based on the notion that the business and political worlds, while offering the surest means to progress, were nevertheless arenas of competition and strife, which if carried to excess would result in the eventual dissolution of society. Balancing this tremendous potential for progress (and harm) was the conservative influence of the home, the destruction of which would mean the destruction of the social order. The home would be destroyed if the distinction between male and female spheres were eradicated, and there was no surer way for this to occur than for women to deny the primacy of the family as the social unit by demanding to be recognized as individuals in their own right.[29]

Kraditor believes that the Antis opposed the vote for women rather than other advances because they feared that the franchise would "dissolve society into a heterogeneous mass of separate persons, whose individual rather than family interests would thenceforth receive political representation."[30] In this view, the vote was not just another addition to all the other rights women had gained but a qualitative change in the social and familial role of women.

> If antifeminism is understood as largely representing fear of social disorder, the contradiction and the anomaly disappear. It was not that social order required the subordination of women, rather, to the conservatives it required *a family structure* that involved the subordination of women.[31]

Another aspect of this conservative social philosophy was the antisuffragist belief that the disfranchisement of women "was necessary to the governmental stability that depended upon the exclusion of 'unfit' men." At this point, however, Kraditor takes the Antis at face value. Woman suffrage would dilute the electorate and change it from a "militia on inactive duty" against the potential internal enemy. To the person of conservative persuasion, the "enemy" was apparent everywhere: in the South, the black; in the Northeast, the Democratic machines and the immigrant; in the West, the frontier riffraff and prostitutes.[32] From the conservative viewpoint, the poor, ignorant, and immoral, if allowed to vote, would not only outnumber, but would also outweigh, the intelligent patrician.

Viewing the Antis as exponents of a conservative social philosophy helps to explain some of the inconsistencies in their position. For example, it now becomes possible to understand why they insisted that the differences between the sexes were so great that women *could not* participate in government, yet at the same time indicated that these differences were so fragile that to preserve them women *must not* participate in government.[33] Maintaining the traditional distinctions was the only way to ensure that women would remain in their place as the "symbol and center of the one institution that prevented society from flying apart."[34]

By the same token, if the Antis were motivated primarily by their class bias, as social conservatives their attitude toward legislation becomes somewhat more explicable. It is now possible to understand why they tried to convince working women that legislation was irrelevant to their needs and at the same time foretold the demise of the American way of life if legislation were in the hands of a predominantly working-class electorate.[35]

This approach also provides a larger perspective from which to view both Antis and suffragists. Seen against the backdrop of social conservatism, broad areas of agreement between the two begin to emerge, and the differences that

211

remain are sharpened. For example, very few suffragists were actually radicals. As Kraditor indicates, most simply wanted to participate more fully in affairs of government, the basic structure of which they accepted.[36] On the other hand, Antis and suffragists diverged considerably in their conception of the role of women in public life.

Both accepted the cult of domesticity and the doctrine of inherent sexual differences in temperament and talents. Even their attitude toward undesirables was shaped by a class bias that saw the uneducated, the indigent, and the immigrant as a threat. The only difference here was the suffragists' insistence that enfranchisement of women would increase the preponderance of fit voters,[37] while the Antis maintained that woman suffrage would hand the reins of government over to the unfit.

Both Antis and suffragists had benefited from advances in women's rights such as higher education, access to the professions, and control over their property; therefore, there was hardly any difference between them regarding the desirability of women's rights—in all areas that is, except the vote. But, according to Kraditor, the significance of the latter for the feminists was that it represented *autonomy*, the desire to be recognized in economic, political, and social realms as individuals in their own right. It was this, rather than a redefinition of woman's proper sphere, that loomed as the feminist objective and served to differentiate feminists and suffragists from Antis.

> Such a recognition could be consistent with a distinction between men's and women's "spheres," even with a continued subordination of the feminine "sphere," as well as with a merging of men's and women's "spheres." The essential change demanded has always been that women's "sphere" must be defined by women. The questions have always been: What is women's proper sphere? and even more, Who should decide what that sphere is?[38]

The Antis, like Memmi's colonized, were quite willing to allow men to define that sphere for them.

Kraditor is not alone in emphasizing the peculiar ambiguities surrounding women in this country. William O'Neill has also pointed out that by the end of the nineteenth century there was little difference between feminists and Antis, due to the conservatism that came to characterize the woman's movement during its later phase. This conservatism, he believed, can be traced to the involvement of radical feminist Victoria Woodhull in the scandalous Beecher-Tilton affair, as a consequence of which many women were affirmed in their conviction that suffrage politics and radical speculations, particularly involving marriage and the family, did not mix.[39]

Furthermore, according to O'Neill, feminism as a product of the Victorian age became increasingly conservative, consonant with the general tightening of morals and manners, the acceptance of Victorian stereotypes, and the rejection of radical ideas about the condition of women. Consequently, the woman's movement tended to emphasize the most conservative aspects of the suffrage question. In other words, by the last quarter of the century, feminism had lost enough of its radical impulse to become respectable. It no longer challenged the traditional orthodoxies concerning woman's place and even began to insist that maternity operated as a "unifying force" and "enabling principle" that made the entrance of women into public life imperative. Feminists fully accepted the Victorian mystique that woman's unique power was rooted in the mystery of her life-giving capacities. Thus, although winning the vote was ostensibly a feminist victory, "it had not been won for feminist reasons."[40] In O'Neill's view the suffragists had merely persuaded the organized middle-class women who had become a potent force for reform that they needed the vote to secure the broader domestic life that was their objective.

Once most feminists had succumbed to the "domestic mythology," however, it became increasingly difficult to tell them apart from the Antis.[41] Even woman's social justice activities were viewed as a logical extension of her mothering role. The fact of the matter was that these social justice activities occupied the Antis to the same extent as the feminists. But Antis and suffragists were "social feminists"—urban upper- and middle-class women whose social worlds often overlapped through their activities as clubwomen. Thus, in addition to the fact that these social justice activities became the principal justification for feminism, most of the organization Antis were also clubwomen (see Biographical Appendix).

Perhaps one of the most challenging aspects of this approach is that as the differences between Antis and suffragists become increasingly obscured, the old definitions no longer hold. It is no longer accurate to define the Antis simply as women who were opposed to suffragism or feminism. Now one has to take into account the fact that often both Antis and suffragists shared a similar worldview and possibly even a similar experience. In many cases it was only their solutions that differed. Furthermore, this approach enables one to view both suffragism and antisuffragism simply as variations of a new and growing trend toward activism among women. Looked at this way, Antis and suffragists had more in common with each other than with the aggregate of women in general. In any event, it becomes necessary to delineate more flexible denominators in dealing with women's behavior in groups than simply saying that some were pro and some were anti; this must be done so that the commonality of shared experience is not obscured by the differences that divided them.

> Women have been the only subordinated group that has belonged to the same families as its rulers. The ambiguous status of well-to-do women, as both ruler and ruled, generated contradictions and ambiguities in both feminists' and antifeminists' attitudes toward women.[42]

As the differences between Anti and suffragist become blurred, it also becomes increasingly difficult to categorize the Antis. The Antis felt that their ideological position differed profoundly from that of the suffragists, yet they hedged when it came to calling themselves true conservatives. The Antis maintained they were devoted to "progressive conservatism." In one of their publications they referred to a cartoon that had appeared in *Punch*, showing President McKinley holding back the wild and screaming flight of the "Bird of Freedom." In their view this described the antisuffrage attitude toward the suffragists.

> To us the demand for suffrage seems, like the demand for war, sure to plunge the country into new danger, and very far from sure to bring it new blessings. . . . It is all the more important that we should show ourselves actively interested in everything that promotes a real progress. Do not let us leave to our opponents the forward movements in patriotism, in education, in temperance, in philanthropy, in social questions. A true conservative should be in the front rank of progress; for only by growth can we preserve the healthy life of the community. Whenever it is possible let us work with the Suffragists, side by side, so that they may understand that it is not progress we are opposing, but its opposite, and seeing us as ardent as themselves for advancement, they may perhaps ask if theirs is the only forward path.[43]

The Antis did in fact share characteristics in common with both the Progressives and with those whom O'Neill calls the "moral conservatives." With the Progressives they believed in the efficacy of an enlightened public opinion created through education and nurture. Unlike them, however, the Antis had less faith in the perfectibility of the system or of the individuals who kept it in operation. They feared the effects of unrestrained individualism, believing that the "evils of society" resulted from the "evil in individuals."[44] Whereas they seemed to assume an ideal of moral perfection, they were suspicious of the moral absolutist who believed that the perfectibility of man was possible, once the appropriate solutions had been found. The liberal, in contrast, was one for whom the view of the ideal was incidental to his or her belief in the perfectibility of the individual.

Perhaps the best illustration of the Antis as moral conservatives is the similarity of their position to those who were opposed to divorce reform. Apparently the conservatives on the divorce issue were as vehement in their denunciation of the feminists as were the Antis. According to O'Neill the critics of divorce were almost all antifeminists, whereas its defenders "invariably sympathized with the woman movement." "Nothing," says O'Neill, "was fraught with more confusion or invested with greater importance than the role—actual and ideal—of woman in this process."[45] Given the prevalent belief that women were uniquely responsible for the family and that they therefore bore a special responsibility for its failure, it was no wonder that the Antis attacked women for not doing their job and that the divorce critics blamed them for the increase in divorce.

In O'Neill's view, the divorce controversy was *not* waged between two sets of groups with contradictory "status anxieties," since most of the protagonists on both sides belonged to the same social group. The real conflict was

> between those who wished to maintain the traditional family structure and those who supported the newer, more egalitarian family . . . between those who argued that the needs of society took precedence over those of the individual, and those who believed the reverse. The traditional conservative insistence on order was set against the historic liberal appeal for freedom.[46]

Evidently divorce was another issue that involved an apparent conflict between the public welfare and individual rights.

According to O'Neill, the fundamental conviction that informed almost every attack on divorce

> was the belief that the family was the foundation of society . . . and that divorce destroyed the family as an institution and consequently threatened the existence of that larger entity of which it was the basic unit.[47]

The Antis shared with the divorce conservatives the belief that more was at issue than mere principle. The arguments of both groups indicated that they genuinely believed that their existence was at stake. For example, both Antis and divorce critics spoke of race suicide and the threat of Mormonism to modern civilization.[48] Furthermore, some of the same individuals—Margaret C. Robinson, Felix Adler, and Lyman Abbott—supplied the rhetoric for both Antis and divorce critics.

The real enemy for both groups, however, were the radical "isms" that they believed were threatening to engulf the nation. For the divorce critics these were particularly individualism, socialism, and feminism. The conservatives, says O'Neill, saw individualism and socialism as complementary, if not identical, impulses. Moral conservatives regarded themselves as guardians of communal values threatened by the new emphasis on the individual as against the family and the community. Thus, in their eyes the emancipated woman was the embodiment of "false democratic ideals" that created an imperfect sense of social responsibility. Rousseau was the arch villain who had propagated these ideals at the expense of the social order.[49]

Apparently, moral conservatives believed that radical writings were actually a cause of the rising divorce rate.[50] For the Antis, the radical writings were allied with suffragism but were not as clearly viewed as a cause by themselves. In fact, the Antis spent very little time trying to analyze the factors that promoted suffragism. In both cases, however, the association of the radical movements with the enemy—in the one with the proponents of divorce and in the other with the suffragists—tended to have both a negative and positive effect. On the one hand, it galvanized conservative resistance by creating the impression that these radical elements were plotting the destruction of marriage and the family. It also embarrassed the moderates (divorce proponents and suffragists) who continually had to dissociate themselves from the extremists. On the other hand, it made divorce reform (as distinct from the movement to do away with marriage altogether) and suffragism seem mild responses compared to the more radical solutions proposed by the extremists.[51]

Helen K. Johnson integrated both strands—the position taken against divorce reform and that taken against woman suffrage—in her condemnation of the suffragists for their stand on divorce. One of the earliest demands made by the suffrage association, she said, was for a law allowing divorce for drunkenness, soon followed by demands for divorce for other causes. She believed that when suffragists urged the passage of bills seeking divorce for drunkenness, this was but an "entering wedge for the radical divorce measures that have been advocated in Suffrage conventions. This matter of easier divorce has been pressed steadily from the beginning, but with very little of the result that the Suffragists desired."[52]

For O'Neill, moral conservatives were "typically American" in that they "instinctively looked for legal solutions to their problems." Yet it is one of the inconsistencies in both the moral conservatives and the Antis that they maintained that legislation alone could not create change because one could not legislate morality, and at the same time they looked for legal solutions to their problems. Thus moral conservatives argued against federal divorce legislation because "legislation can promote morality only when it is in harmony with a substantially unanimous public opinion—which would perhaps be as effective without legislation as with it."[53] And the Antis, faced with the suffragists' contention that women would uplift public life by voting for "good" laws, argued that morality could not be legislated. Yet both Antis and divorce critics were willing to resort to legal solutions when it served their purposes—either to obtain uniform divorce laws or to indicate, by the numerous laws that had been enacted on her behalf, woman's advance without the ballot. "The real test of the working of woman suffrage," said Johnson, "is to be found in the answer to the question whether better laws have been framed as a consequence."[54]

The Dialectical Approach

From a purely philosophical perspective it may be difficult to imagine antisuffragism as the working out of the synthetic phase in a system of Hegelian dialectics. Nevertheless, this paradigm is indeed relevant. During the second half of the nineteenth century, numerous changes were taking place in women's status and role that made women more conspicuous than they had ever been. They were achieving advances on many levels, entering new trades, receiving professional education, undertaking philanthropic work, creating the social service professions, and writing profusely. There was also a growing number of single women who were no longer able to be absorbed in the domestic industries and homes of relatives and who had no alternative but to become self-supporting. In consequence, as the century wore on, women were no longer conforming to type. "In this way," says Viola Klein, "women became a problem for philosophers, psychologists and sociologists."[55]

Although this period of rapid transformation may have introduced the "woman problem" as a subject for serious study, it also witnessed the tendency to crystallize the myths surrounding woman's identity, as if to preserve them from change. The need to "define" woman probably owed less to a sentimental reverence for the past than to a genuine anxiety about the changes taking place in the present. At any rate, women were living in a world of two contradictory social ideals—the ideal of full expression of human potentialities, and that of the stereotypically true woman.

In Hegelian terms, the solidification of the myth of true womanhood at the very time that changes were altering woman's traditional role may be said to represent the thesis and antithesis. Antisuffragism was the reunification principle, the synthesis that resulted from the interaction of the former.

The work of both Aileen Kraditor and Viola Klein offers clues to the dynamics that were involved in creating this synthesis. For Kraditor, the rise of the suffrage movement challenged the Antis to formulate the traditional assumptions of woman's place. These, in turn, defined the context in which suffragists pleaded their cause. The antisuffrage ideology that crystallized in reaction to the threat of feminism was not an end in itself, but went on to define the context within which the suffragist ideas developed. Kraditor believes it posed problems that suffragists had to solve and asked questions they had to answer, and that in response to the suffrage assault on traditional ideas and institutions, the Antis made those ideas explicit and rationalized the institutions.[56]

It is also possible that antisuffrage activity was generated by the need of many women to reinforce the distinctions between themselves and the "new women." The latter, more a creature of the times than of feminism per se, was nevertheless popularly regarded as an offspring of the movement. Beneath the dire mutterings of the Antis always lurked the spectral presence of the "new woman."

Even more limiting, according to Viola Klein, was that as "a child of the Victorian era, it [feminism] presented woman as a sort of sexless creature, as a mere abstraction without flesh and blood."[57] It is no wonder that many women were unable to relate to a model that was cold and unfamiliar and, in consequence, rejected the feminist ideal of womanhood. By contrast, the antisuffragists were fleshed out according to the only models then available and justifiably strove to do all in their power to thwart the sinister influence of the "new woman."

The idea that woman suffrage would turn women into "female men" was so widely taken for granted that even in the twentieth century it continued to be a regular features of the antifeminist arsenal. In *The Nature of Woman*, J.

Lionel Tayler, a London University extension and tutorial lecturer on biology and society, viewed the woman suffrage campaign as an effort on the part of women to give women status that would fit in with their conception of a woman as a "female man." Tayler, however, took issue with the suffragist contention that if woman had not been kept in subjection she would have been able to be a real female male. In his view, man had done all the truly creative things since the beginning of the world and should not bear the blame for shutting woman out, since "Genius makes its own opportunity." Woman, he felt, has shown no inclination toward creative works, although in her own way she has given a magnificent account of herself and therefore should remain unchanged. The world did not need a female man, but did need a "womanly woman."[58]

It was difficult for most women to accept the feminist critique of marriage at a time when marriage was not only the most common career for women but still the major way for women to achieve a sense of social usefulness. To the feminist, who had the same needs as most women, the idea of developing herself as a commodity in order to secure the benefits of marriage was a degradation not only of marriage but of herself as well. Since love and marriage were the main concern of women, it was natural that their revolt contained expressions of protest against the humiliation of having to barter their love for income and social status. But it is also understandable that many women found it psychologically impossible to accept an analysis of their situation that demanded that they accept responsibility for complicity in undertaking a demeaning relationship. To accept the feminist analysis meant acquiescing in the notion that marriage served other than the sublime purpose for which it was supposedly intended.

The fact that the advocates of free divorce were allied to the feminists was another reason for the Antis to reject the feminist analysis of marriage. One of the major free divorce arguments was that it would liberate women from sex. Apparently these people believed that carnal passions were inherited characteristics and therefore laws that forced women to remain married to lustful men and bear them children "passed on the taint to each new generation." Liberal divorce laws alone could stop the production of these "children of lust."[59] This belief coincided with the feminist view of marriage, particularly as explicated by Charlotte Perkins Gilman. She regarded marriage as an exchange of sex capital for security, a situation that exaggerated sexuality and created an impure and commercial relationship.

The antisuffrage movement seen from this perspective was a reaction against a whole "new feminine type."[60] This new type was distinct from the prevailing Victorian ideal of the submissive and "respectable" wife whose activities were limited to *kinder*, *küche*, and *kirche*. It was a reaction against the rejection of mother-women as the ideal.

> These were women who idolized their children, worshipped their husbands, and esteemed it a holy privilege to efface themselves as individuals and grow wings as ministering angels.[61]

Christopher Lasch does not mention the Antis in his study of the new radicalism in America, but his analysis of feminism inadvertently provides an illustration of the dialectical process at work. Lasch feels that American feminism is preoccupied with the question of sexual identity—not simply with what roles women and men ought to play, but of the respective nature of the sexes, what it means to be feminine or masculine.

> The intensity of the speculation about these questions discloses anxieties which lie much deeper than anything associated with the greater leisure of the modern woman or the flight of housework from the home.

Thus, for example, he sees Jane Addams, left after surgery unable to bear children, confronted with the dilemma of her *femininity*.

> Cut off now from a whole range of feminine experience, she must have begun to wonder whether she was not in danger of losing touch with her femininity altogether. A woman bent on a man's career, committed to her father's unyielding masculine example, she now ran the risk of finding herself altogether unsexed.

To Lasch, she was "in danger of losing contact with one whole side of her nature."[62]

In a world in which a "double standard of experience" prevailed, the thinking woman faced a cruel dilemma: to adhere to the prevailing model of femininity that was all but bankrupt, offering her only a secondhand world, where woman's life was but a rough translation of the real thing; or accommodating to the man-world of face-to-face encounter with life.

The lowest common denominator of the feminist revolt was simply a revulsion, formed early in life, against the sheer silliness of the life which a girl was expected to lead and which most girls apparently did lead.[63]

Women had paid an extravagant price for their emancipation, having lost touch with the active, immediate emotional lives led by their grandmothers and great-grandmothers. For many, therefore, a "masculine" career offered the only way of being true to themselves. And, to Lasch, this explains the paradox that being a "true woman" forced one to lead a man's life. What Lasch overlooks is that for many women being a "true woman" forced them into antisuffragism.

Lasch does not underestimate the conflict that would ensue if women to be true to themselves were to lead a man's life. He realized a "true woman" could not lead a man's life with impunity. For Jane Addams, it took its psychic toll in a suspicion that obsessed the feminist imagination: "in pursuing a masculine ideal she had betrayed her own femininity." For Inez Haynes Gillmore, a feminist and career woman, it resulted in a sense of alienation:

I hang in a void, midway between two spheres—the man's sphere and the woman's sphere. A professional career . . . puts me beyond the reach of the average woman's duties and pleasures. The conventional limitations of the female lot put me beyond the reach of the average man's duties and pleasures.[64]

Whether or not the majority of women experienced the sensation of hanging in the void, many women could not help but be aware of the alternatives they faced and of their limitations. Feminism, even though it seemed to open up a new dimension, failed to provide a third alternative because it was simply a new way of reaffirming the male world. Even Lasch admits that although the feminists emphasized the creation of a new "human sex," they were really not interested in the act of personal relations. "They were more interested in asserting their right to enjoy the privileges formerly monopolized by man." Antisuffragism was the reaffirmation of a female world, the beginning of consciousness that women had a culture all their own.

The Sociological Approach

Antisuffragism was by and large a creature of its culture. Not a major force in itself, it was swept along by various other currents that not only helped to

221

shape it but also began to merge with it, thus bringing it into the mainstream of American social history. The points at which the antisuffrage movement intersected with larger social trends were as follows: the Antis were the auxiliaries of numerous conservative social forces;[65] they were members of the old aristocracy that was suffering the pangs of status displacement;[66] they were involved in what has been called a general revolt against men;[67] and they were symptomatic of the middle-class woman's drive to activism.[68]

The view of the Antis as the ladies' auxiliary of special interest groups owes its plausibility to historians who have tended to view the opposition as consisting primarily of liquor interests and politicos.

> The party bosses, the liquor and brewing interests, the uneducated, the foreign-born, apathetic and indifferent women, and men habituated to superior status coalesced into one enormous hostile "they."

Grimes fails to include women who were actively and overtly *hostile* to woman suffrage. In fact, he overlooks the Antis altogether. Consequently, he tends to view the issue of woman suffrage as a conflict over social values in the community, affected less by class differences than by differences in styles of life or modes of existence.

> On the one side was the older, conservative, rural, essentially Protestant and Puritan way of life which the native-born liked to think of as typically American; on the other side was the new or "faster" style of life that accompanied late nineteenth century urbanization, and was ostentatious, crude but sophisticated, and enthusiastically wet.[69]

The former, says Grimes, was nourished by farms, small towns, and the traditional way of life; the latter, by mining, factories, immigrant labor, and new modes of wealth. By making the difference one of "social values," however, his categorization does not apply to the Antis. Even though their values were synonymous with those who favored the traditional way of life, their economic status often derived from new modes of wealth (see Biographical Appendix). The Antis, therefore, bridged both groups. Furthermore, if the difference between Anti and suffragist were simply one of social value, then it would not be difficult to explain the fact that both groups felt themselves threatened by identical forces. In 1885, the Reverend Josiah Strong, a supporter of woman suffrage, wrote in *Our Country* that the evils facing the country could be summed up under the headings Romanism,

Mormonism, Immigration, Socialism, Urbanization, and Intemperance.[70] There were few Antis who would not have agreed.

By 1915, however, one could begin to discern two distinct camps facing each other over the issue of woman suffrage. Both sides retained a nucleus of native American middle-class women, but their allies served to differentiate them. On the side of the feminists were the prohibitionists, trade unionists, social reformers, and socialists. Allied with the Antis were certain large manufacturers and industrialists, railroads and oil interests, and of course the liquor lobby.

According to Grimes, the woman suffrage movement was really a Puritan crusade dedicated to the proposition that American politics was in need of uplifting and that women were singularly well equipped to do the job. Those who most felt this need were the professional middle-class losers in the status revolution—the lawyers, Protestant clergy, university professors, and teachers.[71]

Basically Grimes's thesis is that woman suffrage in the four western states where it was first adopted was never really treated as an isolated issue or decided on its own merits. It was used as a way to gain various other ends. Woman suffrage was the "ethic of this Puritan, middle-class, native, American, feminine reformation" and part of the larger goal of purifying American politics by restoring political power to people and taking it out of the hands of the corrupt.[72] Similarly, the reverse may help to explain its failures in the East. That is, resistance to woman suffrage was often based on the assumption that to delay it would prove beneficial to other causes. Here again this leads right into the ideological camp of the Antis. The only difference this time is that one emerges with a view of antisuffragism as a means rather than as an end. Thus the Antis would appear to be the handmaidens of business groups who feared an alliance between suffragists and reformers, of textile interests who feared that woman suffrage would result in minimum wage legislation, of the liquor interests who feared that an enfranchised woman would usher in prohibition, and of the southern states' rightists who feared that a federal amendment would close all of the loopholes they had worked out to enable them to avoid implementing the Fourteenth and Fifteenth amendments. Looked at this way, the struggle over woman suffrage becomes a battle of the giants, a struggle of *men* for status and power, with the role of the suffragists and the Antis reduced to that of a ladies' auxiliary.

According to Gerda Lerner, these misgivings also motivated the opposition of politicians, party machines, and entrenched hierarchies on every level of government, who feared that " 'the hand that rocks the cradle' might, given suffrage, also rock the boat." All the opponents of woman suffrage had one thing in common—they were conservative in their social outlook. Lerner does not regard the female antisuffragists as a force in and of themselves. She tends instead to relegate them to an auxiliary status.

> The effectiveness of the "antis" is debatable, but they did give legislators added arguments for delaying discussion of or decision on the issue.

In fact, her view of the opposition on the whole is that it served only to delay the advent of woman suffrage by several decades; it could not block the changes transforming American society and with it American women. These changes, in turn, made enactment of woman suffrage inevitable. In effect, Lerner tends to diminish the importance of both the suffrage and the antisuffrage movements. She feels that suffrage was forced to be subordinated to other issues that were taking priority in the public mind.

> Women, as well as men, were more absorbed with the great changes wrought in their society by industrialization, and with taking advantage of technological innovations and educational opportunities. These proved to be of more lasting significance in changing the status of women than the organized movement for suffrage.[73]

Eleanor Flexner is also of the opinion that the female antisuffragists played only a peripheral role. She believes that the major opposition to woman suffrage consisted largely of those who regarded suffrage as a threat to their vested interests. Flexner tends to discount the impact of conservative opinion, distaste for women in new social roles, and feelings concerning the sanctity of motherhood or the sacredness of the home. She does not, however, underestimate the total impact of the organized opposition to women as voters, which she regards as highly organized and articulate, becoming "increasingly intemperate as woman suffrage spread slowly from one state to another."[74] By comparison, protests against women in education or professional work were guerrillalike.

Behind the antisuffrage organization, the witnesses at legislative and congressional hearings, the newspaper articles and advertisements, Flexner detects a sinister and well-organized influence that paid the bills and bought the referendum votes and the immigrant and saloon votes in various cities. But she also adopts the suffragists' point of view that the Antis were barely effective on their own, serving mainly as a front for more potent forces, particularly the liquor interests.[75]

The reason, according to Flexner, that the corporate interests such as railroads, oil companies, and other manufacturers opposed giving women the vote was their resistance to any changes that appeared to threaten their vested interests. These same forces bitterly resisted as "communistic" the Sixteenth Amendment in 1913, which authorized the federal income tax, the Seventeenth Amendment of the same year, which provided for the popular election of United States senators, as well as other elements of the "New Freedom" such as the Federal Reserve banking system, Tariff Commission, and the Federal Trade Commission, the new antitrust legislation and the movement for initiative and referendum.

> In such circumstances, addition of a large body of new voters, control of which appears uncertain and many of whose leaders were vocal in the cause of further reform, presented a fresh menace. What might not such an infusion into the body politic do to the enormous advantage concealed in grants to railroads, franchises of various kinds, and rate schedules?[76]

There was also a strong feeling in some industries that women would use the vote to improve the conditions of working women, says Flexner, citing the legislative records of some states where women had been enfranchised for a number of years. Flexner again depends too heavily on the suffragist interpretation of events, for the franchise for women could benefit women only if they voted as a sex. As the Antis pointed out, class interests were bound to offset sex interests.

James Kenneally, in his mammoth and painstaking study of the antisuffrage movement in Massachusetts, feels that in that state antisuffragism was part of the conservatism and mistrust of the democratic experiment that developed in reaction to the far-reaching changes that accompanied the Civil War. He detects in certain Brahmin families an almost hereditary attitude of profound opposition to any extension of the democratic process. Opposed to the participation of the masses in the government, they naturally resisted the extension of the ballot to the unenfranchised. In Kenneally's view, the tenacity with which the Brahmins clung to this position was increased by their insecurity as they saw political power passing into the hands of immigrants and Catholics.[77]

Thus, their position derived from fear that a social, political, and even religious revolution would be engineered by the immigrant classes through the medium of woman suffrage, a theme that underlies many antisuffrage arguments. In fact, Kenneally points out, Mrs. Charles Eliot Guild, as president of MAOFESW, testified before the Massachusetts legislature in 1898 that fear of the immigrant vote led to the establishment of her organization.[78]

Although Kenneally meticulously cites all of the many women in Massachusetts who were active in writing and remonstrating against suffrage, as well as describes the vast network and efficacy of their organization, he does not view antisuffragism as a women's movement. For him the Antis were simply the spokeswomen of their own particular class interests, a militant and effective arm of the Brahmin counterrevolution.[79]

Helen Papashvily maintains that all women throughout this period were in revolt against men. The difference between active feminists and other women was that feminists brought their revolt into the open. That very few women would go to such lengths to achieve their ends was evidenced by the fact that at the peak of the suffrage movement they had the active support of less than 10 percent of the women in the United States. Nevertheless, insists Papashvily, *all* women were involved in revolt against men, in a "devious, subtle, undeclared war." All women had endured and resented masculine domination, and it was this sense of a common cause that underlay the actions of all women throughout the century.

> The smaller differences in religion, color, nationality, age, class, culture pattern were forgotten—all women—all enchanted—all enchained. How to be free, that was now the question.[80]

Of course, this does not explain why so many women, despite their common grievances, regarded the principal leaders and events of Seneca Falls with so much distrust. What it does suggest, however, is that the antisuffrage emphasis on extolling womanhood for all the ways it was so different from and "superior" to maleness may have been just a disguised version of the revolt against man.

> The common woman was always glorified, her every thought, action, gesture, chance word fraught with esoteric meaning and far-reaching influence; her daily routine . . . imbued with dramatic significance; her petty trials and small joys magnified to heroic proportions.[81]

The sentimentality of the day, says Papashvily, merely served to cloak the horror, revolt, and determination to destroy the common enemy—man. And thus in fiction by women authors man appears either as invalid, corrupt, unregenerate, or a failure, but never whole.

According to Papashvily, women even rejected the philosophy and possibility of compromise. They regarded the days of yielding and submission as over. The women who read novels did not want their faults discussed or their behavior corrected.

> Equality might have satisfied that vociferous minority agitating far and wide for women's rights but the quiet, sweetly smiling ladies at home sought, though perhaps unconsciously, another goal—complete domination.[82]

If the women Papashvily writes about who read and wrote the novels popular throughout this period were representative, it would seem to indicate that the antisuffrage conception of womanhood was but a variation, although a subtle one at that, of the revolt against men.

The drive to activism among American women can probably be traced back to the beginnings of the nineteenth century. According to Jill Conway, however, it took on a new meaning for women born between 1880 and 1920. These women, college educated and in some cases professionally trained, were less isolated than their predecessors from the mainstream of American life. Nevertheless, they were faced with a serious problem. They had inherited from their forebears a strong sense of mission, which was reinforced by the dominant philosophy of the day that the value of knowledge lay in its social utility. Unfortunately, they were faced with limited or nonexistent avenues for using their acquired talents. As a result, these educated middle-class women experienced a sharp sense of unreality and frustration.

> Education was a positive aid in raising the race and it was to be assessed by the degree to which it allowed the recipient to participate in the struggle for survival. This utilitarian notion of the education they had received added to the burden of guilt of post-Civil War American women. Every powerful force in their culture urged that they should pursue active and socially beneficial careers, yet their society provided no such outlet.

This sense of guilt was probably exacerbated by the fact that the average middle-class woman found herself with an abundance of leisure and considerable wealth in a world where the dominant values were those of "frontier activism" and the "Puritan ethic."

Wealth and leisure for the urban middle class raised anguishing problems for women unused to seeking public roles, and unable because of America's predominantly frontier culture to conceive of nonactivist roles for women. A Puritan ethic made leisure for these unhappy ladies an object of restless guilt; *hence the frenetic and pathetic search of urban leisured women for release from their privileged inutility.* Spencer was a torment to them. Reality lay in participation as an individual unit in the struggle for survival.

Although Conway's focus here is on explaining the drive of women such as Jane Addams to explore new avenues for the expression of women's sense of mission and urge to activism, it also helps to explain the antisuffrage movement. The Antis were not exempt from the pressures besetting the urban middle-class woman. If anything, the Antis typify the wealthy leisured woman to an even greater extent than most women. As Conway points out, the problem of wealth in a democratic society has particular implications for women. "For women it was *unearned* wealth and carried with it guilt and feelings of obligation to society which must be reconciled."[83] In one sense the Antis saw the opportunity to justify their existence and fulfill their obligation to society by elevating to a code of conduct and making as an end in itself the creation and nurture of future citizens.

What both Antis and suffragists failed to realize was that women in the late nineteenth century had two legitimate alternatives. Faced with a rejection of the image of the functionless woman, women activists should have been able to choose either the feminists' model of full equality or the Antis' upgrading of the traditional role of woman. However, the choices were not clear-cut, nor were they presented as alternatives by any of the major political parties. Thus it was easy for the suffragists to assume they had a monopoly on the true emancipatory process for women. The Antis, as fully active as the suffragists, were unwilling to accept the feminist goal; instead, out of their own needs and anxieties they felt that an alternative existed for women who were dissatisfied with the only model that had hitherto been presented. Consequently, the Antis had less invested in the status anxieties or social roles of men and were more immune to the feelings of alienation or displacement that may have threatened the suffragists. The suffragists, identifying with the male culture and with male representatives of their class whose social values were being threatened, faced the prospect of a relative decline in political status at a time when the status of women was rising (and becoming more comparable to man's) in other fields. Therefore, for the suffragists, the withholding of political rights was an even greater injustice than it had been under previous conditions.

The Antis believed they were in the mainstream of the women's movement. They were unwilling to consider themselves as either throwbacks or as members of a fringe group and resented the implication that the suffragists were the self-styled protectors of womanhood. In fact, the Antis considered themselves "the defenders of the true progress and advancement of women."[84] Furthermore, they did not feel that they were alienated from the main currents of American history. If anything, the Antis believed they were direct continuators of the social traditions and political philosophy espoused by the country's founders.

> Why is this agitation in favor of Suffrage called pre-eminently the woman movement, as though advocated by all women and supported unanimously by them? Why should not the movement, slow, perhaps, of growth, but supported by some of the largest and most important States of the Union, which opposes the thrusting of political duties and responsibilities upon women without their demand or consent, be likewise recognized as a woman movement?
> . . . we affirm that if any movement should practically be known as the woman movement, it is that affirmative one which upholds woman as the origin and moral savior of the race.[85]

As activists, both Antis and suffragists shared a deep concern for the well-being of society. The Antis, however, were willing to make it their supreme goal, while the suffragists, without disputing it, tended to emphasize the well-being of the individuals (including women) who made up the larger society and believed that only with full legal equality would women be able to make their contribution as individuals. For the Antis, however, the two were mutually exclusive, since they believed that to give woman full equality would deprive the social order of woman's traditional services; equality meant making women less like women and more like men.

It is impossible to determine whether the vast majority of American womanhood was more in sympathy with the Antis or the suffragists. It would seem, however, that part of the reason for the Antis' success in delaying the enactment of woman suffrage was that their position reflected the feelings of a large segment of the public, and particularly the female segment. As activists, however, the Antis were closer to the suffragists than to the majority of women who, consonant with the Antis' basic philosophy, eschewed all forms of public life while they concentrated on woman's true role. It was inevitable, however, in a culture in which the values were predominantly male, that the antisuffrage ideal of a womanhood true to itself would in the end fail.

229

Epilogue

In November 1920, twenty-six million women were eligible to vote in the presidential election, and the number has grown steadily. But it was not until 1956 that women voted in equal numbers with men in national elections.[1] That at first only a small proportion of women were willing to avail themselves of the ballot is not surprising in view of the basic conservatism of most women. The suffragists, after all, were only a handful of activists in relation to the total female population. But the question most germane to this study is what became of the women who worked so long and so hard to prevent the enfranchisement of their sex. Without actual figures of their voting behavior, one can only speculate. It seems likely that the Antis availed themselves of the ballot, if for no other reason than self-defense.[2] Having operated on the assumption that woman suffrage would bring in its wake all the evil effects of widescale democratization, the Antis must have felt the need of doubling their husband's vote in order to preserve their own social and class interests against the threat posed by the enfranchised masses.

For some women who had responded to antisuffragism because it provided a refuge against the more liberal movements of the day, passage of the Nineteenth Amendment marked only the beginning of a new surge of activity. Through *The Woman Patriot*, which continued to be published throughout the 1920s, many former Antis sustained a campaign against both individual feminists and women's groups associated with the peace movement and the labor movement. Significantly, *The Woman Patriot* continued to indicate in its masthead that it was "against Feminism and Socialism."

The Daughters of the American Revolution, which had metamorphosed into a superpatriotic and right-wing organization,[3] also provided an outlet for former Antis interested in red-baiting feminists. One pamphlet distributed by the DAR decried the "six objectives of Communism, Bolshevism, Socialism, Liberalism and Ultra Pacifism" as the abolition of government, patriotism, property rights, inheritance, religion, and family relations.[4] In the view of its authors, the world revolutionary movement operated through more than 200 different organizations, one of which was the Women's International League for Peace and Freedom (formerly the Woman's Peace Party). According to Catt, who continued to feel called upon throughout this period to vindicate the activities of her cohorts, the DAR was also responsible for circulating a pamphlet read into the Senate record by a Senator Bayard on July 3, 1926. Purporting to be in opposition to the Maternity Act, it was instead an attack on the patriotism and honor of individual women and women's organizations and was signed by the "seven directors of the Woman Patriot publishers, all formerly known in the anti-suffrage campaign."[5]

With all the advantage afforded by hindsight, it is easy to see that passage of the Nineteenth Amendment caused neither the millennium anticipated by the suffragists nor the holocaust predicted by the Antis. Nevertheless, throughout the 1920s, individuals prominent in both movements were frequently asked how they viewed the effects of woman suffrage.

After only four years of woman suffrage, Ida Tarbell wrote an article entitled "Is Woman Suffrage a Failure?" In stark contrast to those Antis who continued to voice their abhorrence of feminism and their categorical denunciation of woman suffrage through such vehicles as *The Woman Patriot* and the DAR, Tarbell maintained a characteristically open mind. In her view, many individuals who formerly believed in suffrage were despairing that the world was no better, while many of the women who opposed suffrage were delighting in the fact that suffragist expectations of social betterment were largely unfulfilled. In either case, she felt, this pessimistic approach provided a welcome excuse for women who claimed that they were disinterested or too busy with their personal affairs to take time to vote. For Tarbell, it was the business of every woman to vote as wisely and unselfishly as possible, "if only to counteract the mass of feminine unintelligence and selfishness certain to be mobilized by the always active forces of self-interest."[6]

As to whether woman suffrage was indeed a failure, Tarbell cautioned her readers not to conclude that it was a total failure just because it did not prove itself the miracle worker its advocates thought it would be.

As one who has ever been lukewarm toward suffrage and who regarded the argument that quick and drastic remedial results were sure to come from it as mischievous and dishonest, I want to say that I believe something has happened—something rather more in the time than I at least thought probable—and that something is spreading.

Tarbell's judgment was based on direct observations of what women were doing in public affairs, made during three months of travel throughout the country. The first question she sought to answer was whether women's interest in public matters was more general and natural than before suffrage.

> Everywhere the women I met as individuals and as groups—many of them formerly anti-suffragist—invariably soon turned the conversation to law enforcement, the oil scandal, the regulation of industry, the League of Nations, Coolidge, Smith, McAdoo, and there was always more or less appeal to principle—quite as much as in a similar group of men—and less acrimony—which surprised me.[7]

Though not denying that in every community there had always been informed women who were interested in political affairs, Tarbell felt that there were more of them now.

In Tarbell's view, women were, if anything, more conservative than men, more addicted to law and order and particularly concerned with the question of the integrity of public officials. Especially heartening was the almost universal conviction among women that the proposed equal rights amendment to the Constitution would have a negative effect on women and children in industry. All of this indicated that many women were manifesting a lively and healthy interest in political affairs. Furthermore, she pointed out that increasing numbers of women were seeking public office.

> They come, as they ought to, naturally, like men, through the automatic working of the machinery opened to them—not because they are women, but because they are human beings.

Tarbell had no patience for the "old-style professional suffrage agitators" who resented the women who unobtrusively entered politics and went about their business rather than use their political position to vindicate their sex. On the whole, Tarbell felt it was still too early to tell whether women legislators would contribute something different from men to public life. Nevertheless, she believed that in certain offices, they were proving themselves superior to men, particularly as guardians of public record.

> They are different, neat, exact. They respect their records, take pride in knowing them and in guarding them—and they banish the spittoon![8]

On the negative side, Tarbell cited the lack of innovation among women. "Generally speaking it is the same old thing—activity in party organization, fine party loyalty, faith in politics, and politics alone." Only rarely did women use their collective voting power to defy the local party machines. The women in local politics who merely rushed from convention to convention were not able to galvanize the voting strength of the women who stayed at home. What was missing was an inspired and meaningful leadership.

Consistent with the views she held throughout her life, Tarbell concluded by reiterating that politics was not the way to salvation. Ultimately regeneration depended on "education, discipline, character, hard thinking, hard labor . . . not in conferences, elections, resolutions, legislation." Tarbell was willing to admit, however, that as a secondary tool, suffrage was still a powerful force.

> Constant exercise of the voting power as intelligently and disinterestedly as we are able, with thoughtful study of the effects, the mistakes made, is a part of a woman's business.

The only real failure in woman suffrage was the failure to exercise it. It was much too early to denounce it, she said, since it takes time to learn to use new tools.

> Political experience must be judged not by decades, but rather by centuries. In fifty years from now we may certainly be able to appraise woman's suffrage fairly—we certainly can not now.[9]

Biographical Appendix

The process of compiling background information on the Antis presents certain challenges. Many women who were active in the antisuffrage movement had little other claim to fame, and as a result often were not included in contemporary biographical accounts of prominent persons. On the other hand, when Antis were included, it was usually by virtue of their social prominence. Therefore, whereas it becomes possible to acquire at least some skeletal data on the leading Antis who were also socially prominent, it is often impossible to do the same for many of the lesser luminaries of the movement. In addition, not many of the leading Antis were given to introspection; therefore, there is very little in the way of autobiographical material such as memoirs, diaries, or letters to work from in helping to form some understanding of the personality or motivation of a particular Anti.

Because most of the spokeswomen of the antisuffrage cause and the officers of the various associations were members of the social elite, the Antis were extremely sensitive to charges that they were unrepresentative of the large body of women. Consequently, it is difficult to trust the accuracy of their descriptions since their propaganda were often devoted to conveying a public image of themselves as representing a cross section of society. The Antis were undoubtedly proud of the fact that many women active in the movement also held public service positions of importance and responsibility; but at the same time they made an effort to demonstrate that their adherents were not "of only one class or type." In "Who the Massachusetts Anti-Suffragists Are" (*Anti-Suffrage Essays by Massachusetts Women*), Mrs. John Balch, president of the Massachusetts Women's Anti-Suffrage Association, wrote:

> An examination of our enrollment reveals among our members not only the very large group of homemakers, but also authors, doctors, lawyers, teachers, librarians, newspaper-writers, stenographers, social service workers, cooks, housemaids, nurses, milliners, insurance agents, restaurant-keepers, clerks, shop-keepers, private secretaries, dressmakers, seamstresses.

Many of our leaders are prominent in public welfare activities. The late Mrs. Charles D. Homans, one of the founders of our organization, was an active and important member of the Massachusetts Prison Commission. Mrs. James M. Codman, our beloved ex-President, has served twenty years on the State Board of Charities, was one of the first women overseers of the poor ever elected in this state, and has long been one of the managers of a large private hospital. Miss Mary S. Ames, a former President, is a member of the Executive Council (New England section) of the National Civic Federation, Chairman of the Committee on Practical Training for Girls, a Trustee of the Boston Home for Incurables, one of the managers of the Women's Free Hospital, a director of the Brook House Home for Working Girls, a member of the Easton Agricultural Vocational Training Committee, a Trustee of Unity Church (Easton), and a member of the Advisory Board of the Belgian Relief Committee. . . .

Antisuffragism seemed to appeal primarily to urban upper-class white women. In Massachusetts, as elsewhere, officers of the association were predominantly Protestant, although by the second decade of the twentieth century some attempt was being made to attract leading Catholic women. In New York, the association's roster contained the names of several socially prominent Jews. Throughout the movement as a whole, Jews, like Catholics, represented a distinct minority. Unlike the Catholics, however, Jews seemed to have much less at stake in the outcome of the suffrage issue. Consequently, one finds little evidence of Jewish pressure groups involving themselves one way or the other in the suffrage struggle.

Antisuffragism made little effort to reach out to women from ethnic or racial minorities. Antisuffrage writings reflect an unmistakable class consciousness and racial bias that left no doubt as to who the Antis believed to be the only women capable of exercising the ballot. Immigrant women and blacks were definitely not considered among the "better" class of women. Furthermore, twenty years of antisuffrage racist propaganda designed to strengthen southern opposition to woman suffrage by inflaming racial passions could not have endeared the Antis to black women. Therefore, it is all the more surprising that a group of black women in Massachusetts actually sought to associate itself with the MAOFESW. By the beginning of 1913, a black women's antisuffrage organization, calling itself the Back Bay Pilgrims, was represented at a Massachusetts legislature hearing. This group eventually expanded into a statewide organization and, although never very active, remained in existence until the Nineteenth Amendment was enacted. The MAOFESW, however, never integrated the Pilgrims' membership lists or catalogs with their own, occasioning continual complaints by their sister organization. Perhaps this was the only way the Antis were able to reconcile their continued propaganda against the black vote in the South with their growing desire to win the adherence of black women in the North.

To illustrate the problem of finding material on the Antis in standard biographical works, it is perhaps noteworthy that no Antis were included in Mary A. Livermore and Frances Willard's *A Woman of the Century* (1893), a compilation of 1,470 biographical sketches; the only Anti mentioned in *The Biographical Cyclopaedia of American Women* (1925), was Alice Hay Wadsworth (Mrs. James W. Wadsworth, Jr.); and even the three-volume *Notable American Women, 1607-1950* (1971) omitted such important Antis as Helen Kendrick Johnson, Alice George, Annie Nathan Meyer, Mrs. James W. Wadsworth, Jr., Mrs. Gilbert E. Jones, and many others.

The biographical dictionary that has proved the most helpful is *Woman's Who's Who of America, 1914-1915*. This is due in part to the fact that the editor chose to include at least a hundred women "solely for their prominence as exponents of either side of the suffrage question." Furthermore, he made it a point to query his respondents as to their position on the suffrage question. Of the 9,644 women included in this work, 4,787 declared themselves in favor of woman suffrage, 773 opposed, and 4,084 either neglected to record their views or indicated they were indifferent. Apparently this latter group included several women who "wrote letters asking that nothing be said about their suffrage views, for personal or business reasons."

In tabulating the results, the editor regarded as prosuffrage those women who either said they were or indicated that they were members of purely suffrage organizations. In other words, he did not include in this category women who were merely members of the Progressive or Prohibition parties. However, he did count those who declared themselves socialists, as well as women who advocated restricted suffrage for both men and women. In determining those who were antisuffrage, he counted respondents who declared themselves against woman suffrage or belonged to antisuffrage organizations, as well as those who proposed to confine woman suffrage to school or municipal questions or to taxpaying women. Interestingly, Ida Tarbell is among the women who chose not to indicate their position on the issue.

In the biographies that follow, every effort has been made to include information supplied by the Antis that reveals something about themselves as individuals. Since this has not always been possible, the descriptions vary considerably in their length and content.

Emily Perkins Bissell (1861-1948), first daughter and second child of a banker and real estate investor, lived most of her life in Wilmington, Delaware. She was an active opponent of woman suffrage, testifying before congressional committees and speaking in various states, often in association with Josephine Marshall Dodge, president of the National Association Opposed to Woman Suffrage. Bissell was active in numerous public welfare activities. Her most influential role was in organizing the Delaware Chapter of the American Red Cross and in initiating the antituberculosis Christmas Seal campaign. She was the first president of the Consumers' League of Delaware (1914) and instrumental in securing passage of Delaware's first child labor law and the state's first maximum-hour law for women in industry. She wrote articles, stories, and poems, usually under the pen name of Priscilla Leonard. Her antisuffrage essay, "A Talk to Women on the Suffrage Question," was published by the New York State Association Opposed to Woman Suffrage in 1909 and circulated widely by the Antis.

Minnie Bronson graduated from Upper Iowa University and in 1892 received a Master of Arts degree. She taught mathematics at St. Paul (Minnesota) High School from 1889 to 1899. In 1900 she served as assistant in the Department of Education of the U.S. Commission to the Paris Exposition. At the Pan-American Exposition of 1901 she was director of the Educational Department, and in 1904 served as superintendent of elementary and secondary education at the St. Louis Exposition. In addition to other positions of this nature, Bronson was appointed special agent of the U.S. Bureau of Labor to investigate the conditions of women and children from 1907 to 1909. From March to July 1909, she served as special agent for the Department of the Interior at the Alaska Exhibit of the Seattle Exposition. During the Shirt Waist Makers strike, she was a special agent of the U.S. Bureau of Labor, January to June 1910. Her primary written contributions to antisuffragism consisted of her essays on women and labor.

Caroline Fairfield Corbin (Mrs. Calvin Richard Corbin) was born in Pomfret, Connecticut, in 1835. Her father was Jason Williams. She was educated at the Brooklyn Female Academy and was the author of several works, of which the most well known was probably *Letters from a Chimney Corner*. She was founder and president of the Illinois Association Opposed to Woman Suffrage and the author of numerous antisuffrage pamphlets published by the Illinois Association. She was one of the founders of the Association for the Advancement of Women.

In 1888, Corbin wrote "An Open Letter to My Dear Friend and Sister Frances E. Willard," in which she described some of her basic beliefs regarding woman's role in society. Following a caustic reply from Willard, Corbin wrote "A Rejoinder to Frances Willard," in which she elaborated on the position she had set forth earlier.

> Twenty years ago I was tolerant of woman suffrage, because I felt the need of something to open a wider door for woman, and lift her to a better comprehension of her own powers and worthiness. But . . . mischievous teachings were coming in thick and fast; . . . false ideals were luring women from the natural and holy ministries of the home, and promoting a coarse and selfish individualism. . . .

She went on to say that it took her a long time to trace the source of the miasma to woman suffrage,

> . . . a movement which called itself a reform, and claimed kinship with so much that was good and excellent. Accident or Providence led me at last to a thorough study of Socialism, of which woman suffrage is a vital and integral part, and I felt that therein I had found the key to the mystery.

Corbin feared that if the natural relationship of the sexes was so perverted as to provide for equal labor and equal pay for men and women, and equal political rights, "What guarantee have we that its demand for equal purity would not quickly degenerate to the Socialistic standard of equal license?"

In closing, Corbin described with apocalyptic fervor her vision of the millennium for women.

> My dream for woman is of a day when she shall cast off her low and materialistic views of life and its concomitants, her groveling desires and earthly ambitions, and rise to the spiritual heights of her nature and destiny, as God has ordained them. Then will she be revealed in a glory fitly symbolized by the vision of the Revelator, and which Murillo has reproduced in his incomparable Madonna, of a woman clothed with the sun, and having the moon under her feet. It is to such an apotheosis as this that I believe God is calling her to walk through the pathway of obedience, humility, and love.

Josephine Dodge (Mrs. Arthur M. Dodge) was born in Hartford, Connecticut, in 1855. Her father, Marshall Jewell, a native of New

Hampshire, traced his ancestry to Thomas Jewell, one of the founders of Massachusetts Bay Colony. In 1869, her father served the first of three terms as governor. In 1873, he was appointed minister to Russia, and in 1874 became postmaster general under President Grant. Josephine attended Hartford public schools and spent three years at Vassar. In 1875, she married Arthur Murray Dodge, a wedding attended by members of the Cabinet and many of the country's financial leaders. Her husband was the son of William E. Dodge, one of New York's wealthiest merchants and head of Phelps, Dodge and Co., one of the first directors of the Erie Railroad. The Dodge family traced its ancestry to the settlement of Salem in 1629. Mrs. Dodge and her husband settled in New York and had six sons. In 1896, Josephine Dodge was left a widow.

Dodge's main interest was the day-nursery movement. She sponsored Virginia Day Nursery, founded in 1878 in the slums for the children of working mothers. In 1888 she founded the Jewell Day Nursery to help create an environment in which children of immigrant working classes could be inculcated with middle-class American values. In 1890 she founded and became first president of the Association of Day Nurseries of New York City and in 1898 of the National Federation of Day Nurseries. In contrast to most women of her generation whose concern for working women and immigrants made them sympathetic to woman suffrage, she became actively opposed.

In 1899 she testified in Albany against a limited suffrage bill. Then in 1911 the National Association Opposed to Woman Suffrage was formed in her Park Avenue apartment, with Dodge as its first president. She was also first vice president and chairman of the Executive Committee of the New York State Association Opposed to Woman Suffrage. In articles and speeches at congressional hearings and in *The Woman's Protest*, which she edited, she created a forum for her views. She believed that woman suffrage was unnecessary since the civil and legal rights of women had already been established by state legislatures without woman's vote, the nation's best protective and child labor legislation and the first minimum-wage law for women had been enacted by the male-suffrage state of Massachusetts. It would be ineffective because it would not change the moral and intellectual level of the electorate, and undesirable because partisanship would undermine the influence of women as social reformers. In 1917, when the suffrage struggle became centered in Congress and the headquarters of the National Association was transferred to Washington, D.C., Dodge was succeeded as president by Mrs. James W. Wadsworth, Jr.

Dodge was active in the Presbyterian church and the Colony Club of New York. During World War I, she served as a member of the Women's Committee of the Connecticut Division of the Council of National Defense, which brought her into contact with suffrage leaders.

Alice N. George (Mrs. Andrew J. George) was born in Milford, Massachusetts, in 1866. She was a Wellesley graduate (1887), had one son, and was active and held office in numerous organizations, such as the National Trust (English) for Preservation of Historical Places, the College Club, the Research Committee of the Educational and Industrial Union, the Welfare Department of the National Civic Federation, the Woman's Trade Union League, the American Association for Labor Legislation, and the Massachusetts Child Labor Committee. Her husband, Dr. Andrew J. George, was a professor of literature at Wellesley. George was devoted to the antisuffrage cause and for many years she served as organizing secretary of the MAOFESW and field secretary of the National Association. She was the author of numerous antisuffrage articles and pamphlets. She was Episcopalian.

Jeannette L. Gilder was born in Flushing, New York, in 1849. Her father was the Reverend William Henry Gilder. She was active throughout her life as a critic, editor, and author. With her brother, Joseph B. Gilder, she founded *The Critic* in 1880, of which she was associate editor until it merged in 1907 into *Putnam's Monthly*. In *Woman's Who's Who of America* she did not indicate her position on the suffrage question. Nevertheless, she wrote an essay entitled "Why I am Opposed to Woman Suffrage" (1894), from which the following is taken:

I speak from experience when I say that I don't see how women can cultivate home life and enter the political arena. Circumstances forced me to go out into the world to earn my own bread and a part of that of others. When my mother was living, she made the home, and all went well. But after that, after marriages and deaths, a family of four small children came to me for a home. I don't mean for support, for they had a father living, but for a home. I had to take, as far as possible, the place of my sister, their mother. To do my duty by them and by my work was the most difficult task I ever undertook. I had to go to my office every day and leave them to the care of others. Sometimes the plan worked well, but oftener it worked ill—very ill indeed. I had seven people doing, or attempting to do, what I and two others could have done had I been able to be at home and look after things myself. Suppose that politics had been added to my other cares? Suppose that I had had meetings to attend and candidates to elect, perhaps to be elected myself? What would have been the result? Even direr disaster! We cannot worship God and Mammon; neither can we be politicians and women.

A further clue to Gilder's personality is provided by Ida Tarbell, who admired her greatly as "one of the most interesting women in the literary world of that day." Tarbell, reminiscing about the Gilder she knew in 1898, said she "carried to perfection the then feminine vogue for severe masculine dress: stout shoes, short skirt, mannish jacket, shirt, tie, hat, stick. They were the last word in style . . . but the masculinity was all on the surface." Gilder was a member of the Colony Club.

Louise Caldwell Jones (Mrs. Gilbert E. Jones) was born in Buffalo, New York, and educated in Europe. Her husband, a banker, was the son of George Jones, founder of *The New York Times*. She had two sons. She was founder and president of the National League for the Civic Education of Women, an antisuffrage "front" organization, and an active speaker and writer against woman suffrage. She wrote a couple of plays and numerous antisuffrage pamphlets. She was a member of the New York State Federation and the New York City Federation of Women's Clubs. She was Episcopalian and a member of the Colony Club.

Edith Melvin was educated in the public and private schools of Concord, Massachusetts, and by her father, James Melvin. In the introductory notes to Melvin's essay, "A Business Woman's View of Suffrage," one learns that as a result of the Civil War, her father had become an invalid "confined to his bed for many years before his death, when he left a widow and an only child dependent upon themselves for support."

With training only in stenography and typing, Melvin entered the law office of Judge Prescott Keyes. In 1916, she had been in his law office more than twenty years, "a position of ever increasing responsibilities requiring steady and efficient study and thought." Despite her considerable legal experience, which was apparently sufficient to have qualified her to pass the bar, Melvin claimed that she never applied for admission because she did not believe in women becoming lawyers.

Other of her activities included serving as president of the Guild of the First Parish (Concord) and secretary of the South Middlesex Federation of Young

People's Religious Unions. She was an officer and active member of Old Concord Chapter of the DAR, and was herself a householder and taxpayer. Apparently Melvin was not entirely happy with her lot as an "emancipated" woman. After more than twenty years as a professional woman, she wrote,

> I regret to state, my life has been more that of a man than of a woman. A home-supporter by the actual work of my hands and my brain, rather than a home-maker; my life has been past [sic] amid the heat and turmoil of business life, working shoulder to shoulder with men, pitting my brain against the brains of men; and having no male relative to represent me in the business of the government, a taxpayer "without representation."

Melvin did not deny that she derived satisfaction from the turmoil of business life, but to do so, she had been "forced to summon up the determination, the endurance, the physical and mental labor, which by all the laws of nature belong not to the 'female of the species' but to the male." She felt no desire to "assist the male sex in the business of government, nor do I think I am fitted so to do."

Even though Melvin felt that her professional experience offered her a special advantage when it came to using her mind "in matters pertaining to law and business," she was insistent that "the average business woman cannot make such a study or engage in politics without interference not merely with her physical, but with her mental business life." For Melvin, that only a very small number of women reached the top level of success in the business world was not the result of male prejudice, but rather an example of "the physical and mental limitations of the members of the female sex."

> The trivialities of the afternoon tea are too often present in the work of the wage-earning woman—too often she has too slight a regard of her duty to return full value for the pecuniary consideration she receives. The career of too many wage earning women is now entirely haphazard, the result of necessity rather than well-grounded choice. It is fair to assume that political matters would receive the same degree of smattering knowledge and thought as is too often received by the daily occupation into which many women drift.

What emerges from Melvin's arguments is an attitude of mind that can best be described as "Aunt" Tomism. Obviously she did not consider herself a typical woman performing her "natural function." She seemed to take pleasure instead from the fact that she was anything but typical. Nevertheless, she made a clear distinction between the feminine role, which she had been unable to pursue, and femininity, which she regarded as especially necessary for women forced into the wage-earning world.

The instability of the female mind is beyond the comprehension of the majority of men. The charm, the "sweet unreasonableness," the lack of power of consecutive thought upon any intricate problem, which mark the average woman are sometimes attractive and in personal or family relations not without compensating advantages. In the business world, however, these attributes are wholly detrimental.

Annie Nathan Meyer was born in New York City in 1867. She married Dr. Alfred Meyer and had one daughter. Self-taught, she took an examination at Columbia University one year before Barnard College was founded. In 1888, she began the work that led to the founding of Barnard College in 1889 and subsequently became one of the original trustees of the college. She was the author of several plays and novels, among them *The Dominant Sex* (play) and *Helen Brent, M.D.* (novel). She projected and edited *Woman's Work in America*. She was an outspoken opponent of woman suffrage and frequently contributed antisuffrage articles to newspapers. She was also active in the New York State Association Opposed to the Extension of Woman Suffrage.

M. G. van Rensselaer (Mrs. Schuyler van Rensselaer) was born in New York City, privately educated, and in 1910 received an honorary Litt. D. from Columbia University. She was the author of *History of the City of New York in the Seventeenth Century, English Cathedrals*, and other works. Her major contribution to the antisuffrage cause was her essay "Should We Ask for the Suffrage?" which was widely distributed.

Molly Elliot Seawell was born in Gloucester County, Virginia, in 1860. Her father was John Tyler Seawell, a nephew of President Tyler. She was active throughout her life as a novelist and playwright, winning numerous prizes for her literary works. She was opposed to woman suffrage, a position she elaborated in *The Ladies' Battle*. This book was very popular among the Antis, often quoted, and widely distributed.

Alice Hay Wadsworth (Mrs. James W. Wadsworth, Jr.) was born in Cleveland, Ohio on January 6, 1880. She was the daughter of John Hay, who began his public career as secretary to President Lincoln, eventually becoming secretary of state under President Hayes, and from 1887 to 1890 serving as ambassador to the Court of St. James's. Her husband was U.S. senator from New York. She had two children, a daughter and a son. She was a member of the Visiting Board Craig Colony for Epileptics, a position to which she was appointed by the State Charities Association. In addition, she belonged to numerous women's clubs and civic organizations. She was a member of the New York State Association Opposed to Woman Suffrage and president of the National Association from 1917 to 1920. She wrote and spoke frequently on behalf of antisuffragism. Wadsworth was Presbyterian and a member of the Colony Club. She was the only major Anti included in *The Biographical Cyclopaedia of American Women*.

Notes

ABBREVIATIONS

MAOFESW   Massachusetts Association Opposed to the Further Extension of Suffrage to Women
MHS   Massachusetts Historical Society
MSL   Massachusetts State Library
NAWSA   National Woman Suffrage Association
NYPL   New York Public Library
SSC   Sophia Smith Collection, Smith College

EDITOR'S INTRODUCTION

1. Edward T. James, Janet Wilson James, and Paul S. Boyer. eds. *Notable American Women, 1607-1950: A Biographical Dictionary*, 3 vols. (Cambridge: Harvard University Press, 1971); Barbara Sicherman and Carol Hurd Green, eds., *Notable American Women, the Modern Period: A Biographical Dictionary* (Cambridge: Harvard University Press, 1980).
2. New York: R.R. Bowker, 1979.

INTRODUCTION

1. Aileen S. Kraditor, *The Ideas of the Woman Suffrage Movement* (Garden City, N.Y.: Anchor Books, 1971); William L. O'Neill, *Everyone Was Brave* (Chicago: Quadrangle Books, 1969).
2. Confidential to "My dear Fellow Suffragists," September, 1, 1915, Carrie Chapman Catt Papers, Empire State Campaign Committee, NYPL. This was released to 700 clubs and committees ten weeks before New York State voted on the woman suffrage amendment.
3. It is virtually impossible to arrive at an accurate number of state associations. In the last issue of *The Woman's Protest* (February 1918), the Antis claimed 25 state associations serving their purpose. Nevertheless, it is doubtful that all of these states had fully constituted statewide organizations such as those of Massachusetts

or even New York. Many of them were probably no more than committees. Furthermore, the list omits the Tennessee chapter, which became one of the more active state groups. Until further work is done on each state association, one can only estimate the extent of the antisuffrage organization.

4. The term *Antis* is capitalized when it refers to the *women* who were actively involved in opposition to the extension of suffrage to women. Male opponents of woman suffrage are designated as antisuffragists.

5. Most of the sources for the Antis' beliefs consist of pamphlets written by individual Antis and either published by or circulated under the auspices of one of the various antisuffrage associations. This makes it fairly easy to generalize when speaking of the Antis' attitudes or beliefs, since it may be assumed that any pamphlet under the imprimatur of an antisuffrage association reflected official thinking on the issue.

CHAPTER ONE

1. Some individuals deliberately exploited the relationship between suffragism and feminism, arguing that the ballot for women would lead inevitably to the latter. The Men's League Opposed to Woman Suffrage, "Brief Argument against Woman Suffrage" (Philadelphia 1913) MHS.

2. James McGrigor Allan, *Woman Suffrage Wrong in Principle, and Practice* (London: Remington and Co., 1890), p. 23; Mrs. A. J. George, "Suffrage Fallacies," *Anti-Suffrage Essays by Massachusetts Women* (The Forum Publications of Boston, 1916), p. 29.

3. Mrs. Herbert Lyman, "The Anti-Suffrage Ideal," *Anti-Suffrage Essays by Massachusetts Women*, pp. 118-22; Goldwin Smith, "Woman Suffrage," *Essays on Questions of the Day* (New York: Macmillan & Co., 1894), pp. 183-218.

4. MAOFESW, "The Equal Custody of Children by Parents," pamphlet, n.d., Houghton Library.

5. James Cardinal Gibbons, letter to Mrs. Robert Garrett of Baltimore, April 22, 1913, printed and circulated by The Man-Suffrage Association, *The Case Against Woman Suffrage* (New York, 1915), p. 18.

6. M. G. van Rensselaer, "Should We Ask for the Suffrage?" MAOFESW, n.d., p. 40.

7. Mrs. Charles Burton Gulick, "The Imperative Demand Upon Women in the Home," *Anti-Suffrage Essays by Massachusetts Women*, pp. 128-34.

8. Lyman, "The Anti-Suffrage Ideal."

9. Mrs. Estelle R. McVickar, "What is an Anti-Suffragist?" Read by the author before the Mount Vernon Auxiliary of the Society Opposed to the Extension of Suffrage to Women, n.d.

10. Catharine E. Beecher, "Suggestions Respecting Improvements in Education," Hartford, 1829, in Aileen S. Kraditor, ed., *Up from the Pedestal* (Chicago: Quadrangle Books, 1968), p. 85.

11. James Cardinal Gibbons, Letter to Mrs. Robert Garrett. The cardinal concluded by citing the story of the Roman matron Cornelia.

> If Cornelia, instead of shaping the minds and hearts of her sons to deeds of virtue and patriotism at home, had wasted her time in the Roman Forum, history would never have recorded the noble exploits of the Gracchi.

Perhaps not, but history might have recorded the noble exploits of the Gracchi women.

12. Mrs. Charles P. Strong, "Woman Suffrage and War," *Anti-Suffrage Essays by Massachusetts Women*, p. 75.

13. In Elizabeth Cady Stanton's words, "It is evident the time has come to hunt man into his appropriate sphere." *Eighty Years and More* (New York: Schocken Books, 1971 [1898]).

14. Mrs. Horace A. Davis, "The True Function of the Normal Woman," *Anti-Suffrage Essays by Massachusetts Women*, p. 127.

15. Mrs. William Lowell Putnam, "Suffrage and the Sex Problem," *Anti-Suffrage Essays by Massachusetts Women*, pp. 138, 139.

16. O'Neill, *Everyone Was Brave*, p. 36. To illustrate the feminist position, O'Neill quotes Susan B. Anthony, who said in 1901:

> Responsibilities grow out of rights and powers. Therefore before mothers can rightfully be held responsible for the vices and crimes, for the general demoralization of society, they must possess all possible rights and powers to control the conditions and circumstances of their own and their children's lives.

17. Putnam, "Suffrage and the Sex Problem," p. 137.

18. Lyman, "The Anti-Suffrage Ideal," p. 120.

19. Lily Rice Foxcroft, "Why Are Women Opposing Woman Suffrage?" *The Wellesley Alumnae Quarterly* (April 1917), republished by the Women's Anti-Suffrage Association of Massachusetts.

20. Illinois Association Opposed to Woman Suffrage, *Fifteenth Annual Report*, December 1911. Other statements reflecting these and similar sentiments include the following:

> If men are doing poorly—it is due to the women who trained them. We need better voters, not more voters.

Alice N. George, "Woman's Rights vs. Woman Suffrage" (New York: National Association Opposed to Woman Suffrage, 1913), p. 8.

> If women had conquered their own part of life perfectly, one might wish to see them thus leave it and go forth to set the world to rights. But on the contrary, never were domestic conditions so badly attended to. Until woman settles the servant question, how can she ask to run the government?

Emily Bissell, "A Talk to Women on the Suffrage Question" (New York State Association Opposed to Woman Suffrage, 1909), p. 5.

21. The Reverend Charles H. Parkhurst, "The Inadvisability of Woman Suffrage," *Supplement to the Annals of the American Academy of Political and Social Science* 35 (May 1910), pp. 36-37.
22. Jeannette L. Gilder, "Why I Am Opposed to Woman Suffrage," *Harper's Bazaar* (May 19, 1894), reprinted and bound by MAOFESW, *Why Women Do Not Want the Ballot*, vol. 1, no. 20.
23. Margaret C. Robinson, "Woman Suffrage a Menace to Social Reform," *Anti-Suffrage Essays by Massachusetts Women*, pp. 98-117. By way of illustration, Robinson pointed to the case of Julia Lathrop, suffragist and head of the Federal Children's Bureau, maintaining that she continued to hold her job when the Republicans were replaced by the Democrats only because she was a woman and a nonpartisan. Every man at the head of a similar bureau, she pointed out, lost his job.
24. Rensselaer, "Should We Ask for the Suffrage?" p. 37.
25. Mary A. J. M'Intire, Letter to Editor, *Boston Sunday Herald*, reprinted as "Of No Benefit to Woman: She is a Far Greater Power Without Suffrage," n.d., Houghton Library.
26. Robinson, "Woman Suffrage a Menace to Social Reform," p. 14.
27. George, "Woman's Rights vs. Woman Suffrage," p. 14
28. Foxcroft, "Why Are Women Opposing Woman Suffrage?"
29. Emily P. Bissell, "A Talk to Every Woman," The Virginia Association Opposed to Woman Suffrage, n.d., p. 16.
30. Ibid., p. 17.
31. Robinson, "Woman Suffrage a Menace to Social Reform."
32. Mary Beard, "Legislative Influence of Unenfranchised Women," *Annals of the American Academy of Political and Social Science* (November 1914).
33. Bissell, "A Talk to Every Woman," p. 21. What Bissell seems to be expressing here is not only a plea for power, or rather the fear of sacrificing a familiar source of immediate influence for the sake of an unknown and possibly ineffectual power, but also a less than complimentary view of man's world. "Woman does not need the vote, if she has the voter," wrote Bissell, echoing the belief of thousands of Antis. This is all the more surprising coming from Bissell, who remained single all her life, and presumably never "had the voter."
34. Robert F. Cholmeley, "The Women's Anti-Suffrage Movement" (London: National Union of Women's Suffrage Societies, 1908).
35. Robinson, "Woman Suffrage a Menace to Social Reform," p. 103.
36. Mrs. Richard Watson Gilder [H. de K. G.], "A Letter on Woman Suffrage," MAOFESW, April 1894, p. 12. It would seem as if the writer was deliberately choosing *not* to exchange her familiar behind-the-scenes power of the boudoir for an unknown and questionable numerical advantage.
37. Robinson, "Woman Suffrage a Menace to Social Reform."
38. Ibid.
39. Gilder, "Why I am Opposed to Woman Suffrage."
40. George, "Suffrage Fallacies," p. 26.

41. Ibid., p. 27.
42. Mrs. Gilbert E. Jones, "Some Impediments to Woman Suffrage," *North American Review* (August 1909).
43. Joseph G. Pyle, "Should Women Vote?" (New York: National Association Opposed to Woman Suffrage, 1913), quoted in Mrs. Thomas Allen, "Woman Suffrage vs. Womanliness," *Anti-Suffrage Essays by Massachusetts Women*, p. 80.
44. Rt. Rev. John S. Foley, bishop of Detroit, from a newspaper interview, reprinted in "Some Catholic Views on Woman Suffrage," National Association Opposed to Woman Suffrage.
45. Catharine E. Beecher, *Woman's Profession as Mother and Educator* (Philadelphia: George Maclean, 1872), p. 10.
46. Allen, "Woman Suffrage vs. Womanliness," pp. 77-78.
47. Mrs. Augustin H. Parker, "Are Suffragists Sincere Reformers?" *Anti-Suffrage Essays by Massachusetts Women*, pp. 81-84.
48. Ernest Bernbaum, Introduction, *Anti-Suffrage Essays by Massachusetts Women*, p. xv.
49. Carroll S. Rosenberg, "The Female Animal, A Medical and Biological View of Women and Women's Role in Nineteenth Century America" (Philadelphia: University of Pennsylvania, 1971), p. 1.
50. Dr. Charles L. Dana, letter to Alice Hill Chittenden, president of the New York State Association Opposed to Woman Suffrage, printed by the Man-Suffrage Association, *Case Against Woman Suffrage*, pp. 15-16 (my italics). Also circulated separately under the title "Suffrage A Cult of Self and Sex." Dr. Dana was a professor of physiology at Woman's Medical College from 1880 to 1886; professor of nervous diseases at Bellevue Hospital Medical School and at Cornell Medical College; and accounted by the Antis "One of the world's leading neurologists." MAOFESW, 1915-16 campaign material, MHS.
51. Jill Conway, "Stereotypes of Femininity in a Theory of Sexual Evolution," *Victorian Studies* (September 1970), p. 48.
52. George, "Woman's Rights vs. Woman Suffrage."
53. Lyman, "The Anti-Suffrage Ideal," p. 121. The suffragists had their own battery of medical and biological specialists drafted to uphold their side of the woman question. For example, Dr. Dudley A. Sargent of Harvard University was reported to have said:

> Pound for pound the average normal woman in good health can endure more pain, discomfort and fatigue, and can expend more muscular energy than the average normal man of similar condition.

Sargent went on to emphasize that women should make every whit as good soldiers as men, a pressing issue in 1917:

> Withstanding cold, or thirst, or hunger, or physical privation of any sort, a woman can outlast a man. Nine times out of ten woman, from the standpoint of physical endurance should make as good a soldier as man. . . . Woman of necessity comes nearer the primitive type than man. She is biologically more

of a savage, more of a barbarian, and she has therefore greater physical endurance.
The Vanguard, vol. 2, no. 6 (December 1917).

54. Rosenberg, "The Female Animal," pp. 2-4.
55. M'Intire, Letter to Editor.
56. Men's League, "Brief Argument." An arch antisuffragist and well-known upholder of the status quo argued:

Woman, if she becomes a man, will be a weaker man. Yet she must be prepared to resign her privileges as a woman. She cannot expect to have both privilege and equality. *To don the other sex she must doff her own.*

Goldwin Smith, "Woman Suffrage."
57. Allan, *Woman Suffrage Wrong*, p. 5.
58. Mrs. Gilbert E. Jones, "The Position of the Anti-Suffragists," *Supplement to the Annals of the American Academy of Political and Social Science* (May 1910), pp. 18-22.
59. Edith Melvin, "A Business Woman's View of Suffrage," *Anti-Suffrage Essays by Massachusetts Women*, p. 41. Melvin, an active career woman, was herself not free to become involved in these activities. Might not this provide a clue to understanding the attitude of those professional women who opposed woman suffrage, feeling that they would be left out as political life became possible only for the leisured class of women?
60. Gilder, "A Letter on Woman Suffrage," p. 13.
61. MAOFESW, "Facts and Figures About Woman Suffrage" (Boston: January 1915), MHS.
62. American Constitutional League, "Home Rule," Brief Submitted to U.S. Senate, January 1919, Against Proposal for Constitutional Amendment Compelling States to Adopt Woman Suffrage (NAWSA, Misc. Papers, Box 7, NYPL).
63. Gilder, "A Letter on Woman Suffrage," p. 15.
64. George, "Woman's Rights vs. Woman Suffrage," p. 9. That women were too personal to engage in political life was a view often expressed. Mrs. George, a paid antisuffrage spokeswoman, reportedly said at a Massachusetts State House hearing on woman suffrage that women "do not view life from a broad general standpoint; too many think merely of their own individual wrongs." At this same hearing, Mrs. L. R. Stone argued that a great objection to investing women with political power was that they did not possess the "logical faculty," the power of balancing questions as did men. Houghton clippings, unidentified newspaper, n.d.
65. Beecher, "Suggestions Respecting Improvements in Education," p. 85.
66. Jones, "The Position of the Anti-Suffragist."
67. Smith, "Woman Suffrage." Smith significantly fails to consider the possibility of paying a needlewoman like a tailor.
68. Lyman, "The Anti-Suffrage Ideal," p. 120.
69. Bissell, "A Talk to Women on the Suffrage Question," p. 4. Within a patriarchal system "male superiority depends much less on what the male *is* than on what the

female isn't." Myron Brenton, *The American Male* (Greenwich, Conn.: Fawcett Publications, 1966), p. 198.

70. Rensselaer, "Should We Ask for the Suffrage?," p. 32.
71. Bissell, "A Talk to Every Woman," p. 18.
72. Rensselaer, "Should We Ask for the Suffrage?," p. 32.
73. Caroline F. Corbin, "Equality" (Chicago: Illinois Association Opposed to Woman Suffrage, 1910).
74. Rensselaer, "Should We Ask for the Suffrage?," p. 35.
75. Illinois Association Opposed to the Extension of Suffrage to Woman, "An Appeal to the Common Sense and the Educated Thought of Men and Women Against the Proposed Extension of Suffrage to Women," n.d.
76. Agnes Irwin, Address to the Annual Meeting of MAOFESW, *Eleventh Annual Report*, 1906.
77. Rensselaer, "Should We Ask for the Suffrage?," p. 35.
78. Mary A. Jordan, Address to the Annual Meeting of MAOFESW, *Eleventh Annual Report*, 1906.
79. Dr. S. Weir Mitchell, Address to Radcliffe, January 17, 1895, MHS.
80. Ibid. (my italics).
81. Dr. Edward H. Clarke, *Sex in Education* (Boston, 1872).
82. Ibid., p. 180. The argument that the biological differences between the sexes indicate a cultural difference as well and that these differences should be reflected in the education given each sex still has its adherents. For example, Dr. Philip Rhodes, professor of obstetrics and gynecology at the University of London, argues that the problem of the education of "girls" today is that it is still run by academics who place too high a premium on academic achievement. About 90 percent will have children "and for this, academic attainment however desirable for other reasons is not necessary. The sexes should be kept separate in their formal education because of "very great physiological differences in girls and in their vocational and games and play needs." *Woman: A Biological Study of the Female Role in Twentieth Century Society* (London: Corgi Books, 1969), p. 174.
83. Smith, "Woman Suffrage."
84. W. S. Tyler, "The Higher Education of Women," *Scribner's Monthly* (February 1874), p. 458. See also Ely van de Walker, *Woman's Unfitness for Higher Co-education* (New York, 1903).
85. Mitchell, Address to Radcliffe.
86. Ibid. By the turn of the century some of the ambivalence concerning the nature and purpose of higher education for women may have reflected the fact that women still had few opportunities available to them for using their education. Adele Simmons, "Education for What?" Paper delivered to the Eastern Sociological Association, April 1971.
87. Lyman Abbott, quoted in "Letter to the Voters of New York State" by "A Woman of the Common Class" (October 21, 1971), SSC.
88. Richard Barry, "Why Women Oppose Woman Suffrage," *Pearson's Magazine* (March 1910).

89. Ibid.
90. Bissell, "A Talk to Women on the Suffrage Question," p. 4.
91. Lyman, "The Anti-Suffrage Ideal."
92. Mrs. A. J. George, "Why We Are Anti-Suffragists," *The Woman's Protest*, vol. 7, no. 6 (October 1915).
93. In a letter to Eliza Osborne (niece of Lucretia Mott and eldest daughter of Martha C. Wright) written on November 12, 1891, Elizabeth Cady Stanton castigated her for writing to a mutual friend after having met Stanton and asking her why the latter had such a solemn countenance. Stanton's reply was direct to Osborne. She said she was disappointed that one of her background and beauty should waste her time engaged in the "ten thousand digital absurdities" of knitting, tatting, embroidering, and so on. (Osborne was knitting a washrag at the time of their meeting.) For Stanton this was a base use for the optic nerves, "when they were designed by the Creator to explore the planetary world, with chart and compass to guide mighty ships across the sea, to lead the sons of Adam with divinest love from earth to heaven." *Eighty Years*, pp. 435-36.
94. George, "Suffrage Fallacies," p. 27.
95. Bissell, "A Talk to Every Woman," p. 22. Ida Tarbell also shared this opinion. In her view:
    Insisting that women do the same things that men do, may make the two exteriorly more alike—it does not make them more equal. Men and women are widely apart in functions and in possibilities. They cannot be made equal by exterior devices like trousers, ballots, the study of Greek. *The effort to make them so is much more likely to make them unequal.*
    The Business of Being a Woman (New York: Macmillan, 1912), pp. 212-13 (my italics).
96. Gilder, "A Letter on Woman Suffrage," p. 16.
97. Ibid., pp. 12, 10 (my italics).
98. Ibid., p. 14.
99. Ibid., pp. 10, 17.
100. Ida Tarbell, *The Ways of Woman* (New York, 1915), p. 45.
101. Gail Hamilton, Letter, printed by MAOFESW, n.d. (my italics).
102. James Cardinal Gibbons, letter to Mrs. Robert Garrett, pp. 17-18 (my italics).
103. Lyman, "The Anti-Suffrage Ideal," p. 120.
104. George, "Why We Are Anti-Suffragists."
105. Viola Klein, *The Feminine Character* (New York: International Universities Press, 1946), p. 29.
106. Careful not to confuse subservience with inferiority, antisuffrage polemicists tried to bolster their position by recourse to divine authority.
    . . . in the origin of civilization there is every evidence (see *Genesis*) that woman was given by the Creator a position that is inseparable from and is the complement of man. She was made man's helper, was given a servient place (not necessarily inferior) and man the dominant place (not necessarily superior) in the division of labor.

Man-Suffrage Association Opposed, *Case Against Woman Suffrage*, p. 31.
107. Bissell, "A Talk to Every Woman," pp. 14-16, 19-20.

CHAPTER TWO

1. Richard H. Dana, quoted by Man-Suffrage Association, *The Case Against Woman Suffrage*, p. 16. According to Dana, lawyer, author, and editor, this counsel comes from "inspired instinct" rather than from "labored reasoning."
2. Illinois Association, "An Appeal."
3. Ibid.
4. McVickar, "What is An Anti-Suffragist?"
5. George, "Suffrage Fallacies," p. 25.
6. Foxcroft, "Why Are Women Opposing Woman Suffrage?"
7. Lyman, "The Anti-Suffrage Ideal," p. 119.
8. M'Intire, Letter to Editor.
9. George, "Suffrage Fallacies," p. 25.
10. Illinois Association, "An Appeal."
11. John C. Ten Eyck, "Suffrage and Government" (New York: The Guidon Club, 1914), p. 3 (my italics).
12. Ibid.
13. See also George, "Woman's Rights vs. Woman Suffrage," p. 7.
14. Bissell, "A Talk to Every Woman," p. 20.
15. Elizabeth Jackson, "Suffrage and the School Teacher," *Anti-Suffrage Essays by Massachusetts Women*, pp. 85-86.
16. It is remarkable how infrequently the Antis resorted to characterizing the suffragists according to the usual stereotypes of unfulfilled spinsters who were rebelling against domesticity in theory because they had never known it in practice. Davis, "The True Function of the Normal Woman," said that the suffragists were turning to new ideals because they had never tried the old, but remarks like this were very rare.
17. George, "Suffrage Fallacies," p. 28.
18. Allen, "Woman Suffrage vs. Womanliness," p. 79.
19. Putnam, "Suffrage and the Sex Problem," p. 139.
20. Ibid., p. 136.
21. Men's League, "Brief Argument."
22. Rensselaer, "Should We Ask for the Suffrage?," p. 17.
23. Ibid., p. 24.
24. Bulick, "The Imperative Demand Upon Women in the Home," p. 128.
25. Jackson, "Suffrage and the School Teacher," p. 86.
26. Illinois Association Opposed to Woman Suffrage, *Fifth Annual Report*, 1901.
27. Letter to Editor, Chicago *Record-Herald*, May 17, 1911.
28. The Antis believed implicitly that the female sex had always advanced in accordance with the male. It was all part of the unity of the race and the ebb and

flow of civilization. Helen K. Johnson, *Woman and the Republic* (New York: The Guidon Club, 1913), p. 6.

29. Bissell, "A Talk to Women on the Suffrage Question," p. 4; see also Ellen Mudge Burrill, "Some Practical Aspects of the Question," *Anti-Suffrage Essays by Massachusetts Women*, pp. 43-52.

30. John R. Dos Passos, "Equality of Suffrage Means the Debasement Not Only of Women But of Men" (New York: The National Association Opposed to Woman Suffrage, n.d.), p. 7.

31. Beecher, *Woman's Profession*, p. 6. Other expressions of the view that the vote was but the first step into political life include: Foxcroft's "The opportunity to vote would involve the obligation to vote." "Why Are Women Opposing Woman Suffrage?" She felt that public opinion would force women to vote. The Illinois Association Opposed to Woman Suffrage in its *Fifteenth Annual Report* made the point that

> The holding and managing of caucuses, conventions, primaries, courts and legislatures, are all involved in the simple casting of a ballot and these are labors which call forth the extreme of man's physical and intellectual power.

32. The letter was reprinted by both the Women's Anti-Suffrage Association of Massachusetts and the Man-Suffrage Association.

33. Melvin, "A Business Woman's View of Suffrage," p. 40.

34. Bissell, "A Talk to Women on the Suffrage Question," p. 7.

35. Jeannette L. Gilder, quoted in Man-Suffrage Association, *The Case Against Woman Suffrage*, p. 18.

36. Barry, "Why Women Oppose Woman Suffrage," p. 330.

37. Foxcroft, "Why Are Women Opposing Woman Suffrage," p. 6.

38. Annie Nathan Meyer, "Woman's Assumption of Sex Superiority," *North American Review* (January 1904), reprinted by MAOFESW, *Why Women Do Not Want the Ballot*, vol. 1, no. 60.

39. Jill Conway, "The Woman's Peace Party and the First World War," J.L. Granatstein and R. D Cuff, eds., *War and Society in North America* (Canada: Thomas Nelson and Sons, 1971), p. 52.

40. Strong, "Woman Suffrage and War," pp. 67-76.

41. Rossiter Johnson, *Helen Kendrick Johnson* (New York: Publishers Printing Company, 1917), pp. 17, 32, 33.

42. Ibid.

43. Ibid., pp. 63-64.

44. Ibid., p. 36. Johnson even here was concerned lest the stigma of politics invade the genteel refinement of her club and subvert all that was ladylike. However, there is no evidence that the club engaged in antisuffrage activities. Politics and sectarian religion were excluded from the discussions by an "unwritten law."

45. Ibid, p. 35.

46. "Suffrage Appeals to Lawless and Hysterical Women," an interview with Helen K. Johnson in *The New York Times*, March 30, 1913.

47. One of the contributors was Elizabeth Cady Stanton, who wrote an article entitled "Our Proper Attitude toward Immigration," an attitude that was probably shared by both suffragists and antisuffragists alike.
48. Johnson, *Helen Kendrick Johnson*, p. 49.
49. Ibid., p. 52.
50. Johnson, *Woman and the Republic*, pp. 12, 13, 27, 29-30.
51. Ibid., pp. 69, 61, 49, 65.
52. Ibid., p. 66.
53. Ibid., p. 325.
54. Ibid., pp. 356-57, 360.
55. Illinois Association, "An Appeal."
56. Horace A. Hollister, *The Woman Citizen* (New York: D. Appleton and Company, 1918), pp. 83-98.
57. Agnes Irwin, Address to the Annual Meeting of the MAOFESW, *Eleventh Annual Report*, 1906; M'Intire, Letter to Editor.
58. Lyman, "The Anti-Suffrage Ideal." The major similarity between suffragism and socialism, according to the Antis, was the insistence of both on regarding the individual, rather than the family, as the unit of society.

CHAPTER THREE

1. *The Woman's Protest*, vol. 1, no. 1 (May 1912), p. 3.
2. Bernbaum, Introduction, *Anti-Suffrage Essays by Massachusetts Women*, p. xxi.
3. George, "Woman's Rights vs. Woman Suffrage," p. 4.
4. Rensselaer, "Should We Ask for the Suffrage?," pp. 11-12.
5. Kate Gannet Wells, "An Argument Against Woman Suffrage, Before a Special Legislative Committee," MAOFESW, *Why Women Do Not Want the Ballot*, vol. 1, no. 12, n.d.
6. George, "Suffrage Fallacies," p. 28; Man-Suffrage Association, *The Case Against Woman Suffrage*, p. 6.
7. George, "Woman's Rights vs. Woman Suffrage," p. 3 (my italics).
8. Helen Kendrick Johnson Papers, NYPL.
9. Ibid.
10. "Women Actively Oppose the Suffrage Bill," unidentified Boston newspaper, n.d. [ca. 1895], Houghton Library.
11. Robinson, "Woman Suffrage a Menace to Social Reform," pp. 99, 102.
12. Ibid.; Rensselaer, "Should We Ask for the Suffrage?," p. 47.
13. Rensselaer, "Should We Ask for the Suffrage?," p. 47.
14. Ibid., p. 49.
15. Robinson, "Woman Suffrage a Menace to Social Reform"; Beecher, *Woman's Profession*, p. 11; Bissell, "A Talk to Women on the Suffrage Question"; Foxcroft, "Why Are Women Opposing Woman Suffrage?"; Rensselaer, "Should We Ask for the Suffrage?," p. 52.

16. Rensselaer, "Should We Ask for the Suffrage?," p. 50.
17. Ibid., pp. 9, 10, 14.
18. The Antis feared that if women were given the vote, the larger number of degenerate or wrong-minded women would vote against the reform measure of "good" women, who would have only a few ballots to cast. Robinson, "Woman Suffrage a Menace to Social Reform," p. 106.
19. Rensselaer, "Should We Ask for the Suffrage?," p. 52.
20. The article from which this excerpt was taken was printed in the Cambridge Chronicle (October 16, 1915). It was republished by the Women's Anti-Suffrage Association of Massachusetts and excerpted by Robinson in "Woman Suffrage a Menace to Social Reform," p. 107.
21. Quoted in Carrie Chapman Catt and Nettie Rogers Shuler, Woman Suffrage and Politics (New York: Charles Scribner's Sons, 1923), p. 233.
22. Robinson, "Woman Suffrage a Menace to Social Reform," p. 106.
23. Foxcroft, "Why Are Women Opposing Woman Suffrage?," p. 4.
24. Rensselaer, "Should We Ask for the Suffrage?," p. 52.
25. Beecher, Woman's Profession, p. 11. Beecher's choice of words is very revealing. If by "distinctive power of their sex" she means sexuality or even feminine wiles, why is this assumed to be such a deleterious influence on public life? She does not explain. Others certainly shared her feelings, yet none of the female Antis addressed herself to just how this evil influence would operate. Does this perhaps reflect the fear that women free to engage in public life might use their sexual attractiveness to allure other women's husbands? We have only the male reaction of historian and antisuffragist Francis Parkman, who felt that their sex would give women a political advantage. Women would be free to be aggressive and even attack the men, while the latter, out of chivalry, would be unable to be forthright and fight back. Man-Suffrage Association, "Some of the Reasons Against Woman Suffrage," n.d., reprinted by MAOFESW, Why Women Do Not Want the Ballot, vol. 1, no. 7.
26. George, "Woman's Rights vs. Woman Suffrage," p. 14.
27. Bissell, "A Talk to Women on the Suffrage Question," pp. 6-7.
28. Davis, "The True Function of the Normal Woman," p. 126. It was much more usual for the Antis to allow that men were doing their job well and that government should remain in the hands of those with power to enforce its laws.
29. Ibid., p. 124.
30. Foxcroft, "Why Are Women Opposing Woman Suffrage?," p. 7.
31. Barry, "Why Women Oppose Woman Suffrage," p. 329.
32. Foxcroft, "Why Are Women Opposing Woman Suffrage?," p. 11.
33. Catt and Shuler, Woman Suffrage and Politics, pp. 108-10.
34. Helen K. Johnson, "Woman's Progress versus Woman Suffrage," New York Association Opposed to Woman Suffrage, n.d., pp. 4, 5.
35. Ibid., p. 4.
36. Jones, "Some Impediments to Woman Suffrage," p. 159.

37. Illinois Association Opposed to the Extension of Suffrage to Women, "The Woman Movement in America," n.d. [ca. 1902], p. 1.
38. MAOFESW, *Eleventh Annual Report*, 1906, p. 4.
39. According to Lois Merk, non-property-holding women did pay a poll tax. "Boston's Historic Public School Crisis," *The New England Quarterly*, vol. 31, no. 1 (March 1958), pp. 172-99.
40. See also "Municipal Woman Suffrage, Argument of Clement K. Fay, esq. for Remonstrants" (Brookline: The Chronicle Press, 1887), for a list of legislation on behalf of women enacted by the Massachusetts legislature between 1873 and 1886.
41. Rensselaer, "Should We Ask for the Suffrage?," p. 26.
42. Monica Foley, "How Massachusetts Fosters Public Welfare," *Anti-Suffrage Essays by Massachusetts Women*, p. 56. Leonard was active in the antisuffrage movement in Massachusetts from the very beginning. In 1883, although unable to attend a hearing on municipal suffrage, a letter presenting her arguments was read to the legislature. In 1896 when the Massachusetts Antis were formally organized, she became a member of the Executive Committee, a position she retained until her death in 1904, when she was succeeded by her daughter. Katherine H. Leonard, *Clara Temple Leonard: A Memoir of Her Life by Her Daughter* (Springfield: Loring, Astell Co., 1908).
43. Burrill, "Some Practical Aspects of the Question," p. 49 (my italics).
44. It is difficult to understand how the Antis failed to regard this situation as anything but obvious tokenism. Perhaps from the vantage point of that period, however, this did represent an advance for women.
45. Mrs. Charles E. Guild, "The Present Status of Woman Suffrage in the United States," n.d., Houghton Library.
46. Jones, "Some Impediments to Woman Suffrage," p. 168.
47. James J. Kenneally, "The Opposition to Woman Suffrage in Massachusetts, 1868-1920" (Ph.D. dissertation, Boston College, 1963), pp. 252, 418.
48. Foxcroft, "Why Are Women Opposing Woman Suffrage?," p. 5. The failure of Massachusetts women to exercise the school franchise has been explained by Lois Merk as due to the fact that women voters were peculiarly handicapped in ways that men were not. For example, women without taxable property had to pay a poll tax, while those with taxable property had to present a sworn statement of its value and a receipt for payment of taxes; women had to go to the city or town hall to be assessed a poll tax; women had to give a statement of all their property under oath; registrars hostile to woman suffrage might drop their names from the voting lists; many thought it unfair that property-holding women could vote without paying a poll tax while poor women had to pay; and women were not admitted to the caucuses at which men of the political parties made the nominations for school committee. Merk, "Boston's Historic Public School Crisis," pp. 172-73.
49. Kenneally, "Opposition to Woman Suffrage," p. 253.

50. Johnson, *Woman and the Republic*, p. 89; Johnson "Woman's Progress versus Woman Suffrage," p. 5; Molly E. Seawell, *The Ladies' Battle* (New York: The Macmillan Company, 1911), pp. 103-4; Bissell, "A Talk to Every Woman," p. 23.
51. MAOFESW, "Woman Suffrage in Practice," a criticism of George Creel, "What have Women Done With the Vote," *The Century Magazine* (March 1914), MHS.
52. District of Columbia Association Opposed to Woman Suffrage, "Article on Woman Suffrage," introduced in U.S. Senate by James E. Martine, senator from New Jersey, February 25, 1915. He requested that it be printed in the record, MHS.
53. Robinson, "Woman Suffrage a Menace to Social Reform"; George, "Suffrage Fallacies"; Mrs. Henry Preston White, "The Ballot and the Woman in Industry," *Anti-Suffrage Essays by Massachusetts Women*; *The Woman's Protest*.
54. Man-Suffrage Association, *The Case Against Woman Suffrage*, p. 32. According to William O'Neill, Colorado was a good example of how the suffragists' expectations failed to materialize. Apparently woman suffrage did not raise the pay of women workers, produced no special reforms, and did not purify politics. In 1911, the Colorado legislature legalized race track gambling with the four women members voting in favor. Denver voted down prohibition by a margin of two to one. *Everyone Was Brave*, pp. 60-61.
55. Jones, "The Position of the Anti-Suffragists," pp. 18-22. If Priest were substituted for Elder and Massachusetts for Utah, the Antis could have been speaking here about the Boston Irish, whom they saw manipulated by a foreign priesthood and a corrupt political machine. Mrs. James B. Wells, "Why I am Opposed to Woman Suffrage," Address before the Texas Senate, February 23, 1915, SSC.
56. Jones, "The Position of the Anti-Suffragists"; Johnson, *Woman and the Republic*, p. 95.
57. Jones, "The Position of the Anti-Suffragists."
58. Mrs. Frederick M. Colburn, *Brooklyn Daily Eagle*, October 4, 1915, MHS.
59. Robinson, "Woman Suffrage a Menace to Social Reform," p. 104. In 1913, conservatives led by militant women induced the newly elected Democratic legislature to pass a law extending Nevada's resident requirement from six months to one year. Two years later, however, after a stormy legislative debate, the more lenient requirement was restored. William L. O'Neill, *Divorce in the Progressive Era* (New Haven, 1967), p. 236.
60. *The Anti-Suffragist*, vol. 1, no. 1 (July 1908).
61. Burrill, "Some Practical Aspects of the Question," p. 52.
62. Tennessee Division Southern Women's League for the Rejection of the Susan B. Anthony Amendment, "Mrs. Catt and the Woman Suffrage Leaders Repudiate the Bible," 1920.
63. Kenneally, "The Opposition to Woman Suffrage in Massachusetts," pp. 520-21; Margaret C. Robinson, "Woman Suffrage in Relation to Patriotic Service," Public Interest League of Massachusetts, 1917, SSC; *Woman Patriot*.
64. NAWSA Papers, Box 7, NYPL.

65. Conway, "The Woman's Peace Party and the First World War." Throughout this period it was also a regular feature of antisuffrage campaign tactics to attempt to direct toward NAWSA the antagonism aroused by the *militant* tactics of the Congressional Union. Catt and Shuler, *Woman Suffrage and Politics*, p. 243. The British League for Opposing Woman Suffrage also seemed to concentrate its attention in pamphlets and the press on the activities of British militants. "Black Tuesday," no. 42, November 21, 1911, MHS.

66. Mrs. James W. Wadsworth, Jr., "Case Against Suffrage," *The New York Times Magazine*, September 9, 1917, SSC.

67. Catt Papers, Empire State Campaign Committee News Release, October 25, 1915.

68. Johnson "Woman's Progress versus Woman Suffrage."

69. Allan, *Woman Suffrage Wrong in Principle*, p. 25.

70. Parker, "Are Suffragists Sincere Reformers?," p. 81.

71. Quoted in *The Anti-Suffragist*, vol. 2, no. 1 (September 1909), p. 81.

72. For example, see discussion of Katherine Anthony's *Feminism in Germany and Scandinavia* in "The Feminist Program," *The Unpopular Review* (April-June 1916), republished by the Women's Anti-Suffrage Association of Massachusetts. Anthony was a member of the Woman's Political Union and the Woman Suffrage Party of New York City.

73. Man-Suffrage Association, *The Case Against Woman Suffrage*, p. 45.

74. Lily Rice Foxcroft, "Suffrage a Step Toward Feminism," *Anti-Suffrage Essays by Massachusetts Women*, p. 144.

75. Henrietta Rodman and Fola LaFollette (whose worst crime cited was that they married but retained their maiden names); Edna Kenton (for her article in *The Century*, November 1913); Rosalie Jones ("of 'hiking fame' who is now breaking into the automobile business"); Inez Boissevain; Rheta Childe Dorr; Susan Fitzgerald (for her article in the opening issue of *Femina*); Alyse Gregory; Mrs. Havelock Ellis; and Eleanor Gates.

76. Johnson "Woman's Progress versus Woman Suffrage."

77. George, "Why We Are Anti-Suffragists."

78. Harold Owen, article in *London Daily Chronicle*, reprinted in *The Remonstrance*, n.d. Foxcroft, writing about the feminist theory of "economic independence," pointed out that Gilman was its "most distinguished American champion." "Why Are Women Opposing Woman Suffrage," p. 8. Quoting Gilman, she indicated what she believed were the latter's central thoughts: "The woman should be in the home as much as the man is, no more"; women should "come out of their little monogamous harems"; "The home of the future is one in which not one stroke of work shall be done except by professional people who are paid by the hour." "Suffrage a Step Toward Feminism," p. 142.

79. Wells, "Why I Am Opposed to Woman Suffrage."

80. Gilder, "A Letter on Woman Suffrage."

81. George, "Woman's Rights vs. Woman Suffrage," pp. 12-13.

82. Annie Bock, "Woman Suffrage"; Corbin, "Equality"; Illinois Association Opposed to Woman Suffrage, "Socialism vs. Legal Marriage."
83. Illinois Association Opposed to Woman Suffrage, *Fifteenth Annual Report*, 1911.
84. Jones, "Some Impediments to Woman Suffrage."
85. Annie Bock, "Address to the U.S. Senate Committee on Woman Suffrage, Opposing a Federal Woman Suffrage Amendment," presented 1913, 63rd Congress.
86. A. Elizabeth Taylor, *The Woman Suffrage Movement in Tennessee* (New York: Bookman Associates, 1957), p. 43.
87. September 30, 1917, NAWSA Papers, Box 7, NYPL.
88. *The Woman's Protest*, vol. 1, no. 1 (May 1912).
89. David Goldstein and Martha M. Avery, *Bolshevism: Its Cure* (Boston, 1919).
90. Drawing by E. Voos, after a design by Mrs. A. J. Leatherbee, published by the Women's Anti-Suffrage Association of Massachusetts and issued by the Pennsylvania Association Opposed to Woman Suffrage, January 1915, MHS.
91. Uncatalogued pamphlets, NYPL.
92. Johnson "Woman's Progress versus Woman Suffrage," p. 4.

CHAPTER FOUR

1. MAOFESW, *Twelfth Annual Report*, 1907.
2. Unless otherwise indicated, the material concerning Massachusetts is based on Kenneally, "The Opposition to Woman Suffrage in Massachusetts."
3. A draft of the letter is available in Houghton Library.
4. MAOFESW, Announcement of Standing Committee Meeting, May 21, 1895.
5. Ibid.
6. Article III of the Massachusetts constitution, revised in 1820, limited the entire state franchise to males. For Massachusetts women to secure the franchise, therefore, their only alternatives were obtaining a federal amendment, abrogating Article III of the Massachusetts constitution, or obtaining whatever suffrage (such as municipal or school) was *not* specifically prohibited by the constitution. Enactment of presidential suffrage in Massachusetts did not require an amendment to the state constitution, but could be accomplished by legislative action.
7. Kenneally, "The Opposition to Woman Suffrage," p. 82.
8. An unidentified and undated newspaper clipping from the Houghton collection illustrates perfectly this advantage:
   So long as opposition was confined to the members of the other sex there was about it the appearance of a selfish defence; but under these new conditions the argument can be fairly used by legislators that this is a question upon which the women themselves are materially divided, and hence, until they can get together, is one in which the men have no right to interfere.

In reviewing Helen K. Johnson's *Woman and the Republic*, the Philadelphia *Lutheran Observer* said that it exposed the views of woman suffrage advocates to merciless criticism, which,

coming from a woman, is all the more severe than if it came from a man. Indeed it is more than doubtful that a man would dare to deal so strongly and severely as the author has done.

Johnson Papers.

9. "History of Anti-Suffrage in Massachusetts," *Woman's Protest*, March 1916; *Woman's Journal*, March 11, 1882.
10. Kenneally, "The Opposition to Woman Suffrage," p. 99.
11. Ibid., p. 273.
12. The suffragists were opposed since they were not sure that enough women were independent enough to vote yes. The Antis were afraid they would have to violate their basic tenets and actually go to the polls in order to defeat it. A short notice in the *Boston Herald*, referring to the forthcoming elections, described the difficult position of women opposed to municipal suffrage. It said that they were being forced to go to the polls to register a no vote. They would do better not to go at all and reduce the total number of the vote, thereby nullifying the value of the vote as an indicator of the public's wishes. October 12, 1895, Houghton Library.
13. Kenneally, "The Opposition to Woman Suffrage," pp. 322-23.
14. MAOFESW bylaws.
15. Ibid.
16. Ibid.
17. Kenneally, "The Opposition to Woman Suffrage," pp. 370, 433.
18. Ibid., p. 417.
19. *Anti-Suffrage Bulletin*, April 1918; Executive Committee meetings, September 20 and November 15, 1918, MAOFESW Misc. Papers, Box 2, MHS. MAOFESW handouts found their way into Tennessee during the campaign over ratification of the Nineteenth Amendment. Typical were the following: 1) A picture of a man coming home from work to find his two children alone in the house, forlorn and weeping. On the wall tacked to a poster reading "Votes for Women" was a note from his wife saying "Back some time this evening." 2) A picture of a hen and a rooster, entitled "America When Feminized." The hen was wearing a "Votes for Women" ribbon and walking away from her nest of eggs. The rooster was saying, "Why Ma, these eggs will get all cold!" to which the hen replied, "Set on them yourself, Old Man, my country calls me!" An elaborate explanation for the cartoon read, "The more a Politician Allows Himself to be Henpecked, the more Henpecking We Will Have in Politics; A Vote for Federal Suffrage is a Vote for Organized Female Nagging Forever."
20. Minutes of the New England Anti-Suffrage League, April 23, 1914, MAOFESW Misc. Papers, Box 1, MHS.
21. Illinois Association, "The Woman Movement in America."

22. Apparently three antisuffrage associations formed almost simultaneously, in Albany, New York City, and Brooklyn. Lois Bannister Merk, "Massachusetts and the Woman Suffrage Movement" (Ph.D. dissertation, Radcliffe, 1956), p. 292.

23. Francis M. Scott, Speech before Committee on Suffrage of New York Constitutional Convention, June 14, 1894. Issued by Man-Suffrage Association, reprinted by MAOFESW, *Why Women Do Not Want the Ballot*, vol. 1, no. 21. The argument that the suffragists claimed to want equality but in fact desired supremacy, or that woman suffrage would mean male abdication of power in favor of female, was used by male antisuffragists and by the Man-Suffrage Association. Female Antis could not in good conscience have based their resistance on this argument since one of their implicit goals was to enlarge the sphere of woman's influence and power while confining man to his.

24. The situation was undoubtedly complicated by the fact that the Woman's Party actually began to make an impact on politics in 1913 by using female voting power to oust candidates unsympathetic to woman suffrage. If nothing else, the rhetoric of the party's spokeswomen must have given the Antis pause. Following is an extract from the keynote speech made by Maud Younger when the National Woman's Party was formed.

These [12] states with their four million women constitute nearly one-fourth of the electoral college and more than one-third of the votes necessary to elect a President. With enough women organized in each state to hold the balance of power, the women's votes may determine the presidency of the United States.

Eleanor Flexner, *Century of Struggle* (New York: Atheneum, 1968), p. 276. It is no wonder that the Antis were never fully able to dispel the fear that women would vote as a sex.

25. The Men's League, "Brief Argument."

26. Illinois Association, "The Woman Movement in America."

27. When the resolution was about to be implemented, it was discovered that the word "resident" had been used instead of the correct term "citizen." Consequently, the entire resolution was declared void and was made inoperative.

28. Illinois Association, "The Woman Movement in America."

29. Ibid.

30. Illinois Association Opposed to Woman Suffrage, Description of Association, 1900, NYPL.

31. Illinois Association, *Third Annual Report*, 1906, NYPL.

32. The *Seventh Annual Report* of MAOFESW, 1902, indicated that during the year the Antis had supplied the Massachusetts legislature with "certain important papers and aside from legislatures of other states where the question was imminent, and Committees of the National Congress, we have sent to individuals and to clubs and to the Branches, according to requests received." The Report went on to enumerate: 4,681 copies of the *Remonstrance* were sent to various legislators during the winter and 10,000 leaflets and *Remonstrances* have "gone out in other channels."

33. According to MAOFESW's *Second Annual Report,* 1897, members were appearing regularly before legislative committees.
34. Mrs. Francis M. Scott, "Address Delivered Before the Judiciary Committee of the New York Senate," April 10, 1895, reprinted by MAOFESW, *Why Women Do No Want the Ballot,* vol. 1, no. 22.
35. MAOFESW, *Second Annual Report.*
36. In 1870, when Congress passed the Fifteenth Amendment, most suffragists were bitterly disillusioned that Congress would enfranchise the Negro and deny the same privileges to white women. It was therefore inevitable that white women would turn from the federal government to the states to seek enfranchisement. Catt and Shuler, *Woman Suffrage and Politics,* p. 162. From that time until ratification of the Nineteenth Amendment in 1920, suffrage efforts to achieve enfranchisement by means of state referenda went on concurrently with attempts to win passage of a federal woman suffrage amendment:
    > I don't know the exact number of States we shall have to have, said Miss Anthony once in a musing hour, but I do know that there will come a day when that number will automatically and resistlessly act on the Congress of the United States to compel the submission of a federal suffrage amendment. (p. 227)
37. Ibid., p. 230.
38. Susan B. Anthony and Ida Husted Harper, eds., *History of Woman Suffrage,* 1885-1900, vol. 4 (Rochester: NAWSA, 1902), p. xiii. In a number of states, limited enfranchisement, such as presidential or municipal suffrage, could be conferred on women by an act of the legislature. This authority derived from the fact that control over municipal suffrage was possible in certain states through the authority of the legislature over city charters. The right to enact presidential suffrage belonged to the state legislatures through the provision in the Constitution, which states that each state should
    > appoint, in such manner as the Legislature thereof may direct, a number of [presidential] electors, equal to the whole number of Senators and Representatives to which the state may be entitled in Congress.
39. Catt and Shuler, *Woman Suffrage and Politics,* p. 163.
40. Ibid., p. 107.
41. Kenneally, "The Opposition to Woman Suffrage," p. 435. The *Woman's Journal,* the major suffrage organ, dismissed the new organization as one whose birth
    > will be received with joy by the promoters of the white slave traffic, the exploiters of child labor, the liquor interest, the gambling fraternity, and all the enemies of good government.
    December 9, 1911.
42. *The Woman's Protest,* vol. 1, no. 1 (May 1912), p. 3.
43. The objectives of the National Association can be ascertained from the organization's letterhead:
    > Stands for *home* and *national defense* against suffrage, Feminism and Socialism. For *Manpower* in government because Democracy must be *strong* to be

safe. For the preservation of the established foundation of the American Republic. For the *enforcement* of the *Constitutional Right* of each state to settle the question of woman suffrage for itself. For efficiency and progress, without waste and duplication in government. For the *conservation* of the best Womanhood of all conditions and stations of life. For the ultimate *union* of women of all classes and creeds along *non partisan* lines, so that the interests of womanhood, childhood, and civilization may be advanced *free* from the strife and division of politics, factions and parties. For the retention of the best *ideals* of the past adapted to women under modern conditions, so that the *fundamental principles* of Morality, of Patriotism, and of World Progress may be more firmly established in the present and future generations. MAOFESW Misc. Papers, Correspondence, Box 2, MHS.

44. *The Woman's Protest*, vol. 1, no. 1 (May 1912), p. 3.
45. Kenneally, "The Opposition to Woman Suffrage," p. 346.
46. Merk, "Massachusetts and the Woman Suffrage Movement," p. 293.
47. *The Remonstrance* (April 1910).
48. Ibid., n.d.
49. *The Anti-Suffragist*, vol. 1, no. 1 (July 1908).
50. O'Neill, *Everyone Was Brave*, p. 228.
51. Ibid., pp. 228-29.
52. *The Reply* (May 1913), pp. 1-2.
53. Merk, "Massachusetts and the Woman Suffrage Movement," p. 287.
54. Ibid.
55. One picture on a card issued by the New York State Association Opposed to Woman Suffrage showed a woman rocking and holding in her arms a bundle that looks like an infant, swaddled and labeled the "Ballot." The caption reads, "Hugging a Delusion."

I found calendars published by the Women's Anti Suffrage Association of Massachusetts for 1915, 1916 and 1917. Following are examples of the poems for January and April 1915:

When man becomes the nursemaid every day,
And wifie's marching with her flag unfurled,
There's just one thought to chase his gloom away,
"The hand that rocks the cradle rules the world!"

Five and four good Senators,
Seated in a row;
Along came the Suffragists
And said that they must go.
"We'll make a little black-list,
And unseat them in a trice;
The fact that they're our ablest men
With us will cut no ice.
The Constitution to amend

These men have dared refuse;
They think each State should have the say,
But they don't suit our views."
56. Judging from the photo, by no stretch of the imagination could one say the woman in the picture was being "accosted." Nor does the man in question appear to be a "worker." That the Antis interpreted the scene in such a way suggests either an obsessive fear of exposure to the unknown or a case of wishful thinking, or both.
57. Kenneally, "The Opposition to Woman Suffrage," p. 442.
58. Catt and Shuler, *Woman Suffrage and Politics*, p. 446.
59. NAWSA Misc. Papers, 1 of 2, Box 7, NYPL.
60. Ibid.
61. Ibid. In *Woman Suffrage and Politics*, Carrie Chapman Catt identified the league as the former Men's Anti-Suffrage League (p. 446). Apparently it also formed a branch in Nashville, where its members were mainly politicians who used the organization to bombard prosuffrage legislators.
62. *The Anti-Suffragist*, vol. 1, no. 2 (December 1908), p. 2.
63. Jones, "Some Impediments to Woman Suffrage."
64. *The Anti-Suffragist*, vol. 1, no. 2 (December 1908), p. 2.
65. Johnson Papers, postcard.
66. Mrs. Julian Heath, Letter to Helen K. Johnson, Johnson Papers. A list of lectures for 1909 scheduled to be given in New York City was published in *The Anti-Suffragist* (December 1908), p. 31. It included several well-known Antis, such as Margaret Deland, Annie Nathan Meyer, Mrs. Winslow Crannell, Rev. Howard Duffield, D.D., and Caroline Corbin. Among the list of topics were "The Constitution," "Woman and the Vote," "The Change of the Feminine Ideal," "Woman's Legal Rights in New York State," "Women's Opportunities and Vocations Without the Ballot."
67. *The Anti-Suffragist*, vol. 1, no. 2 (December 1908).
68. Ibid. On March 30, 1913, the Sunday *New York Times Magazine* featured an interview with Mrs. Johnson. The article began, "The Guidon Club is New York's most important organization in opposition to woman suffrage."
69. *The Woman's Protest*, vol. 3, no. 1 (May 1913), p. 14.
70. Johnson Papers, Letter dated May 26, 1915.
71. *The Reply* (May 1913), p. 13.
72. *New York Times Magazine*, interview with Johnson.
73. Many of the MAOFESW's supporters were businessmen and lawyers closely allied to corporations, some of whom would eventually make a career out of politics. Kenneally, "The Opposition to Woman Suffrage," p. 297.
74. Ibid., p. 296.
75. Kenneally suggests that perhaps they feared that knowledge of their meetings would create the impression that the MAOFESW was controlled by men, especially since many of the association's financial backers were men. Ibid., pp. 356-58.

76. MAOFESW, Executive Committee Meetings, October 27, November 10, 1915, pp. 72, 77-78, 115-16, MHS.
77. Kenneally, "The Opposition to Woman Suffrage," p. 438.
78. MAOFESW, Executive Committee Minutes, September 25, December 11, 19, 31, 1915, Misc. Papers, Box 2, MHS.
79. Man-Suffrage Association, *The Case Against Woman Suffrage*.

CHAPTER FIVE

1. Catt and Shuler, *Woman Suffrage and Politics*, pp. 110-292 passim.
2. NAWSA Papers, Letters from Congressmen, State Ratification Correspondence, Box 1, NYPL.
3. Catt and Shuler, *Woman Suffrage and Politics*, p. 134. See also Alan P. Grimes, *The Puritan Ethic and Woman Suffrage* (New York: Oxford University Press, 1967), p. 82.
4. The WCTU was organized in 1874 by Frances Willard. By 1900 it had established chapters in 10,000 towns and cities and had a dues-paying membership of 300,000. The Prohibition Party, supported by the WCTU, adopted a woman suffrage plank as early as 1869 and continued to endorse woman suffrage thereafter except in 1896. Grimes, *Puritan Ethic*, pp. 81-83.
5. *National Forum* (June 25, 1909), pp. 10, 11.
6. Charges that the Antis were tools of the liquor interests were made in 1895, when the suffragists blamed defeat in Massachusetts on liquor interests. Kenneally, "The Opposition to Woman Suffrage," pp. 287-88.
7. Ibid., p. 493. Kenneally says that there is no evidence of Massachusetts liquor dealers' opposition and that according to *The American Brewer*, journal of the national association, the National Association of Brewers was noncommittal in 1915.
8. A letter, dated June 7, 1908, from Alice H. Wilbur, a Portland, Oregon Anti, to a Mrs. Phillips is instructive. Reporting on a recent antisuffrage victory in Oregon, she wrote:

   . . . we worked up to the last minute and the reward is almost overwhelming. Our majority is now over 20,000 with ten more small counties to hear from . . . so far they [suffragists] have carried but one county out of the six accounted for. . . . It must show what cumulative work will do, and it ought to be a tremendous help to all the rest of you.

   She went on to report that Mrs. Duniway [presumably Abigail Scott Duniway] . . . printed another vicious epistle calling me the cat's paw of the Liquor Dealer's Association in one paragraph, and maintained that Prohibition defeated them in another. She and other suffragists will probably exploit the liquor proposition, and I have no doubt the liquor men do oppose it, but by this election there are over twenty-one "dry" counties in this State so that the liquor element can hardly be counted on as a winning power. They may be part of the opposition but *the bulk of it comes from the common sense of the masses*. Of course under the initiative it is possible for them to try again, but I doubt if they do, for only the fanatics could believe in their getting it now. Johnson Papers, New York State Association Opposed to Woman Suffrage folder (my italics).

9. *Woman's Protest*, vol. 9, no. 4 (August 1916), p. 14.
10. Ibid.
11. Ibid., vol. 1, no. 6 (October 1912).
12. In Catt's view, if there had been no prohibition movement, women would have been enfranchised two generations earlier. Catt and Shuler, *Woman Suffrage and Politics*, p. 279.
13. Foxcroft, "Why Are Women Opposing Woman Suffrage?," pp. 5-6.
14. Flexner, *Century of Struggle*, pp. 296-97.
15. Catt and Shuler, *Woman Suffrage and Politics*, pp. 110-277 passim.
16. Ibid., p. 133.
17. The liquor and brewing companies exerted considerable influence over politics through the large revenues they provided the federal and state government and as the best market for farmers' grain. Grimes, *Puritan Ethic*, p. 83.
18. Catt and Shuler, *Woman Suffrage and Politics*, p. 156.
19. Ibid., pp. 274-76.
20. Ibid., p. 204. The bill was passed 19 to 17 in the Senate, February 14, but lost in the House. A referendum did take place that year on the presidential suffrage bill, which was defeated by a majority of 144,000 (p. 206).
21. *National Forum* (June 25, 1909), p. 7.
22. Ibid., p. 9; also pp. 7, 11.
23. Grimes, *Puritan Ethic*, p. 81; Flexner, *Century of Struggle*, p. 298.
24. Catt and Shuler, *Woman Suffrage and Politics*, p. 136.
25. Ibid., pp. 150-52.
26. Grimes, *Puritan Ethic*, p. 82.
27. Catt and Shuler, *Woman Suffrage and Politics*, pp. 141-47.
28. Flexner, *Century of Struggle*, pp. 299-301.
29. Catt and Shuler, *Woman Suffrage and Politics*, p. 335.
30. Flexner, *Century of Struggle*, p. 302.
31. Ibid.
32. *Woman Citizen* (October 26, 1918), p. 429, cited in ibid., p. 310.
33. Merk, "Massachusetts and the Woman Suffrage Movement," p. 309.
34. Kenneally, "The Opposition to Woman Suffrage," p. 358.
35. Merk, "Massachusetts and the Woman Suffrage Movement," p. 310. Merk suggests that conversion of this family to the antisuffrage side may have been related to the spread of woman suffrage ideas among workingmen and -women. This would appear to be substantiated if one examines the number of individuals who combined antilabor and antisuffrage activities, even working directly to defeat the shorter-hour bill, as in the case of the Arkwright Club members.
36. Catt and Shuler, *Woman Suffrage and Politics*, pp. 147-48.

37. Mary Daly, *The Church and the Second Sex* (New York: Harper & Row, 1968).

38. James J. Kenneally, "Catholicism and Woman Suffrage in Massachusetts," *Catholic Historical Review*, vol. 53, no. 1 (April 1967), p. 43.

39. For example, the Episcopal church, Baptists, and Congregationalists continued to oppose woman suffrage, while the Quaker, Unitarian, Methodist, and Universalist churches began to accept it. Kenneally, "The Opposition to Woman Suffrage," pp. 317-19.

40. Kenneally, "Catholicism and Woman Suffrage in Massachusetts," p. 43.

41. Anthony and Harper, *History of Woman Suffrage*, vol. 4, pp. 1079-80.

42. Kenneally, "Catholicism and Woman Suffrage in Massachusetts," p. 47.

43. Ibid., p. 44; Flexner, *Century of Struggle*, p. 369 (footnote).

44. *Boston Herald*, February 15, 1885, cited by Kenneally, "Catholicism and Woman Suffrage in Massachusetts," p. 45.

45. Octavius B. Frothingham, et al., "Woman Suffrage Unnatural and Inexpedient," Boston, 1894, reprinted by MAOFESW, *Why Women Do Not Want the Ballot*, vol. 1, no. 13.

46. Kenneally, "Catholicism and Woman Suffrage in Massachusetts," p. 46.

47. Ibid., p. 54.

48. *Catholic Encyclopedia* (1912), vol. 15, p. 694, quoted in National Association Opposed to Woman Suffrage, "Some Catholic Views on Woman Suffrage," SSC.

49. Kenneally, "Catholicism and Woman Suffrage in Massachusetts," p. 49 (footnote 29).

50. Kenneally, "The Opposition to Woman Suffrage," pp. 378-79.

51. Kenneally, "Catholicism and Woman Suffrage in Massachusetts," p. 45.

52. National Association Opposed to Woman Suffrage, "Some Catholic Views on Woman Suffrage"; "Eminent Catholic Prelates Oppose Woman Suffrage"; "Cardinal Gibbons Says Women Should Keep from the Polls"; " 'Sinister Feminism' is Due to the Abdication of Man, Says Cardinal O'Connell" (SSC).

53. *The Anti-Suffragist* (June 1909).

54. MAOFESW, Monthly Reports for 1915, Misc. Papers, Boxes 1 and 2, MHS.

55. John H. Vincent, Letter to Reverend Dr. J. M. Buckley, April 18, 1894, reprinted by MAOFESW, *Why Women Do Not Want the Ballot*, vol. 1, no. 19. The Reverend Lyman Abbott, author and editor of *The Outlook*, was another influential Protestant clergyman who became an avid spokesman for the Antis. His wife was one of the organizers of the New York State Association Opposed to Woman Suffrage. Through *The Outlook*, he was able to bring the antisuffrage message to a wide audience. Lyman Abbott, "Why Women Do Not Wish the Suffrage," 1903, reprinted by MAOFESW, *Why Women Do Not Want the Ballot*, vol. 1, no. 59.

56. Illinois Association Opposed to the Extension of Suffrage to Women, "Woman Suffrage and the Labor Unions" (Chicago, 1900), p. 4.

57. Albany Auxiliary Association, "Woman Suffrage and Wages," no. 1, reprinted by MAOFESW, n.d., MSL.

58. Minnie Bronson, "Woman Suffrage and Child Labor Legislation," National Association Opposed to Woman Suffrage, 1914, SSC.

59. Minnie Bronson, "The Wage-Earning Woman and the State," MAOFESW, 1910, p. 1.
60. MAOFESW, "The Wage-Earning Woman and the State, A Reply to Misses Goldmark and Mrs. Kelley," July 1912.
61. Bissell, "A Talk to Every Woman," n.d., p. 10.
62. Mrs. George A. Caswell, "Address in Opposition to Woman Suffrage," MAOFESW, n.d. [ca. 1913], p. 9.
63. Albany Auxiliary Association, "Woman Suffrage and Wages."
64. Ibid. See also Mrs. George F. Arnold, "Ignorance of the Real Issues at Stake," *The Woman's Protest*, vol. 6, no. 6 (April 1915); Illinois Association, "Woman Suffrage and the Labor Unions," p. 5.
65. Albany Auxiliary Association, "Woman Suffrage and Wages." The Antis spun out this line of argument to an even finer point and maintained that as working women took jobs away from men or by competing for the same jobs forced a reduction of wages, they were also impairing their chances for marriage: "Jobless men dare not marry, and the social evil flourishes." Arnold, "Ignorance of the Real Issues at Stake," p. 14.
66. "Woman Suffrage and Wages," no. 2.
67. Ten Eyck, "Suffrage and Government," p. 8.
68. Johnson, "Woman's Progress vs. Woman Suffrage," p. 8; White, "The Ballot and the Woman in Industry"; Rensselaer, "Should We Ask for the Suffrage?"; Bronson, "The Wage-Earning Woman and the State"; Illinois Association, "Woman Suffrage and the Labor Unions"; MAOFESW, "The Wage-Earning Woman and the State."
69. Illinois Association, "Woman Suffrage and the Labor Unions," p. 5. The Antis even went so far as to popularize the notion that

    as women enter into competitive industrial life with men, just so does the death rate of little children increase and the birth rate decrease.

    Jones, "The Position of the Anti-Suffragists."
70. Jones, "The Position of the Anti-Suffragists."
71. Mary Dean Adams, "Wages and the Ballot," New York State Association Opposed to Woman Suffrage, 1909, NYPL.

CHAPTER SIX

1. Kenneally, "The Opposition to Woman Suffrage," pp. 419, 422, 443.
2. Ibid., pp. 446-47.
3. Ibid., p. 449.
4. In the 1913 legislature, the Drury Bill was proposed, which would have given Massachusetts women a chance to vote on woman suffrage. The Antis contended that the suffragists were afraid to let women vote on the question and that they worked against the bill. *Anti-Suffrage Essays by Massachusetts Women*, p. xii. In any event, the bill was defeated.

5. Kenneally, "The Opposition to Woman Suffrage," p. 463.
6. Ibid., p. 499.
7. Ibid., pp. 502, 507.
8. Flexner, *Century of Struggle*, p. 271.
9. Ibid.; Kenneally, "The Opposition to Woman Suffrage," p. 509.
10. *Anti-Suffrage Essays by Massachusetts Women*, pp. xi, x.
11. Kenneally, "The Opposition to Woman Suffrage," pp. 510, 517, 523, 524.
12. In 1913, Illinois women lawyers formulated a bill granting all forms of suffrage to women. It provided for a vote on presidential electors, important county officers, all city, town, and village officers (except police magistrates). The bill was passed, and shortly afterward, a municipal election was held in Chicago with one-quarter of a million women voting. Catt Papers, Box 2, "Historical Data."
13. Flexner, *Century of Struggle*, pp. 290, 291.
14. On December 12, 1866, the first vote was taken in Congress on woman suffrage, on the issue of whether to enfranchise the women of the District of Columbia. Nine senators voted for and 37 against the proposed bill. *Congressional Globe.* There is no record of any organized opposition at that time.
15. Johnson, *Woman and the Republic*, p. 349.
16. Ida Husted Harper records the year as 1878. *History of Woman Suffrage*, vol. 5 (New York: NAWSA, 1922), p. 678.
17. *The Woman's Protest*, vol. 1, no. 1 (May 1912).
18. Kenneally, "The Opposition to Woman Suffrage," p. 529. On January 10, 1878, A.A. Sargent introduced in the Senate a proposal for a federal woman suffrage amendment. While an adverse report was made, a minority report was presented by Senator George F. Hoar of Massachusetts on behalf of a women suffrage amendment. Also at issue was whether the suffrage petitioners would be allowed to present their case before the Senate. Their request was denied. *Congressional Record*, January 10, 1878.
19. In 1887, when Senator Hoar became chairman of the Senate Committee on Woman Suffrage, the committee secured a vote on the issue: 16 yes, 34 no, and 26 absent. In the debate, southern senators laid out the arguments upon which northern opposition would be based through the coming years. There were no Antis present, although a letter from Mrs. Clara T. Leonard and excerpts of a pamphlet by A. D. T. Whitney were read. January 25, 1887, 49th Congress, 2d session.
20. Anthony and Harper, *History of Woman Suffrage*, vol. 4, p. 381.
21. Kenneally, "The Opposition to Woman Suffrage," p. 532.
22. *The Woman's Protest*, vol. 1, no. 1 (May 1912).
23. Harper, *History of Woman Suffrage*, vol. 5, pp. 391ff.
24. U.S., Congress, Senate, Committee on Woman Suffrage. Hearing Before Committee on Woman Suffrage, Senate, 63d Cong., 1st sess., 1913.
25. Kenneally, "The Opposition to Woman Suffrage," pp. 538, 539.
26. MAOFESW, *Second Annual Report*, 1897.

27. Kenneally, "The Opposition to Woman Suffrage," p. 534. The suffragists had little success in influencing the platform committees of the major political parties (Republican, Democrat, Populist). They tended to fare better in the lesser parties, which needed their support (Prohibition, Greenback, Labor, Socialist). Grimes, *The Puritan Ethic*, p. 81.

28. This defeat "was due to opposition from a combination of the New England states and the Democratic South—a coalition of conservatism, states' rights, and possibly cotton industry interests." Gerda Lerner, *Women in American History* (New York, 1971), p. 170.

29. Flexner, *Century of Struggle*, p. 310.

30. *The Vanguard*, vol. 3, no. 2 (February 1918), p. 6, NYPL, uncatalogued pamphlets.

31. Ibid., p. 5.

32. American Constitutional League, "Home Rule," Brief Submitted to U.S. Senate, January 1919, NAWSA Papers, Misc. Fliers and Printed Matter, Box 7, NYPL.

33. Flexner, *Century of Struggle*, p. 314.

34. According to Flexner, " 'States' rights' had become the magic touchstone which united all the opponents of votes for women." Ibid., p. 310.

35. Kenneth R. Johnson, "Kate Gordon and the Woman-Suffrage Movement in the South," *Journal of Southern History* 38 (August 1972), pp. 365-92.

36. Ibid., pp. 371, 374.

37. Ibid., pp. 380, 386.

38. Ibid., pp. 391-92.

39. Here an old argument also took on a new twist. The league argued that the whole experience of the race had fitted the mother for unselfish devotion to her children to the point where they should and did come first with her. But this very element, at the same time, unfitted her for political life, where a disinterested and objective viewpoint was essential.

40. American Constitutional League, "Home Rule."

41. Flexner, *Century of Struggle*, p. 275.

42. The South feared not only the black woman vote but also enforcement of the Fourteenth Amendment providing for reduction of the basis of representation of a state denying the right of suffrage to male citizens. In other words, Southerners dreaded anything that called attention to the right of suffrage and that could possibly have an effect on the voting body.

43. U.S. Congress, Senate, 49th Cong., 2d sess., January 25, 1887, *Congressional Record*.

44. Taylor, *The Woman Suffrage Movement in Tennessee*, p. 112.

45. Ibid.

46. Ibid.

47. George Robinson Lockwood, "Woman Suffrage a Menace to the South—A Protest Against Its Imposition Through Federal Authority" (St. Louis, 1917), MSL.

273

48. Ibid. Not wanting to appear an enemy of "that race," Lockwood included a disclaimer at the end of his treatise in which he tried to distinguish between sentimental regard for the blacks he had known in his youth (slaves of his family) and his unalterable opposition

> to anything approaching social equality between whites and blacks, and any and everything that may lead to, or further, such equality, or may give political power to the negro.

49. Senators Wadsworth of New York and Reed of Missouri took the states' rights position to the extreme and declared they would vote against a federal amendment *forbidding* woman suffrage. Flexner, *Century of Struggle*, p. 304.

50. At the 1916 Republican Convention in Chicago, Lodge offered to compromise on the woman suffrage plank

> to favor extension of the suffrage to women, but *recognize the right of each state to settle this question for itself.*

This was accepted by a final vote of 35 to 11. Catt and Shuler, *Woman Suffrage and Politics*, pp. 253-54. The Democrats also hedged in this issue. Only the Progressive Party advocated granting of full political rights to women by both state *and* federal action.

51. Hollister, *The Woman Citizen*, p. 45.

52. Henry St. George Tucker, *Woman's Suffrage by Constitutional Amendment* (New Haven: Yale University Press, 1916).

53. Ibid., pp. 142, 145. Both the Fourteenth and Fifteenth amendments refer to the "right to vote." This by itself had radical implications for those, like the Antis, who regarded suffrage as a privilege rather than a right.

54. Ibid., p. 70.

55. Passage of the Eighteenth Amendment in December 1917, imposing prohibition on the states, effectively destroyed the states' rights arguments against woman suffrage. This did not stop the American Constitutional League or the southern states from continuing to oppose a federal woman suffrage amendment as an infringement of states' rights. It did, however, reduce the number of theoretical papers written to uphold this view.

56. Tucker, *Woman's Suffrage*, p. 72.

57. Ibid., pp. 44-45.

58. Ibid., pp. 105-6.

59. Ibid., p. 113.

60. In support of his position that there was no popular movement for black suffrage, Tucker pointed out several facts, among them that 27 of the 37 states of the Union in the decade prior to 1867 either adopted new constitutions or amended their old ones, and in not one of the 27 was suffrage extended to blacks, while in every case where it was attempted, it was denied (ibid., p. 81). Even as late as December 1863, Lincoln's Reconstruction plans for the South excluded blacks from voting, while the Congressional Reconstruction Bill passed by the Senate on July 2, 1864, provided suffrage for whites only. In that year too, Lincoln was renominated, but neither his platform nor that of the radical Republicans called for black suffrage.

Furthermore, also in that year, Connecticut, Kansas, Nevada, Pennsylvania, and Rhode Island adopted new constitutions or amended old ones, but none involved black suffrage. Tucker speculated that had a vote been taken at the time of its adoption, the Fifteenth Amendment would not have received popular approval.

61. Carrie Chapman Catt, reporting on her first three months as president of NAWSA, pointed out that a federal amendment appealed to women of states whose constitutions made a successful referendum impossible. Flexner, *Century of Struggle*, p. 274. It was not long, however, before Catt realized that the enemy was as much the power structure as the system.

62. Tucker, *Woman's Suffrage*, p. 51.

63. Ibid., p. 55.

64. Ibid., p. 94.

65. Ibid., p. 60.

66. Flexner, *Century of Struggle*, p. 320.

67. Taylor, *The Woman Suffrage Movement in Tennessee*, p. 75.

68. *Nashville Banner*, January 16, 1913, cited ibid., p. 76. The idea that woman suffrage was not native to the South was expressed even later. In a January 19, 1917, debate before the Tennessee House, members spoke in support of the antisuffrage position. P. B. Keith of Winchester argued that woman suffrage "came from the West and the North, like most of our troubles have come" (p. 96).

69. Ibid., p. 80.

70. *Woman's Protest*, vol. 8, no. 6, p. 13.

71. *Nashville Tennessean*, April 11, 1916, cited in Taylor, *The Woman Suffrage Movement in Tennessee*, p. 80.

72. *Woman's Protest*, vol. 9, no. 1, p. 13.

73. *Nashville Tennessean*, May 3, 1916, cited in Taylor, *The Woman Suffrage Movement in Tennessee*, p. 81.

74. Ibid.

75. Ibid.

76. Ibid., pp. 105, 110.

77. *Woman Patriot*, vol. 3, no. 35, p. 7. Apparently the one thing on which both Antis and states' rights suffragists could agree was rejection of a federal amendment. As indicated, the states' rights theme attracted many who were not necessarily against suffrage. Laura Clay of Kentucky, formerly active in NAWSA, had broken with the suffrage association on this issue and actually showed up in Tennessee to fight ratification. Flexner, *Century of Struggle*, p. 322.

78. A Tennessee Constitutional League had been formed to oppose ratification as a violation of the state constitution, but it was not nearly as active as the Southern Women's Rejection League. Taylor, *The Woman's Suffrage Movement in Tennessee*, p. 140 (footnote).

79. Ibid., p. 116.

80. *Nashville Tennessean*, August 13, 1920, cited ibid.

81. Ibid., p. 117. Catt immediately issued a statement that she had never advocated intermarriage and that she considered such a union an "absolute crime against nature."
82. Ibid., p. 119.
83. Allegedly antisuffrage politicians did not hesitate to threaten members of the legislature who favored woman suffrage with ruin of their business and political careers. Another tactic they supposedly used was to ply the prosuffrage legislators with liquor in an effort to keep them from voting. Flexner, *Century of Struggle*, p. 322.
84. Taylor, *The Woman Suffrage Movement in Tennessee*, p. 119.
85. *Nashville Tennessean*, August 22, 1920, cited ibid., p. 121.
86. Ibid., p. 122.
87. Ibid., p. 124.
88. *Leser v. Garnett, U.S. Supreme Court Reports*, U.S. pp. 257-59 (October term, 1921).

CHAPTER SEVEN

1. Ida M. Tarbell, *All in a Day's Work* (New York, 1939), p. 9.
2. Ibid., pp. 29-30.
3. Ibid., pp. 30, 26.
4. Ibid., pp. 31, 32, 33. Henry Ward Beecher was having an affair with Elizabeth Tilton, wife of Theodore Tilton, a liberal editor and friend of Elizabeth Cady Stanton. The affair was publicized by the free-love advocate Victoria Woodhull, who struck back at her critics by writing a lurid account of Beecher's relations with Tilton in *Woodhull's and Claflin's Weekly*. Beecher's friends defended him by smearing not only Woodhull but also Stanton and her suffragist associates. O'Neill, *Divorce in the Progressive Era*, p. 207; Johanna Johnston, *Mrs. Satan, the Incredible Saga of Victoria Woodhull* (New York: Popular Library, 1967).
5. Tarbell, *All in a Day's Work*, p. 34.
6. Ibid., pp. 34 (my italics), 35, 36.
7. Tarbell, *The Business of Being a Woman*, pp. 6, 49.
8. Ibid., p. 26.
9. Tarbell's ambivalence, and also a sense of bitterness, comes across in her description of the "new gospel" of the "uneasy woman":
    She will be a "free" individual, not one "tied" to a man. The "drudgery" of the household she will exchange for what she conceives to be the broad and inspiring work which men are doing. For the narrow life of the family she will escape to the excitement and triumph of a "career."
    Ibid., p. 27.
10. Tarbell, *All in a Day's Work*, pp. 40, 46. Coeducation was repugnant to most Antis, who felt that the opening of certain large universities to women did not represent a gain in the higher education of women. Tarbell specifically chose a "man's

college" even though "co-education was an advanced step and there were plenty of people in my environment to hint to me that it was not 'respectable' although my father and mother stoutly defended me in the adventure." Letter to John S. Phillips, n.d., pp. 2-3, SSC. It was therefore probably on the basis of her own experience that she wrote in *The Business of Being a Woman* that the coeducational experience had shown that college cannot "entirely rub femininity out and masculinity into a woman's brain" (p. 39).

11. Tarbell, *All in a Day's Work*, pp. 54, 31.
12. Ibid., pp. 56, 57 (my italics).
13. Ibid., p. 63.
14. Ibid., pp. 86, 87.
15. Ibid., p. 87.
16. Ibid.
17. Ibid., p. 85.
18. In *The Business of Being a Woman*, Tarbell wrote that woman's method was to plunge into action without discussion of ideas. "A woman rarely feels uncertainty about methods" and has not patience with other points of view. "Only by man and the rare woman is it accepted that talk is a good enough end in itself" (pp. 32-33). It would seem that she considered herself the "rare woman."
19. Tarbell, *All in a Day's Work*, p. 85.
20. Ibid., pp. 142-43 (my italics).
21. Ibid.
22. Tarbell, Letter to John S. Phillips, Ida Tarbell Papers, SSC. Again, this raises the question of how Tarbell viewed her own situation. Her life was a testimony to the concept of individuality. Tarbell must have realized that she was an exception, and yet her view of the exceptional was anything but complimentary. Did she regard herself as "sexless" and not to be trusted? Or was she an exception even to her exception? She hinted at what this exception to the exception might have been.

    A few women in every country have always and probably always will find work and usefulness and happiness in exceptional tasks. They are sometimes women who are born with what we call "bachelor's souls"—an interesting and sometimes even charming, though always an incomplete possession!

    Business, pp. 241-42.
23. Tarbell, *All in a Day's Work*, pp. 125, 143.
24. Ibid., p. 139
25. Ibid., p. 144.
26. Ibid., pp. 278-79.
27. Ibid., pp. 318-20.
28. Ibid., pp. 320, 326
29. Ibid., p. 327. It is possible that Tarbell was speaking here of here association with the Antis.
30. Ibid., p. 327; see also *Business*, pp. 218, 222.
31. Tarbell, *All in a Day's Work*, p. 327. In the Introduction to *The Business of Being a Woman*, Tarbell wrote,

the object of this little volume is to call attention to a certain distrust, which the author feels in the modern woman, of the significance and dignity of the work laid upon her by Nature and by society. (p. vii)

32. Tarbell, *All in a Day's Work*, p. 327 (my italics). Either she forgot that she was once listed as a member of the New York State Association Opposed to Woman Suffrage Executive Committee or else she regarded her involvement as minimal.

33. Ibid., pp. 405, 399, 407.

34. Tarbell, Letter to *The Sun*, quoted in *The Anti-Suffragist*, vol. 1, no. 2, December, 1908 (my italics).

35. Johnson Papers, New York State Association Opposed to Woman Suffrage, Executive Committee Letterhead, 1909. Tarbell delivered an address before Mrs. Mackay's suffrage society on Women of the French Revolution. Before closing, she made it clear to her audience that her researches had actually strengthened her objection to woman suffrage. Apparently, she emphasized the fact that "Women have always loved their own individual group more than any great mass." *The Anti-Suffragist*, vol. 3, no. 3 (March 1911), p. 5.

36. *The Woman's Protest*, vol. 1, no. 3 (July 1912), p. 11.

37. Harriet Burton Laidlow, letter to editor, *The New York Times* (May 26, 1912), quoted ibid.

38. Ibid. How, unmarried and childless, was Tarbell able to consider herself an expert on the subject?

39. Ida M. Tarbell, "The American Woman," *The American Magazine*, 6 installments, beginning vol. 69 (November 1909).

40. This theme was taken up in *The Business of Being a Woman* in her chapter of the same title in which she wrote that the change in women's education occurred in the nineteenth century with the realization that to make real democrats and fulfill the spirit of the Declaration of Independence, one had to begin with the child and therefore with the mother (p. 75).

41. Ibid.

42. Ibid.

43. Ibid. It is interesting to compare Tarbell's view of woman's role in the Civil War with that of Helen K. Johnson, who felt that the war brought women into an "unnatural relationship to society." *The New York Times*, interview, March 30, 1913.

44. Tarbell, "The American Woman" (my italics). Tarbell went on to elaborate:
    . . . the body of women will never demand anything because it is a right, but . . . when they need it to accomplish some good for which they feel themselves responsible, they will seek it—and get it. Necessity is what forces new tools into human hands—not argument and agitation.

45. Ibid. Tarbell was consistent in refusing in her own life to "exploit indiscriminately any unusual activity of women"; she refused President Wilson's invitation to become a member of his Tariff Commission for just this reason. Dorothea Dix was an inspirational model for other Antis besides Tarbell. Helen K. Johnson, for

example, could not resist drawing a comparison between what she regarded as the idle actions of the feminists and the concrete and humane endeavors of Dix. At the very time when Elizabeth Cady Stanton and Lucretia Mott were writing that indictment against the United States Government [Declaration of Sentiments], Dorothea Dix was presenting a memorial to the National Congress asking for an appropriation of five hundred thousand acres of the public lands to endow hospitals for the indigent insane. *Woman and the Republic*, pp. 51-52.

46. Tarbell, "The American Woman." In Tarbell's view, women were not the enduring victims of universal male oppression, but rather accomplices in perpetuating a system that gave them what they wanted. Tarbell's attitude toward the matter of female industry apparently was formed during her years at Allegheny. Although she entered the college a radical feminist—taking for granted the need to revolutionize the plight of downtrodden womanhood—she left with the view that it was not just women who suffered but that the weaker in general were universally the victims of the strong and powerful. *Business*, pp. 228-31; letter to Phillips. Thus, throughout most of her life she held that the question of injustice was a human, rather than a sex, question.

47. Tarbell, *Business*, pp. 16, 23.

48. Tarbell, "The American Woman," installment 5, "Her First Declaration of Independence" (my italics). See also *Business*, pp. 25-26.

49. Tarbell, "The American Woman," installment 6, "Those Who Did Not Fight."

50. Ibid. See also *Business*, p. 164:
   The Woman's Business has always suffered from lack of facility in adapting itself to new forms of expression. . . . The woman usually is as fixed as a star in its orbit. She resents changes of method, new interpretations, and fresh expressions. *It is she, not a man who stands an immovable mountain in the path of militant feminism.* (My italics.)
   In other words, woman follows her instinct to preserve the thing she is making. "Man, an experimenter and adventurer, cannot." Ibid., p. 166.

51. Tarbell, "The American Woman," installment 6.

52. Ibid.

53. Sarah Josepha Hale, *Woman's Record: or Sketches of All Distinguished Women from "the Beginning" Till A.D. 1850* (New York, 1853).

54. Ibid.

55. Tarbell, "The American Woman," installment 6.

56. Ibid.

57. Tarbell, *Business*, p. 167.

58. Ibid., p. 2. Three years later in *The Ways of Woman*, Tarbell warned that the "new woman" was "bent on making over the sex" (p. 63).

59. Tarbell, *Business*, pp. 52, 218. It would have been so much easier for Tarbell if she had arrived at the opposite conclusion. For by elevating woman's traditional role, she forced the question of whether her own was valid.

60. Ibid., pp. 63-70.

61. Ibid., p. 77.
62. Ibid., p. 199.
63. Ibid., pp. 80-81.
64. In her opening chapter entitled "The Uneasy Woman," Tarbell disparaged self-discussion as the most conspicuous occupation of American women in her time:
    Chronic self-discussion argues chronic ferment of mind, and ferment of mind is a serious handicap to both happiness and efficiency. (p. 1)
65. Ibid., pp. 78-80. Tarbell shares the basically moralistic outlook common to the muckrakers—the idea that man could be made "good." However, her solution embodied more than just passing laws to change the condition that made man "bad." With the Antis she believed that public opinion was the motivating force that would induce the electorate to pass the laws necessary for change. Public opinion was for Tarbell the final arbiter, and where but in the atmosphere of a stable and secure home was an enlightened public opinion able to be formed?
66. Ibid., p. 82. Tarbell even went so far as to say that the real service of a woman's higher education was to "fit her intellectually to be a companion worthy of a child" (p. 74).
67. Ibid., pp. 87, 88-89, 92.
68. Ibid., p. 51.
69. Ibid.
70. Ibid., pp. 137-38.
71. Davis, "The True Function of the Normal Woman," pp. 125-26, quoting Tarbell, *Business*, pp. 211-12.
72. Tarbell, *Business*, pp. 42, 43, 45.
73. Ibid., pp. 41-42.
74. Letter to John S. Phillips, n.d., p. 2, SSC. The letter began "To the Editor-in-Chief of the American Magazine" but does not seem to have been intended for publication. Undated, it was composed sometime between 1909 and 1920, probably after publication of *The Ways of Woman* in 1915.
75. Ibid., p. 4.
76. Ibid.
77. Tarbell indicated that Helen Keller said this to her. Ibid., p. 1.
78. Ibid., pp. 9-10.
79. Ibid., pp. 11, 13-14.

CHAPTER EIGHT

1. One of the earliest notices of the Antis by the suffragists occurred in *The Woman's Journal*, vol. 13, no. 10 (March 11, 1882). On that occasion the suffragists were more than generous in describing their opponents:
    They are women as intelligent, as philanthropic and as well educated as those who petition for Woman Suffrage; and there are more of them. There is

nothing new about this fact . . . that the majority of women are opposed to suffrage up to this time.
Thirteen years later a more typical suffrage reaction was condescension. By 1895 the suffragists were no longer willing to admit that the Antis represented the majority of women. In fact, in terms of sheer numbers they believed they had the advantage and were beginning to talk about feeling sorry for the remonstrants. *The Woman's Journal*, vol. 26, no. 24 (June 15, 1895), p. 138.

2. See *The Woman's Journal*, April 21, 1894; March 20, 21, April 20, May 18, 25, June 15, October 25, November 2, 23, 1895; December 5, 1905; February 2, 1907.

3. *The Woman's Journal*, March 7, 1885, quoted in Merk, "Massachusetts and the Woman Suffrage Movement," p. 67. According to Merk, in the minds of the suffragists, the Massachusetts Antis embodied the woman's antisuffrage movement even after 1895, when other associations were formed (p. 293).

4. Nashville *Tennessean*, August 30, 1914, quoted in Taylor, *The Woman Suffrage Movement in Tennessee*, p. 86.

5. Ibid., April 23, 1916.

6. Ibid., June 18, 1916.

7. "Anti-Suffrage Periscope Detected Showing Which Way the Wind Blows," typed ms., probably intended as a news release, NAWSA Papers, Box 7. Wheeler was chairman of the Man-Suffrage Association.

8. NAWSA news release, October 2, 1917, NAWSA Papers, Box 7, 1 of 2.

9. "Mrs. Catt Quotes John Hay Against Antis' Contention That to Believe in Peace is to Be a Traitor to Country," November 1, 1917. Press release, NAWSA Papers, Box 7. The attack and rebuttal occurred on the eve of the New York State election that granted enfranchisement to women. It was probably a last-ditch effort by the Antis to prevent New York State from becoming an equal suffrage state.

10. "Wanted—More Patriots Like Mrs. Carrie Chapman Catt," typed ms., NAWSA Papers, Box 7. Catt continued her rebuttal of the antisuffrage smear campaign against her and other leading feminists in the prosuffrage *Woman Citizen*: "John Hay, Mrs. Catt and Patriotism" (November 10, 1917); "Lies at Large" (June 1927), p. 10; "An Open Letter to the D.A.R" (July 1927), p. 10.

11. Mrs. Mary Sumner Boyd to Mr. Frederick Whitin, March 17, 1916, NAWSA Papers.

12. Whitin to Boyd, June 21, 1916, NAWSA Papers.

13. "Effects of Woman's Suffrage on the Political Situation in the City of Chicago," n.d, NAWSA Papers, 1 of 2, Box 7.

14. NAWSA Misc. Papers, Box 7.

15. Both women were directors of the Department of Social Investigation in the Chicago School of Civics and Philanthropy. Their pamphlet was published by the Boston Equal Suffrage Association for Good Government sometime after 1911, since in it they refer to both Washington and California as woman suffrage states.

16. Florence Kelley and Pauline and Josephine Goldmark, "The Truth About Wage-Earning Women and the State, A Reply to Miss Minnie Bronson" (Concord,

N.H.: Equal Suffrage Association, June 1, 1912). The "truth" of their argument was that improvements in laws affecting wage-earning women between 1908 and 1910 were due not to the spontaneous action of legislators in nonsuffrage states but to the action of the United States Supreme Court in a 1908 Oregon case that upheld the ten-hour law for women and removed the barrier to such legislation.

17. William T. Sedgwick, "Feminist Revolutionary Principle Biologically Unsound," *New York Times* (January 18, 1914), reprinted by the Man-Suffrage Association as "Principles of Feminism Biologically Unsound." Dr. Sedgwick was on the staff of the Massachusetts Institute of Technology.

18. Dr. Frederick Peterson, "Normal Woman Not Neurotic," NAWSA, March 1914, NYPL, uncatalogued pamphlets.

19. Empire State Campaign Committee Press Release, August 23, 1915, Catt Papers.

20. Empire State Campaign Committee Press Release, August 24, 1915, Catt Papers.

21. Some of the speakers and their titles were: Charlotte Perkins Gilman, "Woman Suffrage Would Unsex Women"; George Houghton Gilman, "Woman Suffrage Would Increase Divorce"; Beatrice Forbes-Robertson Hale, "Indirect Influence is Enough"; Harriet B. Laidlaw, "Women are Different from Men"; Fola La Follette, "Women Would Take the Offices from the Men"; Hutchins Hapgood, "It Would Make Woman Less Attractive"; Inez Milholland, "Woman's Place Is in the Home"; Sadie American, "Women Are Already Overburdened"; Inez Haynes Gillmore, "The Ballot Means the Bullet"; Maude E. Miner, "Undesirable Women Chiefly Would Use the Vote"; Lincoln Steffens, "Woman Suffrage Would Increase Corruption"; Maud Nathan, "Women Cannot Defend Their Right to Vote"; Gilbert E. Roe, "There Are Too Many Voters Already"; Morris Hillquit, "Woman Suffrage is Just But Not Expedient"; Frederic C. Howe, "Women Don't Understand Politics." NAWSA, n.d.

22. Alice Stone Blackwell, "Objections Answered," NAWSA, n.d.

23. Blackwell went on to quote Julia Ward Howe:

Out of our 46 states only four have Anti-Suffrage Assns. Tiny anti-suffrage "committees" exist in four states more. There are Suffrage Assns. in 33 states and several territories.

In New York, at the time of the last constitutional convention, the suffragists secured more than 300,000 signatures to their petitions; the anti-suffragists, only 15,000. The woman suffrage petitions presented to the recent constitutional convention in Michigan bore 175,000 signatures. There were no petitions on the other side. In Chicago, not long ago 97 organizations, with an aggregate membership of more than 10,000 women, petitioned for a woman suffrage clause in the new city charter, while only one small organization of women petitioned against it. In Maine, Iowa, Kansas, in short, in every state where petitions for suffrage and remonstrances against it have been sent to the legislature, the petitioners have always outnumbered the remonstrants, and have generally outnumbered them 50 or 100 to one. On the occasion when the government took an official referendum among women on the subject (in Mass. in 1895), the women's vote was in favor of suffrage 25 to one.

Most women are as yet indifferent on the suffrage question; but, of those who take any lively interest in it either way, the great majority are in favor. *The Woman's Journal*, August 1, 1908.

24. Blackwell, "Objections Answered."
25. Carrie Chapman Catt, ed., *Woman Suffrage by Federal Amendment* (New York: NAWSA, 1917).
26. Ibid., p. 72.
27. Ibid., p. 73.
28. Ibid., pp. 74-75, 77. Catt even enlisted as an ally Walter E. Clark, chief justice of the Supreme Court of North Carolina, who argued that the only way to secure the South against the eventuality of readmitting blacks to the polls was by gaining the added strength supplied by the white woman vote. In his words, "The votes of 260,000 white women can be relied on to stand solid against any measure or any man who proposes to question Anglo-Saxon supremacy" (p. 79).
29. Carrie Chapman Catt, Letter to the Speakers in New York campaign, October 9, 1915, Catt Papers.
30. Carrie Chapman Catt, Letter to the Mrs. Sarah Clay Bennett, August 1, 1931, Catt Papers.
31. Lerner, *Women in American History*, pp. 170-71.
32. Carrie Chapman Catt, Telegram to Governor William D. Stevens of California, July 9, 1920, NAWSA Papers, Box 1.
33. Taylor, *The Woman Suffrage Movement in Tennessee*, p. 107.
34. Ibid.
35. *The Boston Saturday Evening Gazette*, editorial, n.d., Houghton Library.
36. *The Boston Herald*, Letter to Editor, 1898.
37. L. M. Haskins, Letter to Helen Mansfield, January 29, 1898, Houghton Library.
38. Catt and Shuler, *Woman Suffrage and Politics*, p. 234. According to Gerda Lerner, the woman suffrage movement was in its doldrums from 1890 to 1915. By 1912, after sixty-four years of organized effort, only nine states allowed women to vote, and all of these were in the West, for a total of forty-five electoral votes. This period also witnessed the death of three of the suffragists' outstanding leaders: Lucy Stone in 1893, Elizabeth Cady Stanton in 1902, and Susan B. Anthony in 1906. In Lerner's view, woman suffrage was simply superseded in the popular imagination at that time by other more urgent problems, such as American expansion in the Caribbean and Pacific and the domestic problems of rapid urbanization, industrial exploitation, and agrarian stress. *Women in American History*, pp. 159-61.

According to Alan P. Grimes, woman suffrage ebbed and flowed with the successes of third parties. In the 1890s in Colorado and Idaho it was supported by Populists, who needed voters. The passing of Populism as an effective force in American politics accounted for the fact that the woman suffrage movement lost momentum, and for fourteen years following its triumphs of 1896 met with only a dreary succession of defeats. For Grimes, it was not until the Progressive movement developed in 1910 that suffrage referenda began to be successful in other states. Between 1910 and 1914 the success of woman suffrage in the West was due to its association with the Progressive movement. *Puritan Ethic*, pp. 94-101.

Furthermore, in Congress, too, the suffrage cause underwent a decline during this period. Between 1900 and 1913 the annual suffrage bill proposing a constitutional amendment was never even reported out of committee. Johnson, "Kate Gordon and the Woman-Suffrage Movement," p. 366.

39. Catt and Shuler, *Woman Suffrage and Politics*.
40. Theodore Roosevelt, Letter to President of National Norwegian Woman Suffrage Association, May 6, 1910, NAWSA Papers.
41. Quoted in Catt and Shuler, *Woman Suffrage and Politics*, p. 238.
42. Stanton, *Eighty Years and More*, p. 451.
43. Kenneally, "The Opposition to Woman Suffrage," p. 443.
44. Catt and Shuler, *Woman Suffrage and Politics*, p. 330.
45. Ibid., p. 109.

CHAPTER NINE

1. John Stuart Mill and Harriet Taylor Mill, *Essays on Sex Equality*, ed. Alice S. Rossi (Chicago: University of Chicago Press, 1970), pp. 238, 173, 168.
2. Ronald V. Sampson, *The Psychology of Power* (New York, 1966), pp. 100-102.
3. In *The Pursuit of Loneliness* (1970), Philip E. Slater maintains that at the core of our culture is the assumption of scarcity and that, consequently, competition becomes necessary for individuals to get a share of the fixed pie. In this situation inequality becomes inevitable. In the family, he believes, the mother exploits her child to fulfill her own thwarted dreams and blocked talents and impresses on her child the old cultural value that he must be "best." An extract from "An Open Letter to My Dear Friend and Sister Frances E. Willard" (1888) by antisuffragist Caroline Corbin bears testimony to this hypothesis:

When a woman bears a household of boy babies, strong, turbulent, hot-blooded even in infancy, and brings them up, every one of them, to a simple, strong, and noble manhood, as thousands of women have done all over the land, she learns some things about the nature of men . . . and one of these things is that if you, a woman, wish to employ force in your system of government, you may do it safely and wisely before your boy has outgrown his knickerbockers, but *not* after that time. Every forceful method, every arbitrary restriction, on the part of his mother after that harms your boy. From the time when manhood begins to stir in his veins, he realizes more or less clearly that he was born to physical and intellectual mastery over women, and the more manly the boy the clearer will be this sense in him.

4. Mill and Mill, *Essays on Sex Equality*, pp. 140-41.
5. Sampson, *Psychology of Power*, p. 101.

6. Ibid., p. 63.
7. O'Neill, *Everyone Was Brave*, pp. 64, 412.
8. Ibid., pp. 412, 56.
9. Klein, *The Feminine Character*, pp. 4, 5.
10. Georg Simmel, "Das Relative und das Absolute im Geschlechterproblem," *Philosophische Kultur* (Leipzig, 1911), in Klein, ibid., p. 82.
11. Klein, *The Feminine Character*, pp. 82, 23.
12. Sheri Fenwick Naditch, "Women and Psychopathology," Cornell University, 1972, p. 5.
13. Judith Bardwick, *Psychology of Women: A Study of Bio-Cultural Conflicts* (New York: Harper & Row, 1971).
14. Matina S. Horner, "Woman's Will to Fail," *Psychology Today*, vol. 3, no. 6 (November 1969), p. 36.
15. Barry, "Why Women Oppose Woman's Suffrage," pp. 326-27.
16. Gilder, "A Letter on Woman Suffrage," p. 11.
17. Parker, "Are Suffragists Sincere Reformers?," p. 83.
18. Albert Memmi, *The Colonizer and the Colonized* (New York: The Orion Press, 1965), pp. 70-71.
19. Ibid., pp. 71, 89.
20. Ibid., p. 85.
21. Ibid., pp. 91, 114. Kate Millett points out that "In terms of industry and production, the situation of women is in many ways comparable both to colonial and to pre-industrial peoples. Although they achieved their first economic autonomy in the industrial revolution and now constitute a large and underpaid factory population, women do not participate directly in technology or in production." Even when they do participate in production of commodities, they do not "own or control or even comprehend the process in which they participate." Furthermore, women's distance from technology "is sufficiently great that it is doubtful that [in the absence of males] they could replace or repair such machines on any significant scale. If knowledge is power, power is also knowledge, and a large factor in their subordinate position is the fairly systematic ignorance patriarchy imposes upon women." *Sexual Politics* (Garden City, N.Y.: Doubleday & Company, Inc., 1970), pp. 41-42.
22. Memmi, *Colonizer and Colonized*, pp. 116, 95.
23. Mary Wollstonecraft, writing in 1792, was concerned about the fact that masculine virtues seemed excessively valuable to early feminists. Women resemble soldiers, she wrote, in that, "They both acquire manners before morals and a knowledge of life before they have, from reflection, any acquaintance with the grand ideal outline of human nature." *A Vindication of the Rights of Woman* (New York: W. W. Norton & Company, Inc., 1967), p. 40.
24. Memmi, *Colonizer and Colonized*, p. 96.
25. Ibid., p. 99.
26. Ibid., p. 121.
27. Ibid., p. 128.

28. Ibid., p. 138.
29. Kraditor, *Up from the Pedestal*, p. 13.
30. Kraditor, *Ideas*, p. 25.
31. Kraditor, *Up from the Pedestal*, p. 14.
32. Kraditor, *Ideas*, pp. 34, 27.
33. Ibid., pp. 34-35.
34. Kraditor, *Up from the Pedestal*, p. 13.
35. Kraditor, *Ideas*, p. 35.
36. Ibid.
37. Ibid., p. 32.
38. Kraditor, *Up from the Pedestal*, p. 8.
39. William L. O'Neill, "Feminism as a Radical Ideology" in *Dissent, Explorations in the History of American Radicalism*, ed. Alfred F. Young (DeKalb: Northern Illinois University Press, 1968), p. 281.
40. Ibid., pp. 283, 287.
41. O'Neill, *Everyone Was Brave*, p. 51.
42. Kraditor, *Up from the Pedestal*, p. 10.
43. MAOFESW, *Third Annual Report*, 1898.
44. Lyman, "The Anti-Suffrage Ideal," p. 120.
45. O'Neill, *Divorce in the Progressive Era*, pp. 266, 82.
46. Ibid., p. 268.
47. Ibid., p. 58.
48. Ibid., p. 50.
49. Ibid., pp. 72-74.
50. Ibid., p. 77.
51. Ibid., pp. 91, 203.
52. Johnson, *Women and the Republic*, p. 174.
53. O'Neill, *Divorce*, pp. 78, 249.
54. Johnson, *Women and the Republic*, p. 178.
55. Klein, *The Feminine Character*, p. 20.
56. Kraditor, *Ideas*, pp. 42, 14.
57. Klein, *The Feminine Character*, p. 24.
58. J. Lionel Tayler, *The Nature of Woman* (New York: E. P. Dutton & Co., 1913).
59. O'Neill, *Divorce*, p. 210.
60. Klein, *The Feminine Character*, p. 18.
61. Kate Chopin, *The Awakening* (New York: Capricorn Books, [1899] 1964) p. 19.
62. Christopher Lasch, *The New Radicalism in America 1889-1963* (New York: Vintage Books, 1965), pp. 56-57, 17-18.
63. Ibid., p. 67.
64. Ibid., pp. 65, 58.
65. Grimes, *The Puritan Ethic*; Lerner, *Women in American History*; Flexner, *Century of Struggle*.
66. Kenneally, "The Opposition to Woman Suffrage."
67. Helen Waite Papashvily, *All the Happy Endings* (New York, 1956).

68. Jill Conway, "Jane Addams: An American Heroine," in *The Woman in America*, ed. Robert J. Lifton (Boston: Beacon Press, 1967).
69. Grimes, *The Puritan Ethic*, pp. 94, 89.
70. Ibid., p. 111.
71. Ibid., pp. 134, 118. It should be noted that quite a few members of the Man-Suffrage Association as well as the husbands of numerous leading Antis were university professors.
72. Ibid., pp. 118-19.
73. Lerner, *Women in American History*, pp. 140, 110.
74. Flexner, *Century of Struggle*, p. 294.
75. Ibid., pp. 295-96.
76. Ibid., pp. 301, 302.
77. Kenneally, "The Opposition to Woman Suffrage," p. 166.
78. Ibid., pp. 188-89.
79. Distrust of the democratic experiment in the late nineteenth century was not limited to the Boston Brahmins, but was apparently a growing concern of a large segment of the population. Even the suffragists were aware of this attitude and characteristically used it to explain their continuing lack of success. They believed that "a modern skepticism as to the supreme merit of a democratic government and a general disgust with the prevalent corruption" had come about and made the struggle to extend the franchise even more difficult. Anthony and Harper, *History of Woman Suffrage*, vol. 4, p. xxvi.
80. Papashvily, *All the Happy Endings*, pp. 23, 24, 14.
81. Ibid., p. xvi.
82. Ibid., p. 57.
83. Conway, "Jane Addams," pp. 248, 257, 259 (my italics).
84. Illinois Association, "The Woman Movement in America."
   In a special way the struggle for woman's enfranchisement became the symbol of women's entry into public life—an event that affirmed her abandonment of the desire to be completely confined to the home in dependence, idleness, or duty. It gave sign instead of her dedication to higher and broader levels of individual and social responsibility.
   Janet Giele, "Social Change in the Feminine Role: A Comparison of Woman's Suffrage and Woman's Temperance, 1870-1920" (Ph.D. dissertation, Radcliffe, 1961), p. 21.
85. Illinois Association Opposed to Woman Suffrage, *Fifteenth Annual Report*, 1911.

EPILOGUE

1. Flexner, *Century of Struggle*, p. 325.
2. At a 1917 meeting of the New York State Association Opposed to Woman Suffrage, after the state had given women the vote, Mrs. Arthur M. Dodge introduced the following resolution:

> While the Committee still believes that suffrage is not an inherent right, nevertheless, having once been conferred, it becomes a duty and a responsibility, and as such must be exercised.

"Anti-Suffragists and Suffragists in New York," *The Outlook* 117 (November 28, 1917), p. 487.

3. Margaret Gibbs, *The DAR* (New York: Holt, Rinehart and Winston, 1969), pp. 100-117.
4. "The Common Enemy," pamphlet distributed by DAR, n.d., NAWSA Papers.
5. Carrie Chapman Catt, statement in response to DAR, Catt Papers.
6. Ida Tarbell, "Is Woman Suffrage a Failure?," *Good Housekeeping* (October 1924).
7. Ibid.
8. Ibid.
9. Ibid.

Bibliography

ABBREVIATIONS

MAOFESW   Massachusetts Association Opposed to the Further Extension
           of Suffrage to Women
MHS   Massachusetts Historical Society
MSL   Massachusetts State Library
NAWSA   National Woman Suffrage Association
NYPL   New York Public Library
SSC   Sophia Smith Collection, Smith College

PRIMARY SOURCES

Manuscript Collections

Anti-Suffrage Material. Fliers, pamphlets, "Some Catholic Views on Woman
    Suffrage," etc. SSC.
Catt, Carrie Chapman. Papers, letters, Empire State Campaign Committee
    material, etc. NYPL.
Johnson, Helen Kendrick. Papers, letters, etc. NYPL.
Leatherbee, Mrs. Albert T. Scrapbook, papers of the Massachusetts Association
    Opposed to the Further Extension of Suffrage to Women. MHS.
Massachusetts Association Opposed to the Further Extension of Suffrage to
    Women. Miscellaneous papers to 1898. Houghton Library, Harvard
    University.
Massachusetts Association Opposed to the Further Extension of Suffrage to
    Women. Papers, journals, reports, campaign materials, newspaper clippings,
    manuscript letters, diaries, leaflet publications. MHS.

National American Woman Suffrage Association. Papers, miscellaneous fliers and printed matter, news releases, letters from congressmen, state ratification correspondence, etc. NYPL.
New York State Association Opposed to Woman Suffrage. Fliers, postcards, etc. MAOFESW Papers, MHS.
Tarbell, Ida. Papers, letters, etc. SSC.
Woman Suffrage Scrapbooks. NYPL.

Annual Reports of Antisuffrage Associations

Illinois Association Opposed to Woman Suffrage
  Third Annual Report, 1899.
  Fifth Annual Report, 1901.
  Fifteenth Annual Report, 1911.

MAOFESW
  First Annual Report, 1896.
  Second Annual Report, 1897.
  Third Annual Report, 1898.
  Seventh Annual Report, 1902.
  Eleventh Annual Report, 1906.
  Twelfth Annual Report, 1907.

Public Documents

Congressional Globe, Minority Report to the U.S. Senate. December 12, 1866.
Congressional Record, 49th Cong., 2d sess., January 25, 1887.
Congressional Record, 66th Cong., 1st sess., June 3, 4, 1919.
Hearing Before the U.S. Senate Committee on Woman Suffrage, 49th Cong., 2d sess., January 25, 1887.
Hearing Before the U.S. Senate Committee on Woman Suffrage, 63d Cong., 1st sess., April 19, 21, 26, 1913.
Leser v. Garnett, U.S. Supreme Court Reports, U.S. 257-59, October Term, 1921.

Journals, Magazines, and Newspapers

Anti Suffrage Bulletin, April 1918.
The Anti-Suffragist, July, December 1908; September 1909.
The Boston Herald, October 12, 1895, 1898.
The Boston Saturday Evening Gazette, editorial, n.d., Houghton Library.
Brooklyn Daily Eagle, October 4, 1915.
Chicago *Record-Herald*, May 17, 1911.
Nashville Tennessean, August 30, 1914; December 19, 1915; April 23, June 18, 1916.
National Forum, June 25, 1909.
The New York Times, January 18, 1914; November 25, 1917.
The *Remonstrance*, October 1909; January, April, October 1910.
The Reply, May 1913.
The Vanguard, December 1917; February 1918.
Woman Citizen, November 10, 1917; June, July 1927.
The Woman Patriot, vol. 3, no. 35.
The Woman's Journal, March 11, 1882; April 21, 1894; February 16, March 21, 30, April 20, May 18, 25, June 1, 15, October 25, November 2, 23, 1895; December 5, 1905; February 2, 1907; December 9, 1911.
The Woman's Protest, May, July 1912; May 1913; March, August 1916.

Pamphlets

Abbott, Edith, and Sophonisba P. Breckinridge. "The Wage-Earning Woman and the State: a Reply to Miss Minnie Bronson." Boston Equal Suffrage Association for Good Government, n.d.
Abbott, Lyman. "Why Women Do Not Wish the Suffrage," 1903. MAOFESW, *Why Women Do Not Want the Ballot*, vol. 1, no. 59.
Adams, Mary Dean. "Wages and the Ballot." New York State Association Opposed to Woman Suffrage, 1909. NYPL.
Albany Auxiliary Association. "Woman Suffrage and Wages," no. 1. Reprinted by MAOFESW, n.d. MSL.
———. "Women Suffrage and Wages," no. 2.
American Constitutional League. "Home Rule." Brief Submitted to U.S. Senate, January 1919 Against Proposal for Constitutional Amendment Compelling States to Adopt Woman Suffrage. NAWSA Papers, NYPL.

"An Appeal to Congressmen and Representatives from New England Wives and Mothers." MAOFESW, March 17, 1913.

Bissell, Emily P. "A Talk to Women on the Suffrage Question." New York State Association Opposed to Woman Suffrage, 1909.

_____. "A Talk to Every Woman." The Virginia Association Opposed to Woman Suffrage, n.d.

Blackwell, Alice Stone. "Objections Answered." NAWSA, n.d.

Bock, Annie. "Address to the U.S. Senate Committee on Woman Suffrage, Opposing a Federal Woman Suffrage Amendment." 1913, 63rd Congress.

_____. "Woman Suffrage," n.d.

The British League for Opposing Woman Suffrage. "Black Tuesday." No. 42, November 21, 1911, MHS.

Bronson, Minnie. "The Wage-Earning Woman and the State." MAOFESW, 1910.

_____. "Woman Suffrage and Child Labor Legislation." National Association Opposed to Woman Suffrage, 1914, SSC.

Caswell, Mrs. George A. "Address in Opposition to Woman Suffrage." MAOFESW, n.d. [ca. 1913].

Cholmeley, Robert F. "The Women's Anti-Suffrage Movement." London: National Union of Women's Suffrage Societies, 1908.

Corbin, Caroline. "An Open Letter to My Dear Friend and Sister Frances E. Willard." 1888, NYPL.

_____. "Equality." Illinois Association Opposed to Woman Suffrage, Chicago, June 1910.

Crosby, John F. "The Advisability of Inserting the Word Sex Before the Word Race in the Fifteenth Amendment to the Constitution of the United States. Washington, D.C.: Georgetown University, 1910.

DAR. "The Common Enemy." NAWSA Papers, n.d., NYPL.

District of Columbia Association Opposed to Woman Suffrage. "Article on Woman Suffrage." Introduced in U.S. Senate by Hon. James E. Martine, senator from New Jersey, February 25, 1915, MHS.

Dos Passos, John R. "Equality of Suffrage Means the Debasement Not Only of Women But of Men." New York: The National Association Opposed to Woman Suffrage, n.d.

Fay, Clement K., Esq. "Municipal Woman Suffrage, Argument of Clement K. Fay, Esq. for Remonstrants." Brookline: The Chronicle Press, 1887.

"The Feminist Program." The Unpopular Review, April-June 1916. Republished by The Woman's Anti-Suffrage Association of Massachusetts.

Frothingham, Octavius B., et al. "Woman Suffrage Unnatural and Inexpedient." Boston, 1894.

George Alice N. "Woman's Rights vs. Woman Suffrage." New York: National Association Opposed to Woman Suffrage, 1913.

Gilder, Jeannette L. "Why I am Opposed to Woman Suffrage." *Harper's Bazaar*, May 19, 1894. MAOFESW, *Why Women Do No Want the Ballot*, vol. 1, no. 20.

Gilder, Mrs. Richard Watson [H. de K. G.]. "A Letter on Woman Suffrage." MAOFESW, April 1894.

Hamilton, Gail. Letter. Printed by MAOFESW, n.d.

Hewitt, Hon. Abram S. "Statement in Regard to the Suffrage." Issued by the New York State Association Opposed to the Extension of the Suffrage to Women, n.d.

Howe, Marie Jenney, "An Anti-Suffrage Monologue." New York: NAWSA, 1912.

Illinois Association Opposed to the Extension of Suffrage to Women. "An Appeal to the Common Sense and the Educated Thought of Men and Women Against the Proposed Extension of Suffrage to Women." N.d.

_____. "Socialism vs. Legal Marriage."

_____. "The Woman Movement in America." N.d. [ca. 1902].

_____. "Woman Suffrage and the Labor Unions." Chicago, 1900.

Illinois Association Opposed to Woman Suffrage. Description of Association. 1900, NYPL.

Johnson, Helen K. "Woman's Progress versus Woman Suffrage." New York Association Opposed to Woman Suffrage, n.d.

Kelley, Florence, and Pauline and Josephine Goldmark. "The Truth About Wage-Earning Women and the State, A Reply to Miss Minnie Bronson." Concord, N.H.: Equal Suffrage Association, June 1, 1912.

Knapp, Adeline. "An Open Letter to Mrs. Carrie Chapman Catt." New York State Association Opposed to the Extension of Suffrage to Women, November 10, 1899.

Leatherbee, Mrs. Albert T. "Woman Suffrage Does Not Mean Prohibition." Vermont Association Opposed to Woman Suffrage, n.d. [ca. 1915].

Lewis, Mrs. Helen Arion. "Woman Suffrage a Menace to the Nation." Nebraska Association Opposed to Woman Suffrage, n.d.

Lockwood, George Robinson. "Woman Suffrage a Menace to the South—A Protest Against Its Imposition Through Federal Authority." St. Louis, 1917, MSL.

McVickar, Mrs. Estelle R. "What is an Anti-Suffragist?" Read by the author before the Mount Vernon Auxiliary of the Society Opposed to the Extension of Suffrage to Women, n.d.

MAOFESW. "Woman Suffrage in Practice." A criticism of George Creel, "What have Women Done with the Vote," which appeared in *The Century Magazine*, March 1914, MHS.

_____. "The Equal Custody of Children by Parents." N.d., Houghton Library.

_____. "Suffrage and the Saloons." Republished from The *Remonstrance*, October 1914.

_____. "The Wage-Earning Woman and the State. A Reply to Misses Goldmark and Mrs. Kelley." July 1912.

Marshall, Edward. "A Woman Tells Why Woman Suffrage Would Be Bad." New York State Association Opposed to Woman Suffrage, n.d., Houghton Library.

The Men's League Opposed to Woman Suffrage. "Brief Argument Against Woman Suffrage." Philadelphia, 1913.

M'Intire, Mary, A. J. Letter to Editor, *Boston Sunday Herald*. Reprinted as "Of No Benefit to Woman: She is a Far Greater Power Without Suffrage." N.d., Houghton Library.

Meyer, Annie Nathan. "Woman's Assumption of Sex Superiority." *North American Review* (January 1904). MAOFESW, *Why Women Do Not Want the Ballot*, vol. 1, no. 60.

Mitchell, Dr. S. Weir. "Address to Radcliffe." January 17, 1895, MHS.

NAWSA. "Socialism Bolshevism Feminism Negro Rule and States Rights." May 1919.

_____. "The Truth vs. Richard Barry." A refutation of "What Woman Have Actually Done When They Vote," originally published in *Ladies Home Journal*, no. 1, 1910. NAWSA, n.d., SSC.

Parkman, Francis. "Some of the Reasons against Woman Suffrage." N.d. MAOFESW, *Why Women Do No Want the Ballot*, vol. 1, no. 7.

Peterson, Dr. Frederick. "Normal Woman Not Neurotic." NAWSA, March 1914, NYPL uncatalogued pamphlets.

Pyle, Joseph G. "Should Women Vote." New York: National Association Opposed to Woman Suffrage, 1913.

Rensselaer, M. G. van. "Should We Ask for the Suffrage?" MAOFESW, n.d.

Robinson, Margaret C. "Woman Suffrage in Relation to Patriotic Service." Public Interest League of Massachusetts, 1917, SSC.

Root, Elihu. "The Federal Amendment—A Destruction of the Right of Self-Government, Statement Read at National Anti Suffrage Convention." New York, 1917.

Scott, Francis M. Speech before Committee on Suffrage of New York Constitutional Convention. June 14, 1894. Man-Suffrage Association.

Scott, Mrs. Francis M. "Address Delivered Before the Judiciary Committee of the New York Senate." April 10, 1895. MAOFESW, *Why Women Do Not Want the Ballot*, vol. 1, no. 27.

Sturtevant, Mrs. Mary. "An Answer to Common Objections to Woman's Suffrage." Paper read before the Newport County Woman's Suffrage League, March 16, 1913, SSC.

"Tell the Truth! What Will Woman Suffrage Cost Our Country?" Massachusetts Public Interests' League, February 1920.

Ten Eyck, John C. "Suffrage and Government." New York: The Guidon Club, 1914.

Tennessee Division Southern Women's League for the Rejection of the Susan B. Anthony Amendment. "Mrs. Catt and the Woman Suffrage Leaders Repudiate the Bible." 1920.

"Twenty-five Answers to Antis." NAWSA, n.d.

Vincent, John H. Letter to Reverend Dr. J. M. Buckley, April 18, 1894. MAOFESW, *Why Women Do No Want the Ballot*, vol. 1, no. 19.

Wells, Mrs. James B. "Why I Am Opposed to Woman Suffrage." Address before the Texas Senate, February 23, 1915, SSC.

Wells, Kate Gannett. "An Argument Against Woman Suffrage, Before a Special Legislative Committee." MAOFESW, *Why Women Do Not Want the Ballot*, vol. 1, no. 12.

"Woman Suffrage and the Liquor Question." New York: Women's Anti-Suffrage Association, July 1, 1915.

"Woman Suffrage and Wages." No. 2, MSL.

Women's Anti-Suffrage Association of Massachusetts. "An Anti-Suffragist Creed." May 1914.

Books by Antis and Suffragists

Allan, James McGrigor. *Woman Suffrage Wrong in Principle, and Practice* London: Remington and Co., 1890.

Anthony, Susan B., and Ida Husted Harper, eds. *History of Woman Suffrage, 1885-1900.* Vol. 4. Rochester: NAWSA, 1902.

Beecher, Catharine E. *Woman's Profession as Mother and Educator.* Philadelphia: Geo. Maclean, 1872.

Bernbaum, E., ed. *The Case Against Woman Suffrage.* New York: The Man-Suffrage Association, 1915.

Bowditch, William I. *Woman Suffrage a Right, Not a Privilege.* Cambridge: University Press, 1892.

Brown, Charles Brockden. *Alcuin: A Dialogue.* New York: Grossman Publishers, [1798] 1971.

Buckley, James M. *The Wrong Peril of Woman Suffrage.* New York, 1909.

Bushnell, Horace. *Women's Suffrage: The Reform Against Nature.* New York, 1869.

Catt, Carrie Chapman, ed. *Woman Suffrage by Federal Amendment.* New York: NAWSA, 1917.

Catt, Carrie Chapman, and Nettie Rogers Shuler. *Woman Suffrage and Politics.* New York: Charles Scribner's Sons, 1923.

Chopin, Kate, *The Awakening.* Capricorn Books, [1899] 1964.

Clarke, Dr. Edward H. *Sex in Education.* Boston, 1872.

Duniway, Abigail S. *Path Breaking, An Autobiographical History of the Equal Suffrage Movement in Pacific Coast States.* 2d ed. New York: Source Book Press, [1914] 1970.

Fuller, Margaret. *Woman in the Nineteenth Century.* New York, W. W. Norton & Company, [1855] 1971.

Gilman, Charlotte Perkins. *The Home: Its Work and Influence.* New York, 1902.

_____. *Women and Economics.* Boston: Small, Maynard & Company, 1898.

Goldstein, David, and Martha M. Avery. *Bolshevism: Its Cure.* Boston, 1919.

Goodwin, Grace. *Anti-Suffrage, Ten Good Reasons.* New York, 1912.

Haien, J. A., ed. *Anti-Suffrage Essays by Massachusetts Women.* Boston: The Forum Publications, 1916.

Harper, Ida Husted, ed. *History of Woman Suffrage, 1900-1920.* Vol. 5. New York: NAWSA, 1922.

Hollister, Horace A. *The Woman Citizen*. New York: D. Appleton and Company, 1918.

Hubbard, B. V. *Socialism, Feminism and Suffragism, The Terrible Triplets, Connected by the Same Umbilical Cord, and Fed from the Same Nursing Bottle*. Chicago, 1915.

Johnson, Helen K. *Woman and the Republic*. 3rd ed. New York: The Guidon Club, 1913.

Johnson, Rossiter. *Helen Kendrick Johnson*. New York: Publishers Printing Company, 1917.

Leatherbee, Mrs. Albert T. *Anti-Suffrage Campaign Manual*. Boston, 1915.

Leonard, Katherine H. *Clara Temple Leonard: A Memoir of Her Life by Her Daughter*. Springfield: Loring, Astell Co., 1908.

Massachusetts Association Opposed to Further Extension of Suffrage to Women, *Why Women Do Not Want the Ballot*. 3 vols. MSL.

Owen, Harold. *Woman Adrift*. New York: E.P. Dutton & Co., 1912.

Pellew, George. *Woman and the Commonwealth: Or a Question of Expediency*. Boston: Houghton Mifflin Company, 1892.

Putnam-Jacobi, Mary. *"Common Sense" Applied to Woman Suffrage*. New York: G. P. Putnam's Sons, 1915.

A Reply to John Stuart Mill on the Subjection of Women. Philadelphia: J. B. Lippincott & Co., 1870.

Roland, Madame. *The Private Memoirs of Madame Roland*. Chicago: A. C. McClurg and Co., [1795] 1900.

Seawell, Molly E. *The Ladies' Battle*. New York: The Macmillan Company, 1911.

Stanton, Elizabeth Cady. *Eighty Years and More*. New York: Schocken Books, [1898] 1971.

Tarbell, Ida M. *All in a Day's Work*. New York, 1939.

_____. *The Business of Being a Woman*. New York: The Macmillan Company, 1921.

_____. *Madame Roland*. New York: Charles Scribner's Sons, 1896.

_____. *The Ways of Woman*. New York, 1915.

Tayler, J. Lionel. *The Nature of Woman*. New York: E.P. Dutton & Co., 1913.

Tucker, Henry St. George. *Woman's Suffrage By Constitutional Amendment*. New Haven: Yale University Press, 1916.

Walker, Ely van de. *Women's Unfitness for Higher Co-education*. New York, 1903.

White, Carlos. *Ecce Femina: An Attempt to Solve the Woman Question.* Hanover, N.H., 1870.

Wollstonecraft, Mary. *A Vindication of the Rights of Woman.* New York: W. W. Norton & Company, Inc., 1967.

The Woman's Book. 2 vols. New York: Charles Scribner's Sons, 1894.

Articles on Woman Suffrage Pro and Con

Abbott, Lyman. "Answer to Arguments in Support of Woman Suffrage." *Significance of the Woman Suffrage Movement. Annals of the American Academy of Political and Social Science, Supplement.* Philadelphia, 1910, pp. 28-32.

_____. "Why Women Do Not Wish the Suffrage," *Atlantic Monthly* 92, 1903, pp. 289-96.

Arnold Mrs. George F. "Ignorance of the Real Issues at Stake." *The Woman's Protest,* vol. 6, no. 6, April 1915.

Barry, Richard. "Why Women Oppose Woman Suffrage." *Pearson's Magazine,* February, March 1910.

Beard, Mary. "Legislative Influence of Unenfranchised Women." *Annals of the American Academy of Political and Social Science* (November 1914).

Chittenden, Alice Hill. "Woman Suffrage a Mistaken Theory of Progress." *The Woman's Protest,* September 1912, p. 8.

Deland, Margaret. "The Change in the Feminine Ideal." *Atlantic Monthly* 105, 1910, pp. 289-302.

_____. "The New Woman Who Would Do Things." *Ladies Home Journal* 24, 1970, p. 17.

Foxcroft, Frank. "The Check to Woman Suffrage in the United States." *Nineteenth Century* 56, 1904, pp. 833-41.

Foxcroft, Lily Rice. "Why Are Women Opposing Woman Suffrage?" *The Wellesley Alumnae Quarterly,* April 1917. Republished by the Women's Anti-Suffrage Association of Massachusetts.

George, Mrs. A. J., "Why We Are Anti-Suffragists." *The Woman's Protest,* vol. 7, no. 6, October 1915.

Jones, Mrs. Gilbert E. "The Position of the Anti-Suffragists." *Annals of the American Academy of Political and Social Science, Supplement.* Philadelphia, 1910.

_____. "Some Impediments to Woman Suffrage." *North American Review*, August 1909.

Owen, Harold. Article in *London Daily Chronicle*. Reprinted in the *Remonstrance*, n.d.

Parkhurst, The Rev. Charles H. "The Inadvisability of Woman Suffrage." *Annals of the American Academy of Political and Social Science, Supplement*. Philadelphia, 1910.

Robinson, Margaret C. "The Feminist Program." *The Unpopular Review* 5 (1916).

Smith, Goldwin. "Woman Suffrage," *Essays on Questions of the Day*. New York: Macmillan, 1894.

"Suffrage Appeals to Lawless and Hysterical Women." An Interview with Helen K. Johnson in the *The New York Times*, March 30, 1913.

Tarbell, Ida M. "The American Woman," *The American Magazine*, 6 installments, beginning vol. 69 (November 1909).

_____. "Is Woman's Suffrage a Failure?" *Good Housekeeping*, October 1924.

Tyler, W. S. "The Higher Education of Women." *Scribner's Monthly*, February 1874.

The Unpopular Review. Discussion of *Feminism in Germany and Scandinavia*, by Katherine Anthony, April-June 1916.

Wadsworth, Mrs. James W. Jr. "Case Against Suffrage." *The New York Times Magazine*, September 9, 1917, SSC.

Watson, Annah R. "The Attitude of Southern Women on the Suffrage Question." *Arena*, vol. 11 (1894-95), pp. 363-69.

"Women Actively Oppose the Suffrage Bill." Unidentified Boston newspaper, n.d. [ca. 1895]. Houghton Library.

SECONDARY SOURCES

Books

Bardwick, Judith. *Psychology of Women: A Study of Bio-Cultural Conflicts*. New York: Harper & Row, 1971.

Beard, Mary R. *On Understanding Women*. London: Longmans, Green and Co., 1931.

Bebel, August. *Woman Under Socialism*. New York: Schocken Books, [1883] 1971.

Brenton, Myron. *The American Male*. Greenwich, Conn.: Fawcett Publications, 1966.

Chalmers, David M. *The Social and Political Ideas of the Muckrakers*. New York: The Citadel Press, 1964.

Cott, Nancy F., ed. *Root of Bitterness. Documents of the Social History of American Women*. New York: E.P. Dutton & Co., Inc., 1972.

Daly, Mary. *The Church and the Second Sex*. New York: Harper & Row, 1968.

Davies, Wallace Evan. *Patriotism on Parade The Story of Veterans' and Hereditary Organizations in America 1783-1900*. Cambridge, Mass.: Harvard University Press, 1955.

Ditzion, Sidney. *Marriage, Morals and Sex in America*. New York, 1953.

Farber, Seymour M., and Roger H. L. Wilson, eds. *The Potential of Woman*. New York: McGraw-Hill Book Company, 1963.

Fiedler, Leslie A. *Love and Death in the American Novel*. Rev. ed. New York: Dell Publishing Co., 1966.

Figes, Eva. *Patriarchal Attitudes*. New York: Stein and Day, 1970.

Flexner, Eleanor. *Century of Struggle*. New York: Atheneum, 1968.

Gibbs, Margaret. *The DAR*. New York: Holt, Rinehart and Winston, 1969.

Gillette, William. *The Right to Vote: Politics and the Passage of the Fifteenth Amendment*. Baltimore: Johns Hopkins Press, 1965.

Goldman, Eric F. *Rendezvous with Destiny*. New York: Vintage, 1958.

Gornick, Vivian, and Barbara K. Moran, eds. *Woman in Sexist Society: Studies in Power and Powerlessness*. New York: Basic Books, Inc., 1971.

Higham, John. *Strangers in the Land Patterns of American Nativism 1860-1925*. New York: Atheneum, 1963.

James, Henry. *The Bostonians*. New York: Macmillan, 1886.

Johnston, Johanna. *Mrs. Satan, The Incredible Saga of Victoria C. Woodhull*. New York: Popular Library, 1967.

Kraditor, Aileen S. *The Ideas of the Woman Suffrage Movement 1890-1920*. Garden City, N.Y.: Anchor Books, 1971.

Kraditor, Aileen S., ed. *Up from the Pedestal*. Chicago: Quadrangle Books, 1968.

Klein, Viola. *The Feminine Character*. New York: International Universities Press, 1946.

Lasch, Christopher. *The New Radicalism in America 1889-1963*. New York: Vintage Books, 1965.

Lederer, Wolfgang. *The Fear of Women*. New York: Harcourt Brace Jovanovich, Inc., 1968.

Leopold, Richard W. *Elihu Root and the Conservative Tradition*. Boston: Little, Brown and Company, 1954.

Lerner, Gerda. *The Grimké Sisters from South Carolina*. New York: Schocken Books, 1967.

_____. *Women in American History*. New York, 1971.

Lifton, Robert Jay, ed. *The Woman in America*. Boston: Beacon Press, 1965.

Lubove, Roy. *The Professional Altruist: The Emergence of Social Work as a Career 1880-1930*. Cambridge, Mass.: Harvard University Press, 1965.

May, Henry F. *The End of American Innocence: A Study of the First Years of Our Own Times*. New York: Knopf, 1959.

Memmi, Albert. *The Colonizer and the Colonized*. New York: The Orion Press, 1965.

Mill, John Stuart and Harriet Taylor Mill. *Essays on Sex Equality*. Edited by Alice S. Rossi. Chicago: University of Chicago Press, 1970.

Millett, Kate. *Sexual Politics*. Garden City, N.Y.: Doubleday & Company, Inc., 1970.

Myrdal, Gunnar. *An American Dilemma*. New York: Harper & Row, 1944.

O'Neill, William L. *Divorce in the Progressive Era*. New Haven, 1967.

_____. *Everyone Was Brave*. Chicago: Quadrangle Books, 1969.

_____. *The Woman Movement: Feminism in the United States and England*. London: George Allen and Unwin Ltd., 1969.

Papashvily, Helen Waite. *All the Happy Endings*. New York, 1956.

Parker, Gail, ed. *The Oven Birds: American Women on Womanhood 1820-1920*. Garden City, N.Y.: Doubleday, 1972.

Putnam, Emily James. *The Lady*. Chicago: University of Chicago Press, [1910] 1970.

Rham, Edith de. *The Love Fraud*. New York: Pegasus, 1965.

Rhodes, Dr. Philip. *Woman: A Biological Study of the Female Role in Twentieth Century Society*. London: Corgi Books, 1969.

Riegel, Robert E. *American Woman: A Story of Social Change*. Rutherford, 1970.

Rossiter, Clinton. *Conservatism in America*. New York: Vintage Books, 1962.

Sampson, Ronald V. *The Psychology of Power*. New York, 1966.

Scott, Anne Firor. *The Southern Lady from Pedestal to Politics, 1830-1930.* Chicago: University of Chicago Press, 1970.

Scott, Anne Firor, ed. *The American Woman: Who Was She?* Englewood Cliffs, N.J.: Prentice-Hall, Inc., 1971.

Shaw, Bernard. *The Intelligent Woman's Guide to Socialism and Capitalism.* New York: Brentano's Publishers, 1928.

Sinclair, Andrew. *The Better Half: The Emancipation of the American Woman.* New York: Harper & Row, 1965.

Slater, Philip E. *The Pursuit of Loneliness.* 1970.

Taylor, A. Elizabeth. *The Woman Suffrage Movement in Tennessee.* New York: Bookman Associates, 1957.

Taylor, William R. *Cavalier and Yankee: The Old South and the National Character.* New York: 1963.

Articles and Essays

Adams, Margaret, "The Compassion Trap." *Woman in Sexist Society*, edited by Vivian Gornick and Barbara K. Moran. New York: New American Library, 1972.

Conway, Jill. "Jane Addams: An American Heroine." Robert Jay Lifton, ed., *The Woman in America.*

_____. "Stereotypes of Femininity in a Theory of Sexual Evolution." *Victorian Studies* (September 1970).

_____. "The Woman's Peace Party and the First World War," J. L. Granatstein and R. D. Cuff, eds., *War and Society in North America.* Canada: Thomas Nelson and Sons, 1971.

_____. "Women Reformers and American Culture, 1870-1930." *Journal of Social History*, vol. 5, no. 2 (Winter 1971-72), pp. 164-77.

Goldberg, Philip. "Are Women Prejudiced Against Women." *TransAction* 55 (April 1968), pp. 28-30.

Graham, Billy. "Jesus and the Liberated Woman." *Ladies Home Journal*, December 1970.

Hochschild, A. "The American Woman: Another Idol of Social Science." *Trans Action*, vol. 8, no. 1/2 (Nov./Dec. 1970).

Horner, Matina S. "Woman's Will to Fail." *Psychology Today*, vol. 3, no. 6 (November 1969).

Johnson, Kenneth R. "Kate Gordon and the Woman-Suffrage Movement in the South." *Journal of Southern History* 38 (August 1972).

Kenneally, James J. "Catholicism and Woman Suffrage in Massachusetts." *Catholic Historical Review*, vol. 53, no. 1 (April 1967).

Maslow, A. H. "Self-Esteem (Dominance-Feeling) and Sexuality in Women." Hendrik M. Ruitenbeek, ed., *Psychoanalysis and Female Sexuality*. New Haven: Yale University Press, 1966.

Melder, Keith E. "Ladies Bountiful: Organized Women's Benevolence in Early 19th Century America." *New York History*, vol. 48, no. 3 (July 1967), pp. 231-54.

Merk, Lois. "Boston's Historic Public School Crisis." *The New England Quarterly*, vol. 31, no. 1 (March 1958).

O'Neill, William L. "Feminism as a Radical Ideology." Alfred F. Young, ed., *Dissent: Explorations in the History of American Radicalism*. DeKalb: Northern Illinois University Press, 1968.

Rosenberg, Carroll Smith. "Beauty, the Beast and the Militant Woman: A Case Study in Sex Roles and Social Stress in Jacksonian America." *American Quarterly*, vol. 23, no. 4 (October 1971), pp. 562-84.

Sakol, Jeannie. "The Pussycat League." *McCalls*, February 1970.

Schlesinger, Elizabeth Bancroft. "The Nineteenth-Century Woman's Dilemma and Jennie June." *New York History*, vol. 42, no. 4 (October 1961), pp. 365-79.

Veblen, Thorstein. "The Barbarian Status of Women." *American Journal of Sociology*, January 1899, pp. 503-14.

Welter, Barbara. "The Cult of True Womanhood: 1820-1860." *American Quarterly* 18 (Summer 1966), pp. 151-74.

Bibliographic Dictionaries

Brown, John Howard, ed. *Lamb's Biographical Dictionary of the United States*. Boston, 1900.

Cameron, Mable Ward, and Emma Conkling Lee, eds. *The Biographical Cyclopaedia of American Women*. 2 vols. New York: 1924, 1925.

Hale, Sara Josepha. *Woman's Record: or Sketches of All Distinguished Women from "the Beginning" Till A.D. 1850*. New York, 1853.

James, Edward T., ed. *Notable American Women, 1607-1950*. 3 vols. Cambridge: Harvard University Press, 1971.

Leonard, John William. *Woman's Who's Who of America 1914-1915*. New York: The American Commonwealth Company, 1914.
Livermore, Mary A., and Frances Willard, eds. *A Woman of the Century*. Buffalo, 1893.

Unpublished Materials

Bridenthal, Renate. "Beyond Kinder, Kuche, Kirche: Weimar Women at Work." Paper presented at the 86th meeting of the American Historical Association, New York City, December 29, 1971.
Giele, Janet. "Social Change in the Feminine Role: A Comparison of Woman's Suffrage and Woman's Temperance, 1870-1920." Ph.D. dissertation, Radcliffe, 1961.
Kenneally, James J. "The Opposition to Woman Suffrage in Massachusetts, 1868-1920." Ph.D. dissertation, Boston College, 1963.
Koonz, Claudia. "After the Vote: Women and 'The Woman Question' in Weimar Politics." Paper presented at the 86th meeting of the American Historical Association, New York City, December 29, 1971.
Merk, Lois Bannister. "Massachusetts and the Woman Suffrage Movement." Ph.D. dissertation, Radcliffe, 1956.
Naditch, Sheri Fenwick. "Women and Psychopathology." Cornell University, 1972. Mimeographed.
Rosenberg, Carroll S. "The Female Animal, A Medical and Biological View of Women and Women's Role in Nineteenth Century America," Philadelphia: University of Pennsylvania, 1971. Mimeographed.
Simmons, Adele. "Education for What?" Paper presented to the Eastern Sociological Association, April 1971.

Index

Abbott, Edith
  and "The Wage-Earning Woman and the State: a Reply to Miss Minnie Bronson," 184-85
Abbott, Lyman
  antisuffrage speeches of, 192
  antisuffrage support of, 270n
  and opposition to divorce reform, 216
Adams, Abigail, xv
Adams, John, xv
Addams, Jane
  Christopher Lasch on, 220, 221
  influence of on Ida Tarbell, 176
  and Ida Tarbell's refusal to serve on the Tariff Commission, 156
  pacifism of, 65, 72
  and women's drive to activism, 228
Adler, Felix
  and opposition to divorce reform, 216
African-American Chatauqua Circle, xvii
Alabama
  antisuffragism in, 130
  and the Southern Women's Rejection League, 140
Albany Anti-Suffrage Association
  constitutional amendment campaign of, 83
Albany Association Opposed to Woman Suffrage
  and *The Anti-Suffragist*, 90
Allan, James McGrigor
  on women, 5
Allegheny College
  Ida Tarbell's attendance at, 148, 149, 279n
All in a Day's Work (Ida Tarbell), 146
American Constitutional League
  antisuffrage support of, 274n

as an antisuffrage front organization, 94, 95-96
  and campaigns against the federal woman suffrage amendment, 129-30
The American Magazine
  editorial conflicts at, 174
  and excerpts from *The Business of Being a Woman*, 161
  Ida Tarbell's purchase of, 155
  and Ida Tarbell's series on "The American Woman," 162-64
  Ida Tarbell's writings for, 158
American Red Cross
  Emily Bissell's work for, 238
American Woman's Journal
  Helen Kendrick Johnson's editorship of, 43, 44
American Woman Suffrage Association
  and split of the woman suffrage movement, 147
Ames, Mary S.
  public activism of, 236
Anthony, Susan B.
  death of, 283n
  on the federal amendment campaign, 265n
  and *History of Woman Suffrage*, 110
  influence of on Ida Tarbell, 175
  on motherhood, 249n
  and suffragist appeals to Congress, 124
Anti-Suffrage Essays by Massachusetts Women, 235
Anti Suffrage Notes
  and creation of the *Woman Patriot*, 91
"Anti-Suffrage Periscope Detected Showing Which Way the Wind Blows"
  and ridicule of male antisuffragists, 181
"The Anti-Suffrage Rose," 92

Employment
See Occupations
England
    antisuffragism in, 13
    militant suffrage tactics in, 91
English Cathedrals (M. G. van Rensselaer),
    244
Equality League of Self-Supporting Women
    and support for woman suffrage, 126
Equal Rights Amendment (ERA)
    arguments against, xxv-xxvi, 233
Equal Rights Association Club, 128
Evolution
    and colonialism, 206
    and democracy, 45
    influence of on Ida Tarbell, 146
    and separate spheres, 58
    and sex differentiation, 22-23, 31, 32
    and women's entry into politics, 42
    and women's superiority over men, 167

Fairchild, Charles S.
    and American Constitutional League, 95
Family
    as analogous to the state, 6-7, 26, 41, 69,
        74-75
    and antisuffragist appeals to working
        women, 118-19
    and public morality, 9
    radical elements as a threat to, 216
    and Anna Howard Shaw on woman
        suffrage, 14
    Ida Tarbell on, 168
    woman suffrage as a threat to, 19, 84,
        134-35, 136, 140, 210-11
    and women's political activism, 15
Farley, John Cardinal
    antisuffrage support of, 114
Father Abraham (Ida Tarbell), 155
Femininity
    and antisuffragism, 204
    and feminist dilemma, 220-21
    and psychology of antisuffragism, 210
    and separate spheres, 25-26
    and sex-role stereotyping, 204
    woman suffrage as a threat to, 19-20, 67
    women's rights as a threat to, 166, 168
    and working women, 243-44

Feminism
    and alienation, 221
    and antisuffragism, 6, 60, 125, 139, 265n
    and antisuffragist appeals to working
        women, 118
    and attacks on woman suffrage, 67, 72,
        73, 91
    and autonomy for women, 212
    and birth control movement, 112
    Catholic Church's opposition to, 114
    and critiques of marriage, 219
    and divorce reform, 215-17, 219
    and equality, 27-28
    Christopher Lasch on, 220-21
    and male antisuffragists, 79
    and the new woman, 218
    Helen Papashvily on, 226-27
    post-1920 attacks on, 231, 232
    and psychology of antisuffragism, 208-9
    and sexuality, 37
    and social accountability of mothers, 9
    and support for woman suffrage, 248n
    Ida Tarbell on opposition to, 279n
    and Victorian morality, 213
    and women's drive to activism, 228
    and women's economic independence, 68-
        70
    and women's history, xxv
Feminists
    as aberrants, 202-3
    Mary Wollstonecraft on, 286n
Fifteenth Amendment
    federal woman suffrage amendment
        compared to, 135-37
    and the woman suffrage movement, 264n-
        65n
Fitzgerald, John T.
    antisuffrage support of, 112
Flexner, Eleanor
    on the peripheral role of female
        antisuffragists, 224-25
Florida
    antisuffragism in, 140
Foley, John S., Rt. Rev.
    antisuffrage support of, 114
Ford, Mrs. Edward
    congressional testimony of, 125
Ford Peace Party
    suffragist support for, 72

Hale, Annie Riley
  and antisuffragist attacks on Carrie
  Chapman Catt, 182
  and woman suffrage debates in Tennessee,
  138
Hale, Beatrice Forbes Robertson
  and *What Women Want*, 73
Hale, Sarah Josepha
  on women and religion, 167
Hanna, Phil
  and "The Anti-Suffrage Rose," 92
Hapgood, Norman
  on woman suffrage and feminism, 68
Harding, Nelson
  and "Ruthless Rhymes of Martial
  Militants," 93
Harman-Brown, Helen S.
  and editorship of *The Reply*, 91
Haskins, L. M.
  antisuffrage support of, 195
Hay, John, 244-45
  suffragist attacks on, 182-83
Hayes, Rutherford B., 244
Hegel, Georg, 217, 218
He Knew Lincoln (Ida Tarbell), 155
Helen Brent, M.D. (Annie Nathan Meyer),
  244
Henry Street Settlement
  Helen Kendrick Johnson's work for, 44
Hewitt, Mrs. Abraham
  antisuffragist protest of, 44
Higgins, Joseph C.
  and ratification of the federal woman
  suffrage amendment, 140
*High Tea at Halekulani: Feminist Theory and
  American Clubwomen* (Margit Misangyi
  Watts), xviii-xix
Hilquit, Morris
  and support for woman suffrage, 73
Hinding, Andrea, xii
*History of the City of New York in the
  Seventeenth Century* (M. G. van
  Rensselaer), 244
The History of the Standard Oil Company (Ida
  Tarbell), 151, 155
The History of Woman Suffrage, 44
  on immigrant opposition to woman
  suffrage, 110

Hoar, George F.
  and proposals for a federal woman suffrage
  amendment, 272n
Homans, Mrs. Charles D.
  public activism of, 236
The Home (Charlotte Perkins Gilman), 69
*The Home, Heaven and Mother Party: Female
  Anti-Suffragism in America, 1868-1920*
  (Thomas J. Jablonsky), xvi-xvii
Home Training for Citizenship (Helen
  Kendrick Johnson), 43
Houghton, Elizabeth
  and publication of antisuffrage pamphlets,
  92
Houghton Mifflin Co.
  and antisuffrage pamphlets, 92
Howe, Julia Ward, xvi
  on small numbers of antisuffragists, 282n-
  83n
"How Many of These Will Your County and
  State Produce Under Federal Suffrage?"
  and racist antisuffrage, 131

Idaho
  divorce law in, 64
  effects of woman suffrage in, 62, 64, 189
  and Populist support for woman suffrage,
  284n
Ideology
  of antisuffragism, 210-17
Illinois
  antisuffragism in, 85, 89, 194, 197, 282n-
  83n
  suffrage victory in, 123
  woman suffrage campaigns in, 272n
Illinois Association Opposed to Woman
  Suffrage
  and Caroline Fairfield Corbin, 238-39
  founding of, 85
  and link between suffrage and socialism,
  70
  socialist smear tactics of, 85-86
Illinois Industrial School, 12
Immigrants
  and antisuffragism, 53-54, 113, 125, 211,
  212, 222, 226, 236, 260n
  and arguments for woman suffrage, 137
  as a national threat, 223
  and political power in Massachusetts, 225

INDEX

Elizabeth Cady Stanton on, 256n
suffragist fear of, 110
in suffragist propaganda, 188-89
and suffragist support for prohibition, 102
An Improved Woman: The Wisconsin Federation of Women's Clubs, 1895-1920 (Janice Steinschneider), xviii
Indiana
antisuffragism in, 197
Industrialization
Ida Tarbell on, 149-50
International Workers of the World (IWW)
and antisuffragist attacks on Carrie Chapman Catt, 182
Iowa
antisuffragism in, 110, 194-95, 197, 283n
suffrage victory in, 127
"Is Woman Suffrage a Failure?" (Ida Tarbell), 232-34

Jablonsky, Thomas J., xvi-xvii
Jackson, Elizabeth
on the functioning of government, 36-37
Jacoby, Robin Miller, xvii-xviii
James, Janet, xii
Jefferson, Thomas
on the will of the majority, 46
Jewell, Marshall, 239-40
Jewell, Thomas, 240
Jews
and antisuffrage recruits, 236
Johnson, Helen Kendrick, 237
on alliances of suffragists, 73
biographical information on, 43
congressional testimony of, 45
on Dorothea Dix, 278n-79n
and Guidon Club, 97-98
on suffragist support for divorce reform, 216-17
on women's economic independence, 68
on women's influence without suffrage, 58
on women's role in the Civil War, 278n
and *Woman and the Republic*, 44-47, 52-53, 91, 262n
Johnson, Rossiter, 43
Jones, George, 242

Jones, Louise Caldwell (Mrs. Gilbert E. Jones), 237
biographical information on, 242
and National League for the Civic Education of Women, 96
Julian, George W.
congressional testimony of, 124
Jury Duty
and antisuffragism, 15, 20, 29, 59
Juvenile Delinquency
suffrage as a stimulus to, 62

Kansas
antisuffragism in, 104, 283n
effects of woman suffrage in, 189
Keith, P. B.
antisuffrage support of, 275n
Keller, Rosemary, xv
Kelley, Florence
influence of on Ida Tarbell, 176
and "The Truth About Wage-Earning Women and the State, A Reply to Miss Minnie Bronson," 185
Kenneally, James
on antisuffragism in Massachusetts, 225-26
Kentucky
antisuffragism in, 192
Keyes, Prescott, 242
Klein, Viola
on effects of out-group membership on women, 203-4, 207
on growing conspicuousness of women, 217
on limits of Victorian feminism, 218
on women's claim to protection, 31
Know-Nothings
See Nativism
Kraditor, Aileen
on interactions between suffragists and antisuffragists, 218
on motivation of suffragists, 212
on social philosophy of antisuffragists, 210-11

Labor Party
suffragist lobbying of, 273n
The Ladies' Battle (Molly Seawell), 244

314

biographical information on, 244
New York City lectures of, 267n
on women's character, 42
Michigan
antisuffragism in, 103, 105, 110
suffrage victory in, 126
Milholland, Inez
on antisuffragist alliance with liquor
dealers, 103
Mill, John Stuart
and "Subjection of Women," 199-200,
201, 202
Millett, Kate
on women's position under patriarchy,
285n
Minnesota
suffrage victory in, 127
Mississippi
antisuffragism in, 129, 140
Missouri
antisuffragism in, 110
suffrage victory in, 127
Mitchell, S. Weir
on education suitable for women, 23-24,
25
Radcliffe College address of, 163
Moeller, Archbishop
antisuffrage support of, 114
Montana
suffrage victory in, 103
woman suffrage granted in, 57
Morality
and antisuffragism, 215-17, 229, 266n
and antisuffragist appeals to working
women, 118
and attacks on suffragists, 64, 65-66
and prohibition, 106
and social improvement, 37
Ida Tarbell on, 171, 176
woman suffrage as a threat to, 19, 85, 111
and women's influence on government,
35, 47
and women's instincts, 42
and women's political activity, 13-14, 16
and women's responsibility as mothers, 8-
11
and women's role in politics, 84
Morgan, J. P., 108

Morgan, Senator
on the types of women who vote, 55
Mormonism
and antisuffragism, 216
as a national threat, 223
woman suffrage linked to, 70, 73
Motherhood
and antisuffragism, 29, 228, 229, 241-42,
249n, 273n
antisuffragist praise for, 20
and career path of antisuffragists, 145
Caroline Corbin on, 284n-85n
and education suitable for women, 23-25
and feminism, 213
and immunity from suffrage, 34
as an inalienable right, 39
and importance of proper moral growth,
37
and psychology of antisuffragism, 201,
202, 205
Philip E. Slater on, 284n
and support for woman suffrage, 249n
Ida Tarbell on, 162, 170, 171-73, 176
woman suffrage as a threat to, 18-20, 85,
94
and women's influence on government,
56, 64
and women's inherent weakness, 20-22
and women's political activism, 15
and women's special role in society, 8-11
Mott, Lucretia, 253n
antisuffragist attacks on, 279n

Naditch, Sheri
on cultural stereotypes of female inferiority, 205
Napoleon: with a Sketch of Josephine (Ida
Tarbell), 155
National American Woman Suffrage
Association (NAWSA), 14
antisuffragist attacks on, 181-83, 260n
and campaigns for ratification of the
woman suffrage amendment, 193
and Catholic Church, 111-12
and liquor dealers, 106
lobbies Democratic Party, 129
pamphlets published by, 188
socialist support for, 72

and men's depravity, 30
and men's fitness for politics, 22
and sex differentiation, 6
and support for woman suffrage, 212
Ida Tarbell on, 168
woman suffrage as a protector of, 27
woman suffrage as a threat to, 20
and women's influence, 32
and women's influence on government, 47
and women's political activity, 13, 14, 16, 48-49
and women's special role in raising children, 8-11
Settlement Houses
and charges of socialism, 44
Sex and Character (Otto Weininger), 26
Sex Differentiation
drawbacks of, 26-27
and education, 253n
and equality, 28, 30-31
and evolution, 22-23, 31, 32
and female superiority, 6
and occupations, 24, 25
and suffragist propaganda, 186
value judgments about, 28-29, 30
and women's participation in government, 211
Sex in Education (Edward H. Clarke), 24
Sexuality
and advocates of free divorce, 219
and feminism, 37
and men's self-control, 9
and politics, 154
Otto Weininger on, 26
and women's influence on public life, 258n
Shaw, Anna Howard
antisuffragist attacks on, 26
as portrayed in suffragist propaganda, 181
on socialist support for woman suffrage, 72
on woman suffrage, 14
and the Woman's Committee of the Council of National Defense, 156-58
Sherman, Mrs. William T.
petitions Congress, 124
"Should We Ask for the Suffrage?" (M. G. van Rensselaer), 244

Simmel, Georg
on women's subordinate status, 203
Sklar, Kathryn Kish, xiii
Slater, Philip E.
and The Pursuit of Loneliness, 284n
Slavery, xiv-xv
Smith, Al, 233
Smith, Goldwin
on education suitable for parents, 25
Socialism
and antisuffragism, 125, 126, 139, 216, 265n
and antisuffragist appeals to working women, 118
and attacks on woman suffrage, 85-86, 91, 96, 97, 98
and birth control movement, 114
Catholic Church's opposition to, 113
and links with woman suffrage, 47, 49, 66, 140, 223, 239, 257n
as a national threat, 223
post-1920 attacks on, 231
and settlement houses, 44
woman suffrage as a tool of, 67, 69-73, 74-75
Socialist Party
suffragist lobby, 273n
Social Reform
and antisuffragists as aberrants, 202
antisuffragist support, 88
and better class of women, 53
effects of partisanship on, 240
majority disapproves, 190
and Massachusetts antisuffragists, 79
and motherhood, 213
suffragist view of, 48
and support for woman suffrage, 223
and sinister influence of socialists, 47
Ida Tarbell on, 163
woman suffrage as a threat to, 55, 139, 257n
woman suffrage not a part of, 37
and women's citizenship, 33-34
and women's drive to activism, 227-28
and women's influence without suffrage, 11-15, 31-32, 57-58, 67, 74
and women's lack of capacity for organizing, 21
and women's political activism, 107

Scholarship in Women's History: Rediscovered and New

GERDA LERNER, Editor